D0608145

PIRET'S

THE GEORGE and PIRET MUNGER · COOKBOOK ·

GEORGE
AND
PIRET
MUNGER

HOUGHTON

MIFFLIN

COMPANY

BOSTON

1985

Copyright © 1985 by Piret Munger and George Munger

All rights reserved. No part of this work may be reproduced or transmitted in any form or by any means, electronic or mechanical, including photocopying and recording, or by any information storage or retrieval system, except as may be expressly permitted by the 1976 Copyright Act or in writing from the publisher. Requests for permission should be addressed in writing to Houghton Mifflin Company, 2 Park Street, Boston, Massachusetts 02108.

Library of Congress Cataloging in Publication Data

Munger, George.
    Piret's: the George and Piret Munger cookbook.
    Includes index.
    1. Cookery, American.   I. Munger, Piret.
II. Title.
TX715.M93   1985   641.5   85-10871
ISBN 0-395-35634-2
ISBN 0-395-39501-1 (pbk.)

Printed in the United States of America

HM10 9 8 7 6 5 4 3 2 1

*To
Cecil,
Frank,
and
Jerry
Munger*

CONTENTS

Acknowledgments · ix

Preface · xi

I OUT OF THE PERFECT PAN · I

2 BEGINNINGS · 23
   Appetizers and First Courses · 26
   Soups · 47

3 SALADS · 65
   Vinegars and Vinaigrettes · 67
   Piret's Salads · 76

4 CHARCUTERIE · 99
   Quiches · 102
   Pizzas · 113
   Sausages · 122
   Pâtés and Terrines · 130
   Spreads and Relishes · 149

5 PIRET'S BISTRO · 159
   Entrées · 162
   Pasta · 185
      Tomato Sauces · 198
   Accompaniments · 203

6 ENTRÉES FOR ENTERTAINING · 217

7 PÂTISSERIE · 255
   Tarts · 258

Cakes, Pastries, and Cookies · 265
Cream and Fruit Desserts · 286
Ice Creams and Sorbets · 291
Dessert Sauces and Sweet Toppings · 303

8 THE PERFECT PAN SCHOOL OF
COOKING · 309
Stocks · 312
Sauces · 320
Pastry · 336
The Basic Kitchen · 349

ACKNOWLEDGMENTS

So many people have contributed to the making of this book it is as if each page is filled with unseen footsteps and shadows of bygone days.

Our cookbook would not exist without Liz Johnson, who sensed the unique direction it might take and became our agent. Her lively imagination, determination, and unwavering belief in us and the business we had created helped to convince Houghton Mifflin Company to undertake the project.

During the past two years, I have come to regard my editor at Houghton Mifflin, Linda Glick Conway, as a fairy godmother. She has stood behind a novice author with unlimited faith and patience.

Marjorie Rice, whom we hired as consulting editor after she had moved from San Diego to become assistant features editor at the *San Francisco Examiner,* has been an unfaltering friend. For nearly a year, she flew to San Diego almost every weekend to help edit the recipes so they could be clearly understood by cooks at every level of expertise. Patty Andrews Studer's skills on the word processor and relentless pursuit of recipe testers' progress kept us on schedule.

Very special thanks are due Lois Stanton, Jack Monaco, and Dan Belajack, who answered countless technical questions at all hours of the day and night. Without their counsel, this book would be yet another year in coming.

We were many times blessed by being able to draw on Diana Hewett, former director of The Perfect Pan shops, and chefs Ben Patterson and Jim

Hill for testing recipes. Their skills are the very soul of this book. Other recipe testers to whom we are indebted are Dee Biller, Suzy Eisenman, Judy Goldman, Mac Millhone, and Patty Andrews Studer. Pastry expertise was provided by Dan Mooney, Jenny Saar, Dinah and Charles Schley, Jay Weinisch, and Mark Zadarnowski.

Among the individuals whose personal philosophies and cooking styles have most influenced Piret's and this book are Dan Belajack, Nadia Frigeri, Jim Hill, Patty McDonald, Jack Monaco, Maurice Moore-Betty, Anne Otterson, Ben Patterson, Jacques Pépin, Lois Stanton, Jerrie Strom, and Paula Wolfert. Others whose recipes appear here or who inspired our own adaptations of their dishes include Frank Arrington, Dee Biller, Giuliano Bugialli, Biba Caggiano, Hugh Carpenter, André Daguin, Suzy Eisenman, Rebecca Evans, Marie-Christine Forester, Bill Glasgow, Lorenzo Gunn, Fran Jenkins, Madeleine Kamman, Diana Kennedy, Mary Knight, Alice Medrich, Marc Meneau, Judy Miller, Katie Millhiser, Roberta Silberman, and Virginia Thomas.

Janet Silver, manuscript editor at Houghton Mifflin, has been invaluable in making this book more readable, and thanks to her, too, our readers are spared lapses in recipe directions.

Finally, The Perfect Pan shops, Piret's, and this cookbook would never have come into being without George Munger. The ideas for all these undertakings were his, and his eternal optimism, encouragement, and love have made our culinary odyssey possible. And we are both indebted to Ron Evans, who created Piret's dynamite logo and whose friendship is special to us.

P R E F A C E

The last twenty years have seen an extraordinary change in the way Americans view food and cooking. Even before George and I opened The Perfect Pan in 1975, a transformation was beginning to take place. Where before George was the only man in our circle of friends who cooked, more and more of our male friends were starting to experiment in the kitchen, and their wives, too, were becoming increasingly adventurous. There is to my mind a logical connection between the women's movement and the emergence of two-career marriages, and recent developments in the culinary world — at least among the marketing segment now known as the "yuppies."

When we opened The Perfect Pan shop and cooking school, *Gourmet* magazine was the single eloquent monthly voice and resource for the gifted home cook and earnest food professional. Williams-Sonoma, through its well-conceived catalogue and sophisticated merchandise, was virtually the only source for culinary gear. James Beard was the established father of American cookery. Through his weekly syndicated columns and ever-expanding library of cookbooks, he inspired confidence among hobbyist cooks, would-be restaurateurs, teachers, and food writers. In 1961, Julia Child with Simone Beck and Louisette Bertholle had introduced Americans to classic French dishes and techniques with *Mastering the Art of French Cooking, Volume I,* and nine years later she and Beck completed the work with *Mastering the Art of French Cooking,*

Volume II. I don't know of a single devoted cook who does not regard these two volumes as the cornerstone of his or her cookbook collection. But it was Julia's lively, instructional cooking series, appearing weekly on public television beginning in the sixties, that brought good cooking methodology to millions of Americans.

The early seventies brought a veritable explosion of quality cookbooks and the debut of a covey of cooks whose names today are synonymous with culinary excellence. In 1972, Diana Kennedy published her splendid *Cuisines of Mexico,* and the following year Paula Wolfert gave us *Couscous and Other Foods from Morocco.* In 1975, Jacques Pépin wrote *A French Chef Cooks at Home* and Marcella Hazan introduced us to the foods of Northern Italy with *The Classic Italian Cookbook.* Craig Claiborne was a prolific presence throughout the decade, and his *New York Times Cookbook* is a classic. *From Julia Child's Kitchen* was one of many books written to coincide with her TV series. Cooking schools, mostly in the form of good cooks teaching in their home kitchens, were popping up across the country.

It was, I believe, Gael Green of *New York Magazine* who first dubbed the emerging bands of food gurus and their zealous followers "foodies." These aficionados resided mainly on the Eastern seaboard, but there were other enclaves here and there. In Berkeley, Alice Waters held forth at Chez Panisse and is today credited with training many of California's outstanding chefs. Nathalie Dupree in Atlanta established one of America's foremost cooking schools at Rich's, while New Orleans' Paul Prudhomme schooled Americans in Cajun cooking first at Commander's Palace and later at K-Paul's. In San Diego, George and our Perfect Pan School of Cooking directors Anne Otterson and Lois Stanton became a culinary focal point.

One of the most important catalytic events was the introduction of the Cuisinart food processor in America by Carl Sontheimer, a brilliant engineer and a marketing genius. Carl allied himself with the professionals who immediately grasped the significance and impact the food processor would have in the home kitchen. Recipes that had previously been impractical because of the time and work involved could now become everyday fare in the home. By Christmas 1977, demand for the Cuisinart food processor was so great that The Perfect Pan and other cookware retailers were selling "almost empty boxes" containing a gift certificate promising February delivery. It was a retailer's nightmare but an inspired stunt on Carl's part.

By the late seventies, the nation's culinary media had burgeoned. Aimed at the upscale, affluent market, the very turf that had belonged to *Gourmet* as a birthright, we now had *Bon Appetit, Cuisine, Food and Wine,* and Carl Sontheimer's *Pleasures of Cooking.* Writer/cooks could now quickly spread the word about trends and fads such as *nouvelle cuisine, cuisine minceur, cuisine bourgeoise,* American cuisine, and California cuisine. "Gourmet" shops popped up everywhere, and cooking teachers moved out of their home kitchens into more elaborate school settings. Department stores jumped on the bandwagon with spiffed-up housewares departments, food demonstrations, celebrations, festivals, and celebrity chef appearances. Restaurateurs, notably Patrick Terrail of Ma Maison in Los Angeles, had their chefs, Wolfgang Puck among them, teach cooking classes. Others presented special dinners cooked by chefs from France. Charitable organizations, noting their patrons' growing interest in food and wine, began to offer wine auctions, celebrity cooking classes and cook-offs, and door prizes with a gastronomic bent.

Today in the eighties, a major effort is under way to demystify the enjoyment of good food and wine and their preparation and to encourage a broader public to give it a whirl. Among the leaders of this movement is none other than Julia Child. No longer just the darling of the PBS crowd, she can regularly be seen on "Good Morning America," and her monthly food section in *Parade* magazine reaches millions in their Sunday newspapers. Food pages in local newspapers are significantly improved from the days when canned cream of mushroom soup postured as a sauce and tuna casseroles were de rigueur. Craig Claiborne, food editor of the *New York Times,* has always promoted a sophisticated approach to food, but he was the exception and not the norm. A more striking example on the local level is Antonia Allegra, food editor of the *Tribune* in San Diego, who has studied cooking extensively in France and Italy and was a widely admired cooking teacher before becoming a journalist. The knowledge she and food editors like her bring to readers is all but revolutionary. Similarly, the nation's mass-appeal magazines — *Better Homes and Gardens, Family Circle, Woman's Day,* and *Redbook* among them — are emphasizing the use of fresh ingredients and classic cooking techniques. These food editors are making classically prepared dishes approachable to millions of people who may have been put off by foreign terminology, unfamiliar ingredients, and the aura of elitism that has traditionally been associated with haute cuisine.

The new egalitarian trend can be seen in the birth of such organizations as the American Institute of Wine and Food, to be housed on the campus of the University of California, Santa Barbara, whose members include young chefs, home cooks, cooking teachers, food writers, and noted authorities. The International Association of Cooking Schools, founded in 1978, is not only concerned with setting standards of professional excellence for cooking-school owners and teachers (also making it possible for a student to appraise a school), but it also provides an invaluable forum for networking.

This book is intended to chronicle the gradual emergence of a culinary tradition in America, which celebrates both our enormous bounty of fresh foodstuffs and the wonderful regional cooking that has always been with us, as well as the new foods and unfamiliar ingredients introduced in recent years. Yet this book is also personal, a microcosm of the larger picture with fond remembrances of the people George and I have come to know and love. Certainly we feel that our primary contribution has been in bringing together a collection of people and ideas in situations that encourage us all to grow.

The recipes we present here are quite literally from all over — from our cooking teachers, guest chefs, author/cooks, and our own working chefs. They come from our cooking school, our Lunch at The Perfect Pan series, and Piret's special caterings, daily menus, and take-out foods. Other recipes come from friends, the George Munger Cook-Offs, and family. We have been careful to credit the source of every recipe, at least *our* source, realizing that in some cases a recipe given to us or taught by one chef actually may have originated with another. Every recipe comes directly from our files, has been tested at least once, and edited as many as a dozen times. Our concern has been to be as clear as possible in describing preparations and to present each recipe so that you, at home, will be able to prepare it successfully.

The book contains some three hundred recipes culled from many thousands. We chose those recipes we felt most represented our organization and philosophy, and as you page through this book, we think you will find a continuity of style and approach. Though our cooking school offers many classes in ethnic cuisines, microwave cooking, vegetarian/dietetic preparations, and other specialty styles, if you were to come to Piret's or The Perfect Pan, you would immediately sense that our roots are in French country foods, with some updates, Americanisms, and regionalisms thrown in. Also, George and I are practical people and a two-career couple. With few exceptions, which we could not resist because they are worth the effort, the recipes in this book are practical in the context of a normal lifestyle, with its time and financial constraints. Many of the dishes can be made ahead, and even taste better made ahead. Where alternative ingredients are appropriate, we suggest them, knowing all too well that not everything is available everywhere or in all seasons.

All of the chefs whose recipes we've included encourage experimentation, although none of them would hail the born-again chefs who think that simply putting odd ingredients together constitutes a new "cuisine." Few of the recipes here are strikingly new and original in that way. The idea is to be creative with good fundamentals. And remember that elegant does not have to mean complicated or expensive. If you have a good grasp of the basics, you can make a simple family stew as elegant as a lavish carpaccio with caviar sauce. Above all, we hope to inspire you to be adventurous in the kitchen, to be open to new food experiences, and to take a joyful approach to cooking.

PIRET MUNGER

San Diego
1985

1

OUT OF THE
PERFECT PAN

IN THE SUMMER OF 1974, the idea of our first foray into the food business, The Perfect Pan, was born. George had wanted to try a Jacques Pépin recipe from the Time/Life *Foods of the World* series and he needed a high-sided flan pan. We looked everywhere. Driving back to San Diego from a business trip to Los Angeles, we stopped to browse in a shopping center and came upon a shop called Skillets. It was closed, but inside was the pan! Skillets was a delightfully well-put-together shop, with antique country French and English dining furniture, kitchen accessories, cookware, and utensils. All the way home, George talked about opening a place like Skillets in San Diego. We began scouring California for similar shops. There weren't many. One day we stopped to look at the Pottery Barn near UCLA. George decided to shoot a few pictures of displays, while I meandered around the tableware department upstairs. Suddenly I became aware of three clerks eyeing me with alarm and soon heard booming voices downstairs. One boomer was George. The other was Dick Friedman, at that time owner of the West Coast Pottery Barn shops. Dick was not impressed with George's story about opening a pan shop in San Diego and thought we were casing his store with robbery in mind. We beat a hasty retreat to a shop next door.

From these inauspicious beginnings emerged The Perfect Pan, so named because some dishes require a "perfect pan" — like the high-sided flan pan.

Our intent was to stock *everything* a cook could

want. This was an ambitious goal, in light of our initial investment: $20,000 from George and me and $10,000 from George and Kim Gilmore, our original partners. George was our only employee and he was unpaid. I continued with my work as a freelance public relations consultant to support our household. At night and on weekends, I became The Perfect Pan's unpaid bookkeeper, display- and odd-jobs person. I wrote advertising copy for the first time in my life and wrote the cooking school's quarterly class schedule. The Gilmores did everything from selling, to painting, to unpacking and pricing merchandise. Our friend Ron Evans, a graphic designer, created the logo for The Perfect Pan and, later, Piret's. We opened the store on September 8, 1975.

From the start we had envisioned a cooking school and a prix fixe lunch menu of classic French country dishes served weekdays to sixteen guests. Neither was long in coming. Cooking classes began in November and Lunch at The Perfect Pan was launched the following spring. George not only did all the buying and running of the shop, he was our only cooking teacher. Virginia Thomas joined him several months later to teach baking and was our first "professional" teacher. In the spring of 1976, George and San Diego restaurateur Giuseppe Ferrare teamed up for an Advanced French Cooking series. The cooking school at that time was in the middle of the shop, with students crowded around a butcher-block work center — standing, mind you. With George popping in and out taking care of customers and Giuseppe in a frazzle over his new restaurant, the classes could be more accurately described as Advanced Chaos. Looking back, it's a wonder the cooking school survived.

Our first paid employee lasted but a few weeks, the frenetic goings-on not quite her speed. Our first official employee was Judy Miller (see her Hungarian Rolled Stuffed Cabbage Leaves, page 166). In 1976, Anne Otterson, who had been teaching in her La Jolla home kitchen for years, joined us as director of the cooking school. Anne's culinary style reflected our own — country French dishes utilizing classic cooking techniques. And Anne was quick to pick up on George's style: "Go for it. Don't worry about it! We can handle it."

Anne's personal style was much like our own as well, with ten projects going at once. Between delivering one child to his singing lesson or another to a birthday party, she'd be racing off to Jurgensen's, a La Jolla food market, to pick up needed ingredients on her way to class. One day while paying the bill, she instructed the bag boy to put the groceries in the trunk of the gray Mercedes. Arriving at the school, she opened the trunk to find it empty. A frantic call was made to Jurgensen's and it was discovered the boy had put the groceries in the wrong Mercedes. Jurgensen's called a cab for the missing groceries and they arrived in the nick of time.

Anne brought us a great collection of resident teachers, many of whom are still with us today. Among the most durable of our resident professionals are Patty McDonald, who specializes in ethnic cuisines, vegetarian and health-oriented menus, and specialty techniques; Jerrie Strom, who often teams up with Fran Jenkins for classes in Mexican and Chinese cookery; Grace Wheeler, an expert in microwave cooking; Nadia Frigeri, whose specialty is Northern Italian cuisine; and, of course, Virginia Thomas, whose baking classes are ever popular. Anne, a great networker, also became an informal booking agent for Eastern writer/cooks, French chefs, and other traveling food authorities. She was responsible for bringing us — and much of the West Coast — Jacques Pépin, Paula Wolfert, Diana Kennedy, Anne Willan, and Irene Kuo, to name just a few. She persuaded Marc Meneau, the celebrated three-star chef/owner of L'Esperance, to come to San Diego. He was so well received that we later invited Alain Dutournier, André Daguin, Jacques Cagna, and Michel Pasquet to teach and cook dinners. Other notables stemming back to the Anne Otterson era include Marcella and Victor Hazan, Giuliano Bugialli, Biba Caggiano, Ken Hom, and Barbara Tropp.

Anne was the cornerstone on which our school was built; Lois Stanton, her successor, has built the school into a thriving organization. George's and my role has been simply to support and encourage these capable women and, to the best of our ability, provide the resources they have needed to build a standard for excellence. Over four thousand classes have been held at The Perfect Pan School of Cooking with some fifty thousand students enrolled. Today we have three school locations, each seating from eighteen to thirty students. We've come a long way from ten students standing around George's butcher-block counter, thanks to both Anne and Lois and to all of our teachers locally and from around the country. And thanks, too, to all the students, who want to eat well at home. The recipes they have learned in class are found throughout this book, along with those from the chefs at Piret's and Lunch at The Perfect Pan.

During Anne's era as director, our whole organization and the school was free-wheeling and experimental — everything about it had the newness and exuberance of young love. As we opened more school locations and offered more and more classes, it was obvious that more structure was needed. Lois Stanton was the perfect person to take us into the new era. She is organization-plus and has developed a solid teacher-assistant's program, routines for scheduling classes and processing recipes, and accounting procedures. New teacher candidates are screened before a gallery of our current teachers. Our kitchens are well equipped, well stocked, and spotless. Lois, like Anne, is a networker, with her finger on the pulse of culinary trends and up-and-coming food personalities. Both have been key to the development of the International Association of Cooking Schools and the American Institute of Wine and Food. Lois founded the Southern California Culinary Guild, which provides excellent technical programs for cooking teachers and chefs.

Maybe it's good Midwest blood that has made the cooking school, The Perfect Pan shops, and Piret's what they are. Anne was born in Minnesota, Lois grew up in Kansas, and George was born and raised in Wisconsin — lands of plenty and plenty of energy. George's forebears arrived in America in the 1600s from England, and his grandparents went by covered wagon to Nebraska. His grandfather was an engineer on the Burlington Railroad and his grandmother grew her own chickens and killed them for dinner well into her dotage. She stopped driving at the age of eighty-five when the town of Hastings, Nebraska, petitioned that her license not be renewed, and she died a few weeks before her one hundredth birthday. George's father, Frank, full of wanderlust, spent his early years roaming from Colorado, where he had a restaurant, to New York, where he learned photography, and finally to Milwaukee, where he settled. There he married Cecil, George's mother, a splendid-looking woman, nearly six feet tall, and of good German stock.

The family home included a huge garden of vegetables, berries, and fruit-bearing trees. Frank and Cecil were both excellent cooks and shared the kitchen, taking full advantage of the garden's bounty. Among my favorite dishes from this early era is Frank Munger's Spaghetti and Meatballs. The recipe was given to him by a conductor of the Denver Symphony and it was not written down until George and I left Milwaukee bound for San Diego in 1963. Since both Cecil and Frank worked, they didn't have time to cook down pounds of tomatoes for a simple family spaghetti dinner; this recipe, which is delicious, takes shortcuts with excellent results. The meatball recipe makes terrific meatloaf as well. Just place the mixture in a bread pan, tamp it down to remove any air pockets, cover the top with strips of raw smoked bacon to keep it moist and flavorful, and bake at 425° for about 1 hour and 45 minutes.

FRANK MUNGER'S SPAGHETTI AND MEATBALLS

Makes 8 servings

The sauce reheats beautifully and tastes best if made in advance so the flavors can mingle.

TO PREPARE THE SAUCE

3 strips smoked bacon, minced

1 small yellow onion, chopped

¼ pound mushrooms, cleaned, cut in quarters and halves

2 cans (6 ounces each) tomato paste

Salt and freshly ground pepper, to taste

1. Brown the bacon in a large sauté pan. Remove the bacon from the pan and cook the onions in the bacon fat until they are translucent. Add the bacon, mushrooms, tomato paste, salt, pepper, and chili powder, and stir in the spaghetti sauce with meat. Stir the sauce well and bring it to a slow boil. Reduce the heat, and simmer the sauce for 1 hour.

2. Add the Parmesan cheese and enough water to keep the mixture the consistency of heavy cream. Continue simmering the sauce for 30 minutes more.

½ teaspoon chili powder
1 can (12 ounces) spaghetti
  sauce with meat
¼ pound freshly grated
  Parmesan cheese

TO PREPARE THE MEATBALLS

2 pounds ground beef
½ pound pork sausage
1 teaspoon salt
¼ teaspoon freshly ground
  pepper
½ teaspoon oregano
½ cup saltine crackers,
  crumbled fine
2 whole eggs
2 cans (8 ounces each)
  tomato sauce
1 medium yellow onion,
  minced
Milk
Bacon fat, for frying

Cooked spaghetti
Freshly grated Parmesan
  cheese

1. Mix the beef, sausage, salt, pepper, oregano, crackers, eggs, one can of tomato sauce, and onions. Add enough milk to make the mixture slightly moist and pliable. Form the meat into 1½-inch balls. Brown the meatballs in the bacon fat.

2. Preheat the oven to 425°. Place the meatballs in an ovenproof casserole and pour the second can of tomato sauce over them. Cover the casserole with aluminum foil and bake for 45 minutes. Reduce the heat to 400°, and bake the meatballs, uncovered, another 30 minutes.

3. Serve the sauce and meatballs over spaghetti, cooked al dente. Pass freshly grated Parmesan cheese separately.

George's tastes run a crazy-quilt gamut from simple home cooking to the grand and grandiose. Grandiose is a tradition on his birthday, which he shares with Ron Evans. On their fortieth birthdays, they decided to host a dinner for twelve at our house. Ron arranged for a string quartet to play during dinner. All guests contributed to the meal. As guest Bill Glasgow described it in *San Diego Magazine,* it was "The Ultimate Potluck Dinner" for which he prepared himself by reading Veblen's *Theory of the Leisure Class* and Spengler's *Decline of the West* "to assuage any guilt feelings that threatened to arise."

The guests arrived on time, for a change, Bill noted. And the dinner was on:

Maine Lobster with
  Mayonnaise
Beluga Caviar
Fresh *Foie Gras*

Stolichnaya Vodka
Reims Brut Champagne, George Goulet

Truffle Soup, Paul Bocuse

Cold Poached Trout with   *Bâtard Montrachet, Louis Jadot, 1976*
    Caper Vinaigrette

Boeuf Richelieu with   *Musigny, Comte Georges Vogue, 1974*
    Madeira Sauce   *Chambertin Clos de Bèze, Duroche, 1961*
Château Potatoes   *Clos des Lambrays, Madame Cosson, 1937*
Stuffed Tomatoes
Braised Lettuce
Stuffed Mushrooms

Green Salad   *Graves Grand Cru, Château Oliver, 1976*

Cheeses

Riz à L'Impératrice   *Kiedricher Gräfenberg Reisling Eiswein Beerenauslese*
                              Erzeugerabfullung, estate bottled by Dr. R. Weil

Coffee   *Grande Champagne Cognac du Logis de la Mothe*

Bill favored the Cold Poached Trout with Caper Vinaigrette. To make this delicious
fish course, poach one trout per person in court bouillon (page 319) for 7 to 8
minutes. Remove the trout from the poaching liquid and allow it to cool slightly.
When the trout are cool enough to handle, remove the skin, head, and tail, and all
bones. Serve two fillets per person, at cool room temperature, napped with Caper
Vinaigrette.

CAPER VINAIGRETTE

Makes about 1 cup (4 servings)

½ tablespoon salt
Pinch freshly ground pepper
2 tablespoons crushed capers
1 teaspoon minced fresh
    parsley
1 teaspoon minced fresh
    tarragon
1 teaspoon Dijon-style
    mustard
1 onion, minced
2 tablespoons white wine
    vinegar
5 tablespoons extra-virgin
    olive oil
Fresh tarragon, for garnish

In a bowl, combine the salt, pepper, capers, parsley,
tarragon, mustard, and onions. While beating the
mixture vigorously with a whisk, beat in the vinegar and olive oil a little at a time. Spoon the sauce
over the fillets and garnish the plate with the sprigs
of fresh tarragon.

Recipes for the Boeuf Richelieu and trimmings, along with the recipe for Riz à L'Impératrice, can be found in *Classic French Cooking* in the Time/Life *Foods of the World* series. The truffle soup is in *Paul Bocuse's French Cooking*.

Over the past ten years, we've cooked and hosted luncheons and dinners for dozens of culinary celebrities. Our very first was for the late James Beard in 1976, following a cooking benefit he and Philip S. Brown put on for San Diego's University Hospital. What on earth do you serve a great cook, a man who has experienced it all? We brooded over the problem for weeks and finally opted for simplicity. In a nationwide column (much to our pleasure and surprise) this is how he described the meal: "We had a delicious lunch with the Mungers. It consisted of asparagus vinaigrette, steak au poivre prepared in the French manner — sautéed very quickly until the outside was brown and crustily peppery and the inside beautifully rare, then flambéed with Cognac and served with appropriate vegetables. This was followed by a luscious strawberry Bavarian cream. All in all, it was a beautifully balanced meal."

GEORGE MUNGER'S STEAK AU POIVRE

Makes 1 serving

You may multiply this recipe at will, but do not overcrowd the pan or the steaks will steam instead of sear. Also, be prepared for lots of smoke in the house, unless your venting system is fabulous, and turn off the smoke alarm if you have one.

1½-inch thick prime
   fillet of beef (about 6
   ounces)
Whole peppercorns
Salt or kosher-style salt
Minced fresh parsley and
   chives, to taste
1 tablespoon butter
1 drop Tabasco
½ teaspoon Worcestershire
   sauce
½ lemon tied in cheesecloth
⅓ cup Cognac
   (approximately)

1. Trim the fillet of all fat and sinew. Coarsely crush the black peppercorns with a mortar and pestle. Press the peppercorns into both sides of the steak so the steak is nicely crusted. (This steak should be quite peppery.) Allow the crusted steak to rest for 30 minutes before cooking.

2. Place enough ordinary table salt or kosher-style salt in a cast-iron skillet to lightly coat the bottom of the pan. Place the skillet over high heat. When the salt begins to "jump" in the pan, sear the steak on one side about 1½ minutes. When you turn the steak, place on top of the seared side the minced parsley and chives, butter, Tabasco, and Worcestershire sauce, and squeeze the juice of the lemon through cheesecloth onto the steak.

3. Turn down the heat, pour the Cognac into the pan, and light it carefully with a long match. When the flames die down, place the steak on a warmed dinner plate and pour over the pan juices. Garnish with additional parsley and serve immediately. We like to serve Steak au Poivre simply, with baby carrots, Chinese pea pods, or another colorful vegetable. This cooking time produces a rare steak, which we prefer, but you can adjust the cooking time according to your own, or your guests', taste.

We first met Jacques Pépin in much the same way we met Jim Beard and Julia Child — by providing the equipment for his cooking classes for charity in San Diego. Jacques first taught at The Perfect Pan in July 1978. For a press luncheon in his honor, our chef for Lunch at The Perfect Pan, Ben Patterson, served Feijoada Completa (page 253), Brazil's national dish. We didn't know it at the time, but we had stumbled on the perfect choice. Jacques's wife, Gloria, is Puerto Rican and Jacques loves Latin food. In San Diego, he invariably chooses Mexican restaurants, and his favorite Piret's *nouvelle* pizza is Pizza Verde with Tomatillo Sauce (page 118).

Jacques has an easy smile and elfin wit. Peggy Roux of the San Diego *Tribune* reported on the 1978 classes, noting that Jacques does not use charcoal briquettes for barbecuing because, he says, they give off tar equivalent to smoking six hundred cigarettes. Instead he uses wood, or sometimes the *New York Times* rolled into logs. He told the class about a recipe for fish he especially liked, in which the fish is wrapped in the *Times* and cooked until the paper burns off. The ink in the *Times,* he noted with a wink, is especially suited to this dish. Jacques once told Eleanor Widmer, restaurant critic for the San Diego *Reader,* how he buys fish: "I go very early to the biggest markets, look the fish in the eye, test the gill, establish rapport with the fish, and then I buy it."

In his classes, Jacques always calls for flexibility in cooking while reminding students that good cooking requires a command of technique and constant tasting. The recipe has to change every time, he says. He does not measure a teaspoon of this or that but stops when his taste buds tell him the dish is right. Eleanor Widmer observed the process in action: "Pépin tastes everything by dipping his finger into the ingredient, then placing it on his tongue. Sometimes he wipes his tongue with a paper towel afterward."

Marjorie Rice, former food editor of the San Diego *Tribune,* once observed that Jacques's classes and books "demystify" French cooking. He teaches techniques that will enable the home cook to succeed and shows how to select the fresh ingredients that will impart the most flavor and texture to the finished dish. There is nothing "precious" about his food — it is good food meant to be enjoyed. Perhaps that is why he is also a popular teacher among men. Ten years ago, few men attended cooking classes. Now a third to one-half of his students at night are men.

It could be fairly said of anyone mentioned in this book that he or she is "passionate" about good food, but to no one is it more applicable than Paula Wolfert. As Gael Greene once said, "To Paula, an overaged string bean is an outrage, a mushy tomato is a personal attack." One of Paula's classes with us in the late seventies lasted over six hours while Paula added new dishes she couldn't resist sharing because the ingredients at the market were especially fresh. She recently told Maureen Clancy, food editor of the *San Diego Union*, "I like real tastes, not whispering ones . . . lusty, rustic food. . . . I'm a cook, not a florist." To underline the point, Maureen describes Paula in action: "Grabbing a hot Potato 'Quercy,' partially roasted in duck fat, and waving it past her wrinkled nose, Wolfert swooned — 'It actually smells like Southwest France.' "

Paula was among the first to predict that *nouvelle cuisine* and all its imitators were becoming too "cute" to last. She packed up her bags and spent six months discovering what was going on in the real kitchens of France. In 1980, she told us the new "new" cuisine would be *cuisine bourgeoise,* real food, honest food, "back of the mouth food." *Cuisine bourgeoise,* she said, would retain the best of *nouvelle cuisine,* such as the crispy vegetables, the reduction sauces, and the beurre blancs. At the same time, it would incorporate traditional slow-cooked braised meats, foods cooked in rendered fat for added flavor, and meats cooked to render out the fat, leaving only the wonderful flavor of fat behind. Paula's critically acclaimed book *The Cooking of Southwest France,* released in 1983, is a celebration of *cuisine bourgeoise* from the region that produces *foie gras,* truffles, ducks, and geese.

In the early seventies, about the same time that Paula taught us about Moroccan food, the subject of her first cookbook, Diana Kennedy taught us to appreciate the regional foods of Mexico. Her first class with us was to be held in our North County Perfect Pan cooking school, before we moved it to our home. Anne Otterson had taken Diana shopping at the outdoor market in Tijuana, and George and I made a final sweep of the classroom later in the day to make sure everything was perfect. To my horror, I happened upon some thoroughly disgusting bananas that seemed to have been forgotten in a drawer for weeks, if not months. I threw out the blackened bananas while congratulating myself on having found them before Diana arrived to teach the following morning. The classes went splendidly, and I heard nothing about bananas until the following year, when I helped Diana set up for class in our Mission Hills school. She turned to me and said, "You know, little hurts stay with me a long time. Like the time last year when someone stole my bananas." I could not bring myself to admit that I was the banana bandit.

Eleanor Widmer described Diana Kennedy in a 1981 article: "She could play with ease the role of the Englishwoman detective in a murder mystery. Her air is absent-minded, her accent crisp, and while she appears slightly befuddled, as if she were wearing mismatched socks under her stocky walking shoes, you know that she is the kind to gather the suspects in the living room, fix them with imperious gaze, and solve the murder in a trice. Detection is really her game, and she has the nose, or more accurately the palate, of a sleuth. She tracks down recipes from the farthest reaches of Mexico, and though she was born in Essex, England, she is regarded as the greatest living authority on Mexican cooking."

For her books on Mexican cooking, *The Cuisines of Mexico, The Tortilla Book,* and *Recipes from the Regional Cooks of Mexico,* Diana was awarded the *Aguila Azteca,* the highest recognition awarded to foreigners by the Mexican government for cultural contribution to the Republic of Mexico.

When she is in San Diego, Diana invariably stays with Jerrie and Maury Strom in Rancho Santa Fe, where she chose to test a recipe for cow-muzzle salad, which appears in her latest book, *Nothing Fancy.* It is not a dish for the timid. First, you must find a cow muzzle (try a slaughterhouse) and then you must deal with the furried thing. Jerrie recalls coming home from a reception to find Diana awash in fur she had shaved off the muzzle. The dish, *Ensalada Trompa de Res, Estilo Chalet Suizo,* was served days later to the regional organizing committee for the International Association of Cooking Schools. It was delicious. The meat, thinly sliced and marinated in a spicy dressing, was served with marinated onion rings.

The biographical material we received about Maurice Moore-Betty prior to his first classes with us in 1977 spoke grandly about his high-society students from the Upper East Side, Long Island, and Palm Beach. We were prepared for someone rather grandly stuffy, perhaps even snooty. We couldn't have been more wrong. Maurice's early career had been in the military. The English-born Moore-Betty, whom one of our students fondly calls Brown-Betty (the name for a famous English teapot), learned to cook because he tired of restaurant food. He convinced the Ritz in London to let him work in the kitchen for $3 a day and stayed there a year. After emigrating to the United States, he became the chef for the executive dining room at American Express. His *Maurice Moore-Betty Cookbook* is eminently usable, with excellent recipes and instructions.

We've collected a wealth of Moore-Bettyisms, all of them as down-to-earth as he is. Among the most typical:

"No matter how old or ugly a butcher, it is your duty to make love to him."

". . . raw roux is the reason one has those terrifying sauces in restaurants."

"Cooking of vegetables has been neglected scandalously."

"Food is to be enjoyed, not worshiped."

Among Anne Otterson's richest contributions to The Perfect Pan were classes and dinners by chefs she discovered on her annual tours of France. Some of these chefs we brought to the United States on our own and, later, through the auspices of L'Ecole de Cuisine La Varenne in Paris.

Marc Meneau, owner/chef of L'Esperance in Saint-Père-sous-Vézelay in France, and his wife, Françoise, taught at The Perfect Pan in 1978. As early as 1975, Marc was regarded by many as the most original chef in France since the venerable Fernand Point of Le Pyramide. That year, at the age of twenty-seven, he became the youngest chef ever to have been awarded two stars by *Le Guide Michelin*. In 1984, he was awarded his third star, the highest attainable ranking.

Marc is rare among French chefs, who typically apprentice at an early age, leaving little time for formal schooling. He did not choose his career as innkeeper and restaurateur until he was twenty-four and well on his way to earning a degree in law. In her interview with the great chef, Marjorie Rice observed that Marc does not believe in working with precise measures when cooking meats and sauces; rather, "You feel, taste, and smell while cooking." He likened his experience of teaching American women to cook to teaching a group of virgins who lack the inner confidence to trust their own judgment. To him, the excitement of the kitchen is in the "idea" of the dish, and it is the combination of flavors and imaginative use of ingredients that makes cooking so special.

While he is a proponent of the *nouvelle cuisine* school of cooking which he learned from André Guillot, a master chef who worked mainly in the kitchens of the wealthy, Marc explained that many of his recipes, though labeled *nouvelle,* are 200 to 250 years old, dating from a time when wealthy people had servants and cooks preparing food in their homes. It could be prepared fresh, for the specific meal, and didn't need long cooking. He blames restaurants for the overcooked foods and belabored sauces simmered hours to avoid spoilage in prerefrigerator days. Those sauces dominated French cuisine until recently.

In keeping with our desire to encourage experimentation and a spirit of adventure, we are including a recipe from Meneau's classes with us, printed in the San Diego *Tribune*. Although Marjorie took meticulous notes in class and later went over each recipe with Marc, she cautions, "The recipes have ambiguous instructions and even more casual ingredient amounts." She suggests trying the recipe out with family first to get a feel for the techniques and ingredients. In other words, cook in the spirit of Meneau by feeling and smelling and tasting as you go.

MARC MENEAU'S PEARS ROSEMONDE

Makes 4 servings

This dessert can be made, for the most part, well ahead of serving time. The pineapple macerates in the rum, then goes into the hollowed-out pears. The sauce, a sabayon, takes a strong arm to whip and must be made at the last minute, since it loses its volume soon after cooking. Whisking from side to side, rather than a circular motion, results in greater volume.

FRUIT

1 cup fresh pineapple cubes
½ cup white rum
4 fresh pears
Lemon juice
½ cup granulated sugar
    (approximately)

SAUCE

6 egg yolks
½ to ⅔ cup sugar
Zest of 1 lime
2 cups Chablis

1. Cut the pineapple into small dice, mix it with the white rum, and set it aside. Peel the pears, leaving the stems attached, and core them by cutting from the bottom to form a generous hollow. Drop the pears into water acidulated with lemon juice to prevent darkening. Place the pears in a saucepan that will hold them in one layer. Sprinkle about ½ cup of sugar over them. Pour on just enough water to keep them from sticking (too much water will dilute the taste of the pears). Cover the pears with aluminum foil, then cover with the saucepan lid. You can add a few sprigs of mint, some candied ginger, vanilla bean, or fresh coriander (cilantro), if you wish. Poach the pears until just tender, but not soft.

2. Fill the pear hollows with the pineapple mixture. Stand the filled pears in a clean dish and chill them.

3. *To prepare the sauce:* In a medium, heavy saucepan, beat the egg yolks, the ½ to ⅔ cup sugar, and lime zest until light and pale. Place the pan over low heat and gradually add the wine, whisking vigorously until it expands in volume, becoming light and airy. Pour the sauce over the pears and serve immediately. (For more detailed instructions on making sabayon sauce, see Zabaglione, page 304).

While the seventies was an era of *nouvelle cuisine* in France, it was also the decade of the Italians — or, more precisely, the Northern Italians. By the early eighties, Americans were awash in pasta mania. Cold pasta salads proliferated, and only in culinary backwaters would anyone admit to using packaged pasta. Pasta machines and pasta shops became the rage, along with porcini mushrooms, sun-dried tomatoes, and heretofore unheard-of Italian cheeses. Naturally, we began to teach Italian cooking at The Perfect Pan. The vigor of the trend for Italian cooking and its durability is underscored by the fact that Nadia Frigeri, our resident Italian-cooking specialist, consistently has long waiting lists for her classes.

Our first guest teacher in Northern Italian cooking was Biba Caggiano. Biba was born in Bologna, where she met and married an Italian-American physician. They subsequently moved to New York City, and in 1970 settled in Sacramento. As Biba tells it, in Bologna she had little interest in cooking, and in New York there were enough good Italian restaurants and shops to make her happy. It was the dearth of good Italian food in Sacramento that provoked her to go back to Bologna to learn the simple, good cooking of her homeland. In Sacramento, she laments, if you put parsley on the steak it is "gourmet."

All successful cooking teachers are part performers, part teachers, and, of course, good cooks. Biba has an infectious enthusiasm, a verve that makes even the most timid cook want to get in there and try. Her food is the sort you love to eat and want to cook. A perfect example of Biba's easygoing style is this roasted bell pepper appetizer: Char red bell peppers over an open flame (or under a broiler) until they are dark brown and the skin is blistered. Place them in a plastic bag and seal the bag so the peppers will sweat. After the peppers cool, peel them and cut them in half, and remove the pith and seeds. Place them on a large serving platter. Combine minced fresh garlic, minced parsley, salt, pepper, freshly squeezed lemon juice, and extra-virgin olive oil to taste. Pour over the peppers and let them stand at room temperature for 30 minutes or longer, to blend the flavors. Serve on their own or with hunks of crusty Italian bread.

Marcella Hazan is a much more formal and formidable presence than Biba. She and her husband Victor, along with the indomitable Maria, Marcella's long-time assistant, arrived as an entourage in the spring of 1979. Husky voiced, aloof, and a rapid-fire chain smoker, Marcella was clearly not one to be tangled with. Victor, suave, handsome, and diplomatic, tended to run interference. Maria, diffident, capable, and fondly protective, seemed determined not to be the cause of any trouble. We all walked on eggs. As it turned out, we and our students had a grand time, and Marcella and Victor even talked about buying a home in the San Diego area.

Marcella has two Ph.D.s, one in biology and another in natural science. After moving to New York with Victor, she did not want to pursue her career in science and, as a lark, enrolled in a course in Japanese flower arranging. Fellow flower arrangers, fascinated with her tales of the lunches she prepared for Victor — multiple small courses to titillate the taste buds but not to overwhelm their trim figures — convinced her to teach her first cooking class.

Marcella is a great believer in the rhythm of an Italian meal, with its sequence of courses, all of equal importance. The first course, *i primi,* consists of pasta, soup, or rice. The second, *i secondi,* is always meat, fish, or poultry, with a vegetable. Dessert, *i dolci,* may be fruit or *gelato,* the Italians' sinfully delicious ice cream.

"Making pasta by hand is a craft, not a recipe," Marcella declares. Her classes for us went off without a snag and the food was fabulous, most of it seemingly easy to prepare.

Giuliano Bugialli earned his Ph.D. in Italian literature and went on to teach at the University of Florence and later at the Dalton School in New York. But he was always happiest in the kitchen, cooking and baking. Combining his love of cooking and a scholarly bent, he became fascinated with the ancient origins of contemporary

Tuscan foods and recipes, spending hours perfecting dishes using the methods and ingredients most closely resembling those of his ancestors. In 1972, he opened a cooking school in Florence while continuing to teach. During the first year he had just nineteen students, he told Eleanor Widmer, "all Americans. Italians do not consider cooking a subject to be learned at school." In 1977, having previously accepted a literature professorship at Dalton, he told his mother he had decided to take up teaching cooking as a full-time profession. "How can you possibly make a living from cooking?" she demanded.

Giuliano received seven hundred responses to the first advertisement for his class. He dedicated his first book, *The Fine Art of Italian Cooking,* a great success, to his mother, "the worst cook in the family." His second book, *Giuliano Bugialli's Foods of Italy,* was one of the most popular cookbooks during the 1984 holiday season at The Perfect Pan, in spite of its $45 price tag.

Giuliano's classes are unique. He makes pasta entirely by hand, for example — a process one would probably not try to duplicate at home, but it is fascinating to watch. The historical and literary perspective he brings to Italian cooking, as well as to certain aspects of French cuisine, makes his classes totally different from Marcella's or Biba's.

Madeleine Kamman first came to teach at The Perfect Pan in 1981, at a time when George and I were out of town. Lois Stanton and our teachers and students all adored her. No one could think of a single criticism. When she returned in April 1984, we saw firsthand why she commands both respect and affection.

Madeleine is a compact woman with glowing skin and softly graying hair. She has a pretty smile and ready wit; however, the authority of her carriage and movements leads one to suspect she could face down a five-star general, if need be. Born in Paris, she began working in her aunt's restaurant at the age of ten and later added to her culinary knowledge through extensive travel as a stewardess on an international airline. After marriage, she moved to Philadelphia and began teaching cooking. When she and her engineer husband moved to Boston, she opened the Modern Gourmet Cooking School and later a professional school of the same name, which was accredited by the Commonwealth of Massachusetts. The following year she added a restaurant, providing her professional students with practical experience in a commercial restaurant setting.

When the state began to require increased enrollments she closed the school in 1979 and took up residence in Annecy, France, where she continues to offer classes for hobbyist and professional cooks. Today she divides her time between Annecy and New Hampshire, offering classes in both locations. She is the author of *When French Women Cook, Cooking Against the Clock, The Making of a Cook,* and *In Madeleine's Kitchen.*

Rigidly following a recipe is for the birds, Madeleine likes to say, but she is a stickler for both fresh ingredients and command of technique. She has little use for anything less than perfection. Here is a quick little nonrecipe Madeleine suggests as a condiment for duck dishes. It would also be delicious with sausages and braised meats.

MADELEINE KAMMAN'S APRICOT AND GINGER COMPOTE

Peel 2 ginger roots (with about 4 "fingers" each) and cut them into paper-thin slices, then 1-inch julienne strips. Blanch the strips in boiling water for 5 seconds, then cook them briefly in a little butter until translucent. Soak 1 pound of dried apricots in cold water to cover for 30 minutes, then pour off the water to remove any sulfur taste. Soak the apricots again in cold water to cover for 30 minutes longer, drain, and save the liquid. Heat the apricots slowly in a small saucepan, in only enough soaking liquid to keep them from sticking. When they start to simmer, add 1 tablespoon honey and cook the apricots until they are very soft. Stir in the ginger, and serve.

In February 1978, George and I went to a housewares show in Cologne, followed by a week in Paris to set up an importing business and to visit charcuteries and pastry and bread shops. I recalled from my childhood in Europe, and, later, living among refugees in the United States, that Europeans combine freshly made carry-out foods with homemade dishes in their everyday meal planning. With more and more two-career families and single-parent households emerging in the U.S., George and I felt Americans would welcome the convenience of quality carry-out dishes, breads, and pastries.

Our trip convinced us of the wisdom of opening a carry-out establishment in the States. In Paris, George and I were like delighted children, exploring cheese shops, charcuteries, and pastry and bread shops. Every neighborhood, it seemed, had a profusion of tiny butcher shops, fishmongers, wine boutiques, and enough chocolate purveyors to satisfy the most addicted chocoholic. We spent a memorable weekend at Princess Marie-Blanche de Broglie's country estate in Normandy and discovered that even tiny villages offered a profusion of such establishments. Marie-Blanche taught at The Perfect Pan in the late seventies and recently published her delightful *Cuisine of Normandy,* a book made more special by her personal recollections of her father and post–World War II France.

When we returned home, we prepared a prospectus offering stock in The Perfect Pan company to raise capital for the development of Piret's charcuterie, boulangerie, and pâtisserie. Our original plan was to model Piret's after the French, with carry-out food counters in front of the shop and a kitchen in back. However, within several months we were offered the possibility of opening a second Piret's shortly after the first, and the added space requirements for the bakery and charcuterie kitchen made the original plan impractical. We opted to relocate our offices and warehouse to a larger facility that would house a central kitchen. From there, the foods made fresh each day were trucked to the retail outlets. We expanded on the French concept by offering customers a full range of foods: pâtés, sausages, and salads; breakfast pastries and breads; dessert pastries; cheeses; chocolates; coffees and teas; a wine boutique; and imported groceries. And since many of the prepared foods we offered were unfamiliar to San Diegans, we thought it would be a good idea to have limited restaurant service, bistro-style, to allow customers to try the new dishes.

We also were in a quandary about locating chefs experienced in French pastry-making and charcuterie. We hired Maybelle Iribe, who had many French connections in the United States and France, to help us. Soon — too soon, since we were months away from opening — the pastry chef appeared at our doorstep. Not wishing to lose him, we busied him in a friend's kitchen making small amounts of pastries which we sold at The Perfect Pan to whet customers' appetites for Piret's. These meager labors allowed him plenty of time to pursue personal hobbies like roller-skating. One day, skating at breakneck speed and out of control, he opted to take to the grass rather than plow into two sailors, whereupon he came to an abrupt halt and broke his leg. We took turns hauling him around and feeding him, praying for the leg to mend quickly.

By summer, Maybelle had also located a *charcutier* in France. We arranged to bring him and his wife to San Diego. Within weeks we discovered that his wife's languor was only partly caused by homesickness (she was very young and until now had not traveled more than ten miles from her village near Lyon). She was pregnant. The *charcutier* and the pastry chef viewed each other with equal distaste.

By the summer of 1979, we were operating the two Perfect Pan shops and cooking schools, trying to cope with our French chefs, and supervising construction at three sites simultaneously. George was our general contractor in addition to handling the buying and managing of the business. By now I had quit my public relations business and was working full-time at The Perfect Pan. Into this maelstrom, we invited Alain Dutournier, the owner/chef of Au Trou Gascon in Paris, to cook several dinners at Piret's just weeks after opening.

The first Piret's was 1,400 square feet and could seat 30 guests. The kitchen was a tiny affair, not designed to accommodate Alain's elegant *nouvelle cuisine* cooking. As much as possible, the food was prepared at the central kitchen and trucked in for last-minute preparations. We hooked a portable salamander (a commercial broiler) to propane gas tanks on the sidewalk. Alain, then a one-star, two-toque chef, coped admirably. One reviewer called his cooking "Genius. Sheer genius. A total tour de force." Eleanor Widmer described his first course of Gulf Shrimp with Saffron and Melon with Fresh Raspberries and Cinnamon Bark as "knock-out gorgeous." Of his Fresh Fruit Soup with Slivers of Cooked Egg White and Almond Sauce, she said, "I have rarely experienced such a remarkable combination of foods." Alain says he dreams of food all the time. When he buys fish, he visualizes how it will taste and the textures and colors of the finished dish. As he shops, he creates a mental image of the day's menu at Au Trou Gascon based entirely on the fresh ingredients available to him.

After opening Piret's, we suspended Lunch at The Perfect Pan, and Jack Monaco, our chef since 1978, became director of Piret's. Jack's interest in food is long-standing. He recalls rolling meatballs and raviolis in a family-owned restaurant at the age of three, and munching on pastries at another family establishment. His father's business required considerable travel, enabling Jack to taste a wide variety of American regional foods. As an art major in Philadelphia, he worked his way through college, cooking at all-night diners, and after serving in the navy in Vietnam, Jack and some friends launched a restaurant in San Diego, which ultimately failed. ("We were having too much fun and not minding the business.") Jack was chef at a bistro popular with the theater crowd prior to joining The Perfect Pan. Today he is director of food operations for Piret's.

Jack gives credit for the Filets Mignons with Roquefort Sauce (page 237) to André Daguin, chef/owner of Mapotel de France, who taught the recipe to him between courses they cooked for a dinner at Piret's in 1980. Jack serves the beef followed by a salad of green beans on Boston lettuce with a tarragon vinaigrette. The salad may be prepared ahead, but Jack warns not to mix the beans and the vinaigrette until just before serving, or the beans will turn gray.

JACK MONACO'S GREEN BEAN SALAD

Serves 6 to 8

MARINATED ONIONS

8 tablespoons extra-virgin olive oil

3 tablespoons tarragon vinegar

Pinch each of dry mustard, sugar, salt, and freshly ground pepper

1 yellow onion, thinly sliced

2 pounds tender, fresh green beans

2 heads Boston lettuce

1 tablespoon minced fresh parsley

1. *To marinate the onions:* Whisk together the olive oil, tarragon vinegar, dry mustard, sugar, salt, and pepper. Pour the mixture over the sliced onion and let stand at least an hour.

2. Remove the ends of the green beans and blanch them in 2 quarts of salted boiling water for 2 to 3 minutes. Quickly refresh the beans in ice water. The beans should be bright green and still very crisp.

3. Wash the lettuce and dry the leaves in a salad spinner, or carefully blot them with paper towels. Ten minutes prior to serving, arrange the lettuce on a platter or individual serving plates, and toss the green beans with the onions and their marinade. Arrange the beans on the lettuce and spoon over the onions and marinade. Sprinkle the salad with the parsley, and serve immediately.

In addition to his day-to-day management tasks, Jack also has had responsibility for Piret's Catering. One of our favorite clients is Tawfiq Khoury, who has one of the finest private wine cellars in the United States. He and his wife, Richel, plan their parties carefully, and the planning begins with the wines he selects for his guests. Our menus are designed around the wines. Robert Mondavi and his wife, Margrit Biever, are favorite and frequent guests at the Khourys'. At a dinner celebrating their wedding, this was the menu prepared by Jack and our chef Andre Pinel.

Reserve Chardonnay Robert Mondavi, 1977	Lemon-Soy Swordfish Steaks with Avocado Butter (page 173)
Romanée Conti, 1937	Squab André de Groot
	Sorbets
Château Mouton Rothschild, 1949	Saddle of Lamb Arlesienne
Château d'Yquem, 1937	Poached Figs with Raspberry Sauce
Cockburn Port (magnum), 1927	Savoury Richel

Another memorable dining occasion, orchestrated by Jack at Piret's, was a series of dinners cooked by Michel Pasquet, owner/chef of the Paris restaurant bearing his name. After only three years in the restaurant business, Michel had earned a Michelin star and two toques from Gault-Millau. That, however, should not be too surprising since he had chosen his professional calling by the age of four. Maureen Clancy described his first course of Flan of Chicken Livers with Port Wine Cream Sauce as "breathtaking" and pronounced his dessert, Orange Sherbet with Grenadine-Soaked Orange Rind in Cookie Tulips, "spectacular."

As is true of most of the young chefs in France and the United States, for Michel, cooking is a passion. If memory serves me correctly, nine chefs toil in his kitchen to serve thirty-eight guests. Among his adages are those shared by many cooks whose recipes appear in this book: Cook with respect for the seasons, using only the freshest meats, fish, and produce. And don't bother to measure things to the teaspoon; cooking should be done to taste.

During Michel's visit to San Diego we were again building, this time in North San Diego County, where in November 1982 we opened a combined Piret's, Perfect Pan shop, and cooking school. We closed our second Perfect Pan shop a few miles south of the new location and, much to our relief, finally moved the cooking school out of our home (where we had moved it a few years earlier to make room for a mini-Piret's carry-out). This was our third Piret's. With a new and major investor, we forged ahead the following year, opening a combined Piret's, Pan shop, and cooking school in Orange County at South Coast Plaza, and a Piret's in East San Diego.

In the spring of 1984, we opened a Piret's unlike any other, this one in the spacious atrium lobby at a San Diego high-rise office building.

Gradually, inspired by our customers rather than by intent, we had become restaurateurs. Each successive Piret's, while including all the original carry-out foods and wines, grew in restaurant seating and size. Each new kitchen became more comprehensive, offering *nouvelle* pizzas, fresh pastas, grilled fish dishes, and giving the chef in each kitchen more latitude with daily specials. We continue to provision Piret's with fresh pastries and charcuterie specialties from the central kitchen each day.

By spring of 1984, George and I realized that what had started out to be a small, hands-on food business had grown willy-nilly to something quite a lot larger than we had envisioned. We could no longer be everywhere, doing everything. We needed computers and systems and back-office support. Venture capital investors, interested franchisees, stockbrokers, and our own shareholders advised us about future financing and needed management skills. Arjun Waney, our major shareholder, discussed the problem with a friend, who suggested a meeting with VICORP Restaurants, Inc., an aggressive restaurant chain out of Denver. In whirlwind negotiations lasting less than a month, Piret's and The Perfect Pan were swept into the VICORP empire. Today there are plans to expand Piret's in Southern California and elsewhere.

George and I are often asked to speak to college students about our careers. How did we end up where we are? What is the secret? As you know from reading this, we certainly didn't have any master plan to speak of. But Julia Child didn't learn to cook until mid-life when she and her husband Paul lived in Paris, where he was in the U.S. diplomatic corps. Marcella Hazan began her career as a scientist. Giuliano Bugialli was a professor of literature who loved food and cooking as a hobby. Jack Monaco was an art major. Ben Patterson's first career was in the theater. Biba Caggiano became a cooking teacher out of desperation when she couldn't find acceptable Italian food in Sacramento. Maurice Moore-Betty was a military man. Diana Kennedy learned to love Mexican cuisine because her late husband, Paul, was a correspondent for the *New York Times* in Mexico. Jacques Pépin could well have been a career-long chef in a fine restaurant instead of an author/teacher. George has a degree in history. Mine is in American literature. Who would suspect, least of all me, the turns our lives would take.

2

BEGINNINGS

APPETIZERS &
FIRST COURSES

SOUPS

APPETIZERS AND FIRST COURSES

Gravlax with Mustard Sauce and Cucumber Salad · Wild Mushroom Walnut Spread on Garlic Toast Rounds · Brie with Roquefort and Herbs · Maurice Moore-Betty's Shrimp Scandia · Marinated Shrimp Stuffed with Chèvre · Coquilles Florentine · Scallops Vesuvio · Fettuccine with Shrimp Sauce · Fettuccine with Caviar · Pasta with Cream Sauce · Carpaccio with Caviar Mayonnaise · Pasta Salad with Smoked Salmon and Sun-Dried Tomatoes · Hugh Carpenter's Pon-Pon Noodle Salad · Escargots Piret's · Calamari Belajack · Duck Breast and Cèpes Salad · Roasted Duck Salad

SOUPS

Fish Soup · Mediterranean Fish Soup with Garlic · Cream of Scallop Soup · Mussel Soup Piret's · New England Clam Chowder · Potato and Cheddar Cheese Soup · Cream of Mushroom Soup · Watercress Soup · Cream of Broccoli Soup · Cream of Artichoke and Chestnut Soup · Onion Soup Piret's · Gazpacho · Minestrone alla Diana · Tomato Consommé · Becky's Klodniak · Peach Soup with Champagne

I N MANY WAYS, the first course, whether soup, salad, or a more elaborate preparation, is the most important part of a meal. It sets the tone and mood for the entire menu. And it should create a balance for what is to come. If the first course is rich, balance it with a light entrée. If the entrée is robustly flavored, a more delicate first course is appreciated. If budget is a concern, serve costly foods such as shellfish in the first course, when portions will be smaller.

When entertaining at home, George and I like to balance the amount of time needed for last-minute preparations. Since most of our friends tend to congregate in the kitchen while we're working there, we plan a first course that will be done at the last minute, while the entrée, salad, and dessert can be prepared almost wholly in advance. This allows us to enjoy our friends with a minimum of absences from the table.

Nearly all of the recipes in this section can become entrées by increasing the quantities (or reducing the number of guests). Certainly many of the soups are substantial enough to make a very pleasant main dish for supper. The variety of these dishes reflects their sources in our cooking school, in Southern California regionalisms, and in the French orientation of Piret's.

APPETIZERS AND FIRST COURSES

GRAVLAX WITH MUSTARD SAUCE AND CUCUMBER SALAD

Makes 16 servings

Choose only the very freshest, firmest salmon for gravlax, and figure about 2 ounces per serving. The salmon must be very thinly sliced. This can best be accomplished by chilling it first and then using a fish filleting knife or any thin-bladed sharp knife that is at least 5 inches long. Wetting the blade will keep the knife from dragging through the delicate fish flesh.

Fresh dill is imperative to the success of this Scandinavian delicacy; do not substitute dried.

2 pounds center-cut fresh
    salmon, unskinned, cut
    into 2 fillets
½ cup sugar
¼ cup kosher-style salt
1 tablespoon freshly ground
    pepper
1 to 2 bunches fresh dill,
    coarsely chopped

1. Place one salmon fillet, skin side down, in a ceramic or glass dish. Sprinkle on half each of the sugar, salt, and pepper, and all of the dill. Top with the second salmon fillet and sprinkle on the remaining sugar, salt, and pepper. Cover the fish with foil, place a board on top, and weight the fish down (a six-pack of beer works well). Refrigerate the fish for at least two days, turning and basting it 3 times a day with the juices that accumulate.

2. To serve, place one salmon fillet skin side down on a board and slice thinly on the diagonal, to, but not through, the skin. Repeat with second fillet. Coat the sliced salmon lightly with mustard sauce. Serve with cucumber salad, the rest of the mustard sauce, and pumpernickel bread.

❦ To maximize the life of fresh dill or any other fresh herb, trim the stems and place the herb bouquet in a small amount of water in a drinking glass in the refrigerator. Change the water daily and trim the stems from time to time.

Mustard Sauce
Makes about 2 cups

4 tablespoons chopped
    fresh dill
1 cup extra-virgin olive oil
6 tablespoons Dijon-style
    mustard
4 to 5 tablespoons white
    wine vinegar
2 to 3 tablespoons sugar
Salt and freshly ground
    pepper, to taste

Whisk all ingredients together to form a smooth sauce. Refrigerate it overnight, covered, to blend the flavors.

Cucumber Salad
Makes 12 to 16 servings

8 cucumbers
Salt
2½ cups white wine vinegar
4 tablespoons soy sauce
10 tablespoons chopped
    fresh dill
½ cup peanut oil
Salt and freshly ground
    pepper, to taste

1. Score the unpeeled cucumbers with a fork and slice them very thinly. Sprinkle the slices liberally with salt and let them drain in a colander for 1 hour. Rinse the cucumbers and pat them dry.

2. Combine the vinegar, soy sauce, dill, oil, salt, and pepper. Toss the dressing with the cucumbers, and chill the salad.

WILD MUSHROOM WALNUT SPREAD ON GARLIC TOAST ROUNDS

Makes 8 servings

3 ounces dried chanterelle
mushrooms (see note)
1½ cups warm water
1 cup heavy cream
3 tablespoons Cognac
8 tablespoons unsalted
butter
1 large clove garlic, minced
1 baguette, sliced in
¼-inch-thick rounds
4 tablespoons virgin or
extra-virgin olive oil
½ cup minced shallots
2 cloves garlic, minced
½ cup minced mixed fresh
herbs (summer savory,
chives, tarragon, thyme,
chervil, etc.)
1 cup minced fresh parsley
Kosher-style salt and freshly
ground pepper, to taste
5 tablespoons cream cheese,
softened
¾ cup toasted, minced
walnuts

1. Soak the mushrooms in the warm water for 30 minutes. Remove them with a slotted spoon, rinse, pat them dry, and coarsely chop them.

2. Combine the cream and Cognac in a small, heavy saucepan and simmer the mixture over medium heat, whisking it occasionally, until it is thickened and reduced by half, about 20 to 25 minutes.

3. Meanwhile, melt the butter in a medium skillet, add the 1 clove minced garlic, and drop in the bread rounds, coating both sides with the garlic butter. Cook the bread until the butter has been absorbed and both sides are golden. Place the toasted rounds on a baking sheet and keep them warm in a 225° oven.

4. Wipe out the skillet with paper towels. Add the olive oil, and sauté the chopped chanterelles, shallots, and remaining garlic over medium heat for 10 minutes. Sprinkle on the mixed herbs and the parsley, tossing to blend.

5. Season the mixture with kosher-style salt and pepper, and stir in the reduced cream and Cognac mixture. Add the cream cheese and walnuts, blending them well.

6. Spread the mushroom mixture on the garlic toast rounds, or spoon it into a crock surrounded by the toast rounds and allow your guests to serve themselves.

NOTE

Morels, cèpes, or shiitake mushrooms may be substituted for the chanterelles. Each ounce of dried mushrooms measures about 1 cup after soaking. Fresh mushrooms also may be substituted: sauté 4 cups chopped mushrooms in the olive oil with the garlic and shallots until all the liquid has evaporated, then proceed as directed above.

🔊 The soaking liquid for dried mushrooms is flavorful. Strained through several layers of dampened cheesecloth, it may be added to pasta sauces, soups, or stocks.

BRIE WITH ROQUEFORT AND HERBS

Serves about 6 people

This is a great savory to serve at a buffet supper or with aged Port after dessert at a formal dinner party. Quantities can vary to suit the number of people you wish to serve. Figure on an 8-inch round of Brie for a party of six. If you're having a crowd, splurge and get a large round (12 to 14 inches). Sometimes we decorate the top of the Brie with fresh fruit such as halved strawberries or kiwi, laid in a pretty concentric pattern.

1 round (8 inches) ripe
    Brie
1 cup Roquefort (or any
    blue-veined cheese)
2 to 4 tablespoons *crème
    fraîche* (page 175)
4 tablespoons chopped fresh
    herbs (such as chives,
    sage, parsley, and basil)
Cracked peppercorns,
    to taste

NOTE

VARIATIONS

Gorgonzola–pine nut filling

1. Place the Brie in the freezer for about 15 minutes to make it firm. With the knife blade parallel to the work surface, cut the Brie in half horizontally. Combine the Roquefort with enough *crème fraîche* to make it spreadable but not runny.

2. Place the bottom layer of Brie, cut side up, on a serving dish. Spread the Roquefort over the Brie. Sprinkle on a liberal layer of chopped herbs and cracked pepper. Cover with the top layer of Brie. Seal the Brie in plastic wrap and refrigerate it overnight. Bring it to room temperature before serving.

For a group of twelve or more, get a 12- to 14-inch Brie, and use about 2 cups of Roquefort, ¼ to ⅓ cup of *crème fraîche*, and ¾ cup of chopped fresh herbs. Below are some favorite variations from Lois Stanton's repertoire of recipes for entertaining. The ingredient amounts are for an 8-inch Brie, and you can easily scale them up for a larger round in proportions similar to those for the basic recipe.

Use 1 cup Gorgonzola cheese, 2 tablespoons *crème*

fraîche, 3 tablespoons fresh minced basil, and ¼ cup toasted pine nuts.

Marscapone and almond filling — Use 1 cup Marscapone cheese, 2 fresh figs, peeled and chopped, and ⅓ cup toasted slivered almonds.

Robiolla and walnut filling — Use 1 cup Robiolla cheese, 1 fresh, ripe pear, peeled and chopped, and ¼ cup of English or California walnuts, chopped.

MAURICE MOORE-BETTY'S SHRIMP SCANDIA

Makes 6 servings

Serve a crisp, dry white wine with this cold shrimp appetizer. Maurice's sauce is similar to the Mustard Sauce we include for Gravlax (page 27). In fact, you may want to try his sauce with the salmon for variety.

SAUCE

1 tablespoon prepared mustard
1 tablespoon sugar (or more, to taste)
1½ tablespoons white wine vinegar
½ teaspoon salt
Freshly ground white pepper, to taste
1 teaspoon lemon juice
1 tablespoon chopped fresh dill
4 tablespoons vegetable oil

SHRIMP

1½ pounds small to medium shrimp (approximately 25 to 30 to the pound), unshelled
2 tablespoons chopped onion
1 rib celery, chopped
1 tablespoon salt
4 whole black peppercorns

1. *To prepare the sauce:* In a jar with a tight-fitting lid, combine the mustard, sugar, white wine vinegar, salt, pepper, lemon juice, dill, and oil. Shake well. Allow the sauce to stand for several hours before serving.

2. Shell and devein the shrimp and rinse them under cold running water. In a medium, enameled cast-iron saucepan, combine the onions, celery, salt, and peppercorns, and fill with cold water to cover. Bring the water to a boil, reduce the heat, and simmer, covered, for 5 minutes.

3. Add the shrimp to the saucepan, bring the mixture back to a boil, and boil the shrimp, covered, for 1 minute. Remove the pan from the heat and allow the shrimp to stand in the cooking liquid for 10 minutes more. Drain the shrimp, and cool.

4. To serve, arrange the shrimp attractively on a serving platter, and pass the sauce for dipping.

MARINATED SHRIMP STUFFED WITH CHÈVRE

Makes 4 servings

Only recently have we had chèvre, or goat cheese, available in the United States in some profusion. Having seen the public enthusiasm for it, some American cheese-makers, notably Laura Chenel in Northern California, are now beginning to make it as well. Goat cheese has a tangier flavor than cow's milk cheeses, providing an interesting counterpoint in cooking and making it a favorite among America's young, experimental chefs. Choose a plain goat cheese rather than one that has been rolled in ashes or herbs.

TO PREPARE THE SHRIMP

1 pound large or jumbo
   shrimp, unshelled
1¼ cups extra-virgin olive
   oil
2 small cloves garlic,
   mashed
1¼ cups raspberry vinegar
¼ to ½ cup mild white
   wine vinegar
1 clove garlic, minced
¼ cup minced fresh parsley
¼ cup minced scallions
1 tablespoon fresh tarragon
   (or 1 teaspoon dried)
Pinch of sugar
Salt and freshly ground
   pepper, to taste

1. Shell the shrimp, reserving the shells (do not devein). Wash the shrimp and refrigerate them while you prepare the shrimp oil.

2. Grind the shrimp shells in a food processor fitted with the steel blade. Place the ground shells in a saucepan and add the olive oil. Cook the mixture over very low heat for 20 minutes. Strain the oil through a fine sieve into a large bowl, pressing the shells to get all the oil.

3. Heat 2 to 4 tablespoons of the shrimp oil (reserve the rest) in a sauté pan, and cook the shrimp with the mashed garlic for 3 to 4 minutes. Remove the shrimp, and place them in a bowl with the reserved shrimp oil.

4. Add the vinegars, minced garlic, parsley, scallions, tarragon, sugar, salt, and pepper to the shrimp and oil. Taste, adjust the seasonings, and refrigerate for 1 hour, stirring occasionally.

TO STUFF THE SHRIMP

1 pound chèvre (goat cheese)
8 to 12 teaspoons heavy
   cream
¼ teaspoon cayenne pepper
Butter lettuce

1. Beat the chèvre with the cream, then beat in the cayenne pepper. Place the mixture in a pastry bag fitted with a ¼-inch star tip.

2. Remove the shrimp from the marinade. Open up the backs of the shrimp (do not cut them all the way through), and pipe in the chèvre mixture.

3. Place the filled shrimp on a plate lined with butter lettuce leaves, drizzle some of the marinade over, and serve.

COQUILLES FLORENTINE

Makes 12 to 14 first-course servings

Over the years, we have found that writers love to cook, and that the best writer-cook combinations seem to have Southern origins. This may be a new myth, but it is certainly true of our friend Bill Glasgow, whose roots are in Arkansas, even though he has spent most of his journalistic life roaming around Europe and the United States.

Bill's Coquilles Florentine makes an excellent appetizer when served on toast rounds, or makes 12 to 14 first-course servings. Serve it in scallop shells for a pretty presentation.

15 ounces frozen leaf spinach
   (or 4 bunches fresh)
1½ pounds fresh mushrooms
4 cups fish stock or bottled
   clam juice
2 cups dry vermouth
½ cup chopped shallots
1½ pounds large shrimp,
   unshelled
1½ pounds scallops
1 cup unsalted butter
2 cups milk
½ cup unbleached,
   all-purpose flour
1 cup heavy cream
2 egg yolks
¾ cup freshly grated Swiss
   cheese
¼ cup freshly grated
   Parmesan cheese
1 tablespoon Pernod
1 cup fresh bread crumbs
1 bunch parsley, chopped,
   for garnish

1. Cook the spinach according to the package directions, drain, and squeeze it dry in a towel. (For fresh spinach: Wash the spinach and put it in a saucepan with only the water that clings to the leaves. Cook it over high heat, covered, for about 30 seconds. Stir the spinach, and continue cooking just until it wilts. Drain and squeeze dry in a towel.) Chop the spinach finely and set it aside. Wipe the mushrooms with a damp towel and remove the stems. Reserve the stems and slice the caps.

2. In a medium saucepan, combine the fish stock or clam juice, the vermouth, the mushroom stems, and the shallots. Bring the mixture to a boil, reduce the heat, and simmer for 5 minutes. Add the shrimp in their shells and simmer until they turn pink, about 5 minutes. Remove the shrimp from the liquid with a slotted spoon and set them aside. Reserve the cooking liquid.

3. Remove and discard the muscles from the scallops. Simmer the scallops in the reserved cooking liquid for 3 to 4 minutes, then remove them with a slotted spoon. Strain the cooking liquid into a clean pan through a double thickness of dampened cheesecloth. Reduce the liquid over high heat to about 3 cups.

4. Melt ½ cup of the butter over medium heat and sauté the sliced mushroom caps for 5 minutes. Put them in a colander to drain.

5. Shell and devein the cooked shrimp, split them lengthwise, and cut them into ¾-inch pieces. Slice the scallops ¼-inch thick. Combine the shrimp, scallops, and mushrooms in a large bowl.

6. Add the milk to the reduced cooking liquid and bring it to a boil. Set the mixture aside. In another saucepan, melt the remaining ½ cup of butter. Add the flour, stirring constantly with a wire whisk until it thickens into a smooth roux. Cook the roux for 2 minutes, whisking all the while. Pour in the hot milk mixture, and whisk the sauce over medium heat until it is smooth and thick (about 8 minutes). Stir in the cream. Lightly beat the egg yolks with a little of the hot sauce, then stir them back into the sauce, whisking until smooth. Stir in the Swiss and Parmesan cheeses until they melt. Add the Pernod and spinach, stirring until smooth.

7. Preheat oven to 450°. Mix the sauce with the shrimp-scallop mixture and spoon it into a buttered gratin dish, if serving on toast rounds, or into 12 to 14 scallop shells. Sprinkle on the bread crumbs and bake for 10 to 15 minutes, until browned. Garnish with chopped parsley, and serve immediately.

SCALLOPS VESUVIO

Makes 4 servings

Jack Monaco came up with this delicious first course. It should be cooked quickly so the tomatoes keep their fresh texture and flavor. Total cooking time for this dish is about 10 minutes. Serve the scallops with hot French bread.

1 pound sea or bay scallops
¼ cup clarified butter (page 239)
8 cloves garlic, mashed
½ teaspoon salt
⅛ teaspoon freshly ground pepper
¼ teaspoon cayenne pepper
1 tablespoon chopped fresh parsley
3 tablespoons lemon juice
2 tablespoons dry vermouth
4 small tomatoes, peeled and seeded
Lemon wedges and sprigs of fresh parsley or cilantro (fresh coriander), for garnish

1. Thoroughly rinse the scallops under cold running water to remove any sand or grit. Remove the small muscle, if it is present, and pat the scallops dry with paper towels.

2. In a large skillet or sauté pan, heat the clarified butter and garlic over medium heat, to soften but not fry the garlic. Add the scallops, salt, pepper, cayenne pepper, parsley, lemon juice, and vermouth, and cook until the scallops are nearly done (they'll turn milky white and lose their translucency). Add the tomatoes during the final minutes of cooking. The tomatoes should retain a fresh appearance and flavor. Take care not to overcook the scallops or they will be tough.

3. Divide scallops among individual serving plates or scallop shells, and garnish with lemon wedges and parsley or cilantro.

❧ The secret to all scallop cooking lies in the freshness of the scallops and quick cooking. Considering the expense, it is worthwhile to deal regularly with a reputable fish market so the staff will sell you only the highest quality available. If you buy the scallops a day ahead, soak them in milk in the refrigerator to keep them sweet and juicy. When preparing the scallops for cooking, remove the tough muscle tissue. And remember, scallops cook very quickly — in less than a minute. Scallops should be milky white, but still slightly translucent, after cooking. At this point they are tender and almost without texture.

We favor sea scallops, because they have more flavor. If a recipe calls for bay scallops and the small size is important to the dish, cut the sea scallops in half horizontally and then into fourths.

FETTUCCINE WITH SHRIMP SAUCE

Makes 6 servings

For a more complex and sophisticated dish, we sometimes serve this sauce with tortellini or ravioli stuffed with a filling of minced fresh fish. This recipe is Nadia Frigeri's.

1 pound small or medium shrimp, unshelled
4 tablespoons butter
4 tablespoons virgin olive oil
1 tablespoon finely chopped scallions
3 tablespoons brandy
¼ cup dry white wine
3 tomatoes, peeled, seeded, and chopped
Pinch of salt and cayenne pepper
1 cup heavy cream
Fettuccine made with 3 cups of unbleached, all-purpose flour and 4 eggs (see Basic Egg Pasta, page 187), or about 1½ pounds dried fettuccine

1. Shell and devein the shrimp, reserving the shells. Set the shrimp aside. Melt 2 tablespoons of the butter with the oil in a heavy skillet. Add the reserved shrimp shells and sauté them over high heat for 3 minutes. Remove the shells with a slotted spoon, allowing the butter and oil to drain back into the pan. Discard the shells.

2. Add to the pan the scallions, brandy, white wine, tomatoes, salt, and cayenne pepper. Simmer the mixture gently over low heat for about 10 minutes, until the liquid is reduced by one-third.

3. Add the reserved shrimp and the cream, and cook the sauce over low heat for 5 to 8 minutes more, or until the shrimp are just cooked. Whisk in the remaining 2 tablespoons of butter.

4. Cook the fettuccine in a large pot of salted boiling water, 2 to 3 minutes for fresh pasta, about 7 minutes for dried. The pasta should be al dente. Drain it well and toss it with the sauce. Serve immediately.

FETTUCCINE WITH CAVIAR

Makes 6 to 8 servings

George served this delicious first-course pasta dish at one of his caviar tastings. You can also use California golden caviar, which has firmer eggs and a pretty color.

1 pound fresh or dried
   fettuccine
¼ cup plus 1 tablespoon
   unsalted butter
1½ cups heavy cream
½ cup freshly grated
   Parmesan cheese
1 can or jar (2 ounces) fresh
   Sevruga caviar (reserve
   1 or 2 teaspoons
   for garnish)

1. Cook the fettuccine in salted boiling water to which 1 tablespoon of butter has been added. Cook 2 to 3 minutes for fresh pasta, about 7 minutes for dried. The pasta should be al dente. Meanwhile, melt the ¼ cup butter in a large skillet. Add the cream and heat it to simmering.

2. Remove the fettuccine from the water with a fork to drain the excess water, but let some moisture cling to the noodles. Place the noodles in the skillet with the butter-cream mixture and toss the pasta gently to coat it with the sauce. At the last minute, add the Parmesan cheese and caviar, stirring gently to blend. Serve the pasta immediately in heated plates or bowls, topping each serving with a little of the reserved caviar.

NOTE

Be sure to serve the cooked pasta immediately after adding the caviar, without heating it further, or the caviar eggs will become hard-boiled.

PASTA WITH CREAM SAUCE

Makes 6 servings

The recipe for this simple, classic sauce was taught to us by Jerrie Strom and Fran Jenkins. It can be doubled for main-course servings.

1 cup heavy cream
3 tablespoons unsalted
  butter
½ pound fresh or dried
  fettuccine or tagliatelle
  noodles
⅔ cup freshly grated
  Parmesan cheese
Freshly ground pepper,
  to taste
Freshly grated nutmeg,
  to taste
Minced fresh Italian parsley,
  for garnish
Freshly grated Parmesan
  cheese

1. Choose a saucepan large enough to accommodate the finished pasta. Combine ⅔ cup of the cream and all of the butter in the saucepan and simmer them over medium heat until the butter and cream have thickened slightly. Remove the pan from the heat.

2. In a large pot, bring 4 quarts of salted water to a boil and add the pasta. Cook the pasta to the early al dente stage (firmer than usual because it will cook some more in the pan with the sauce: 2 to 3 minutes for fresh, about 5 to 7 minutes for dried). Drain the pasta and transfer it to the pan with the butter and cream.

3. Toss the pasta in the butter-cream sauce over low heat until the pasta is evenly coated. Add the remaining cream and the Parmesan cheese, and season with pepper and nutmeg. Toss until the pasta is well coated.

4. Garnish the pasta with parsley, and serve it with additional grated Parmesan cheese on the side.

NOTE

For a flavor variation, and to add some crunch to the pasta, add ¼ cup poppy seeds when tossing the pasta with the sauce.

CARPACCIO WITH CAVIAR MAYONNAISE

Makes 6 servings

George loves carpaccio, and he loves caviar. For the mayonnaise sauce, it is perfectly acceptable to use an ungraded caviar with less than perfect eggs, since incorporating the caviar eggs into the sauce will bruise them slightly no matter how careful you are. Serve this dish with a carafe of good Chianti.

TO PREPARE THE CARPACCIO

1 pound prime shell steak or top round, completely trimmed of fat and sinews (1½ pounds before trimming)
Salt and freshly ground pepper, to taste
Juice of 1 lemon

Slice the meat very thinly, across the grain. (This is easier to do if the meat is thoroughly chilled or even slightly frozen.) Wet the counter and a meat pounder, and pound the slices to about 3 to 4 inches in diameter. The meat should be almost paper-thin. Arrange the meat on a platter. Sprinkle on a small amount of salt, pepper, and the lemon juice. (Remember that caviar is salty, so use only enough salt to flavor the meat slightly.) Cover the meat and keep it chilled until just before serving.

TO PREPARE THE MAYONNAISE

1 egg yolk
2 teaspoons lemon juice
1 cup extra-virgin olive oil
¼ to ½ teaspoon freshly ground pepper
1 tin (1 ounce) Sevruga caviar
1 hard-cooked egg, yolk and white sieved separately
6 scallions, for garnish

1. Whisk together the egg yolk and lemon juice. Drizzle the olive oil into the mixture, starting a few drops at a time and increasing to a very thin stream, whisking vigorously all the while to form a thick, creamy mayonnaise. Season with the freshly ground pepper. Stir in 3 to 4 tablespoons of the caviar, blending gently but thoroughly.

2. To serve, arrange the sliced meat attractively on six chilled dinner plates. Spoon the caviar mayonnaise liberally over the meat. Sprinkle the egg white lightly over the mayonnaise, then add a fine sprinkling of egg yolk. Garnish each plate with a dollop of caviar and a scallion. Serve with crisp Italian bread and unsalted butter.

PASTA SALAD WITH SMOKED SALMON AND SUN-DRIED TOMATOES

Makes 4 to 6 servings

Neither lox nor the "gourmet" smoked side of salmon will work for this salad, since neither one flakes. Almost all Jewish delicatessens and fish markets sell thicker smoked chunks of salmon. If you can't find smoked salmon, smoked tuna in chunks will work equally well.

DRESSING

¾ cup extra-virgin olive oil
4 to 5 tablespoons lemon
   juice
2 tablespoons bottled clam
   juice
1 clove garlic, minced
1 tablespoon minced shallot
1 tablespoon fresh dill weed
   (or ½ teaspoon dried)
Grated zest of 1 lemon
Freshly ground pepper,
   to taste
¼ cup freshly grated
   Parmesan cheese

SALAD

½ pound smoked salmon,
   in chunks
3 cups small shell macaroni,
   cooked, drained,
   and cooled
½ cup mozzarella cheese,
   julienne-cut
½ cup sun-dried tomatoes,
   chopped
½ cup minced fresh parsley

Crisp salad greens
Sun-dried tomatoes,
   for garnish
Freshly grated Parmesan
   cheese

1. *To prepare the dressing:* Whisk together the olive oil, lemon juice, clam juice, garlic, shallots, dill, lemon zest, and pepper, blending them well. Stir in the Parmesan cheese.

2. *To prepare the salad:* Flake the salmon into fairly large pieces. In a large bowl, combine the salmon with the macaroni, mozzarella cheese, tomatoes, and parsley.

3. Add just enough of the dressing to the salmon-pasta mixture to moisten all the ingredients, and toss lightly. Mound the salad on a lettuce-lined platter or in a salad bowl. Garnish with chopped sun-dried tomatoes. Pass freshly grated Parmesan cheese.

HUGH CARPENTER'S PON-PON NOODLE SALAD

Makes 8 servings

Hugh Carpenter is one of the great culinary talents on the West Coast. His specialty is Chinese cuisine. Our students adore him for his mastery of technique and wonderful sense of humor. The ingredients for this recipe are available at Asian and Chinese specialty food shops.

Most of the preparation for this salad can be done several hours ahead of serving time. To keep the noodles from sticking together, toss them with a little peanut oil after they are cooked. The ingredients should not be mixed and dressed until just before serving. Virtually any matchstick-cut vegetable is excellent in this salad.

MARINADE

3 tablespoons hoisin sauce
1 tablespoon oyster sauce
2 teaspoons peanut oil
2 teaspoons chili paste with garlic
1 tablespoon dark soy sauce
1 tablespoon honey

SALAD

3 large chicken thighs
2 large carrots
2 large zucchini
2 cups bean sprouts
½ pound fresh or dried Chinese noodles (see note)
1 tablespoon peanut oil (optional)

DRESSING

2 tablespoons minced fresh ginger
3 medium cloves garlic, minced
3 tablespoons red wine vinegar
1 tablespoon sugar
2 tablespoons mushroom soy sauce
1 tablespoon sesame oil

1. *To marinate the chicken:* Whisk together the hoisin sauce, oyster sauce, peanut oil, chili paste, soy sauce, and honey. Rub the marinade into the chicken thighs, place them in a glass or porcelain dish, and let them stand 30 minutes to an hour. (They can be refrigerated in the marinade overnight.)

2. Preheat oven to 400°. Bake the chicken thighs in the marinade for about 30 minutes, or until they are cooked through. When the chicken is cool enough to handle, remove the meat with the skin from the bones and cut into thin slivers.

3. Cut the carrots on a very sharp diagonal into thin slices, then overlap the slices and cut the carrots into slivers. Cut the zucchini into slivers in the same manner. (Other fresh, crisp vegetables may be substituted for the carrots or zucchini.) Plunge the bean sprouts into boiling water, drain them immediately, and plunge them into ice water to refresh for a minute. Pat them dry with paper towels.

4. Drop the noodles into lightly salted boiling water and cook until they are al dente. Drain the noodles, rinse them briefly under cold water, and drain them again. If you are preparing them ahead of time and the noodles will stand for a while, toss the noodles with the peanut oil.

5. *To prepare the dressing:* Whisk together the minced ginger and garlic, red wine vinegar, sugar,

⅛ teaspoon ground
  Szechwan peppercorns
½ teaspoon salt
2 teaspoons chili paste with
  garlic

¼ cup minced scallion
2 tablespoons minced
  cilantro (fresh coriander)

mushroom soy, sesame oil, Szechwan peppercorns, salt, and chili paste.

6. *To assemble the salad:* Using your fingers, thoroughly blend the chicken, carrots, zucchini, bean sprouts, and noodles. Add the dressing, scallions, and cilantro, mixing the ingredients thoroughly, again using your hands. Serve immediately.

NOTE

Chinese noodles, staple items in any Chinese market, are sold fresh and dried. Cook them as you would spaghetti. In fact, spaghetti may be substituted for the noodles if they are not available in your area.

ESCARGOTS PIRET'S

Makes 6 servings

Jack Monaco and Andre Pinel thought up this ingenious version of escargot wrapped in filo pastry for Tawfiq Khoury, a San Diego wine and food connoisseur. He wanted an extraordinary "finger food" for a meeting he hosted of the La Jolla Wine and Food Society.

TO PREPARE THE SNAIL BUTTER

1 pound unsalted butter, at
  room temperature
¼ cup minced fresh parsley
1 tablespoon minced shallots
1 tablespoon minced
  scallions
10 or more cloves garlic,
  minced (1½ tablespoons)
1½ teaspoons salt
1 teaspoon freshly ground
  pepper

In a mixing bowl, combine the butter, parsley, shallots, scallions, garlic, salt, and pepper. Stir to blend thoroughly. Set the snail butter aside. (The butter may be prepared using a food processor fitted with the steel blade. With the machine running, drop the ingredients, unchopped, through the feed tube in this order: garlic, shallots, scallions, parsley, salt, and pepper. Mince finely. Add the butter, cut into large pats, and process to a smooth paste, stopping to scrape down the sides as needed.)

TO PREPARE THE ESCARGOTS

3 dozen snails (French, from
   a tin, are fine)
1 carrot, diced
1 rib celery, finely sliced
½ onion, diced
2 bay leaves
1 teaspoon dried thyme
1 tablespoon peppercorns
½ cup red wine
¼ cup vegetable oil

36 large mushroom caps (or
   equal to the number of
   snails you use)
1 package filo pastry

1. In a medium saucepan, combine the snails, carrots, celery, onions, bay leaves, thyme, peppercorns, wine, and oil. Add water to cover. Quickly bring the mixture to a boil over high heat, turn the heat to low, and poach the snails for 15 minutes. Drain the snails and set them aside to cool.

2. Wipe the mushrooms clean with a damp towel. Cut 36 3-inch squares of filo. Cover them with wax paper and a damp towel until needed. Lightly butter a baking sheet.

3. Preheat oven to 375°. Place a mushroom cap, upside down, on each filo square. In each mushroom, place a snail and about ½ teaspoon of the snail butter. Wrap the filo like a miniature square egg roll, tucking in the sides to completely enclose the filling. Place the filled filo on the baking sheet. Repeat with remaining filo squares until the snails and mushrooms are all used. (Figure 3 or 4 per person for an appetizer, 5 or 6 per person for a first course.) Leave about a half inch between each filo package. Bake them for 20 to 25 minutes, or until the filo is golden brown. Serve immediately.

❧ Snail butter is great to have on hand. Make it in large batches in the food processor and freeze it in sticks or rolls. It's then easy to slice into pats for escargots, or for melting over grilled steak.

Filo pastry also is a good freezer staple. It thaws in minutes and can be used to wrap savory fillings for quick appetizers. When handling filo, which is paper-thin and fragile, unwrap the package and spread out the dough. Cover the filo with a sheet of wax paper and a damp (not wet) towel and work with only a few sheets at a time, so it won't dry out.

CALAMARI BELAJACK

Makes 6 to 8 servings

For this wonderful squid salad, our executive chef at Piret's, Dan Belajack, uses fresh, tender squid steaks cut into julienne strips. The result resembles chicken strips instead of tentacles. This dish is very fresh tasting and colorful, a nice way to begin a meal.

3 pounds calamari steaks
   (squid)
1 quart court bouillon (see
   page 319)
Juice of 2 lemons
Juice of 3 limes
3 cloves garlic, minced
1 small red onion,
   thinly sliced
2 jalapeño chilies, seeded
   and finely minced
2 teaspoons ground
   cumin
½ bunch scallions,
   thinly sliced
1 red bell pepper, seeded
   and thinly sliced
1 green bell pepper, seeded
   and thinly sliced
1 bunch cilantro (fresh
   coriander), stemmed and
   coarsely chopped
1 tablespoon sugar
1 can (4 ounces) water
   chestnuts, drained and
   thinly sliced
1 can (7 ounces) tomato
   paste
Salt and freshly ground
   pepper, to taste

Watercress
Lime wedges, for garnish

1. Trim the calamari of connective tissue and rinse them under cold water. Simmer the calamari in the court bouillon for 4 to 5 minutes, remove them from the cooking liquid with a slotted spoon, and allow them to cool. Discard the liquid. Cut the calamari into ¼-inch strips.

2. In a large glass or ceramic bowl, combine all of the remaining ingredients, except the watercress and lime wedges. Add the calamari and toss the mixture well. Refrigerate the salad, tightly covered, overnight, to allow the flavors to blend. Serve it on beds of watercress on individual plates, and garnish each serving with a wedge of lime.

DUCK BREAST AND CÈPES SALAD

Makes 4 to 6 servings

Duck is a favorite ingredient of many cooks who have taught at our cooking school. It shows up practically everywhere but dessert. This salad and the one that follows are variations on recipes from Jacques Pépin. They make delicious first courses. One uses duck breast, the other uses the leg and thigh portion. Save the liver for pâté, save the leftover rendered fat for cooking, use the cracklings (crisp skin pieces left from rendering) to sprinkle over salads, and use the carcass for stock. Our chefs invented the word *frugal*—they use everything but the quack.

Porcini mushrooms may be substituted for the cèpes.

1 can (9¾ ounces) whole cèpes

Juice of ½ lemon

3 tablespoons virgin olive oil

1 teaspoon minced shallots

2 teaspoons finely chopped mixed fresh herbs (parsley, chervil, and chives)

Salt and freshly ground pepper, to taste

2 bunches mixed greens (watercress, arugula, mâche)

2 tablespoons butter

1 cup dried white bread cubes (½-inch cubes)

1 clove garlic, peeled and halved

1 tablespoon vegetable oil or rendered duck fat

1 whole duck breast, boned, skinned, trimmed of fat, and cut into long, thin julienne strips

1. Drain the cèpes and cut them into very thin slices. In a small bowl, combine the lemon juice, olive oil, shallots, mixed herbs, salt, and pepper, blending them well. Pour the mixture over the cèpes and refrigerate until ready to serve.

2. Wash and trim the greens; dry them well. About 10 minutes before serving, mix the greens with the cèpes and arrange on serving plates. Heat the butter in a skillet until it just begins to foam, then quickly add the bread cubes and garlic. Fry until the cubes are golden brown on all sides, stirring constantly so they will not burn. Drain, and discard the garlic.

3. In a separate skillet, heat the oil or fat and quickly sauté the duck strips, stirring, for about 5 minutes. Season the duck with salt and plenty of pepper. Scatter the duck over the greens and mushrooms, top with the croutons, and serve at once.

🐚 Ducks are becoming more available both fresh and frozen, but it is still best to order one in advance from your butcher. The best place to buy duck is from a Chinese market — they sell far and away the freshest. The most common American duck is the Long Island duckling, which is in fact a domestically grown Peking duck. This variety is tender and juicy, although all ducks tend to be low on meat, bony, and fatty. As one friend put it, one duck has too little meat for two and too much for one. That's one reason the new duck salads and the *nouvelle* recipes, which use small portions of duck breast, make sense. Wild ducks have a gamier flavor, much favored by connoisseurs; however, this is an acquired taste. Moreover, they are hard to find, unless you know a hunter.

ROASTED DUCK SALAD

Makes 4 servings

TO MAKE THE DRESSING

2 tablespoons heavy cream
1 tablespoon red wine
    vinegar
¼ teaspoon salt
¼ teaspoon freshly ground
    pepper
2 tablespoons vegetable oil

In a small bowl, whisk the cream until it is foamy and slightly thickened. Whisk in the vinegar, salt, and pepper. Add the oil and stir just until mixed. Set aside.

TO PREPARE THE SALAD

4 duck legs with thighs
    attached, boned
½ teaspoon salt
¼ teaspoon freshly ground
    pepper
2 tablespoons Dijon-style
    mustard
1 cup dry bread crumbs
2 medium heads Boston
    lettuce, washed, dried,
    and torn into bite-size
    pieces

1. Remove any excess fat from the duck pieces and reserve it. Sprinkle the salt and pepper evenly over the duck. Heat a large, ovenproof skillet over medium-high heat. Place the duck pieces in the skillet, skin side down, and cook them for 5 minutes, or until they are lightly browned on the bottom (there should be sufficient fat in the skin to keep the duck from sticking; if not, add a little oil or rendered duck fat to the skillet).

2. Preheat oven to 400°. Turn the pieces skin

side up, place the skillet in the oven, and roast the duck for 30 minutes.

3. Remove the duck to a platter to cool. Strain the fat that has melted from the duck into a clean skillet. Add all of the remaining duck fat, and render it over medium-low heat. Add vegetable oil, if necessary, until there is ½-inch of fat in the skillet.

4. Brush the cooled duck pieces with the mustard, using about ¾ teaspoon for each piece, and coat them with the bread crumbs. Heat the rendered fat over medium-high heat to about 375°. Cook the coated duck in the hot oil, turning it often, for about 1 minute, or until the crumbs are nicely browned. Drain the duck on paper towels.

5. *To assemble:* Toss together the lettuce and dressing. Divide the lettuce among four plates, arrange a leg portion on each plate, and serve.

S O U P S

FISH SOUP

Makes 4 servings

Thickened with Neufchâtel, a low-fat cow's milk cheese from Normandy, this is more a stew than a soup. Neufchâtel cheese comes both fresh and ripened. When ripe, it has a more pungent flavor, delicious with this combination of ingredients. However, suit your own taste.

Any firm, white, nonfatty fish, such as snapper or thresher shark, works well.

1 quart fish stock (page 318)
1 whole onion
1 celery heart
2 leeks, white part only, julienne-cut
2 medium carrots, julienne-cut
1 small turnip, julienne-cut
4 pieces white sea bass, cut into small pieces
12 medium shrimp, peeled and deveined
¼ cup Chablis
1 sprig fresh thyme
1 bay leaf
3 ounces Neufchâtel cheese
Dash of cayenne pepper
2 tablespoons chopped fresh parsley or chives
2 to 3 tablespoons fresh lemon juice
Chopped fresh chives, for garnish

1. Combine the fish stock, onion, and celery heart in a medium saucepan, bring to a boil, reduce the heat and simmer the vegetables gently for about 30 minutes. Drain the vegetables, reserving 1 cup of the cooking broth, and set them aside. (The remaining broth can be strained and refrigerated for poaching fish or for other recipes.)

2. In a separate saucepan, boil the leeks, carrots, and turnips in enough water to just cover them, for about 15 minutes. Pour off the cooking liquid, and set the vegetables aside.

3. Preheat oven to 350°. Combine the fish and shrimp in a shallow pan, and add the Chablis, thyme, and bay leaf. Cook them over medium heat, covered, for 2 minutes. Place the pan in the oven, and bake for 20 minutes without removing the cover.

4. Place the cooked celery and onion in a blender with the 1 cup of reserved cooking broth and blend until smooth. Add the Neufchâtel cheese, and blend until smooth. Pour this sauce over the cooked leeks, carrots, and turnips, and simmer the mixture for a few minutes over low heat.

5. When the fish is cooked, remove the thyme sprig and bay leaf. Pour the sauce and vegetables over the steaming fish. Add the cayenne pepper,

parsley or chives, and lemon juice. Simmer the mixture for 2 to 3 minutes over low heat. Taste for
seasoning, and add salt, if necessary. Serve in shallow soup bowls, garnished with chives.

MEDITERRANEAN FISH SOUP WITH GARLIC

Makes 6 servings

The fish stock is an excellent one from Jacques Pépin, which you can use as a base
for any rich fish soup.

Use any firm, meaty, nonoily fish (halibut is a good example) for this flavorful
soup, common in the Mediterranean regions of France and Italy. Ask your fish
market for fish bones; there usually is no charge for them, and plenty of meat is
attached. To save time at the end, we sometimes blanch the potatoes and carrots
while the stock is cooking, then finish cooking them together with the squash and
cubed fish.

A fresh garden salad with a light vinaigrette makes a good accompaniment.

TO MAKE THE TOAST ROUNDS

24 slices French bread,
  ½ inch thick
2 large cloves garlic, peeled
  and halved
½ cup butter, melted
Freshly grated Parmesan
  cheese

Preheat oven to 375°. Rub both sides of the French
bread slices with the cut sides of the garlic. Brush
both sides of the bread with the melted butter, and
sprinkle Parmesan cheese over one side. Place the
bread rounds, cheese side up, on a baking sheet, and
toast in the oven. Set the toast aside to cool.

TO MAKE THE FISH STOCK

3 tablespoons olive oil
1 large onion, diced
1 leek, white part only,
  diced
1 rib celery, diced
½ cup minced fresh parsley
2 carrots, peeled and diced
1 small head of garlic,
  unpeeled
2 tomatoes, seeded and
  coarsely chopped

1. Heat the olive oil in a 4-quart heavy Dutch
oven over medium-high heat. Add the onions, leek,
celery, parsley, and diced carrots, and cook them for
10 minutes. With the head of garlic root side up,
press the garlic against a counter top, using the heel
of your hand, to crush it slightly. Add the garlic to
the pot with the tomatoes, bay leaves, fish bones,
thyme, saffron, and pepper. Stir the mixture and
cook it for a few minutes longer.

2. Stir in the tomato purée, white wine, and
water to cover. Bring the stock to a boil, reduce the

3 bay leaves
3 pounds fish bones,
    thoroughly washed
2 sprigs fresh thyme (or a
    pinch of dried)
Pinch of saffron threads
1 teaspoon freshly ground
    pepper
½ cup tomato purée
1 cup dry white wine
3 quarts water
    (approximately)

heat, and simmer the stock, uncovered, for 30 minutes.

3. Remove the fish bones and bay leaves, and put the stock through a food mill. You should have 1½ to 2 quarts of liquid. Pick off any meat from the fish bones and set it aside.

TO ASSEMBLE THE SOUP

1 cup coarsely sliced carrots
1 cup cubed potatoes
1 cup cubed squash
½ pound fish fillets, cubed
3 cloves garlic, peeled
1 egg yolk
Dash each of salt, cayenne
    pepper, and dry mustard

1. Strain the stock into a large saucepan. Add the sliced carrots and simmer them gently about 5 minutes, or until they begin to soften slightly. Add the potatoes and simmer the soup for another 5 minutes. Add the squash and the cubed fish, and cook the mixture at a very low simmer until the fish is tender (about 10 minutes).

2. Meanwhile, fit a food processor with a steel blade. With the machine running, drop the 3 cloves of garlic through the feed tube to mince them. Add the egg yolk, salt, cayenne pepper, and dry mustard, and process until the sauce is emulsified.

3. Whisk some of the hot broth from the soup into the egg mixture, and then whisk the mixture back into the soup to thicken it slightly. Stir in the fish removed from the bones, heat the soup through (do not let it boil) and serve it immediately with the toast rounds.

CREAM OF SCALLOP SOUP

Makes 6 servings

Jack Monaco serves this rich yet delicate soup as a first course at our more important caterings and dinners. The scallops must be impeccably fresh.

3 pounds bay scallops
Juice of 4 limes
3 tablespoons butter
½ cup chopped green bell
  pepper
6 scallions, including tender
  green, sliced
1 teaspoon minced garlic
6 bottles (8 ounces each)
  clam juice, or 6 cups fish
  stock (page 318)
1 teaspoon Worcestershire
  sauce
1 teaspoon dry mustard
2 egg yolks, beaten
3 cups heavy cream
Salt and freshly ground
  white pepper, to taste
Paprika and chopped fresh
  parsley, for garnish

1. Remove the tough muscle tissue and marinate the scallops in the lime juice for several hours, refrigerated. Drain, and dry them on paper towels.

2. Melt the butter in a large saucepan, and cook the green pepper, scallions, and garlic until soft but not brown. Stir in the clam juice or fish stock, Worcestershire sauce, and dry mustard. Bring the mixture to a boil and add the scallops. Reduce the heat and simmer the scallops for 3 to 4 minutes, being careful not to overcook them. The scallops are done when they are milky white and lose their translucency.

3. Whisk the beaten egg yolks with the cream. Stir ½ cup of the scallop cooking liquid into the egg-cream mixture to warm it, and then stir the mixture into the scallops. Heat the soup, but do not let it boil. Season with salt and freshly ground white pepper. Serve the soup sprinkled liberally with paprika and chopped parsley.

MUSSEL SOUP PIRET'S

Makes 8 to 10 servings

Chef Dan Belajack features the next two recipes as "soups of the day" at Piret's, where they're great favorites with our customers.

2 dozen mussels
1 quart court bouillon (page 319) or bottled clam juice
2 tablespoons unsalted butter
3 tablespoons minced shallots
½ teaspoon minced garlic
1 rib celery, minced
½ cup dry white wine
2 cups heavy cream
Salt and freshly ground white pepper, to taste
Freshly grated nutmeg, to taste
Chopped fresh parsley, for garnish
Croutons (page 57) (optional)

1. Put the mussels in cold water to cover and discard any that float. Scrub the mussels thoroughly under cold running water and pull off any beards. Rinse the mussels as many times as necessary to eliminate all traces of sand or mud.

2. Bring the court bouillon to a boil in a large stockpot. Add the mussels, cover the pot, and bring them to a boil. Reduce the heat and simmer the mussels, covered, for 5 to 6 minutes. Remove the mussels from the cooking liquid with a slotted spoon. If any haven't opened, heat them a minute or two longer. Any that still do not open should be discarded.

3. When the mussels are cool enough to handle, remove the meat from the shells and set the meat aside. Line a strainer with a double thickness of damp cheesecloth and strain the cooking liquid into a clean bowl.

4. Melt the butter over low heat in a medium, heavy saucepan. Stir in the shallots, garlic, and celery, and cook them for 2 to 3 minutes. Add the wine and the reserved cooking liquid, increase the heat, and bring the mixture to a boil.

5. Reduce the heat to low. Stir a ladleful of hot soup into the cream to warm it, and then stir the cream into the soup. Simmer the soup for 10 minutes. Stir in the mussels, and season the soup with salt, white pepper, and nutmeg. Garnish each serving with a pinch of parsley, and top with croutons, if desired.

NEW ENGLAND CLAM CHOWDER

Makes 6 servings

In all cuisines, there are some recipes so integral to the national culture they become synonymous with it. Certainly, New England Clam Chowder is as familiar in Kansas and California as it is on the Eastern seaboard, and equally loved.

¼ pound salt pork, rind removed
1 small yellow onion, diced
1 rib celery, diced
½ green bell pepper, seeded and diced
1½ pounds potatoes, peeled and cut into ½-inch cubes
½ teaspoon fresh thyme, or to taste
1 cup heavy cream
½ to 1 cup dry white wine
1 can (16 ounces) chopped clams in juice, drained
Salt and freshly ground white pepper, to taste
Chopped fresh parsley, for garnish

1. Dice the salt pork finely and cook it in a medium, heavy saucepan over medium heat, stirring, until it is crisp. Transfer the salt pork to paper towels to drain. Pour off all but 2 tablespoons of the fat in the pan. Add the onions, celery, and green pepper to the pan, and cook for 2 to 3 minutes.

2. Stir in the potatoes, thyme, and salt pork, blending them well. Add the cream and wine, bring the soup to a boil, reduce the heat, and simmer it until the potatoes are tender. Add the clams, and season the chowder with salt and white pepper. Serve the soup garnished with chopped parsley.

POTATO AND CHEDDAR CHEESE SOUP

Makes 8 servings

Patty McDonald brought us this interesting variation on vichyssoise, made richer with the addition of a Cheddar cheese sauce.

6 Russet potatoes, peeled and chopped
2 medium onions, chopped
7 tablespoons butter

1. In a 6-quart saucepan or soup pot with a heavy bottom, sauté the potatoes and onions in 4 tablespoons of the butter for 4 to 5 minutes. Add the stock, thyme, and cayenne pepper, and simmer until the potatoes are tender (about 35 to 45 minutes).

2. Working in batches, purée the mixture in a

8 cups rich chicken stock,
    preferably homemade
    (page 317)
2 teaspoons fresh thyme (or
    1 teaspoon dried)
Dash of cayenne pepper
3½ cups milk
Salt and freshly ground
    pepper, to taste
3 tablespoons unbleached,
    all-purpose flour
3 cups freshly grated
    Cheddar cheese
⅛ teaspoon freshly grated
    nutmeg
Minced fresh chives,
    for garnish

blender or food processor fitted with the steel blade. Stir in 1 cup of the milk. Pour the soup into a clean pot and bring it to a simmer. Taste the soup for seasoning and add salt and pepper to taste. Set it aside while you prepare the sauce.

3. Melt the remaining 3 tablespoons of butter in a small saucepan over medium-high heat. Stir in the flour and cook 1 to 3 minutes, but do not let it brown. Whisk in the remaining 2½ cups of milk all at once. Cook the white sauce, stirring it often, until it is thick enough to coat a spoon.

4. Stir the cheese into the white sauce, a little at a time, until it melts and the sauce is smooth. Adjust the seasoning with salt and pepper, and add the nutmeg. Stir the sauce into the soup, bring it to a simmer, and adjust the seasoning again. Serve the soup garnished with a generous pinch of chives.

CREAM OF MUSHROOM SOUP

Makes 6 to 8 servings

1 rib celery, peeled and
    coarsely chopped
1 medium onion, coarsely
    chopped
½ cup unsalted butter
1 pound large mushrooms,
    sliced
Juice of ½ lemon
½ cup dry sherry
1 quart rich chicken stock,
    preferably homemade
    (page 317)
¼ cup unbleached,
    all-purpose flour
2 cups heavy cream
Salt and freshly ground
    white pepper, to taste
Minced fresh chives,
    for garnish

1. Cook the celery and onions in the butter over low heat for 2 to 3 minutes. Add the mushrooms, lemon juice, and sherry. Cook the mixture until the liquid is reduced to a glaze, stirring often to keep it from sticking.

2. Heat the chicken stock in another saucepan.

3. Stir the flour into the mushroom mixture to form a roux, and cook it for a few minutes over medium heat. Stir in the heated chicken stock. Stir a ladleful of the hot soup into the cream to warm it, and then stir the cream into the soup. Cook the soup over medium heat until it is heated through. Season the soup with salt and white pepper. Garnish each serving with chopped chives.

WATERCRESS SOUP

Makes 4 to 6 servings

Diana Hewett, former manager of The Perfect Pan shops, tested many recipes for this book. For this recipe, she was inspired by England's Jane Grigson, who makes this soup with sorrel. Since sorrel is not readily available here, Diana experimented with watercress, which works admirably. She garnishes the soup with tomato and chives — a garden-fresh flavor.

4 tablespoons butter

½ medium onion, minced

2 medium Russet potatoes, peeled and diced

3½ cups rich chicken stock, preferably homemade (page 317)

Salt and freshly ground pepper, to taste

Freshly grated nutmeg, to taste

Pinch of sugar

¾ to 1 pound watercress

4 tablespoons *crème fraîche* or heavy cream

½ cup chopped fresh chives

2 medium tomatoes, seeded and chopped (about ½ cup)

Toasted bread rounds (page 57)

1. In a large, heavy saucepan, melt the butter and cook the onions until translucent. Stir in the potatoes, chicken stock, salt, pepper, nutmeg, and sugar. Simmer the mixture, covered, over low heat until the potatoes are tender (about 30 minutes).

2. Pinch off and discard any thick stems from the watercress and wash the leaves well. Working in batches, purée the cooked potatoes and stock with the watercress leaves in a blender or food processor fitted with the steel blade. The soup will be smooth in texture and bright green. Return the soup to the saucepan and correct the consistency, if necessary, with more stock.

3. Reheat the soup, but do not let it boil or the watercress will darken and become bitter. Stir in the *crème fraîche.* Garnish the soup with the chopped chives, tomatoes, and toasted bread rounds.

NOTE

If more texture is desired, add a few shredded watercress leaves after the soup is puréed. For variety, substitute ¾ pound spinach or sorrel or 2 cups diced beets for the watercress. This soup can also be served chilled: use 1 additional cup of *crème fraîche* and 1 additional cup of stock.

CREAM OF BROCCOLI SOUP

Makes 8 to 10 servings

2 bunches fresh broccoli
½ cup unsalted butter
1 rib celery, peeled and
   coarsely chopped
1 small yellow onion,
   coarsely chopped
1 quart rich chicken stock,
   preferably homemade
   (page 317)
¼ cup unbleached,
   all-purpose flour
2 cups heavy cream
Salt and freshly ground
   white pepper, to taste
Freshly grated nutmeg, to
   taste

1. Wash the broccoli under cold running water. Cut off the florets, leaving about 1 inch of stem attached, and set the florets aside. Peel and roughly chop the broccoli stems, discarding any tough, stringy pieces.

2. Melt the butter in a large, enameled cast-iron saucepan over low heat. Add the celery, onions, and chopped broccoli stems, and cook, covered, for 5 to 7 minutes, stirring the mixture occasionally.

3. Meanwhile, bring the chicken stock to a boil in another saucepan. Add the broccoli florets, and boil them until they are crisp-tender. Remove the florets from the stock with a slotted spoon. Reserve the stock, and keep the florets warm.

4. Stir the flour into the onion-broccoli mixture and blend well. Cook the mixture for a few minutes to remove the raw flour taste. Whisk in the hot chicken stock. Stir a ladleful of the soup into the cream to warm it, and then stir the cream into the soup. Bring the soup to a quick boil, reduce the heat to low, and simmer the soup a few minutes. Season it with salt, white pepper, and nutmeg. Add the broccoli florets, and serve.

CREAM OF ARTICHOKE AND CHESTNUT SOUP

Makes 8 to 10 servings

Dan Belajack served this incredible soup for the first course at a dinner honoring food editors attending the 1984 Pillsbury Bake-Off. Ever since, we've had numerous requests for the recipe from across the country. As you can see, the preparation is simple. The soup may be made ahead and reheated just before serving. The flavor is delicate yet enticing.

1 teaspoon minced shallot
½ cup dry sherry
4 freshly cooked artichoke bottoms (or 4 artichoke bottoms canned in water, drained)
8 fresh chestnuts, peeled (or 1 cup unsweetened chestnut purée)
1 quart rich chicken stock, preferably homemade (page 317)
1 quart heavy cream
1 sprig fresh thyme (or dried thyme, to taste)
Salt and freshly ground white pepper, to taste

1. Cook the shallots and sherry in a 4-quart Dutch oven over medium-high heat until reduced to about 1 tablespoon. Add the artichoke bottoms, chestnuts, and chicken stock, and simmer the mixture for 15 minutes.

2. Purée the mixture in small batches, using a blender, food mill, or food processor fitted with the steel blade.

3. Return the puréed mixture to the pot and bring it to a boil. Stir in the cream and thyme, and simmer the soup until it is reduced to a creamy consistency. Season the soup with salt and white pepper.

ONION SOUP PIRET'S

Makes 8 servings

Piret's Lyon-style onion soup is a favorite year after year. The secret is in the rich stock and our wonderful croutons, which we make ourselves (see below). Don't overdo the cheese. Too often onion soup is so gluey with cheese, it becomes difficult to eat, and the cheese overshadows the soup.

4 cups rich chicken stock, preferably homemade (page 317)

4 cups rich brown stock, preferably homemade (page 313)

1 cup butter

12 medium onions, finely sliced

3 tablespoons sugar (optional)

1 tablespoon chopped fresh thyme (or 1 teaspoon dried)

Salt and freshly ground pepper, to taste

½ cup unbleached, all-purpose flour

2 cups dry red wine

Croutons, for garnish (see below)

Freshly grated Swiss or Gruyère cheese, for garnish

1. Combine the chicken and beef stocks in a large, heavy saucepan. Bring the stock to a simmer while cooking the onions.

2. Melt the butter in a large, heavy stockpot over medium heat. Add the onions and cook them, stirring frequently, until they are evenly browned. If sugar is added to the onions, it will help caramelize them and give the soup a sweeter flavor. Add the thyme, and season with salt and pepper.

3. Reduce the heat to low and stir the flour into the onions, cooking for 2 to 3 minutes. Add the red wine and deglaze the pan by stirring and scraping to bring up any browned bits.

4. Whisk the hot stock into the onion mixture, mixing until the ingredients are well combined. Bring the soup to a boil, reduce the heat, and simmer the soup for 30 to 45 minutes, stirring occasionally. Taste the soup and adjust the seasoning, if necessary.

5. To serve, ladle the hot soup into serving bowls. Float several croutons on the surface and cover the top with the grated cheese. Place the bowls of soup under the broiler until the cheese is browned and bubbly. Serve immediately.

NOTE

A good onion soup requires a rich stock as a base. If your stock needs enrichment, you might add, to taste: soy sauce, Dijon-style mustard, beef or chicken base, or even miso (soybean paste).

⁂ Homemade croutons are a useful way to use up stale bread, and they taste better than the prepackaged store-bought kind. The bread can be fried or oven- or broiler-toasted and cut into cubes for salads, squares to float on onion or other soups, and triangles, rounds, or rectangles for canapés. Garlic toast is a great accompaniment to soups and salads. Make a garlic butter by mashing 1 clove of garlic into 4 tablespoons of butter, spread it on the bread, and toast. White bread is generally used for croutons. Dry-toasted croutons will last as long as a month in an airtight container. Fried croutons should be used immediately, as the butter and oil will become rancid in short order.

Fried croutons	Heat half butter, half oil in a skillet. When the fat is hot, put in the croutons, being careful not to crowd them. When they are brown, turn them over and fry the other side. Drain the croutons on paper towels to remove excess fat. The bread will absorb less fat if you cook it at a medium rather than high heat.
Oven-toasted croutons	Brush melted butter (flavored or unflavored) on the bread and bake at 375° until golden. To make dry toasts, do not butter the bread. Or run the croutons under the broiler for a few minutes on each side.

GAZPACHO

Makes 4 servings

We don't know where this gazpacho recipe originated, but this is how we serve it at Piret's in the summer. The soup must be thoroughly chilled and the vegetable garnishes cold, firm, and crunchy. Our version is quite tangy, but if it's *hot* you like, simply add more Worcestershire sauce and Tabasco. Serve it with homemade crouton rounds.

SOUP

1 cup sliced hothouse
   cucumber (see below)
4 tomatoes, peeled and
   seeded
1 teaspoon salt
1 teaspoon red wine vinegar
4 tablespoons fresh lime
   juice
2 cloves garlic, chopped
1 teaspoon Worcestershire
   sauce
½ teaspoon Tabasco

GARNISH

⅓ cup each: minced green
   bell pepper, celery, and
   cucumber
1 tablespoon chopped cilantro (fresh coriander)

1. Combine all the soup ingredients in a blender or food processor fitted with the steel blade, and process to a smooth consistency.

2. Chill the soup until it is ice cold. After it is chilled, taste the soup for seasoning, and adjust with more lime juice, Worcestershire, and Tabasco as needed. Garnish each serving with a sprinkling of bell pepper, celery, cucumber, and cilantro.

⁂ "Hothouse" cucumbers are known in England and on the East Coast as "burpless" or "English" cucumbers. We advise you to use hothouse cucumbers in most of our recipes because they are meatier, have fewer seeds, and are less bitter than garden-variety or "ridge" cucumbers. They have a thin skin, which can be left on, if desired. You'll usually find these long, narrow cucumbers packaged in plastic shrink wrap to keep them fresh.

MINESTRONE ALLA DIANA

Makes 6 to 8 servings

This is Diana Hewett's version of a great Italian classic.

2 cups dried pinto, navy, or great northern beans

½ cup virgin olive oil

2 cloves garlic, minced

1 medium onion, coarsely chopped

2 ribs celery, chopped

2 carrots, chopped

3 medium White Rose or Russet potatoes, peeled and cubed

2 tablespoons chopped fresh parsley

1 sprig fresh rosemary, minced (or 1 tablespoon dried)

1 sprig fresh thyme, minced (or 1 tablespoon dried)

6 fresh basil leaves (or ½ tablespoon dried)

¼ pound thinly sliced pancetta (Italian bacon) or hickory smoked bacon

½ head cabbage, cored and shredded

2 leeks, white part only, washed thoroughly and finely chopped

4 tomatoes, peeled, seeded, and chopped

2 zucchini, unpeeled and finely chopped

1 cup peas, fresh or frozen

¼ pound fresh mushrooms (any variety), thinly sliced

8 cups rich chicken stock, preferably homemade (page 317)

1. Pick over the beans and wash them thoroughly in several changes of cold water. Place the beans in a bowl with enough cold water to cover them by 2 inches. Soak the beans overnight.

2. The next day, cook the beans in their soaking water until they are tender (about 2 hours). Keep an eye on them during cooking and add water as needed so that the beans will remain covered by 2 inches of water. Drain the beans, reserving the cooking liquid. Purée half of the beans, using a food mill, blender, or food processor fitted with the steel blade. Set the beans and the purée aside.

3. Heat the olive oil in a large soup kettle. Over medium-high heat, cook the garlic, onions, celery, carrots, potatoes, parsley, rosemary, thyme, basil, and pancetta or bacon, until the pancetta is soft and translucent. Stir in the cabbage, leeks, tomatoes, zucchini, peas, and mushrooms. Pour in the chicken stock, then add the puréed and whole beans. The puréed beans give this soup a thicker consistency. If you like it soupier, add some of the reserved bean cooking liquid.

4. Season the soup with salt and pepper. Simmer the soup over low heat for 45 minutes, partially covered.

5. If using pasta, cook it in boiling salted water until it is tender but not soft. Drain the pasta and add it or the cooked rice to the soup. Simmer the soup for 15 minutes more, allowing the pasta to absorb some of its flavor. Serve the soup garnished with freshly grated Parmesan cheese.

Salt and freshly ground
  pepper, to taste
1 cup cooked rice, or 1 cup
  uncooked pasta (optional)
Freshly grated Parmesan
  cheese, for garnish

TOMATO CONSOMMÉ

Makes 6 cups

Maurice Moore-Betty's tomato consommé made with canned Italian plum tomatoes was the basis for this Southern California variation, using pine nuts, Parmesan cheese, and a bit of garlic. When using Maurice's original recipe, we like to serve the consommé cold, because it is light and delicate in flavor. The additional ingredients, however, make for a more complex soup, best served hot.

1 can (16 ounces) Italian
  plum tomatoes, drained
  (about 2 cups)
2 cloves garlic, minced
¼ cup chopped fresh basil
  (or 4 tablespoons dried)
⅓ cup freshly grated
  Parmesan cheese
⅓ cup pine nuts, roasted
  and chopped (optional)
4 cups rich chicken stock,
  preferably homemade
  (page 317)
¼ cup dry white wine
Salt and freshly ground
  pepper, to taste
Coarsely grated zest of 1
  lemon

1. In a large, enameled or stainless steel saucepan, combine the tomatoes, garlic, basil, Parmesan cheese, pine nuts (if desired), and chicken stock. Bring the mixture to a boil, reduce the heat, and simmer for 5 to 10 minutes.

2. Strain the mixture through a fine sieve, pressing the solids with the back of a spoon. Add the wine, and salt and pepper to taste. Serve the soup hot or cold, garnished with grated lemon zest.

BECKY'S KLODNIAK

Makes 16 servings

Rebecca Evans, a gastronomic adventurer of the first order, introduced us to this marvelous chilled soup at a George Munger Cook-Off in the early seventies. She won a major prize, and we won a recipe we've used dozens of times for Lunch at The Perfect Pan and at parties we've catered. Becky's Klodniak is a refreshing first course, and some friends swear it's a first-class cure for a hangover. It is best to refrigerate the soup overnight before serving it, to let the flavors blend. This soup may be stored, refrigerated, for up to a week. We make a rather large batch and use whatever is left over as quick midafternoon pick-me-ups or as an after-work snack.

½ pound small bay shrimp, cooked, shelled, and deveined

2 large cucumbers, peeled, seeded, and minced

2 cups sour cream

5 cups buttermilk

1 cup sauerkraut juice

3 cloves garlic, mashed

¼ cup fresh dill

1 cup minced scallions, white part only

½ tablespoon powdered fennel seed

Salt and freshly ground white pepper, to taste

4 hard-cooked eggs, yolk and white sieved separately, for garnish

9 small sprigs fresh dill, for garnish

1. Combine the shrimp, cucumbers, sour cream, buttermilk, sauerkraut juice, garlic, dill, scallions, fennel seed, salt, and white pepper. Stir the mixture to blend it well, and chill it overnight.

2. Serve the soup in chilled bowls, garnished with a bit of sieved egg yolk and egg white, and fresh dill.

PEACH SOUP WITH CHAMPAGNE

Makes 6 to 8 servings

We serve this refreshing fruit soup as a first course. The recipe is adapted from Jacques Pépin, who serves it for dessert, pouring the soup over pound cake and decorating it with blueberries and piped whipped cream.

1½ cups water
4 whole cloves
¾ cup sugar
1 stick cinnamon, crushed
2 tablespoons cornstarch
2 tablespoons cold water
1½ cups champagne
3½ pounds peaches (about 12 peaches)
1 cup heavy cream
Fresh berries or mint, for garnish

1. Bring the 1½ cups water, cloves, sugar, and cinnamon to a boil in a small saucepan over high heat. Stir together the cornstarch and 2 tablespoons cold water and add them to the boiling syrup. Lower the heat, and simmer the syrup for 10 minutes, stirring it often. Remove the pan from the heat, strain the syrup through a fine sieve, and let it cool to room temperature. Add the champagne and chill the mixture.

2. Peel and seed the peaches, reserving 1 beautiful peach, unpeeled, for garnish. Purée the peeled fruit, using a blender or food processor fitted with the steel blade. Gradually blend in the cold syrup and the cream, then return the mixture to the refrigerator to chill it thoroughly.

3. Serve the cold soup garnished with fresh peach slices, a few fresh berries, or a sprig of mint. This soup is especially pretty when served in chilled glass bowls or red-wine goblets.

3

SALADS

VINEGARS &
VINAIGRETTES

PIRET'S SALADS

VINEGARS AND VINAIGRETTES

Herb Vinegar · Raspberry Vinegar · Spiced Vinegar · Piret's Red or White Vinaigrette · Basic Vinaigrette and Variations · Lemon Vinaigrette with Fresh Herbs · Tarragon Vinaigrette for Vegetables · Basil Vinaigrette · Ravigote Dressing

PIRET'S SALADS

Lima Beans Vinaigrette · Marie-Christine Forester's Lentil Salad · White Bean Salad · Tortelloni Salad · Endive Salad with Walnuts and Goat Cheese · Cauliflower Vinaigrette · Winter Salad · Green Bean Salad with Shrimp and Fresh Tomato Vinaigrette · Artichoke Heart Salad · Cold Beet Salad with Sour Cream–Orange Dressing · Carrot-Ginger Salad · Pea and Snow Pea Salad with Basil Dressing · Tomato and Sorrel Salad · Dee Biller's Tomatoes and Basil with Garlic Vinaigrette · Creamy Cucumbers with Dill · Red and Green Pepper Salad · Piret's Moroccan Carrot Salad · Ratatouille · Watercress and Orange Salad · Orange and Onion Salad with Raspberry Vinaigrette · Anne Otterson's French Summer Salad · Chicken Salad with Potatoes and Beets · Couscous Salad · Mediterranean Salad · Green Cabbage Salad · Tonnato Salad · Pasta Salad with Capers and Basil Dressing · Chèvre Salad with Walnuts

EVERY DAY AT PIRET'S, guests have a choice of four or more charcuterie salads to choose from or to take home. By "charcuterie" we mean vegetable or nonlettuce salads, typically found in French take-out emporiums. These include celery root, baby beet, hearts of palm, cauliflower, artichoke hearts, lentil, new potato, pea, bean, zucchini, eggplant, and lots more.

Some of these salads may be served either hot or cold; Ratatouille is a good example. Most of Piret's salads will hold up well for four to five days refrigerated in air-tight containers. Our nonvegetable-based salads include Couscous Salad (cracked wheat), a variety of pasta salads, and entrée salads. We've included several salads taught in our cooking school to give you a broad range of approaches to salad-making.

We also want to share with you a variety of vinaigrette and other dressings. When you tire of one, try another, or make up your own.

VINEGARS AND VINAIGRETTES

Today there is such an abundance of wonderful vinegars, oils, and mustards available that they simply invite experimentation. Try some of the aromatic wine vinegars steeped with tarragon, dill, basil, raspberries, lemon — even chili peppers. Or make your own at home. For salads, we favor the milder, delicate flavor of a naturally fermented wine vinegar rather than distilled vinegar (more appropriate for pickling, or, perhaps, washing windows!). The finest wine vinegars, such as the heavenly *aceto balsamico* from Emilia Romagna, are fermented in oak, chestnut, mulberry, or ash wood casks and are handled with the care vintners give their choicest wines. Balsamic vinegars are known for their intense color and a complex bouquet that is both tart and sweet. A very old, fine balsamic vinegar is so syrupy that you need only a few drops blended with a less noble vinegar to make a memorable dressing.

Although wine vinegars are the most readily available, vinegars are also made from apples (for cider vinegar), malt, or rice. Rice vinegars are used in Asian cooking. Besides white wine vinegar (flavored or unflavored), you have a choice of rosé, red, and even sherry vinegar. There are a rich variety of oils to choose from as well. Grape seed, peanut, sesame, sunflower, walnut, hazelnut, and extra-virgin or virgin olive oils are excellent in salad dressings. Corn, peanut, sesame, and sunflower oils, and fine grades of olive oil, are all good in cooking and frying. Polyunsaturated oils are delicate in flavor. Cold-pressed extra-virgin or virgin olive oil is mild and sweet, while lower grades pressed under heat with less than choice olives are heavy, with a pungent odor and flavor. It is worth every extra penny that you pay for the top grades, which is why our recipes usually call for extra-virgin or virgin olive oil.

We Americans have been brainwashed by the supposed economy of buying large sizes. But buying in quantity is not at all economical when it comes to oils, unless you have a large family or use an unusually large amount of oil in your cooking. The minute you open that can or bottle of oil, it begins to go rancid. Set it in a sunny window or counter, near your stove or another hot area, and it will spoil very rapidly. So, plan to use it up quickly. Above all, resist the temptation to reserve that expensive walnut, hazelnut, or extra-virgin olive oil for infrequent special occasions.

Mustard adds a nice zest to oil and vinegar dressings. Today's food purveyors offer rich choices of imported and domestic mustards made with white, yellow, black, or brown seeds, and flavored with everything imaginable. Moutarde de Meaux is a whole-seed mustard that is excellent for basting a pork roast or for flavoring sauces as well as dressings. American "hot dog" mustard is made from white or yellow seeds and is mild and sweet. We prefer the darker, more buoyantly flavored mustards for cooking.

Traditionally, ground mustard seeds were blended with unfermented grape juice. Today, though, you will find mustards made with white wine, champagne, vinegar, and citrus juices, and flavored with herbs, spices, fruit, pickles, chilies, garlic — you name it.

If at all possible, use fresh herbs for vinaigrette. In many parts of the country, fresh herbs are available at specialty food markets and even supermarkets. Or you can grow them easily on a sunny window sill.

ᨠ When you must use dried herbs, use half of the measurement given for fresh. For more flavor, buy leaves and grind them just before using with a mortar and pestle or a small electric coffee grinder. Do not, however, use the coffee grinder alternately for grinding coffee and herbs, because coffee beans leave an oily residue, which will taint the herbs.

Paula Wolfert says fresh tarragon sprigs can be frozen with "fabulous" success. They're a great improvement over dried tarragon. To freeze, drop the fresh sprigs into boiling water, remove them at once with a slotted spoon, and plunge them into a bowl of ice water. Drain, pat dry with kitchen cloths, and pack the sprigs in sheets of paper towels by rolling them into cylinders. Pack them in plastic bags and freeze; they'll keep a few months. Use them straight from the freezer; no need to thaw.

HERB VINEGAR

Makes 1 gallon

Katie Millhiser visits us from Berkeley every few years to give terrific classes on preserving and gifts from the kitchen. This recipe for Herb Vinegar and the two flavored vinegars that follow are Katie's creations.

1 gallon cider or white wine
    vinegar
12 peppercorns, slightly
    crushed
1 bunch scallions, including
    tender green, chopped
6 cloves garlic, minced
1 cup fresh tarragon leaves,
    loosely packed
8 sprigs fresh rosemary
8 sprigs fresh thyme
1 cup fresh parsley, loosely
    packed
4 sprigs fresh summer savory

1. Combine all of the ingredients in a 1-gallon glass container, cover it tightly, and let it stand in a cool, dark place for two weeks.

2. Strain the vinegar through cheesecloth. Pour the vinegar into hot, sterilized bottles, and cork them tightly. Store the vinegar in a cool, dark place.

NOTE

Dried herbs should not be substituted for fresh in this recipe.

RASPBERRY VINEGAR

Makes 1 quart

Raspberry-flavored vinegar is wonderful in vinaigrettes and in certain poultry recipes. You can make your own raspberry vinegar for personal use and to give as gifts. Splendid yet inexpensive bottles to present homemade vinegars in are available at specialty shops all over the country, and of course at Piret's.

1½ pounds raspberries, fresh
    or frozen
½ cup sugar
Red wine vinegar

1. Place the raspberries and sugar in a sterilized, dry, large-mouthed 1-quart jar, and fill the jar with red wine vinegar. Place the uncovered jar on a rack in a deep saucepan, and pour enough water into the pan to come halfway up the sides of the jar. Bring

the water to a boil, reduce the heat, and simmer for
10 minutes. Remove the jar from the water bath
and let it cool on a rack or a folded towel in a draft-
free place.

2. When the vinegar is completely cool, close
the jar with an airtight lid and shake it well. Refrigerate the mixture for three weeks.

3. After three weeks, strain the vinegar, pressing
the berries to extract their juice. Discard the pulp.
If the vinegar is too thick, thin it with a little red
wine vinegar. Store the raspberry vinegar, tightly
closed, at room temperature.

SPICED VINEGAR

Makes 1 quart

This is a good, basic recipe, and you can vary the spices to your taste. If you prefer a
bit of "bite," add bruised ginger root or chopped chilies, Katie suggests.

1 quart distilled white
  vinegar
1 cinnamon stick
2 tablespoons mustard seed
2 tablespoons peppercorns
1 tablespoon whole allspice
1 tablespoon crumbled blade
  mace (or ⅛ teaspoon
  dried)

1. Pour the vinegar into a noncorrosive pan
(porcelain, enameled cast iron, or stainless steel).
Put the cinnamon, mustard seed, peppercorns,
allspice, and mace in a cheesecloth bag, and add
them to the vinegar. Cover the saucepan and bring
the mixture almost to the boiling point, but do not
allow it to bubble. Remove the pan from the heat
and let the mixture stand until it is completely cool.
Discard the spice bag.

2. Pour the vinegar into a hot, sterilized 1-quart
bottle (or 2 1-pint bottles), seal, and store the
vinegar in a cool, dark place.

PIRET'S RED OR WHITE VINAIGRETTE

Makes 2 cups

Red Vinaigrette is made with red wine vinegar; White Vinaigrette with white wine vinegar. They are the basic recipes we use for many of the dressings served at Piret's. The flavor can be varied almost endlessly by the addition of different cheeses, anchovies, herbs, and other seasonings. You may also want to play with the basic ingredients, trying flavored vinegars or nut oils, for example. When a recipe in this book calls for "White or Red Vinaigrette," this is the recipe we mean. It will keep, tightly covered and refrigerated, for weeks.

½ cup red or white wine
vinegar
Salt and freshly ground
white pepper, to taste
1 tablespoon sugar
½ teaspoon chopped fresh
tarragon
½ teaspoon chopped fresh
basil
½ teaspoon chopped
fresh dill
½ teaspoon chopped fresh
marjoram
1 shallot, minced
2 tablespoons Dijon-style
mustard
½ cup extra-virgin olive oil
1 cup vegetable oil

1. Whisk together the vinegar, salt, pepper, sugar, tarragon, basil, dill, marjoram, shallot, and mustard, beating until the mixture is thoroughly blended and the salt and sugar are dissolved.

2. Add the olive oil in a slow, steady stream, whisking constantly. Add the vegetable oil in the same manner. Continue whisking until the oil is thoroughly mixed into the dressing.

BASIC VINAIGRETTE

Makes about ½ cup

Many of the variations below are Anne Otterson's.

2 tablespoons white wine
    vinegar or lemon juice
6 to 8 tablespoons olive oil
Salt and freshly ground
    pepper, to taste

Whisk all the ingredients together.

VARIATIONS

Zesty Vinaigrette

Basic Vinaigrette *plus:*
- ½ teaspoon Dijon-style mustard, *or*
- ¼ teaspoon Dijon-style mustard and ¼ teaspoon Moutarde de Meaux, *or*
- ¼ teaspoon Dijon-style mustard and ¼ teaspoon dry mustard.

Herb Vinaigrette

Basic Vinaigrette *plus:*
- Dijon-style mustard, chopped fresh tarragon, or chopped fresh basil (excellent with tomatoes), to taste, *or*
- chopped fresh chives, to taste, *or*
- a mixture of chopped fresh chives, parsley, tarragon, chervil, or other herbs, to taste, but avoid using two strong herbs together.

Creamy Vinaigrette

Basic Vinaigrette *minus:*
- 2 tablespoons olive oil. Substitute 2 tablespoons heavy cream, *crème fraîche,* sour cream, or yogurt.

Curry Vinaigrette (for chicken or fruit)

Basic Vinaigrette *plus:*
- 2 teaspoons minced shallots and ½ teaspoon curry powder.

Garlic Vinaigrette

Basic Vinaigrette (made with red wine vinegar) *plus:*
- 1 to 2 cloves garlic, crushed.

Provençal Vinaigrette

Basic Vinaigrette *plus:*
- 1 anchovy fillet, rinsed and finely ground, and minced garlic, to taste.

Chiffonnade Vinaigrette

Basic Vinaigrette *plus:*
- 1 teaspoon chopped shallots, 1 teaspoon chopped fresh parsley, and 1 chopped hard-cooked egg. (Capers and chopped green olives are optional.)

LEMON VINAIGRETTE WITH FRESH HERBS

Makes 3 tablespoons

Pinch of salt and freshly
  ground pepper
1 teaspoon lemon juice
1 teaspoon minced fresh
  chervil
1 teaspoon minced fresh
  tarragon
1 teaspoon sherry vinegar
2 teaspoons extra-virgin
  olive oil
2 teaspoons vegetable oil

Whisk together the salt, pepper, lemon juice, herbs, and vinegar. Whisk in the oils, a little at a time at first, then in a steady stream, to blend smoothly.

TARRAGON VINAIGRETTE FOR VEGETABLES

Makes about 1½ cups

5 tablespoons tarragon
  vinegar
2 teaspoons salt
1 teaspoon freshly ground
  pepper
½ teaspoon Dijon-style
  mustard
1 clove garlic, minced
⅔ cup extra-virgin olive oil
1 small egg, lightly beaten
⅓ cup half-and-half

Whisk together the vinegar, salt, pepper, mustard, and garlic. Whisk in the olive oil, a little at a time at first, then in a steady stream. When all the oil has been added, whisk in the egg and the half-and-half to make a thick dressing. Serve the dressing over blanched al dente vegetables, garnished with minced parsley.

BASIL VINAIGRETTE

Makes 1 cup

1 shallot, peeled
1 tablespoon fresh basil
   leaves, tightly packed (or
   1½ teaspoons dried)
¾ cup extra-virgin olive oil
¼ cup red wine vinegar
½ teaspoon sugar
½ teaspoon salt
Freshly ground pepper, to
   taste

Using a food processor fitted with the steel blade, drop the shallot through the feed tube with the machine running. Remove the cover and scrape down the sides of the bowl. Add the basil, olive oil, vinegar, sugar, salt, and pepper, and process until the ingredients are well mixed.

RAVIGOTE DRESSING

Makes about 1 cup

¼ cup champagne wine
   vinegar
½ teaspoon salt
⅛ teaspoon freshly ground
   pepper
1 tablespoon minced shallots
1 tablespoon minced capers
1 teaspoon Dijon-style
   mustard
1 cup vegetable oil

Whisk together the vinegar, salt, pepper, shallots, capers, and mustard, whisking the mixture until the salt dissolves. Add the oil in a slow, steady stream, whisking constantly. The dressing will keep, refrigerated in a covered container, for one week. Use as a dressing for green salads, bean salads, or any vegetable salad you fancy, or use as a marinade for barbecued chicken.

PIRET'S SALADS

There's been quite a turnaround in the way Americans eat salad. The traditional Iceberg lettuce salad with bottled dressing served as a first course has given way to cold combinations of pasta and/or vegetables, such as the Pasta Salad with Capers and Basil Dressing you'll find in this chapter. And many Americans have adopted the European custom of serving the green salad after the main course, as a pleasant palate cleanser before dessert.

Whatever the salad and whenever you serve it, there are some components that remain essential, among them a good vinaigrette. In addition to the recipes in the beginning of this chapter you'll find vinaigrette recipes tucked into the salad recipes throughout this section.

LIMA BEANS VINAIGRETTE

Makes 8 to 10 servings

VINAIGRETTE

1 medium red onion, minced
½ cup fresh parsley, coarsely chopped
1 tomato, peeled, seeded, and minced
½ cup vegetable oil
2 tablespoons Dijon-style mustard
1 tablespoon balsamic vinegar
1 teaspoon salt
Freshly ground pepper, to taste

1. Whisk together all the vinaigrette ingredients. Let the mixture stand at least one hour at room temperature to mellow the flavors.

1 pound fresh or frozen lima
 beans

2. Simmer the lima beans in boiling salted water to cover, until they are tender but not mushy. Drain the cooked beans thoroughly, and toss them with the dressing while they are still hot. Serve the salad at cool room temperature.

NOTE

Dried lima beans also may be used. Wash them thoroughly, soak them in water to cover overnight, drain, and combine them with 7 cups cold water and 1 tablespoon salt. Bring them to a boil, reduce the heat, and simmer the beans for 1 to 1½ hours, or until they are tender but not mushy. The cooking time may vary. Drain and use as directed above.

MARIE-CHRISTINE FORESTER'S LENTIL SALAD
(In the style of l'Ambassade d'Auvergne in Paris)

Makes 6 to 8 servings

2 cups uncooked lentils
4½ cups cold water
1 onion studded with 6
 whole cloves
3 bay leaves
1 cup diced cooked ham
½ cup chopped shallots
½ cup chopped fresh parsley
½ cup minced fresh chives
½ cup diced bell pepper
 (red, green, or a
 combination)
2 cloves garlic, crushed
⅓ cup red wine vinegar
⅔ cup extra-virgin or virgin
 olive oil
½ pound bacon, diced and
 sautéed
Butter lettuce

1. In a medium saucepan, place the lentils in the cold water with the clove-studded onion and bay leaves. Bring to a slow boil over medium heat, and simmer for 30 minutes. The lentils should be tender but not mushy. Drain the cooked lentils in a colander, let them cool, then refrigerate them until they are thoroughly chilled (about 2 hours).

2. Add the ham, shallots, parsley, chives, bell pepper, and crushed garlic. Refrigerate the salad.

3. About 15 minutes before serving, add the vinegar, olive oil, and cooked bacon, and toss. Serve slightly chilled on a bed of butter lettuce.

WHITE BEAN SALAD

Makes 6 to 8 servings

1 pound navy beans or other
  small white beans
12 large pitted ripe olives,
  drained and minced
8 pimiento-stuffed green
  olives, drained and
  minced
4 scallions, including tender
  green, chopped
Salt, to taste
1½ cups (approximately)
  White Vinaigrette
  (page 72)

1. Pick over the beans and wash them thoroughly in cold water, then place them in a pan with cold water to cover and let them soak for 2 hours. Bring the beans and their soaking water to a boil, reduce the heat. and simmer the beans, partially covered, until they are tender but not mushy. The beans for this salad should have a little bite to them.

2. Drain the beans and toss them lightly with the ripe and green olives, scallions, salt, and enough White Vinaigrette to coat the salad lightly. The salad will keep, refrigerated and tightly covered, for four to five days.

TORTELLONI SALAD

Makes 6 to 8 servings

Another of our popular charcuterie salads, this is a regular on the Piret's menu. Make it well ahead of serving time to allow the pasta to absorb the flavors of the vinaigrette. Tortelloni are large tortellini, but other forms of pasta may be substituted. Be sure not to overcook the pasta for this and other salads, or it will fall apart when tossed with the other ingredients.

2 pounds green tortelloni
12 large pitted ripe olives,
  halved
2 tomatoes, cored, seeded,
  and cut in ½-inch dice
2 tablespoons chopped fresh
  cilantro (fresh coriander)
½ medium red onion, thinly
  sliced
½ cup freshly grated
  Parmesan cheese
1½ cups (approximately)
  White Vinaigrette
  (page 72)

Cook the tortelloni in boiling salted water until al dente. Drain and cool the pasta. Toss it lightly with the olives, tomatoes, cilantro, onion, Parmesan cheese, and White Vinaigrette to coat, taking care not to break up the pasta. The salad will keep, refrigerated and tightly covered, for four to five days.

ENDIVE SALAD WITH WALNUTS AND GOAT CHEESE

Makes 6 to 8 servings

Jack Monaco has a culinary love affair with Paula Wolfert. He loves her earthy approach and her devil-may-care attitude toward experimenting with dishes both old and new. And he confirms his admiration by using many of her dishes when catering and at Saturday Night at Piret's. This is Paula's recipe as adapted by Jack.

½ cup walnut halves
½ cup walnut oil
4 to 5 heads curly endive (or any bitter greens; Paula likes chicory)
2 tablespoons white wine vinegar
½ teaspoon kosher-style salt
½ teaspoon minced fresh chives
1 baguette, cut in ¼-inch-thick rounds
¼-pound log Montrachet (goat cheese), cut in ¼-inch slices
Finely shredded carrot, for garnish

1. Soak the walnut halves in the walnut oil for 30 minutes. Wash the greens and pat them dry with paper towels.

2. Whisk together the vinegar, salt, and chives. Stir in the walnut halves with the oil. Dip the leaves of endive in the dressing and arrange them on individual serving plates. Reserve the walnut halves for garnish.

3. Preheat oven to 500°. Place 2 bread rounds per person on a baking sheet and toast them in the oven, turning them midway, until golden on both sides. Top each toast round with a slice of the Montrachet. Bake them, or run them under a broiler, until golden. Place two cheese toasts on top of each salad serving, and garnish with the shredded carrot and reserved walnuts.

CAULIFLOWER VINAIGRETTE

Makes 6 to 8 servings

Anne Otterson taught us this delicious vinaigrette. Try it also with broccoli (Anne's preference), Brussels sprouts, green beans, or cherry tomatoes. The salad is delicious as part of an antipasto tray. (This vinaigrette is too rich for lettuce salads.)

2 medium heads cauliflower

VINAIGRETTE

2 teaspoons kosher-style or sea salt
1 teaspoon freshly ground white pepper
½ teaspoon freshly ground black pepper
½ teaspoon dry mustard
1 teaspoon Dijon-style mustard
2 teaspoons minced garlic
5 tablespoons tarragon vinegar
⅔ cup extra-virgin olive oil
1 raw egg, beaten
½ cup half-and-half
¼ teaspoon sugar (optional)
1 hard-cooked egg, minced
1 tablespoon fresh chives, minced
1 tablespoon fresh parsley, minced
2 tablespoons minced green olives
1 tablespoon minced drained capers

1. Break up the cauliflower into florets. Drop the florets into boiling salted water for a few minutes, until they are tender but still resist the bite. Drain, and plunge them into ice water to stop the cooking. Pat the florets dry and arrange them in a shallow serving dish.

2. *To make the vinaigrette:* In a jar with a tight-fitting lid, combine the salt, white and black peppers, dry mustard, Dijon-style mustard, garlic, vinegar, olive oil, raw egg, half-and-half, and the sugar, if it is used. Shake the mixture well. Add the hard-cooked egg, chives, parsley, olives, and capers, and chill the vinaigrette.

3. Toss the dressing with the cauliflower and refrigerate the salad at least an hour to blend the flavors. The salad is better if the vegetable is allowed to marinate in the dressing overnight in the refrigerator.

WINTER SALAD

Makes 6 to 8 servings

VINAIGRETTE

¼ cup tarragon vinegar
2 teaspoons French whole-
    grain mustard
2 teaspoons lemon juice
2 teaspoons salt
Freshly ground pepper, to
    taste
¾ cup extra-virgin olive oil

SALAD

3 ribs celery
½ small head cauliflower
¼ pound mushrooms
1 tablespoon salt
1 pound fresh green beans,
    washed and trimmed
    (or 2 10-ounce packages
    frozen green beans,
    thawed according to
    package directions)
2 tomatoes, peeled, seeded,
    and chopped
3 tablespoons chopped fresh
    parsley
1 medium shallot, minced
    (or 4 scallions, white part
    only, thinly sliced)
1 pound mild white cheese
    (such as Monterey Jack),
    cut into ¼-inch cubes
2 bunches watercress

1. *To make the vinaigrette:* Whisk together the vinegar, mustard, lemon juice, salt, and pepper. Slowly whisk in the olive oil. Set the dressing aside.

2. Using a vegetable peeler, remove the tough fibers from the celery, and slice the ribs on the bias. Break up the cauliflower into florets. Wipe the mushrooms with a damp cloth and slice them very thin.

3. Bring a quart of water to a boil and add the salt. Blanch the celery in the boiling water for 4 minutes. Remove the celery with a slotted spoon, plunge it into ice water to stop the cooking, and drain on paper towels. Using the same water, cook the cauliflower florets and the green beans in the same manner (the cauliflower should boil 4 minutes, the green beans 5 to 7 minutes, or until they are tender but still resist the bite).

4. Toss the cooked vegetables together in a serving bowl. Add the tomatoes, mushrooms, parsley, shallot, and cheese, and toss again. Add enough vinaigrette to coat, and toss once more. Serve the salad on a bed of watercress.

GREEN BEAN SALAD WITH SHRIMP AND FRESH TOMATO VINAIGRETTE

Makes 6 servings

VINAIGRETTE

3 tomatoes (about 1¼
    pounds), peeled, seeded,
    and diced
2 small shallots, minced
2 cloves garlic, very finely
    chopped
4 tablespoons White
    Vinaigrette (page 72)
1 to 2 tablespoons oregano,
    fresh or dried
Freshly ground pepper, to
    taste

2 pounds fresh green beans,
    washed and trimmed
1 can (6 ounces) small
    shrimp, drained (or ½
    pound fresh, cooked)
Red onion, thinly sliced

1. *To make the vinaigrette:* In a medium bowl, combine the tomatoes, shallots, garlic, and White Vinaigrette. Season the mixture with the oregano and pepper. Blend the mixture well and refrigerate it for at least three hours so the flavors can mellow.

2. Blanch the green beans in boiling water for 3 to 4 minutes. Remove them from the water with a slotted spoon and plunge them into ice water to preserve their color and chill them. Drain the beans on paper towels and refrigerate until serving time.

3. At serving time, combine the green beans and shrimp with the tomato vinaigrette, tossing to combine them thoroughly. Serve the salad on a bed of thinly sliced red onion.

VINAIGRETTE VARIATIONS

Creamy mint vinaigrette

Combine ½ cup sour cream, 2 tablespoons plain yogurt, 2 tablespoons chopped mint, and salt and freshly ground pepper to taste.

Sweet dill vinaigrette

Substitute dill for the mint in the original recipe, and add a little sugar.

ARTICHOKE HEART SALAD

Makes 8 servings

4 cups cooked, quartered
   artichoke hearts
½ red bell pepper, seeded
   and thinly sliced
3 scallions, chopped
¼ cup chopped fresh parsley
½ cup White Vinaigrette
   (page 72)
Salt and freshly ground
   pepper, to taste

Toss together the artichoke hearts, bell pepper, scallions, and parsley with enough White Vinaigrette to coat them lightly. Season the salad to taste with salt and pepper. Refrigerate to allow the flavors to blend for at least three hours before serving. This salad will keep, refrigerated and tightly covered, for one week.

COLD BEET SALAD WITH SOUR CREAM–ORANGE DRESSING

Makes 6 servings

This is our adaptation of an Anne Otterson recipe, as is the Pea and Snow Pea Salad on page 84.

2 pounds fresh beets
1 cup sour cream
1 tablespoon grated orange
   zest
1 tablespoon frozen orange
   juice concentrate
½ cup chopped pecans

1. Simmer the unpeeled beets in water to cover for about 40 minutes, or until they are fork-tender. Drain the beets and let them cool. Peel the beets and cut them into ½-inch cubes or in julienne strips. Chill.

2. Stir together the sour cream, orange zest, and thawed orange juice concentrate. Just before serving, toss together the beets and pecans with enough of the dressing to lightly coat them.

CARROT-GINGER SALAD

Makes 6 to 8 servings

This is one of our most popular charcuterie salads. It's crunchy, colorful, and delicious — a great salad for a buffet. The carrots should be sliced into very thin discs; a food processor does it in seconds.

2 pounds carrots (about 6 or 7), peeled and thinly sliced

½ bunch scallions (about 6), including tender green, thinly sliced

1 ounce sesame seeds, toasted

1 piece of ginger about the size of a walnut, ground

1 cup (approximately) White Vinaigrette (page 72)

Toss together the carrots, scallions, sesame seeds, and ginger, blending them thoroughly. Toss the salad with enough White Vinaigrette to lightly coat it. The salad will keep, tightly covered and refrigerated, for one week.

PEA AND SNOW PEA SALAD WITH BASIL DRESSING

Makes 6 servings

DRESSING

1 cup sour cream

1 cup fresh basil leaves (loosely packed)

½ teaspoon salt

Dash of pepper

1 tablespoon chopped scallion

1 package (10 ounces) frozen petite peas, thawed

2 cups (approximately) snow peas (see note)

Boston lettuce leaves

Cooked bacon, crumbled, for garnish

1. *To make the dressing:* Using a blender or a food processor fitted with the steel blade, purée the sour cream, basil, salt, and pepper.

2. Toss the scallion, peas, and snow peas with the dressing. Serve the salad either on individual lettuce-lined plates or in a large salad bowl lined with lettuce leaves. Garnish with crumbled bacon.

Fresh or frozen snow peas may be used. They may be added to the salad raw, or blanched a couple of minutes in boiling water, then quickly chilled in ice water. For more crunch, add ¼ cup or so of sliced water chestnuts.

TOMATO AND SORREL SALAD

Makes 6 servings

This salad is a classic, very popular with our teachers. The basic idea is Jacques Pépin's. To make the chiffonnade, stack 5 or 6 sorrel leaves and tightly roll up the stack lengthwise, cigar fashion. Thinly slice across the roll to cut into fine shreds.

4 medium, very ripe
    tomatoes
15 to 20 fresh sorrel leaves
1 large red onion, thinly
    sliced
10 to 12 ounces quality
    mozzarella cheese, very
    thinly sliced
½ teaspoon salt
¼ teaspoon freshly ground
    pepper
4 tablespoons red wine
    vinegar
½ cup extra-virgin olive oil
2 shallots, minced (optional)
1 hard-cooked egg, yolk and
    white sieved separately,
    for garnish

1. Cut the cores from the tomatoes. Slice the tomatoes crosswise, ¼ inch thick. Reserve the unattractive top and bottom slices for other recipes where looks don't matter. Cut the sorrel leaves into chiffonnade.

2. Arrange the tomato slices on a serving platter in an overlapping pattern, alternating them with slices of onion and cheese. Sprinkle them evenly with the salt and pepper, drizzle with the vinegar and olive oil, and sprinkle on the shallots, if used. Decorate with the sorrel chiffonnade. The salad can stand, unrefrigerated, for up to an hour in a cool kitchen.

4. Just before serving, garnish the salad with circles of sieved egg white and egg yolk. (Capers and strips of anchovy fillets also may be used as a garnish.)

The chiffonnade cutting technique can be used for tender leaves of spinach, basil, lettuce, or any leafy vegetable. The technique keeps the leaves from bruising and being crushed, and the fine shreds make a pretty garnish for soups and salads.

DEE BILLER'S TOMATOES AND BASIL WITH GARLIC VINAIGRETTE

Makes 6 servings

Dee Biller is one of our school's most versatile teachers. In addition to teaching food processor classes, she instructs our "Indispensable" series on quiches, omelets, soufflés, and crêpes. In recent years, she and her husband, Mark, have teamed up for classes on home entertaining, and she and Suzy Eisenman teach our very popular *dim sum* sessions.

TO MAKE THE VINAIGRETTE

3 whole heads of garlic
½ cup extra-virgin olive oil
½ cup red wine vinegar
1 tablespoon Dijon-style
  mustard
1 tablespoon minced fresh
  herbs (such as oregano,
  marjoram, thyme, and/or
  rosemary)
½ cup freshly grated
  Parmesan cheese

1. Break the heads of garlic into cloves, leaving the skins on. Drop the garlic cloves into boiling water and boil them until tender (about 5 to 10 minutes). Drain the garlic in a colander. When it is cool enough to handle, squeeze the garlic cloves out of their skins (they will pop out easily).

2. Place the olive oil, vinegar, mustard, herbs, and Parmesan cheese in the work bowl of a food processor fitted with the steel blade, and process until well blended. Pour the mixture into a bowl, add the garlic cloves, and let the mixture stand at room temperature for at least an hour. (The dressing can be refrigerated for up to twenty-four hours at this point.)

TO ASSEMBLE THE SALAD

1 cup fresh basil leaves
  (tightly packed)
6 ripe tomatoes, cored and
  sliced
Salt and freshly ground
  pepper, to taste

1. Stack 5 or 6 basil leaves, roll them into a tight cigar shape, and slice them very thinly, crosswise, to make a chiffonnade. Repeat with the remaining basil.

2. Divide the tomato slices among six individual serving plates. Scatter the chiffonnade over the tomatoes. Spoon on the garlic dressing, and season the salad with salt and pepper. The salad should be served as soon as the dressing has been added.

CREAMY CUCUMBERS WITH DILL

Makes 6 servings

Cucumbers and dill have an affinity for each other. We recommend using hothouse cucumbers, if you can get them. They're sweeter and have a silkier texture than the more common salad cukes.

3 cucumbers, peeled and
  sliced in ¼-inch-thick
  rounds
1 teaspoon salt

DRESSING

3 tablespoons white wine
  vinegar
3 tablespoons sugar
Salt and freshly ground
  white pepper, to taste
1 tablespoon fresh dill
  (or 2 teaspoons dried)
1 teaspoon dill seed, ground
  in spice grinder
2 tablespoons minced
  shallots
1 cup sour cream
½ cup plain yogurt

1. Toss the cucumber rounds with the 1 teaspoon salt and let them drain in a colander for at least a half hour, to remove any bitterness. Rinse the cucumbers under cold water and pat them dry. (If using hothouse cucumbers, it's not necessary to peel them or mellow them with salt.)

2. *To make the dressing:* Combine the vinegar, sugar, salt, white pepper, dill weed, dill seed, and shallots, whisking until the sugar and salt are dissolved and the spices are blended. Whisk in the sour cream and yogurt, blending thoroughly.

3. Stir the dressing into the cucumbers. This salad will keep, refrigerated, for two to three days.

RED AND GREEN PEPPER SALAD

Makes 6 servings

6 tablespoons extra-virgin or
    virgin olive oil
3 cloves garlic, minced
2 medium onions
1 pound ripe tomatoes,
    peeled, seeded, and
    chopped
Salt and freshly ground
    pepper, to taste
4 large red bell peppers
2 large green bell peppers
¼ cup finely chopped fresh
    basil leaves (about 1
    bunch)

1. Heat the olive oil in a large saucepan. Add the garlic and onions and cook over low heat until the onions are translucent. Stir in the chopped tomatoes, and season the mixture with salt and pepper. Cook it over medium heat for 5 minutes.

2. Remove the seeds and cores from the peppers and cut the peppers into strips. Add them to the tomato mixture with the basil, and cook over low heat, covered, for 30 minutes, or until the peppers are soft. Taste for seasoning and adjust with salt and pepper. The salad can be served hot or cold, and it improves with a day's refrigeration.

PIRET'S MOROCCAN CARROT SALAD

Makes 6 to 8 servings

A food processor's fine slicing blade, or a mandolin, makes quick work of the carrots for this salad. The slices should be very thin so the carrots can absorb the dressing.

VINAIGRETTE

3 tablespoons white wine
    vinegar
Juice of 1 lemon
½ teaspoon ground cumin
Salt and freshly ground
    white pepper, to taste
1 clove garlic, minced
8 to 10 sprigs fresh mint,
    minced
¼ cup honey
¾ cup extra-virgin olive oil

2 pounds carrots, peeled and
    thinly sliced

1. *To make the vinaigrette:* Using a blender or food processor fitted with the steel blade, blend the white wine vinegar, lemon juice, cumin, salt, pepper, garlic, and mint. Slowly add the honey until it is dissolved, then add the olive oil.

2. Toss the carrots with enough vinaigrette to thoroughly coat them, and season the salad with salt. The salad will keep, tightly covered and refrigerated, up to one week.

RATATOUILLE

Makes 6 to 8 servings

This recipe calls for lavender, which is found in premixed herbs such as *herbes de Provence*. You will not find it fresh or dried in grocery stores, but it is available in shops that sell potpourri and in nurseries specializing in herbs.

Ratatouille is also delicious served hot over pasta, topped with freshly grated Parmesan cheese.

2 medium eggplants (about 2½ pounds), unpeeled, cut into ½-inch cubes
4 zucchini, unpeeled, cut into ½-inch cubes
12 tablespoons virgin or extra-virgin olive oil
2 yellow onions, cubed
6 cloves garlic, minced
2 green bell peppers, seeded and cut into small cubes
1 can (1 pound) diced tomatoes with juice (or 1 pound fresh tomatoes, peeled and diced, not seeded)
1 can (28 ounces) tomato purée
Salt and freshly ground pepper, to taste
2 tablespoons *herbes de Provence* (or 1 teaspoon each: oregano, basil, thyme, marjoram, rosemary, and lavender)
2 tablespoons cornstarch mixed with 2 tablespoons water (optional)

1. In a large skillet, sauté the eggplant and zucchini in 6 tablespoons of the olive oil until they are tender but still resist the bite. Set the mixture aside.

2. Cook the onions, garlic, and bell peppers in the remaining 6 tablespoons of olive oil over medium heat until they are soft. Add the tomatoes, tomato purée, salt, pepper, and herbs, and simmer the mixture for 10 minutes, or until thick. (If using fresh tomatoes and the sauce is too thin, stir in the cornstarch paste and simmer the mixture until it is thickened.)

3. Add the eggplant mixture, stirring it thoroughly. Taste for seasoning and adjust with salt and pepper. Refrigerate the mixture, uncovered, until it is thoroughly chilled (cover for longer storage). Serve cold as a salad, or hot as a vegetable side dish.

WATERCRESS AND ORANGE SALAD

Makes 6 servings

Here is a refreshing salad that's especially pleasing with spicy Latin dishes or North African fare, taught by Patty McDonald.

2 navel oranges
4 bunches watercress,
    cleaned and stemmed

VINAIGRETTE

2 tablespoons white wine
    vinegar
8 tablespoons extra-virgin
    olive oil
2 tablespoons lemon juice
Salt and freshly ground
    pepper, to taste
1 large shallot, minced
Scant ½ teaspoon curry
    powder

1. Peel the oranges, removing all traces of white pith. Cut the oranges in half lengthwise, then thinly slice them crosswise. Place the slices in a colander to drain for 15 minutes (catch the juice and reserve it for other recipes). Combine the orange slices with the watercress and refrigerate until serving time.

2. *To make the vinaigrette:* Whisk together the white wine vinegar, olive oil, lemon juice, salt, pepper, shallots, and curry powder. Taste the mixture and correct the seasoning, if necessary. Chill until serving time.

3. To serve, toss the dressing with the oranges and watercress, and serve immediately.

ORANGE AND ONION SALAD WITH RASPBERRY VINAIGRETTE

Makes 6 servings

You may use commercial raspberry vinegar in this recipe, or make your own — it's easy, and a lot less expensive than the purchased version. (For the recipe, see page 70.) Serve this salad with pâtés, with barbecued or grilled meats, or with spicy sausages.

4 thin-skinned oranges, such
    as Valencia
¼ cup hazelnut oil (see note)
1½ tablespoons raspberry
    vinegar
¼ teaspoon sea salt
1 large red onion

1. Working over a bowl to catch the juices, peel the oranges, removing all the bitter white pith, and thinly slice the oranges. Whisk the hazelnut oil, raspberry vinegar, and salt with the orange juice, and let the mixture stand for 10 minutes to develop the flavor.

2. Peel the onion and cut it into thin rings. Ar-

Salad greens, preferably
  curly endive or arugula

range the orange and onion slices in overlapping layers in a glass bowl. Pour on the dressing and let the salad marinate at room temperature for at least an hour.

3. Line serving plates with the salad greens and top with the orange salad.

NOTE

Vegetable oil may be substituted for the hazelnut oil. In that case, add 1 to 2 tablespoons of orange juice and a pinch of cumin to the dressing.

ANNE OTTERSON'S FRENCH SUMMER SALAD

Makes 8 servings

A perfect luncheon entrée salad.

VINAIGRETTE

6 tablespoons white wine
  vinegar
1 teaspoon Dijon-style
  mustard
Salt and freshly ground
  pepper, to taste
1 cup extra-virgin olive oil

SALAD

4 ribs celery (or 2 zucchini),
  julienne-cut
4 whole chicken breasts,
  poached and julienne-cut
½ pound mushrooms, sliced
¼ cup chopped walnuts
¼ pound Roquefort cheese,
  crumbled

1. *To make the vinaigrette:* Whisk together the vinegar, mustard, salt, and pepper. Slowly whisk in the olive oil.

2. If using celery, blanch the julienne strips in boiling water for 1 minute, then plunge them into ice water to stop the cooking (there's no need to blanch zucchini).

3. In a serving bowl, toss together the celery, chicken, and mushrooms. Sprinkle on the walnuts and cheese, and toss the salad with enough vinaigrette to lightly coat it.

CHICKEN SALAD WITH POTATOES AND BEETS

Makes 4 to 6 servings

Anne Otterson says this salad may be varied by substituting game or ham for the chicken, or using a combination of ham and chicken. Vary the other ingredients according to season: for example, use green beans instead of beets in the spring.

VINAIGRETTE

3 tablespoons heavy cream
½ teaspoon Dijon-style
   mustard
2 tablespoons white wine
   vinegar
Salt and freshly ground
   pepper, to taste
3 tablespoons extra-virgin
   olive oil

SALAD

1 cup cooked chicken,
   julienne-cut
2 potatoes, boiled, chilled,
   and julienne-cut
½ cup thinly sliced celery
1 beet, boiled and julienne-
   cut
2 to 3 cornichons or small
   gherkins, chopped
Chopped fresh parsley, for
   garnish

1. *To make the vinaigrette:* Whisk together the cream, mustard, vinegar, salt, and pepper. Slowly whisk in the olive oil.

2. Gently combine the chicken, potatoes, and celery with two-thirds of the vinaigrette. Pour the remaining vinaigrette over the beets. Let both mixtures marinate for an hour.

3. Just before serving, combine the two mixtures, toss gently with the pickles, and garnish with parsley.

❧ When recipes call for the zest of orange, lemon, or lime, take care to remove only the colored part of the citrus peel, which contains the highly flavored oils. The white pithy portion is bitter and should be discarded. Specialty stores have "zesters" available, but you can always use a sharp knife to scrape off the peel, or even a fine grater.

COUSCOUS SALAD

Makes 8 to 10 servings

Couscous grains are like little sponges that soak up flavors without getting mushy in texture. This is one of our most popular salads, a zesty blend that includes crunchy vegetables. To cut the vegetables quickly, use a mandolin or a food processor fitted with the julienne blade.

This is a great salad for summer entertaining, because it can stand unrefrigerated for several hours. Make it ahead of time so the flavors can blend.

DRESSING

Juice and very thinly sliced zest of 1 orange
Juice and very thinly sliced zest of ½ lemon
6 ounces raspberry vinegar
Salt, to taste
1 teaspoon *quatre épices* (or ¼ teaspoon each: freshly ground cinnamon, nutmeg, pepper, and clove)
¼ teaspoon ground fennel
¼ teaspoon turmeric
1 teaspoon ground ginger
2 teaspoons chopped garlic
2 cups extra-virgin olive oil

COUSCOUS

1¼ cups water
2 pounds couscous

VEGETABLES

1 carrot, peeled and julienne-cut
2 zucchini, julienne-cut
3 ribs celery, thinly sliced
1 white onion, thinly sliced
2 tomatoes, cored, seeded, and cut into small dice
1 bunch cilantro (fresh coriander), minced

1. *To make the dressing:* Stir together the orange and lemon juices and zests, and the raspberry vinegar. Whisk in the salt, pepper, *quatre épices,* fennel, turmeric, ginger, and garlic. When the spices are dissolved, drizzle in the olive oil, beating the dressing constantly, until all the oil has been added and the dressing is smooth. Set it aside.

2. *To prepare the couscous:* Bring the water to a vigorous boil and pour it over the couscous in a medium bowl, stirring constantly. The couscous will absorb the water, swelling slightly. Keep stirring the couscous with a fork or your fingers to break up any lumps, until all the water is absorbed and the couscous has cooled.

3. Toss all the vegetables together. Add the couscous, and blend well. Moisten the salad well with the dressing. It will keep, tightly covered and refrigerated, up to one week.

MEDITERRANEAN SALAD

Makes 10 servings

This is a colorful combination that goes particularly well with grilled meats and poultry. Be careful not to oversalt the dressing since the cheeses are salty.

DRESSING

7 ounces feta cheese
1½ ounces blue cheese
4 ounces cream cheese,
    softened
¾ cup sour cream
½ cup plain yogurt
Salt and freshly ground
    pepper, to taste
⅛ teaspoon dried tarragon
⅛ teaspoon dried basil

SALAD

2 green bell peppers, seeded
    and thinly sliced
1 medium red onion, halved
    and thinly sliced
10 cherry tomatoes, halved
20 pitted ripe olives
5 cucumbers, julienne-cut
    (see note)

1. *To make the dressing:* Using a blender or food processor fitted with the steel blade, blend the cheeses, sour cream, yogurt, salt, pepper, tarragon, and basil, and process for 1 minute. The purée should not be completely smooth but should have some texture.

2. Toss together the bell peppers, onion, tomatoes, olives, and cucumbers with enough dressing to thoroughly coat the salad. It will keep, tightly covered and refrigerated, up to one week.

NOTE

If using regular cucumbers, partially peel them, leaving some skin on for color. If using hothouse cucumbers, do not peel them at all.

GREEN CABBAGE SALAD

Makes 8 to 10 servings

DRESSING

3 to 4 tablespoons sugar
Salt, to taste
10 tablespoons (5 ounces)
   white wine vinegar
2 tablespoons Dijon-style
   mustard
⅓ cup vegetable oil
1 ¼ cups mayonnaise
   (page 328)

SALAD

1 medium head green cab-
   bage, cored and shredded
1 carrot, grated
1 small white onion, minced
3 ribs celery, finely diced
½ cup sweet pickle relish

1. *To make the dressing:* Dissolve the sugar and salt in the vinegar. Whisk in the mustard and oil, then the mayonnaise.

2. Combine all the salad vegetables, and toss them with enough of the dressing to thoroughly coat them. The salad may be refrigerated, tightly covered, up to one week.

TONNATO SALAD

Makes 6 servings

The ingredients for this salad can be prepared ahead and layered in the salad bowl. Cover them with plastic and refrigerate until about an hour before serving time. Let the salad come to cool room temperature before serving it.

1 can (1 pound)
   water-packed tuna
¾ pound green beans
1 pound small red (new)
   potatoes
12 large pitted ripe olives
9 cherry tomatoes, halved
2 to 3 anchovies with oil
1 ½ cups White Vinaigrette
   (page 72)

1. Drain and flake the tuna. Cook the green beans in boiling water until tender-crisp, then plunge them into ice water to stop the cooking and set the color. Boil the potatoes until they are tender but not soft, and cut them into quarters.

2. In a salad bowl, layer, in order, the tuna, green beans, olives, potatoes, and tomatoes.

3. Using a food processor fitted with the steel blade, purée the anchovies with their oil. Whisk

them into the White Vinaigrette. Just before serving, drizzle on enough dressing to lightly coat the salad.

PASTA SALAD WITH CAPERS AND BASIL DRESSING

Makes 12 to 14 servings

Be sure to slightly undercook the pasta for this salad. It will soften more as it absorbs the dressing.

VINAIGRETTE

1 ½ ounces (2 to 3 bunches) fresh basil leaves, minced
¾ cup white wine vinegar
1 ½ tablespoons minced garlic
Salt, to taste
2 ¼ cups extra-virgin olive oil

SALAD

2 ½ pounds large pasta shells
1 cup capers, drained
1 large red onion, minced
2 cups freshly grated Parmesan cheese

1. *To make the vinaigrette:* Using a blender or a food processor fitted with the steel blade, finely chop the basil with a little of the vinegar. Blend in the garlic, salt, and the rest of the vinegar. With the machine running, slowly add the olive oil.

2. Cook the pasta shells in salted boiling water until al dente. Rinse the pasta under cold water, drain it completely, and refrigerate until chilled.

3. In a large salad bowl, mix together the capers, onion, and Parmesan cheese. Add the pasta and toss it gently with enough dressing to coat. The salad will keep, tightly covered and refrigerated, up to one week.

CHÈVRE SALAD WITH WALNUTS

Makes 6 servings

VINAIGRETTE

2 tablespoons red wine
vinegar
½ teaspoon salt
Freshly ground pepper, to
taste
½ teaspoon Dijon-style
mustard
½ teaspoon Moutarde de
Meaux
½ cup walnut oil

SALAD

1 log Montrachet (goat
cheese)
1 cup dry bread crumbs,
finely ground
½ cup chopped walnuts
Salad greens (escarole,
endive, arugula,
watercress, and other
flavorful greens should be
used, at least in part)

1. *To make the vinaigrette:* Whisk together the red wine vinegar, salt, and pepper, then add the Dijon-style mustard and Moutarde de Meaux. Whisk in the walnut oil, a little at a time at first, then in a steady stream, until smooth.

2. Cut the cheese into 8 discs and roll them in the bread crumbs to thoroughly coat them. Refrigerate the cheese, covered, until just before serving time.

3. Preheat the oven to 400°. Bake the cheese rounds on a cookie sheet for 2 minutes.

4. Stir the walnuts into the vinaigrette in a large salad bowl. Add the greens and toss to coat. Divide the salad among six individual serving plates. Top each serving with a baked cheese round and serve immediately. You'll have two rounds to spare for hearty appetites.

4

CHARCUTERIE

QUICHES

PIZZAS

SAUSAGES

PÂTÉS & TERRINES

SPREADS & RELISHES

QUICHES

Piret's Quiche Pastry · Basic Custard Quiche · Chèvre Quiche · Cheese and Herb Quiche · Blue Cheese and Walnut Quiche · Mushroom and Cheese Quiche · Quiche Lorraine · Piret's Onion Tart · Piret's Tomato Tart · Tourte au Chou · Woodland Torte · Leek and Sausage Pie

PIZZAS

Piret's Pizza Dough · Smoked Salmon and Goat Cheese Pizza · Three-Mushroom Pizza · Lamb Sausage Pizza · Pizza Verde with Tomatillo Sauce · Scamorze Pizza with Sweet Red Pepper Sauce · Five-Cheese Pizza

SAUSAGES

Basic Sausage · Pork Sausage · Lamb Sausage · Fragrant Fennel Sausage · Boudin Blanc · Patty McDonald's Seafood Sausage

PÂTÉS AND TERRINES

Peppercorn Pâté · Country Pâté en Croûte · French Country Pâté · Duck Pâté à l'Orange · Terrine de Campagne · Duck Terrine with Raisins · Anne's Duck Terrine with Green Peppercorns · Rabbit Liver Terrine · Rabbit Terrine with Tomato Coulis · Salmon Terrine · Galantine of Veal and Pork · Aspic

SPREADS AND RELISHES

Chicken Liver Spread · Paula Wolfert's Salmon Rillettes · Pork Rillettes · Duck Rillettes · Tapenade · Tart Onion Relish Diana Kennedy · Jerrie Strom's Red Onion Relish · Tomato Relish · Red Pepper Confit

WE LOVE THE FOOD served in restaurants in France and Italy; but we also adore the delicious pâtés, sausages, and salads one can purchase at charcuteries, the great breads at nearby bakeries, and the exquisite cheeses one finds in profusion in small specialty shops. All that, topped off with a delightful regional wine and a mouthwatering pastry, is our idea of fine dining. Crazy as it may sound, we have spent days on end in Europe lugging these gastronomic delights to our hotel room, to parks, and the countryside, without once setting foot in a restaurant.

Back home we found slim pickings in prepared carry-out foods, and nowhere the range of wonderfully rich soft goat- and cow's-milk cheeses. Where, oh where, we asked, are the splendid breads of Europe? And why can't we have the luscious cakes and pastries that are commonplace in even the tiniest villages of France?

With that, in 1979, we started Piret's charcuterie, boulangerie, and pâtisserie extraordinaire. And while we were at it, we added a fromagerie (cheese department), a chocolate section, wines, imported and domestic groceries, and a restaurant. We also catered. We intended to be the complete *traiteur*, shopkeeper and caterer, to San Diego.

In France and Italy, the *charcutier*'s cuisine is a cuisine of the working class. Its mainstay is pork, which, combined with other meats and ingredients, becomes pâtés and terrines, delectable sausages, and galantines or ballottines. Over the years, the selection has broadened to include stews, as well as smoked and cured meats and roasted and rotisseried meats. To complete the meal, the *charcutier* may also offer quiches, pizzas, vegetable side dishes, salads, and relishes.

First-class *charcutiers* are expert in buffet dining in the grand manner, creating beautifully decorated roasted meats and *chauds-froids* (cold chicken, fish, or game preparations), coated with aspic or *chaud-froid* sauce, elegant pâtés using game birds, baked in flaky, decorative crust, and silken terrines with *foie gras* and truffles. Each presentation is a feast for the eye as well as the palate.

Q U I C H E S

Piret's charcuterie, like those in France, offers a variety of quiches daily. These come in individual 4-inch crusts or 9- to 11-inch sizes for a whole family or a party. You can also make giant rectangular quiches in a jellyroll pan for a big party. Or use flan rings in various sizes and shapes for an interesting buffet presentation.

A quiche is nothing more than a flaky crust filled with custard and a variety of additional ingredients. We give you a number of recipes, but don't feel bound by them. You can use vegetables, meats, cheeses, fish — whatever you have around or fancy.

The basic dough we use for all our quiches and tarts, and recipes for many of our most popular fillings follow. The pastry can be refrigerated (in a block or precut to fit individual or large tart pans), tightly wrapped in plastic wrap, for one to two days, or frozen for as long as six months. Thaw frozen pastry overnight in the refrigerator before using. The pastry and the filling recipes will make four individual tarts or one big pie (use either a quiche pan or a regular pie pan). Either size can be partially baked (remove them from the oven 10 minutes before they are done), then refrigerated to be finished later.

&❧ If you are entertaining a large group and want to make several quiches ahead of time, prebake them as described above, and refrigerate them until about 30 minutes before reheating time. Allow them to come to room temperature, then bake them in a preheated 350° oven for 15 to 20 minutes, or until they are heated through. Do not use a microwave oven, because reheating in a microwave can make the dough soggy.

PIRET'S QUICHE PASTRY

Fits 11-inch quiche pan, 9-inch pie pan, or four 4-inch tart pans

1½ cups (7 ounces) unbleached, all-purpose flour
½ teaspoon salt
6 tablespoons (3 ounces) chilled unsalted butter, cut into 1-inch pieces
3 tablespoons (1 ounce) shortening, cut into 1-inch pieces
1 egg
3 tablespoons ice water

1. Place the flour and salt in the work bowl of a food processor fitted with the steel blade, and blend them for 1 second. Add the butter and shortening, and process them with 4 or 5 on/off pulses. Small bits of butter and shortening should still be visible. Whisk together the egg and ice water, and add them to the work bowl. Process the dough for 4 or 5 on/off pulses, until the pastry just begins to stick together. Turn the pastry out onto a lightly floured surface and gently press it into a thick disc. Wrap it in plastic wrap and refrigerate for 30 minutes. It also may be wrapped for freezing and frozen at this point. Let it thaw overnight in the refrigerator before rolling. (To mix the dough by hand, stir together the flour and salt, and cut in the butter and shortening with a pastry blender or two knives, until the mixture looks like small peas. Using a fork, add the egg-water mixture and toss until the pastry just holds together. Turn it out onto a lightly floured surface, press it into a thick disc, and refrigerate as directed above.)

2. Roll the pastry no more than ¼-inch thick, and cut it to fit the quiche, pie, or tart pan with a small overhang. Line the pan with the pastry (be careful not to stretch it), pinch up a rim, and prick the bottom all over with a fork.

3. If the filling you are using is very moist, or if you wish to use a filling such as pastry cream or fresh fruit, bake the pastry empty (or "blind"), until it is partially or completely cooked, to seal the bottom so the filling won't make it soggy: Preheat oven to 400°. Fit aluminum foil or parchment paper into the pastry-lined pan and fill it with about ½ inch of dried beans, uncooked rice, or small metal pie weights. For a quiche with a moist filling, bake the pastry partially, for 10 to 15 minutes, then remove the liner and weights. Proceed to fill as indicated. If the pastry shell is to be used with a precooked filling or filled with fresh fruit, remove the liner and weights from the partially baked pastry shell, return the pastry to the oven, and finish baking it, empty, until the pastry just begins to take on a very light beige color (about 10 minutes). Cool the pastry before adding the filling.

BASIC CUSTARD QUICHE

Makes one 9- to 11-inch or four 4-inch tarts

This is the basic custard mixture that goes into many of our quiches. Some of our favorite combinations appear below, but we hope you'll use them as inspiration for your own creations. Just about any combination of grated cheese, vegetables, leftover meat, poultry, or seafood, or whatever else appeals to you can be added to this all-purpose custard. It's a great way to clear out the refrigerator.

1 recipe Piret's Quiche
   Pastry (page 103)

FILLING

3 eggs
2 tablespoons unbleached,
   all-purpose flour
¼ teaspoon freshly grated
   nutmeg
½ teaspoon salt

1. Line the quiche pan with the pastry, pinch up a rim, and prick the bottom all over with a fork. Partially bake the pastry, if you wish, and set it aside.

2. *To make the filling:* Whisk together the eggs, flour, nutmeg, salt, and white pepper. Blend in the cream, and then the milk.

3. Evenly distribute whatever cheese, meat, and/or vegetables you are using in the prepared pastry shell, and pour in the custard filling. (If you are using high-moisture vegetables, such as tomatoes,

½ teaspoon freshly ground
    white pepper
1 cup heavy cream
½ cup milk

1 to 2 cups additional
    cheese, meat, and/or
    vegetables

zucchini, or mushrooms, they should be cooked first to evaporate some of their water content.)

4. Preheat oven to 375°. Place the filled pan on a baking sheet. Generally, custard quiches should be baked for 35 to 40 minutes, or until the custard is just set. Let the quiche rest for 8 to 10 minutes before slicing and serving it.

CHÈVRE QUICHE

Makes one 9- to 11-inch or four 4-inch tarts

1 recipe Piret's Quiche
    Pastry (page 103),
    partially baked

4 ounces Bucheron or
    Montrachet (goat cheese)
4 ounces cream cheese,
    softened
1 tablespoon unbleached,
    all-purpose flour
3 large eggs
1 cup heavy cream
½ cup milk
1 small can (about ¼ cup)
    chopped Anaheim chilies
½ cup sliced pitted ripe
    olives

1. If using the Bucheron chèvre, trim off the rind. Combine the chèvre and cream cheese in the work bowl of a food processor fitted with the steel blade, or in the bowl of an electric mixer, and process or beat until smooth. Add the flour, and process a few seconds to blend. Add the eggs, one at a time, processing a few seconds after each addition. Add the cream and milk, processing until the custard is smooth. Add the chilies, and process 2 seconds to blend.

2. Preheat oven to 375°. Evenly distribute the olive slices in the prepared pastry shell. Gently pour in the custard mixture. Place the filled pan on a baking sheet and bake the quiche for 35 minutes, or until the custard is just set. Let the quiche rest for 8 to 10 minutes before slicing and serving it.

CHEESE AND HERB QUICHE

Makes one 9- to 11-inch or four 4-inch tarts

1 recipe Piret's Quiche
   Pastry (page 103),
   partially baked

4 ounces cream cheese,
   softened
½ cup sour cream
2 tablespoons unbleached,
   all-purpose flour
½ teaspoon salt
½ teaspoon freshly ground
   pepper
⅛ to ¼ teaspoon freshly
   grated nutmeg
2 eggs
1¼ cup milk or
   half-and-half
1½ cups (about 4 ounces)
   freshly grated Swiss or
   Gruyère cheese
2 tablespoons freshly grated
   Parmesan cheese
3 tablespoons sliced scallions
3 tablespoons chopped fresh
   parsley
1 tablespoon fresh chives or
   other herb (such as basil,
   dill, or watercress)

1. Beat together until smooth the cream cheese, sour cream, flour, salt, pepper, and nutmeg. Beat in the eggs, blending them well, then beat in the milk or half-and-half.

2. Preheat oven to 375°. Sprinkle the Swiss and Parmesan cheeses, scallions, parsley, and chives in the prepared pastry shell. Gently pour in the cream cheese mixture. Place the filled pan on a baking sheet, and bake the quiche for 45 minutes, or until the custard is just set. Let the quiche rest 8 to 10 minutes before slicing and serving it.

BLUE CHEESE AND WALNUT QUICHE

Makes one 9- to 11-inch or four 4-inch tarts

1 recipe Piret's Quiche
    Pastry (page 103),
    partially baked

2¼ cups (about 6 ounces)
    freshly grated Swiss or
    Gruyère cheese
½ cup (about 2 ounces)
    crumbled blue cheese
2 tablespoons minced red
    onion
¼ cup chopped walnuts
1 recipe filling for Basic
    Custard Quiche
    (page 104)

1. Combine the Swiss and blue cheeses and sprinkle them in the prepared pastry shell. Sprinkle the red onion and walnuts over the cheese. Gently pour in custard to fill the pastry to the rim.

2. Preheat oven to 375°. Place the filled pan on a baking sheet, and bake the quiche for 35 to 40 minutes, or until the custard is just set. Let the quiche rest 8 to 10 minutes before slicing and serving it.

MUSHROOM AND CHEESE QUICHE

Makes one 9- to 11-inch or four 4-inch tarts

1 recipe Piret's Quiche
    Pastry (page 103),
    partially baked

3 tablespoons butter
¼ cup chopped onion
½ pound mushrooms, sliced
Salt and freshly ground
    pepper, to taste
3 tablespoons chopped fresh
    parsley
1½ cups (about 4 ounces)
    freshly grated Swiss or
    Gruyère cheese
2 tablespoons freshly grated
    Parmesan cheese
1 recipe filling for Basic
    Custard Quiche
    (page 104)

1. Melt the butter in a large skillet. Add the onion and cook until translucent. Stir in the mushrooms and cook until they are soft and their liquid has evaporated. Season the mixture with the salt, pepper, and parsley.

2. Preheat oven to 375°. Sprinkle the Swiss cheese in the prepared pastry shell. Spread the mushroom mixture over the cheese, then sprinkle on the Parmesan cheese. Gently pour in custard to fill the pastry to the rim.

3. Place the filled pan on a baking sheet, and bake the quiche for 35 to 40 minutes, or until the custard is just set. Let the quiche rest for 8 to 10 minutes before slicing and serving it.

QUICHE LORRAINE

Makes one 9- to 11-inch or four 4-inch tarts

1 recipe Piret's Quiche
   Pastry (page 103),
   partially baked

4 ounces bacon, cut in
   1/4-inch pieces
2 ounces cooked ham
2 1/4 cups (about 6 ounces)
   freshly grated Swiss or
   Gruyère cheese
1 recipe filling for Basic
   Custard Quiche
   (page 104)

1. Blanch the bacon in boiling water for 2 minutes, remove it from the water with a slotted spoon, and let it drain and cool in a colander. Grind the ham, using a food processor fitted with the steel blade, or dice it finely by hand.

2. Preheat oven to 375°. Combine the bacon, ham, and Swiss cheese, and sprinkle them in the prepared pastry shell. Gently pour in custard to fill the pastry to the rim.

3. Place the filled pan on a baking sheet, and bake the quiche for 35 to 40 minutes, or until the custard is just set. Let the quiche rest for 8 to 10 minutes before cutting and serving it.

PIRET'S ONION TART

Makes one 9- to 11-inch or four 4-inch tarts

The onions in this tart become sweet and buttery — a great diversion from the custard-based quiche.

1 recipe Piret's Quiche
   Pastry (page 103),
   partially baked

1/4 cup unsalted butter
2 1/2 pounds yellow onions,
   thinly sliced
1 tablespoon chopped garlic
2 teaspoons salt
1 teaspoon freshly ground
   white pepper
1/4 teaspoon freshly grated
   nutmeg
1 cup heavy cream
3 tablespoons arrowroot or
   cornstarch

1. Melt the butter in a large skillet, and cook the onions in the butter over medium heat for 20 to 30 minutes, stirring occasionally, until they are soft and caramel-colored. Add the garlic, salt, white pepper, and nutmeg.

2. Whisk together the cream and arrowroot or cornstarch, adding the cream a little at a time to avoid lumps. Stir the cream into the onion mixture and simmer until it begins to thicken. Pour the onion mixture into a shallow pan to cool.

3. Preheat oven to 400°. Pour the onion mixture into the prepared pastry shell, leveling off the top with a spatula. Place the anchovy fillets on the top like the spokes of a wheel, and arrange the olives,

1 can (2 ounces) anchovy
   fillets, drained
8 pitted ripe olives, halved
2 tablespoons freshly grated
   Parmesan cheese

split side down, over the top. Sprinkle on the Parmesan cheese. Place the filled pan on a baking sheet, and bake the tart for 25 minutes, or until the top is golden brown. Let the tart cool slightly before serving.

PIRET'S TOMATO TART

Makes one 9- to 11-inch or four 4-inch tarts

1 recipe Piret's Quiche
   Pastry (page 103),
   partially baked

½ cup minced onion
4 tablespoons olive oil
1 clove garlic, minced
2 cans (32 ounces each)
   Italian-style tomatoes,
   drained (or 3 pounds
   fresh tomatoes, peeled,
   seeded, and diced [about
   4 cups])
¾ teaspoon salt
   (1½ teaspoons if using
   fresh tomatoes)
¾ teaspoon freshly ground
   pepper
1½ teaspoons dried basil
¼ teaspoon dried thyme
   (optional)
Pinch of sugar
2 tablespoons tomato paste
3 tablespoons butter
2 tablespoons unbleached,
   all-purpose flour
1½ cups hot milk
Salt and freshly ground
   pepper, to taste
1 large or 2 small ripe
   tomatoes, thinly sliced
2 tablespoons freshly grated
   Parmesan cheese

1. Over medium-low heat, cook the onion in the olive oil until soft. Stir in the garlic and cook it for 30 seconds. Add the tomatoes, salt, pepper, basil, thyme, sugar, and tomato paste. Bring the mixture to a boil, reduce the heat, and simmer for 15 to 20 minutes, stirring occasionally, until the liquid has almost completely evaporated. Pour the mixture into a fine sieve to drain the excess liquid.

2. Melt the butter in a medium saucepan. When it begins to foam, whisk in the flour. Cook this roux, whisking it constantly, for 2 minutes. Remove the pan from the heat and whisk in the hot milk, ¼ cup at a time. Return the pan to the heat and cook the sauce, stirring, until it is thick and smooth. Season it with salt and pepper, to taste. (This sauce is called a béchamel; see also page 324.)

3. Preheat oven to 375°. Pour the drained tomato mixture into the prepared pastry shell and level the top with a spatula. Cover the filling with the béchamel sauce, spreading it evenly. Arrange the tomato slices on top and sprinkle on the Parmesan cheese.

4. Place the filled pan on a baking sheet and bake the tart for about 30 minutes, or until the top is golden brown. Cool slightly before serving.

TOURTE AU CHOU

Makes 6 to 8 servings

Our first *charcutier,* who was raised in Nantua and worked in charcuteries in and around Lyon, brought us this recipe for a cabbage pie. It is a robust main dish, with marvelously balanced flavors. If you are using this for entertaining, you may want to bake it several hours earlier in the day, or the day before. Bring it to room temperature and reheat for about 20 minutes in a preheated 350° oven.

1 recipe Classic Puff Pastry (page 342), or 2 recipes Piret's Quiche Pastry (page 103)

½ pound bacon
1 pound ground pork
2 large onions, coarsely chopped
1 large head cabbage, shredded (about 8 cups)
Kosher-style salt and freshly ground pepper, to taste
Egg wash: 1 egg beaten with 1 tablespoon water

1. Roll out half of the dough ¼ inch thick in a circle large enough to fit a deep-dish 10-inch pie pan with an overhang of 1 inch. Fit the pastry into the pan, being careful not to stretch it. Refrigerate the pastry-lined pan. Wrap the remaining pastry in plastic wrap and refrigerate until needed to top the pie.

2. Coarsely chop the bacon and cook it in a large skillet or casserole until it begins to render its fat. Add the ground pork and cook it until it just loses its pink color. Stir in the onions and cook them for 5 minutes. Add the cabbage and plenty of salt and pepper. Cook the mixture over medium-low heat, covered, for 20 to 30 minutes, or until the cabbage is soft. Drain the mixture in a colander and spread it out in a shallow pan so it cools quickly.

3. Preheat oven to 350°. Spoon the cabbage mixture into the prepared pie pan, mounding it in the center. Roll out the remaining pastry to a circle ¼-inch thick and wide enough to overhang the edge by ½ inch. Place the pastry over the pie and brush the top with the egg wash. Fold the bottom overhanging edge of the pastry over the top edge, pressing the edges to seal, then roll the pastry rim to form a thick, ropelike effect. Cut a small hole in the center of the top pastry to allow steam to escape. Brush the top a second time with the egg wash and score the pastry decoratively with the tip of a knife.

4. Bake the pie about 55 to 60 minutes, or until it is well browned. Let the pie stand for 15 minutes or so to firm up, then cut it into wedges to serve.

WOODLAND TORTE

Makes 8 to 10 servings

Piret's Woodland Torte is a hearty, earthy potato and mushroom pie — absolutely divine as a luncheon or supper entrée at a patio party or buffet. You can prepare the whole thing ahead of time and reheat it just before serving: cover the top with parchment paper or aluminum foil to prevent the crust from becoming overly browned, and heat for 20 to 25 minutes at 350°.

Chanterelle, cèpe, or morel mushrooms are available dried and fresh in specialty food shops. They are expensive but add a splendid, woody flavor and interesting texture that you will not have with commercially grown mushroom caps. If you are unable to find the European-style mushrooms, you may want to experiment with an Oriental variety, such as shiitake.

4 tablespoons unsalted butter

2 pounds yellow onions, thinly sliced

1 pound button mushrooms, washed and stems removed (leave the caps whole)

4 ounces chanterelle, cèpe, or morel mushrooms

2 tablespoons unbleached, all-purpose flour

¼ cup dry sherry

1 cup heavy cream, warmed slightly

2 tablespoons chopped fresh parsley

Salt and freshly ground pepper, to taste

3 tablespoons butter, melted

1 recipe Classic Puff Pastry (page 342), or enough for a double-crust 11-inch deep-dish pie

4 to 5 medium White or Red Rose potatoes, sliced ¼-inch thick

1 egg, beaten

1: Melt the 4 tablespoons butter in a heavy skillet over medium heat and cook the onions and mushrooms. When all of the liquid has evaporated, stir in the flour. Add the sherry and warmed cream, blending them thoroughly, and simmer the mixture gently for 8 to 10 minutes, or until it is fairly thick. Season the mixture with the parsley and salt and pepper, and set it aside to cool completely.

2. Choose an 11-inch pie or quiche pan with a removable bottom. Brush it with the melted butter. Roll the pastry into two circles, one 14 inches wide, the other 11 inches. Place the larger puff pastry circle in the pan, pressing it in against the sides and leaving the edge overhanging evenly all around. Place one-third of the potato slices in a single layer of concentric circles, covering the pastry completely. Cover the potatoes with half of the onion-mushroom mixture. Using half of the remaining potatoes, add a second layer of potato slices. Follow this with the remainder of the onion-mushroom mixture, and spread the rest of the potatoes over the top.

3. Preheat oven to 375°. Place the 11-inch circle of puff pastry on top of the potatoes and brush it lightly with the beaten egg. Fold the overhanging edge of the pastry up over the top edge, pressing the

edges to seal, then roll the pastry rim to form a thick, ropelike effect. Cut a small hole in the center of the top pastry to allow steam to escape. Brush the top a second time with the egg, and score the top decoratively with the tip of a knife. Bake the torte for 50 minutes, or until it is golden brown. Let the torte stand for 15 minutes or so to firm up, then cut it into wedges to serve.

LEEK AND SAUSAGE PIE

Makes 6 servings

We love homey, hearty recipes, the kind you like to have on brisk fall nights. This pie, developed by Lois Stanton, has a pastry with a bit of bite from the mustard, and a filling both savory and sweet. It's great served with a mug of dark beer.

TO PREPARE THE PASTRY

1½ cups unbleached, all-purpose flour
Pinch of salt
2 teaspoons dry mustard
2 teaspoons caraway seeds
½ cup unsalted butter, chilled
3 to 4 tablespoons ice water

1. Stir together the flour, salt, mustard, and caraway seeds. Cut in the butter, working the mixture with your fingers or two knives until it resembles coarse meal. Quickly stir in the ice water with a fork. Gather the dough into a flattened disc, wrap it in plastic wrap, and refrigerate for 30 minutes. (The dough can also be made using a food processor: see Piret's Quiche Pastry [page 103], step 1.)

2. Preheat oven to 400°. Following the directions for Piret's Quiche Pastry, fit the pastry into a 9- to 11-inch deep pie pan and bake "blind" for 15 minutes. Remove it from the oven, and reduce the heat to 350°. Place the pastry shell on a baking sheet.

TO PREPARE THE FILLING

2 tablespoons dry bread crumbs
2 tablespoons freshly grated Parmesan cheese
12 ounces bulk sausage
Dried thyme and sage, to taste (optional)

1. Stir together the bread crumbs and the 2 tablespoons of Parmesan cheese and sprinkle them in the pastry shell. Cook the sausage, breaking it up as it cooks. Drain it thoroughly on paper towels. Taste the sausage and season with thyme and sage if

6 leeks

2 tablespoons unsalted
butter

3 large eggs

2 egg yolks

1½ teaspoons Dijon-style
mustard

1 teaspoon salt

¼ teaspoon cayenne pepper

⅓ cup butter, melted

½ cup freshly grated
imported Swiss cheese

2½ cups milk, scalded

¼ cup freshly grated
Parmesan cheese

it tastes bland. Sprinkle the sausage over the bread crumbs and cheese in the pastry shell.

2. Thoroughly wash the leeks, and slice them, taking both the white and the tender green. Melt the 2 tablespoons butter in a skillet over medium heat and cook the leeks until they are soft.

3. Whisk together the whole eggs and egg yolks. Whisk in the mustard, salt, cayenne pepper, melted butter, Swiss cheese, scalded milk, and the cooked leeks. Spoon the mixture into the pastry shell, top with the remaining Parmesan cheese, and bake the pie for 25 minutes, or until the custard is puffed and golden and a knife inserted in the custard comes out clean. Serve the pie warm or at room temperature.

P I Z Z A S

The following pizza dough and toppings are conceptually similar to the pizzas served at Chez Panisse in Berkeley and Spago in Los Angeles, rather than the familiar "Italian" pizza we're all accustomed to. Piret's pizza is 10 to 12 inches in diameter, with a very thin, delicate, crusty dough. One of these makes a nice appetizer for four, or a light lunch or supper for two served with a salad and dessert. When entertaining, we make several with different toppings as an appetizer or for hors d'oeuvres.

The Lamb Sausage Pizza is Greek or Mediterranean in style, and somewhat spicy. Pizza Verde with Tomatillo Sauce, Jacques Pépin's favorite, is quite hot, and Mexican in style. Scamorze Pizza, with mellow red pepper sauce, is sweetly spicy. Five Cheese Pizza is wonderfully mild, yet interesting — a safe bet for any crowd. Smoked Salmon and Goat Cheese Pizza is definitely Scandinavian, definitely different. Three Mushroom Pizza is buttery and elegant.

Our recipes for "California" pizzas were created

by Jenny Saar, a baking adventurer of the first order. At Piret's we grate all the cheeses freshly — it makes all the difference in the world (and it's easy to do in the food processor).

PIRET'S PIZZA DOUGH

Makes six 12-inch pizzas

This recipe makes dough that is quite soft and may seem sticky in the bowl. However, it can be easily handled with a light dusting of flour. Roll out the dough to about half of the desired size. Spinning the dough by tossing it in the air is an ideal way to form the dough to the desired diameter without compressing it too much. For those of us who are less dexterous, the dough may be gently stretched and manipulated by hand to the final size. Drape the rolled dough over the backs of your hands, and pull to stretch it over your knuckles, turning the dough to stretch it evenly. (If the dough seems too elastic, allow it to rest for a few minutes before finishing.) It will benefit in taste and appearance from brushing a light film of olive oil over the surface before adding the toppings of your choice.

We've purposely made this recipe for six pizzas because the dough is easy to freeze and use later for entertaining. To freeze the dough, cut into six portions. Wrap each portion in oiled plastic freezer bags and press out the air. To thaw, leave the dough in the plastic bag and allow it to rise at room temperature, then proceed as directed.

We recommend that you use a pizza stone, quarry tile, or other bread-baking tile when you bake pizza, in order to get the crispy brown crust of pizza baked in commercial ovens.

These pizzas are especially recommended for stand-up cocktail parties for guests who have become jaded with stuffed mushroom caps and celery laden with cream cheese concoctions. Lois Stanton suggests offering a variety of toppings, which guests can assemble for a personalized pizza approach.

2 cups warm (105°) water
1½ tablespoons dry yeast (or
    ¾ ounce cake yeast)
Pinch of sugar
4 tablespoons olive oil
4½ teaspoons salt
6 cups unbleached,
    all-purpose flour

1. Combine the water, yeast, and sugar in a large bowl and let it proof for 5 to 10 minutes. Add the olive oil and salt, then stir in the flour all at once. Stir the mixture with a wooden spoon until it forms a ball of soft dough. Turn the dough out onto a floured surface and knead it for 10 to 15 minutes, or until it is smooth and elastic.

2. Divide the dough into six equal portions and

Cornmeal
Olive oil

form them into balls. Let the dough rest for 10 minutes. Roll each ball of dough to half the desired diameter, and finish forming the circles by pressing them lightly with your hands.

3. Transfer the dough to a thin board or piece of cardboard that has been generously sprinkled with cornmeal. Brush the dough with olive oil, and arrange the toppings of your choice over the dough.

TO BAKE PIZZA

Set the oven at its highest setting (usually 500°) and heat a pizza stone or bread-baking tile on the bottom rack. Tap the board the pizza is on to loosen the pizza, tilt the board slightly, and slide the pizza onto the tile. Most pizzas will bake in 10 to 15 minutes. The pizza is done when the bottom crust is browned and the sauces bubble.

SMOKED SALMON AND GOAT CHEESE PIZZA

Makes one 12-inch pizza

1 recipe Piret's Pizza Dough
   (page 114)

¼ cup freshly grated
   Parmesan cheese
3¼ to 4 ounces goat cheese
   (Montrachet, Lezay, or
   Bucheron)
2½ ounces smoked salmon,
   cut into strips ½- to
   ¾-inch wide
½ red onion, very thinly
   sliced and separated into
   rings
1 to 2 tablespoons chopped
   fresh dill
Olive oil

1. Prepare the dough on a thin board or piece of cardboard generously sprinkled with cornmeal. Preheat the oven and a baking tile at the highest setting, as directed under Piret's Pizza Dough. Brush the dough with olive oil.

2. Sprinkle the dough with 3 tablespoons of the Parmesan cheese, leaving a ½-inch border. If you have a potato ricer, use it to distribute the goat cheese over the pizza; otherwise, crumble it by hand and distribute it as evenly as possible. Arrange the salmon in close parallel rows over the cheese. Spread the onion rings over the salmon.

3. Transfer the pizza to the baking tile and bake it for 10 to 15 minutes, or until the crust is browned on the bottom and the onions are cooked. Return the pizza to its board and cut it into 6 or 8 wedges. Top with the remaining Parmesan cheese, the dill, and a light drizzle of olive oil.

THREE-MUSHROOM PIZZA

Makes one 12-inch pizza

Any combination of mushrooms may be used for this pizza, but do try to use two or more varieties instead of a single type.

1 recipe Piret's Pizza Dough
   (page 114)

¼ cup freshly grated
   Parmesan cheese
1 small clove garlic, minced
1 ounce mozzarella cheese,
   grated
1 ounce Swiss cheese, grated
2 tablespoons minced red
   onion
2½ ounces Marscarpone
   cheese (see note)
2 ounces shiitake mush-
   rooms (1 or 2 mush-
   rooms)
2 ounces oyster or abalone
   mushrooms (1 or
   2 mushrooms)
½ cup enoki mushrooms
   (approximately)
Freshly ground white
   pepper, to taste
2 tablespoons chopped fresh
   sage (or 1 teaspoon dried,
   plus 1 tablespoon
   chopped fresh parsley)
Olive oil

1. Prepare the dough on a thin board or piece of cardboard generously sprinkled with cornmeal. Preheat the oven and a baking tile at the highest setting, as directed under Piret's Pizza Dough. Brush the dough with olive oil.

2. Thoroughly blend 3 tablespoons of the Parmesan cheese with the garlic, and sprinkle the mixture over the dough, leaving a ½-inch border. Combine the mozzarella and Swiss cheeses and sprinkle them over the Parmesan with the onion. Pinch off small pieces of Marscarpone cheese and distribute them over the onion.

3. Wipe the shiitake and oyster mushrooms with a damp towel. Cut off and discard the stems, and thinly slice the mushrooms. Sprinkle them over the pizza. Cut off and discard the yellow part of the enoki mushroom stems. Reserve a small bunch of the enoki mushrooms for the garnish and sprinkle the rest over the pizza. Season the pizza with white pepper.

4. Transfer the pizza to the baking tile and bake it for 10 to 15 minutes, or until the crust is browned on the bottom and the cheeses are melted. Return the pizza to the board and cut it into 6 to 8 wedges. Top with the sage, remaining Parmesan cheese, and a drizzle of olive oil. Place the "bouquet" of enoki mushrooms in the center, and serve.

NOTE

If Marscarpone, a buttery Italian cheese, is unavailable, use the following substitute: Drain ½ cup of sour cream in a colander or cheesecloth for 30 minutes to an hour. Blend the drained cream with 2 tablespoons unsalted butter and 1 teaspoon lemon juice. Refrigerate the mixture until firm.

LAMB SAUSAGE PIZZA

Makes one 12-inch pizza

1 recipe Piret's Pizza Dough
   (page 114)

3 to 4 brine-packed grape
   leaves
¼ cup freshly grated
   Parmesan cheese
2 to 3 ounces feta cheese
½ red onion, very thinly
   sliced and separated into
   rings
1 small tomato (or ½ cup
   cherry tomatoes), thinly
   sliced
3 ounces Lamb Sausage
   (page 126)
⅓ cup pitted Nyons or
   oil-cured olives
1 tablespoon pine nuts
Freshly ground pepper, to
   taste
2 tablespoons chopped fresh
   sage, oregano, or parsley
Olive oil

1. Prepare the dough on a thin board or piece of cardboard generously sprinkled with cornmeal. Preheat the oven and a baking tile at the highest setting, as directed under Piret's Pizza Dough. Brush the dough with olive oil.

2. Thoroughly rinse the grape leaves in hot water and drain them. Pat the leaves dry with paper towels. Cut off the stems and remove the large vein.

3. Arrange the grape leaves over the dough, leaving a ½-inch border. Sprinkle the leaves with 3 tablespoons of the Parmesan cheese. Crumble on the feta cheese, and arrange the onion rings over the cheese. (This looks like a lot of onion, but it will cook down quite a bit.) Arrange the tomato slices evenly over the onion. Break up the sausage into pieces the size of half a walnut, and arrange the sausage and the olives evenly over the tomatoes. Top with the pine nuts and a liberal sprinkling of pepper.

4. Transfer the pizza from the board or cardboard to the baking tile and bake it for 10 to 15 minutes, or until the crust is browned on the bottom and the onions are cooked. Return the pizza to its board and cut it into 6 or 8 wedges. Sprinkle on the fresh herb, remaining Parmesan cheese, and a light drizzle of olive oil.

PIZZA VERDE WITH TOMATILLO SAUCE

Makes one 12-inch pizza

1 recipe Piret's Pizza Dough
(page 114)

¼ cup freshly grated
Parmesan cheese
¾ cup freshly grated
Monterey Jack cheese
¾ to 1 cup Tomatillo Sauce
(recipe follows)
1 small tomato (or ½ cup
cherry tomatoes), thinly
sliced
1 ounce feta cheese
5 to 6 slices *queso fresco*
(Mexican fresh cheese)
(optional; see note)
1 small can (4 ounces) whole
Anaheim chilies
Freshly ground pepper, to
taste
Chopped cilantro (fresh
coriander), for garnish
Olive oil

1. Prepare the dough on a thin board or piece of cardboard generously sprinkled with cornmeal. Preheat the oven and a baking tile at the highest setting, as directed under Piret's Pizza Dough. Brush the dough with olive oil.

2. Sprinkle the dough with 3 tablespoons of the Parmesan cheese, leaving a ½-inch border. Sprinkle the Monterey Jack cheese over the Parmesan. Spread on the Tomatillo Sauce and arrange the tomato slices over the sauce. Crumble the feta cheese over the tomatoes and arrange slices of *queso fresco* over the feta. Place a chili on each slice of *queso fresco* and sprinkle the pizza lightly with pepper.

3. Transfer the pizza to the baking tile and bake it for 10 to 15 minutes, or until the crust is browned on the bottom and the sauce is bubbly. Return the pizza to its board and cut it into 6 or 8 wedges. Garnish with the remaining Parmesan, a light drizzle of olive oil, and the chopped cilantro.

NOTE

According to Diana Kennedy in *Recipes from the Regional Cooks of Mexico, queso fresco,* sometimes called *queso de metate,* is closest to our farmer cheese, sold in bulk form in delicatessens. She finds *queso blanco* unacceptable as a substitute, because it becomes rubbery when heated.

Tomatillo Sauce

Makes 2 to 3 cups (enough for 2 to 3 Pizza Verdes)

Tomatillos are a familiar ingredient to cooks from the Southwest and are popular in many Mexican sauces. They look like small green tomatoes in a papery, brownish skin. However, according to Diana Kennedy, they are part of a fruit family related to green cherries or gooseberries (*Physalis*), not tomatoes.

This sauce may be used for pizza (with Mexican cheese and chilies), and it makes an unusual sauce for broiled fish and chicken.

2 pounds fresh tomatillos (or 2 cans [13 ounces each] tomatillos [see note])
1 teaspoon crushed, dried red pepper
2 teaspoons powdered cumin
¾ teaspoon freshly ground pepper
4 tablespoons vegetable oil (approximately)
1 cup chopped onion (1 medium onion)
3 cloves garlic, chopped
Scant ⅛ teaspoon ground cloves
Pinch of sugar
Salt, to taste
1 bunch cilantro (fresh coriander), chopped

1. If using fresh tomatillos, soak them in warm water for a minimum of 10 minutes to loosen the papery husks. Peel off the husks, rinse the tomatillos in cold water, and slice them.

2. In a sauté pan over medium-high heat, toast the red pepper, cumin, and black pepper, shaking the pan to evenly toast the spices and keep them from burning. Add the oil, onion, garlic, and cloves, and sauté them for 3 to 5 minutes. When the onions are translucent, add the tomatillos, sugar, and salt (omit the salt if you are using canned tomatillos). Cook the mixture about 20 to 30 minutes, or until the tomatillos have released their liquid and are limp but not mushy.

3. Drain the sauce in a sieve to remove any excess moisture. The sauce should be coarse, with the tomatillo slices intact. Allow it to cool, then add the cilantro. Taste the sauce and add more salt or sugar, if necessary.

NOTE

If using canned tomatillos, drain, rinse in cold water, and coarsely mash them.

SCAMORZE PIZZA WITH SWEET RED PEPPER SAUCE

Makes one 12-inch pizza

1 recipe Piret's Pizza Dough
(page 114)

3 tablespoons olive oil
¼ cup freshly grated
Parmesan cheese
2 teaspoons finely minced
garlic
¾ cup Sweet Red Pepper
Sauce (recipe follows)
6 to 8 thin slices smoked
mozzarella cheese
½ medium red onion, thinly
sliced
3 ounces pepperoncini
(sometimes called Tuscan
peppers), stemmed,
seeded, and sliced into
rings
1 tablespoon pitted ripe
olives, sliced or minced
4 ounces pancetta (Italian
bacon), julienne-cut
Salt and freshly ground
pepper, to taste
Olive oil

1. Prepare the dough on a thin board or piece of cardboard generously sprinkled with cornmeal. Preheat the oven and a baking tile at the highest setting, as directed under Piret's Pizza Dough. Brush the dough with olive oil.

2. Sprinkle on half of the Parmesan cheese and all of the garlic, leaving a ½-inch border. Spread on the Sweet Red Pepper Sauce, and arrange the mozzarella cheese slices over the sauce. Arrange the onion over the cheese. Sprinkle on the pepperoncini rings, olives, and pancetta, and season with salt and pepper.

3. Transfer the pizza to the baking tile and bake it for 10 to 15 minutes, or until the crust is browned on the bottom and the sauce is bubbly. Return the pizza to its board, and cut it into 6 or 8 wedges. Top with the remaining Parmesan cheese, and a light sprinkling of olive oil.

Sweet Red Pepper Sauce
Makes about 3 cups

This sauce is also delicious served over pasta.

5 tablespoons olive oil
1 cup chopped onion (about
½ large onion)
2 pounds red bell peppers,
seeded and chopped
2½ teaspoons salt

1. Heat the olive oil in a large skillet or sauté pan and cook the onions over medium heat until they are translucent but not brown. Stir in the red peppers, salt, pepper, paprika, and wine. Simmer the mixture, covered, for 10 minutes, stirring occasionally.

2. Uncover the pan and continue cooking the

1 teaspoon freshly ground
  pepper
½ teaspoon sweet paprika
¾ cup dry white wine

sauce 10 to 15 minutes, or until the liquid evaporates and the sauce thickens.

3. Cool the sauce, transfer it in batches to a blender or food processor fitted with the steel blade, and purée it to a smooth consistency. Taste and adjust the seasonings.

FIVE-CHEESE PIZZA

Makes one 12-inch pizza

1 recipe Piret's Pizza Dough
  (page 114)

¼ cup freshly grated
  Parmesan cheese
1 small clove garlic, minced
  (about ½ teaspoon)
2 ounces mozzarella cheese,
  grated
2 ounces Swiss cheese,
  grated
1 small tomato (or ½ cup
  cherry tomatoes), thinly
  sliced
1 to 2 ounces feta cheese
Freshly ground pepper, to
  taste
2 tablespoons fresh basil (or
  1 teaspoon dried, plus 1
  tablespoon chopped fresh
  parsley)
1 tablespoon freshly grated
  Romano cheese
Olive oil

1. Prepare the dough on a thin board or piece of cardboard generously sprinkled with cornmeal. Preheat the oven and a baking tile at the highest setting, as directed under Piret's Pizza Dough. Brush the dough with olive oil.

2. Thoroughly blend 3 tablespoons of the Parmesan cheese with the garlic and sprinkle the mixture over the dough, leaving a ½-inch border. Combine the mozzarella and Swiss cheeses and sprinkle them over the Parmesan. Arrange the tomatoes over the cheese. Crumble the feta over the tomatoes, and season the pizza liberally with pepper.

3. Transfer the pizza to the baking tile and bake it for 10 to 15 minutes, or until the crust is browned on the bottom and the cheeses are melted. Return the pizza to its board and cut it into 6 or 8 wedges. Top with the remaining Parmesan, a chiffonnade of the basil, the Romano cheese, and a light drizzle of olive oil. (For chiffonnade, roll the basil leaves into a tight cigar shape and cut the cylinder crosswise into fine shreds.)

S A U S A G E S

Thanks to the food processor, which does away with hours of tedious grinding, you can easily make your own sausages and eliminate the preservatives and excessive salt so common in commercially made sausages. You can use just about any sausage mixture to make crépinettes — flat, round patties wrapped in caul fat to hold their shape. Or for a classic sausage shape, use a sausage stuffing tube and some natural or manmade casings.

Quality butcher shops carry sausage casings for home use or can order them for you. For home use, casings are packaged in plastic cups called "hog cups," which provide enough casing for twenty pounds of forcemeat. They come in a variety of sizes depending on the width of the sausage you are making. For link sausages, you want 20 to 22 millimeter; frankfurter size is 22–24 millimeter; and for pudgy sausages, like our Boudin Blanc, 24–26 millimeter. We prefer natural casings to manmade, which don't hold the flavor of the sausage as well and can be tough. Natural casings can be from sheep, pork, and beef. When you buy or order casings, tell the butcher what sort of sausage you are making, as some animal casings are more suitable to certain fillings than others.

Uncooked sausages should be eaten within a week and may be poached, grilled, broiled, sautéed, or pan-fried.

BASIC SAUSAGE

Makes 4 pounds (6 to 8 main-dish servings)

This is the basic sausage we use for all sorts of recipes. It can be varied by the addition of herbs, spices, garlic, or other seasonings.

2 pounds lean pork (or 1 pound cooked ham and 1 pound pork)
1 pound veal
1 pound pork fat
3 teaspoons salt (varies with the amount of ham used)
½ teaspoon freshly ground pepper
¼ teaspoon allspice (or a mixture of ground ginger, nutmeg, and cloves)
Butter
6 to 8 feet natural pork casing
1 teaspoon vegetable oil to lubricate the sausage horn

TO PREPARE THE STUFFING

Cut the meats and the pork fat into 1-inch cubes. Sprinkle the salt, pepper, and spices over the mixture, and grind it using a meat grinder or a food processor fitted with the steel blade. Sauté a small amount of the sausage mixture in a little butter. Taste the cooked sausage for seasoning and adjust as necessary. The mixture can be formed into patties, used as the forcemeat in pâté recipes, or stuffed into casings.

TO STUFF THE CASING

1. Thoroughly rinse the casing to remove any salt or brine. Soak the casing in tepid water for 30 minutes. Ease one end of the casing over a faucet, and run cold water through it for several minutes. Drain it thoroughly, but do not let it completely dry.

2. Slip one end of the casing over the oiled sausage horn of a meat grinder (see note), and push the casing onto the horn, bunching it up until only about 2 inches of casing hangs from the end. Tie the loose end of the casing with kitchen twine. Force the sausage mixture through the grinder, filling the casing. Ease some casing off the sausage horn and continue grinding, filling the casing until it is tightly stuffed to within 3 inches of the end. Detach the casing and knot the end.

3. Using your hands, roll the sausage on a tabletop to evenly distribute the filling. Twist the sausage at 3-inch intervals to form links, twisting each successive link in the opposite direction to keep them from unwinding. Pierce any air bubbles in the casing with a needle. Tie the sausages with 2 knots

at each twist. The sausage may be left in one piece and cooked, then cut into links to serve, or cut between the knots to make individual links.

TO COOK THE SAUSAGE

Place the sausage in a large frypan, pour in about ½ inch water, and simmer the sausage, uncovered, over medium heat, for 30 minutes. The water will evaporate, and the sausage can then brown in its own fat. The cooked sausage will keep, refrigerated and tightly wrapped, up to one week.

NOTE

If you do not have a meat grinder with a sausage horn, a pastry bag may be used to fill the casing. Fit a large pastry bag with a large plain tip. Fill the bag with the sausage mixture. Ease one end of the casing over the pastry tip and gather it onto the tip until only 6 inches remains hanging free. Tie a knot about 3 inches from the free end. Begin squeezing the pork mixture into the casing, pushing it down toward the knot to eliminate air pockets. Ease some of the casing off the tip and continue squeezing the pork from the pastry bag until the casing is tightly stuffed to within 3 inches of the end. Detach the casing and knot the open end. Continue as directed above.

VARIATIONS

- Add 2 to 3 ounces of shelled pistachio nuts to the Basic Sausage recipe.
- Add 2 seeded hot red peppers, 2 cloves garlic, and 2 ounces cumin.
- Add ¼ cup chopped fresh parsley.
- Add 3 tablespoons chopped fresh sage (or 2 tablespoons dried sage).
- Add 3 tablespoons chopped fresh thyme (or 2 tablespoons dried thyme).
- Add 1 clove garlic, minced.
- Add 1 tablespoon cayenne pepper.

Crépinettes

Cut caul fat into 4-inch squares. Soak the squares in water to cover mixed with 1 teaspoon white vinegar, until the fat is pliable. Put a square in the palm of your hand, spoon in a small lump of sausage meat, and wrap it, overlapping the ends. To serve, sauté the crépinettes in a little butter.

PORK SAUSAGE

Makes 2¼ pounds (4 to 6 servings)

2 pounds pork shoulder or
  butt
¼ pound pork fat
1 to 2 tablespoons red or
  white wine
½ teaspoon anise
1 tablespoon paprika
Dash of cayenne pepper
Salt and freshly ground
  pepper, to taste

Butter
3 to 5 feet natural sausage
  casing

1. Cut the meat and fat into 1-inch cubes. Sprinkle the wine and the remaining seasonings over the meat, and grind the mixture using a meat grinder or a food processor fitted with the steel blade. Sauté a small amount of the sausage mixture in a little butter. Taste the cooked sausage for seasoning and adjust as necessary.

2. Fill the casing and cook as directed in the Basic Sausage recipe (page 123).

LAMB SAUSAGE

Makes about 3 pounds (6 to 8 servings)

One of our most popular pizzas features this lamb sausage. We cover pizza dough with a single layer of grape leaves, then sprinkle on lamb sausage, Parmesan and feta cheeses, oil-cured olives, thinly sliced red onions, and pine nuts. Very Mediterranean and very delicious! (The recipe is on page 117.)

The uncooked sausage mixture can be refrigerated for up to three days, or frozen, tightly wrapped, up to four months, before cooking. It can be used as a breakfast sausage, in stuffing, or as a forcemeat, as well as for pizza topping.

2 pounds lean leg of lamb, cut into 1-inch cubes (or 2 pounds lean ground lamb)

¾ pound pork fat, cut into 1-inch cubes

1 medium onion, coarsely chopped

5 to 6 cloves garlic, chopped

½ cup fresh parsley (about ⅓ bunch)

2 tablespoons fresh rosemary (or 1 tablespoon dried)

1 teaspoon fresh thyme (or ½ teaspoon dried)

Crushed soda crackers or dry bread crumbs (for meat grinder procedure)

1 tablespoon salt

½ teaspoon freshly ground pepper

Vegetable oil

MEAT GRINDER PROCEDURE

Using the medium disc, grind the lamb in small batches alternately with the pork fat. Pass through the grinder, in order, the onions and garlic, parsley, rosemary, and thyme. Pass through several crushed soda crackers or dry bread cubes to clean the grinder of any meat and herbs. Season the meat mixture with the salt and pepper.

FOOD PROCESSOR PROCEDURE

1. Spread the cubed pork fat on a cookie sheet. Place it in the freezer for 15 minutes, or until the fat is very cold and firm. Combine 1 cup of the cubed lamb with ½ cup of the pork fat in the work bowl of a food processor fitted with the steel blade. Chop the mixture coarsely, using several on/off pulses. Transfer the mixture to a bowl. Repeat with the remaining lamb and pork, until all of the meat is chopped.

2. Combine the onions, garlic, parsley, rosemary, and thyme in the work bowl of the processor and chop finely. Stir the mixture into the ground meat along with the salt and pepper, blending lightly but thoroughly.

FINAL PREPARATION

1. Sauté a small amount of the sausage mixture in a little oil. Taste, and adjust the seasoning. Keep in mind that the flavors will blend and intensify overnight.

2. Form the mixture into patties. Cook immediately, or freeze. The sausage may also be crumbled onto pizza.

FRAGRANT FENNEL SAUSAGE

Makes 2 pounds (4 to 6 servings)

This is Anne Otterson's delicious variation on the sausage theme. It takes very little time to prepare, and the flavor is marvelous.

1 pound lean pork
1 pound veal
½ pound pork fat
3 shallots, minced
1 teaspoon fennel seed
1 teaspoon chopped fresh
    sage (or ½ teaspoon
    dried)
1 teaspoon chopped fresh
    thyme (or ½ teaspoon
    dried)
1½ teaspoons salt
Freshly ground pepper,
    to taste

Butter
3 to 5 feet natural
    sausage casing

1. Cut the meat and fat into 1-inch cubes. Sprinkle the shallots and the remaining seasonings over the mixture and grind it, using a meat grinder or a food processor fitted with the steel blade. Sauté a small amount of the sausage mixture in a little butter. Taste the cooked sausage for seasoning and adjust as necessary.

2. Fill the casing and cook as directed in the Basic Sausage recipe (page 123).

BOUDIN BLANC

Makes 16 sausages (8 servings)

Boudin blanc simply means "white sausage." This is a fine-grain, delicately flavored sausage. We serve it at Piret's with sautéed fresh apples and heated vinegar-laced red cabbage. For an outdoor party, you may want to grill the sausages, which gives them a whole new flavor.

1 pound boneless, skinless
   chicken breast (about 2
   medium breasts), cleaned
   of all sinew
1 pound pork shoulder
1 pound pork fat
½ medium onion, chopped
1½ teaspoons minced garlic
   (1 to 2 medium cloves)
⅔ cup milk
⅓ cup heavy cream
1½ teaspoon *quatre épices*
   (page 131)
¼ cup Cognac
4 eggs
2 teaspoons salt
¼ teaspoon freshly ground
   pepper

Vegetable oil
6 feet of natural sausage
   casing

1. Thoroughly chill the chicken, pork, and pork fat. Cut the chilled meats into cubes, and combine them with the onions and garlic. Purée the mixture in small batches, using a food processor fitted with the steel blade. Transfer the puréed mixture to a mixing bowl and stir in the milk, cream, *quatre épices*, and Cognac, blending thoroughly. Refrigerate the mixture for 30 minutes.

2. Using a paddle attachment on a heavy-duty electric mixer (or working with a wooden spoon and plenty of elbow grease), blend in the eggs, one at a time, beating thoroughly after each addition. Season the mixture with the salt and pepper. Sauté a small amount of the sausage mixture in a little oil. Taste the cooked sausage for seasoning, and adjust as necessary. Chill until the casing is ready.

3. Prepare and fill the casings as directed in the Basic Sausage recipe (page 123), but make 4-inch links.

4. Gently poach the sausages in simmering water to cover for 45 minutes. Drain them well. At this point they may be refrigerated for four to five days before cooking. To serve, brown the sausages lightly in a little butter.

PATTY McDONALD'S SEAFOOD SAUSAGE

Makes 16 to 20 sausages

You can make a fine-grain sausage by grinding all the ingredients for these recipes, but we prefer the texture and visual interest of whole bay shrimp and other shell-fish. After the sausages have been poached, they may be refrigerated for up to two days.

2½ pounds fresh fillet of
  sole, cut into 2-inch
  chunks
2 eggs
2 shallots, chopped
¾ cup chopped mushrooms
  (about 6 ounces)
1½ cups heavy cream
1 to 1½ teaspoons salt
½ teaspoon paprika
1 teaspoon Tabasco
¾ cup chopped fresh parsley
¾ pound small bay shrimp
6 ounces sea scallops,
  minced

12 feet of 1-inch sausage
  casing
2 tablespoons butter
Herb Sauce (page 323)

1. Place the sole in the work bowl of a food processor fitted with the steel blade. Coarsely chop the sole, using on/off pulses. Add the eggs, shallots, mushrooms, cream, salt, paprika, Tabasco, and parsley, and process the mixture until smooth. Turn the mixture into a chilled bowl and stir in the shrimp and scallops. Chill the mixture until it is very cold (about 30 minutes).

2. Grease the horn of a meat grinder with a stuffing attachment, or a sausage stuffer. Push the sausage casing onto the horn and tie off the end. Place the fish mixture in the machine and stuff the casings, pricking any air bubbles with a needle. Tie off the end, and tie off the casing at 6- to 8-inch intervals.

3. Place the sausage in rapidly boiling water to cover and cook for 15 minutes. Transfer the cooked sausage to ice water to stop the cooking and keep it from drying out. Drain the sausage and cook in the butter over medium heat until it is lightly browned. Serve warm with Herb Sauce.

PÂTÉS AND TERRINES

Today, "pâté" and "terrine" are synonymous. At one time, however, a pâté was baked *en croûte* (in a crust), while a terrine was baked and served out of a clay or porcelain rectangular or oval dish, called a terrine. All pâtés and terrines use a combination of lean and fatty pork as a base. Hence, *pâté de canard* (duck) has pork and duck. The specialties of the charcuterie were designed to use up parts of the pig — parts that would otherwise have been wasted — by grinding up the meats, fats, innards, and brains, and turning them into delicious terrines and sausages. The caul fat (lacy membrane of the stomach) or fatback that terrines are wrapped in is designed to keep the meat moist and flavorful; and when the fat hardens, it acts as a preservative. In their quest for lighter (if not necessarily less caloric) dishes, *nouvelle cuisine* chefs have introduced delicate fish pâtés, which use a mousse or mousseline of various seafoods, and vegetable terrines, which have beautiful, artistic layerings of whole or cut vegetables and various mousses.

With the advent of the food processor, making pâtés and terrines and sausages has become manageable at home. But there are a few rules. To taste the seasonings in a meat mixture, cook a few tablespoons in a frypan, taste, and adjust as necessary. (Never eat raw pork.) Also, remember that you are serving the dish chilled; therefore, you need more seasoning than if you were serving it hot. Pâtés need to rest for three to four days in the refrigerator prior to serving, to thoroughly blend the flavors. Do not freeze pâté; the moisture from defrosting will make it watery.

The pâté must be weighted after you have poured off the fat rendered during baking and while it is resting in the refrigerator, to give it a smooth and compact texture. The weighting draws out excess fat in the pâté, which can be removed easily after it has congealed during refrigeration. Since pâté molds come in all sizes and shapes, you'll have to be inventive about the weighting. Depending on the size of the mold, you want as much as 3 to 7 pounds of weight. The classic weighting object is a board or aluminum foil with a brick on top. Marjorie Rice prefers a board and a six-pack of beer, which fits her mold perfectly. Julia Child recommends a board topped with the parts of a hand meat grinder. If you have a pan correctly shaped for your mold, fill it with water and set that on top of the pâté. (This works very well if your mold is a bread loaf pan.) Large dog-food cans, laid sideways, also work fine.

To unmold the chilled pâté, place it in the sink or in a pan of hot tap water for two minutes. Remove it from the water and run a knife around the edge to loosen the sides. Turn it out on a cutting board and, with your hands or a knife, remove the congealed fat. We have included instructions for making aspic, in case you want to decorate your unmolded pâté.

We refer often in this section to *quatre épices*. You should be able to find this mixture of spices in specialty food shops or, if your town has a French neighborhood, in food shops there, since it is common in French cooking. You can also make it at home, using a small electric coffee grinder. The four spices usually include pepper, cloves, nutmeg, and ginger or cinnamon.

PEPPERCORN PÂTÉ

Makes 16 servings

¼ pound pork liver
1¼ pound very lean pork
   (from pork shoulder)
1 pound pork fat
1 egg
2 teaspoons chopped fresh
   thyme (or 1 teaspoon
   dried)
1 teaspoon *quatre épices*
   (page 131)
1 clove garlic, minced
4 tablespoons minced onion
   (about ½ medium onion)
2 tablespoons heavy cream
1 teaspoon salt
¼ teaspoon freshly ground
   pepper
1 tin (6 ounces) green
   peppercorns, drained
¼ cup dry white wine

Vegetable oil
Caul fat, softened in enough
   water to cover, plus 1
   teaspoon white vinegar

1. Trim the pork liver of all sinews and cut it into 1-inch cubes. Mince the liver, a cup at a time, using a blender, meat grinder, or food processor fitted with the steel blade.

2. Cut the pork and pork fat into 1-inch cubes and grind them using a meat grinder fitted with the medium disc, or a food processor fitted with the steel blade. It may be necessary to do this in batches. The meat should be about the same texture as coarse hamburger.

3. Combine the liver and the pork-fat mixture with the egg, thyme, *quatre épices,* garlic, onions, cream, salt, pepper, green peppercorns, and wine. This can be done using a heavy-duty electric mixer fitted with the paddle, or by hand. Sauté a small amount of the mixture in a little oil. Taste for seasoning and adjust as necessary, keeping in mind that the spices will be muted once the pâté is cooked and chilled.

4. Line a standard 6-cup loaf pan with caul fat, allowing enough to hang over the edges to enclose the top of the pâté. Fill the mold with the pork mixture and bring the edges of the caul fat up over the top. Slam the mold on the counter five or six times to remove any air pockets, and cover it tightly with aluminum foil.

5. Preheat oven to 325°. Place the mold in a roasting pan and pour in enough boiling water to come about 1 inch up the sides of the mold (a bain-marie). Bake the pâté for 1½ hours, or until a meat thermometer inserted in the center registers 160°.

6. Remove the pâté from the oven. Drain the fat from the mold and the water from the roasting pan, and put the mold back in the pan. Weight the pâté and place it, still in the roasting pan, in the refrigerator, to chill overnight.

7. To serve, unmold the pâté and trim off the

excess fat. The pâté will keep, well covered in the refrigerator, for at least a week.

&❧ A bain-marie, or water bath, is essentially a double-boiler, using boiling water to control the heat and maintain an even baking temperature. Chafing dishes set into hot water to keep foods and sauces warm without cooking them are also bain-maries. A bain-marie is used in baking pâtés, mousselines, plum puddings, custards, and, sometimes, soufflés. The molds or terrines are placed in a roasting pan of boiling water to assure a constant temperature of 212° to 250° while baking. Since you don't want to traverse your kitchen with a heavy pan filled with boiling water, whenever you bake anything in a bain-marie first place the roasting pan with the molds in it in the oven, then pour in the boiling water. When the molds or pâté are baked, take them out of the roasting pan and place them on a baking sheet. Allow the water to cool before removing the pan from the oven.

COUNTRY PÂTÉ EN CROÛTE

Makes 10 to 12 servings

Instead of using the forcemeat in this Anne Otterson recipe, you may substitute our Basic Sausage recipe (page 123) or any flavorful pork sausage.

TO MAKE THE FORCEMEAT

2 pounds pork (or 1 pound pork and 1 pound cooked ham)
1 pound veal
1 pound pork fat
1 to 3 teaspoons salt (varies with amount of ham used)
½ teaspoon freshly ground pepper
¼ teaspoon allspice or *quatre épices* (page 131)
Butter

1. Cut the meats and fat into 1-inch cubes. Sprinkle the salt (start with the smaller amount), pepper, and allspice or *quatre épices* over the mixture and grind it using a food processor fitted with the steel blade, or in a meat grinder.

2. Sauté a small amount of the forcemeat in a little butter. Taste it for seasoning and adjust as necessary. This will make more forcemeat than you'll need for this pâté recipe. The remainder may be formed into patties and sautéed, put into casings (see the Basic Sausage recipe, page 123), or used in any recipe calling for pork sausage.

TO PREPARE THE FILLING

1 pound veal, very thinly
   sliced
1 pound cooked ham, very
   thinly sliced
¼ cup Madeira
¼ cup dry vermouth
2 tablespoons Cognac
2 pounds forcemeat (or other
   pork sausage)
2 cloves garlic, minced
¼ teaspoon allspice
¼ teaspoon freshly grated
   nutmeg
1 tablespoon salt
1 tablespoon freshly ground
   pepper

1. Cut the slices of veal and ham into julienne strips and marinate them in the Madeira, vermouth, and Cognac for several hours or overnight, refrigerated. Mix the 2 pounds of forcemeat with the garlic, allspice, nutmeg, salt, and pepper, blending thoroughly.

2. When you are ready to bake the pâté, drain the marinated meat, and add enough of the marinade to the forcemeat mixture to make it moist but not soggy.

TO PREPARE THE PASTRY

2¼ cups unbleached,
   all-purpose flour
1 teaspoon salt
¾ cup unsalted butter,
   softened
2 egg yolks
4 to 5 tablespoons cold
   water
1 egg, beaten

Stir together the flour and salt. Form a well in the middle and add the butter, egg yolks, and water. Stir them into the flour, working from the edges of the well and incorporating the flour gradually. When nearly all the flour has been worked into the dough, pat it together and knead, incorporating the last of the flour, to form a smooth dough. Do not overknead.

TO ASSEMBLE THE PÂTÉ

1. Roll out the pastry to about a 16-inch square. In the center of the square, spread a rectangular layer of the forcemeat mixture, about 9 × 5 inches. Spread one-third of the marinated meat mixture over the forcemeat. Repeat the layers, finishing with a final layer of forcemeat.

2. Loosely fold the dough over the layers, marking where the edges of the dough overlap. Unfold the dough and trim away the overlapping dough, making neat edges. The object will be to make a sort of "box" of pastry, which may be folded up and sealed to hold in the juices while the pâté bakes. At each of the four corners, cut away a square of pastry, so when you bring the side and end pieces up over

the top of the loaf, they just meet at the corners and on the top. Pinch the corner edges together to seal. Pinch the top edges to seal them as well. Turn the loaf over so the long seal is on the bottom, and place it on a baking sheet with a rim (to catch juices that may escape during baking).

3. Preheat oven to 375°. Cut a vent on top of the loaf to allow steam to escape. Roll out any extra dough and cut leaves, flowers, or other shapes. Use them to decorate the top of the pâté. Brush the crust liberally with the beaten egg, and bake the pâté for 1½ hours, or until a meat thermometer inserted in the center registers 160°. Chill the pâté thoroughly before serving. The pâté may be refrigerated about three days; if refrigerated longer, the crust may become soggy.

FRENCH COUNTRY PÂTÉ

Makes 12 servings

There are as many recipes for country pâté as there are country folk. Typically, a country pâté has a rich, coarse texture, unlike the more sophisticated velvety pâtés set in aspic or baked *en croûte*. Lois Stanton taught this version in a class on elegant picnic foods.

6 slices bacon
¼ cup shelled pistachio nuts
¼ pound chicken livers
4 tablespoons butter
½ cup fresh parsley
¼ cup white bread crumbs
    (from ½ slice stale French
    bread)
2 cloves garlic, peeled
1 medium onion, peeled and
    quartered
1½ pounds pork, cut in
    1-inch cubes
1½ pounds veal, cut in
    1-inch cubes
1 pound cooked ham, cut in
    1-inch cubes
3 large eggs
½ cup Cognac
2 teaspoons salt, or to taste
1 teaspoon mixed dried
    herbs (savory, thyme, and
    oregano)
½ teaspoon allspice
½ teaspoon cinnamon
½ teaspoon freshly grated
    nutmeg

Butter
Additional bacon or pork fat
    (optional)

1. Place the bacon slices in cold water to cover, bring them to a boil, reduce the heat to very low, and simmer the bacon for 5 minutes. Drain the bacon on paper towels. Bring a small clean saucepan of water to a boil and blanch the pistachio nuts for 1 minute. Drain the nuts and rub off the skins with a towel. Sauté the chicken livers in 2 tablespoons of the butter until they are barely cooked through. Set them aside.

2. Using a food processor fitted with the steel blade, mince together the parsley and bread crumbs. Put them in a large mixing bowl. Mince the garlic and onion, using the food processor. Heat the remaining 2 tablespoons of butter in a skillet and cook the garlic-onion mixture until it is soft but not brown. Add it to the bread crumbs.

3. Coarsely chop the pork, veal, and ham, using the food processor (you may have to do this in batches). Add them to the bowl. Combine the sautéed chicken livers and 3 slices of the bacon in the work bowl of the processor and purée. Stir the purée into the meat mixture. Thoroughly blend in the eggs, Cognac, salt, herbs, allspice, cinnamon, and nutmeg. Sauté a small amount of the pâté mixture in a little butter. Taste for seasoning and adjust as necessary.

4. Butter a 6-cup terrine mold or loaf pan and line the bottom with parchment paper (or line the bottom and sides of the pan with more bacon or thin

sheets of pork fat). Spoon in the pâté mixture, and bang the pan on the counter a few times to eliminate any air pockets. Top with the 3 remaining bacon slices and cover with the terrine lid or aluminum foil.

5. Preheat oven to 350°. Place the mold in a roasting pan and pour in enough boiling water to come halfway up the sides. Bake for 2½ hours, or until a thermometer inserted in the center of the pâté registers 160°.

6. Remove the mold from the water and let it cool. Remove the lid, if used, and cover with aluminum foil. Place a weight on the foil and, with the weight in place, chill the pâté thoroughly.

7. Serve the pâté from the mold, or unmold it and cut in thin slices. Serve with cornichons and a variety of mustards.

DUCK PÂTÉ À L'ORANGE

Makes 16 servings

We decorate this pâté with very thin slices of orange, leaving the rind on. It's simple and very pretty. Take the duck meat from about half of a 4½- to 5-pound duck.

1 pound boneless, skinless duck meat
¾ pound very lean shoulder pork
¾ pound pork fat
½ pound duck or chicken livers
1 egg
Juice and zest of ½ Valencia orange
1 tablespoon Cognac
1 tablespoon Grand Marnier
2 teaspoons *quatre épices* (page 131)
1 teaspoon salt
¼ teaspoon freshly ground pepper
½ cup shelled pistachio nuts
½ cup coarsely chopped dried apricots

Vegetable oil
Caul fat, softened (see note)

1. Cut the duck, pork, and pork fat into 1-inch cubes. Refrigerate the cubes for 30 minutes, to thoroughly chill them. Grind the cubes using a meat grinder fitted with the medium disc or a food processor fitted with the steel blade. It may be necessary to do this in batches. The ground meat should be the same texture as coarse hamburger. Trim the livers of all sinews, and mince the livers in the food processor using on/off pulses.

2. Combine the meat mixture, livers, egg, orange juice and zest, Cognac, Grand Marnier, *quatre épices*, salt, pepper, pistachio nuts, and apricots. This can be done either in a heavy-duty electric mixer fitted with the paddle, or by hand. Sauté a small amount of the mixture in a little oil. Taste the cooked mixture for seasoning and adjust as necessary, keeping in mind that the spices will be muted once the pâté has been cooked and chilled.

3. Line a standard 6-cup loaf pan with the caul fat, allowing enough to hang over the edges to enclose the top of the pâté. Fill the pan with the meat mixture and bring the edges of the caul fat up over the top, enclosing it completely. Bang the pan against the counter a few times to eliminate any air pockets, and cover it tightly with aluminum foil.

4. Preheat oven to 350°. Place the loaf pan in a roasting pan and pour in enough boiling water to come 1 inch up the sides of the loaf pan. Bake the pâté for 1½ hours, or until a meat thermometer inserted in the center registers 160°.

5. Remove the pâté from the oven. Carefully pour off the fat from the loaf pan. Cover the pâté with buttered wax paper, buttered side down, weight it down, and refrigerate the pâté overnight.

6. To serve, unmold the pâté and trim off any excess fat. The pâté will keep, well wrapped in the refrigerator, for at least one week.

NOTE

To soften the caul fat, soak it in water to cover, plus 1 teaspoon white vinegar.

TERRINE DE CAMPAGNE

Makes 8 servings

½ pound pork shoulder
¼ pound pork fat
½ pound veal
2 tablespoons butter
½ cup minced onion
1 tablespoon salt
1 teaspoon freshly ground pepper
¼ teaspoon allspice or *quatre épices*
½ teaspoon dried thyme
2 cloves garlic, finely chopped
3 tablespoons Cognac
2 large eggs
Butter
12 ounces calf liver, diced
1 pound fatback strips, or caul fat (see note)
1 bay leaf

1. Using a food processor fitted with the steel blade, finely mince the pork shoulder, pork fat, and veal. Combine them in a large bowl.

2. Melt the butter in a small skillet and cook the onions over medium heat until they are soft but not browned. Add the onions to the meat mixture along with the salt, pepper, allspice, thyme, garlic, Cognac, and eggs. Mix well. Sauté a small amount of the mixture in butter. Taste the cooked mixture for seasoning and adjust as necessary. Fold in the liver.

3. Line a terrine mold with the sheets of fat, pressing to seal where they overlap, or use caul fat. Spread the meat mixture into the mold and bang it against the counter a few times to eliminate any air pockets. Place the bay leaf on the terrine and fold the sheet of fat over the top to enclose it completely. Cover the terrine with aluminum foil.

4. Preheat oven to 350°. Place the mold in a roasting pan and pour in enough boiling water to come two-thirds of the way up the sides. Bake the terrine for 2 hours, or until a meat thermometer inserted in the center of the terrine registers 160°.

5. Remove the mold from the bain-marie and weight it down. Let it cool, then refrigerate, still weighted down, to chill thoroughly. Serve either unmolded or directly from the terrine mold. This will keep, covered and refrigerated, about a week.

NOTE

If using fatback, cut it into four 4 × 6 inch rectangles and two 4-inch squares to fit the loaf pan or terrine. If using caul fat, soften it in water to cover, plus 1 teaspoon white vinegar.

DUCK TERRINE WITH RAISINS

Makes 8 servings

This terrine is a variation on a recipe by Michel Guerard. Serve it with crusty French bread and cornichons or one of the relishes found at the end of this chapter.

1 duck (4 to 5 pounds)
6 ounces salt pork, diced
½ pound chicken or duck
   livers
2 teaspoons salt
2 teaspoons freshly ground
   pepper
¼ teaspoon allspice or *quatre
   épices* (page 131)
1 cup heavy cream
4 egg yolks
2 tablespoons Cognac
½ cup golden raisins
2 tablespoons butter,
   softened (for terrine)

1. Skin and bone the duck. Refrigerate the duck meat for 30 minutes. Cut the breast meat into ¼-inch cubes. Coarsely chop the remaining duck meat, using a food processor fitted with the steel blade. Place all of the duck meat in a mixing bowl.

2. Combine the salt pork, livers, salt, pepper, and allspice in the work bowl of the food processor, and process until creamy. Add the cream, egg yolks, and Cognac, and process until the mixture is completely homogenized, about 1 minute. Pass this mixture through a sieve, and stir it into the reserved duck meat. Stir in the raisins.

3. Preheat oven to 400°. Butter a 1½-quart earthenware terrine and pour in the duck mixture. Cover the terrine with aluminum foil, place it in a roasting pan, and pour in enough boiling water to come halfway up the sides of the terrine. Bake for 45 to 60 minutes, or until a meat thermometer inserted in the center registers 160°. Remove the terrine from the bain-marie, cool, then refrigerate overnight.

ANNE'S DUCK TERRINE WITH GREEN PEPPERCORNS

Makes 8 servings

1 duck (4 to 5 pounds)
¼ pound ground veal
¼ pound ground pork
¼ pound pork fat, ground
¼ pound chicken or duck
  livers
1 pound fatback strips or
  caul fat (see note,
  page 139)

MARINADE

½ cup Cognac
½ cup Madeira
½ cup dry vermouth
1 cup minced onion
1 teaspoon dried thyme
½ teaspoon dried basil
2 teaspoons chopped fresh
  parsley
1 bay leaf
3 teaspoons green
  peppercorns
2 teaspoons salt
1 teaspoon freshly ground
  pepper

1. Skin and bone the duck. Refrigerate the duck meat for 30 minutes. Render the fat, if you wish, and use the bones for duck stock. Cut the chilled breast meat into thin, long strips. Combine all the marinade ingredients and pour them over the strips of duck breast. Let them marinate 6 hours to overnight, refrigerated.

2. Using a food processor fitted with the steel blade, coarsely chop the remaining duck meat. Thoroughly combine the chopped duck and ground veal, pork, and pork fat. Drain the duck breast strips, reserving the marinade. Using the processor, purée the liver, adding marinade as needed to make a smooth mixture. Stir the purée into the meat mixture with enough of the marinade to make a moist but not soggy mixture.

3. Line a terrine mold with the sheets of pork fat, pressing them together at the edges to seal, or use caul fat. Spread about one-third of the meat mixture in the mold. Arrange half the duck breast strips over the meat mixture. Repeat the layering, ending with the meat mixture. Cover the top with pork fat, then with aluminum foil.

4. Preheat oven to 375°. Place the terrine mold in a roasting pan and add enough water to come halfway up the sides. Bake the terrine 1 to 1½ hours, or until a meat thermometer inserted in the center registers 160°.

5. Remove the terrine from the bain-marie and weight it down. Let it cool, then refrigerate overnight with the weight in place.

6. To serve, unmold the terrine, trim off the excess fat, and slice. Serve with cornichons and French bread.

RABBIT LIVER TERRINE

Makes 8 to 12 servings

If you happen to visit the San Diego area, treat yourself to a meal at Gustaf Anders in La Jolla, to our mind one of the finest restaurants in the country. Their sautéed rabbit livers, and a chicken liver appetizer at Rex Il Ristorante in Los Angeles, inspired Piret's chef Jim Hill to create this unusual terrine. You may have difficulty finding rabbit livers, so plan ahead by asking butchers in your area to order them for you, or substitute chicken or other poultry livers.

1 pound rabbit livers
1½ cups milk, or enough to
  cover the livers
2½ tablespoons good-quality
  Port
1½ teaspoons salt
¼ teaspoon sugar
½ teaspoon freshly ground
  pepper
½ clove garlic
Scant ⅛ teaspoon *quatre
  épices* (page 131)
¾ cup clarified butter
  (page 239)
Fresh watercress, for garnish

1. Rinse the livers under cool running water and remove any connective tissue. Drain the livers, place them in a glass bowl, and cover them with milk. Refrigerate the livers overnight. Drain and rinse them again, repeating until the water runs clear.

2. In a glass or ceramic bowl, combine 1 tablespoon of the Port with 1 teaspoon of the salt, the sugar, ¼ teaspoon of the pepper, the garlic, and the *quatre épices* to make a marinade. Add the livers, turning to coat each one generously, and refrigerate them overnight. Drain the livers and pat them dry with paper towels.

3. Preheat oven to 300°. Place the livers in a 3 × 5 inch ovenproof terrine mold. Add the remaining ½ teaspoon salt, ¼ teaspoon pepper, and 1½ tablespoons Port. Pour the warm clarified butter over the livers to cover them. Cover the mold, place it in a roasting pan, and pour in enough hot water to come halfway up the sides of the mold. Bake for 15 minutes, or until the livers are cooked but still a bit pink in the center.

4. Take the mold out of the bain-marie. Remove the livers from the butter and let them cool. Strain the butter to remove any liver particles and set the butter aside.

5. Transfer the livers to a deep bowl and pour in enough strained butter to cover them. Cover the bowl tightly with muslin or aluminum foil and refrigerate. Allow the livers to rest for three to four days so the flavors can blend and mellow.

6. To serve, bring the livers to room temperature. Remove all the butter and slice the livers. Arrange them attractively on a plate garnished with fresh watercress. Serve with toasted French bread rounds.

RABBIT TERRINE WITH TOMATO COULIS

Makes 1 large loaf

2 pounds boneless rabbit meat
2 rabbit livers
1 pound veal
1 pound bacon
1 onion, chopped
3 cloves garlic, minced
1 carrot, chopped
3 tablespoons chopped fresh parsley
2 tablespoons chopped fresh tarragon (or 1 tablespoon dried)
2 teaspoons chopped fresh rosemary (or 1 teaspoon dried)
1 tablespoon chopped fresh chervil (or 2 teaspoons dried)
1 teaspoon chopped fresh thyme (or 1 teaspoon dried)
1 teaspoon salt
½ teaspoon freshly ground pepper
¼ teaspoon allspice
¼ cup brandy
1 egg white, lightly beaten
2 to 3 bay leaves
1 to 2 pounds fatback strips, or caul fat (see note, page 139)

1. Using a food processor fitted with the steel blade, finely chop the rabbit meat, livers, veal, and bacon. Stir them together in a bowl, cover, and refrigerate.

2. Combine the onion, garlic, carrot, parsley, tarragon, rosemary, chervil, thyme, salt, pepper, allspice, and brandy, and let them marinate for 3 hours at room temperature.

3. Line a 1½-quart terrine mold or large loaf pan with the fatback strips, reserving a few strips to cover the top, or use caul fat. Stir the marinade and the egg white into the meat mixture, blending thoroughly. Spoon the mixture into the mold and cover with the bay leaves and remaining fatback strips. Cover the terrine securely with aluminum foil.

4. Preheat oven to 350°. Place the mold in a roasting pan and pour in enough boiling water to come up to within an inch of the top of the mold. Bake the terrine for 1½ hours.

5. Remove the mold from the bain-marie and weight it down until cool. Carefully pour off the released liquid, then refrigerate the terrine with the weight in place.

6. To serve, unmold the terrine, cut away the excess fat, and slice. Serve with Tomato Coulis.

Tomato Coulis
Makes about 1½ cups

Coulis is a term that has become topical in recent years, although the French have always associated it with reductions of vegetable sauces.

1 tablespoon extra-virgin
　olive oil
1 onion, finely chopped
1 clove garlic, minced
4 medium tomatoes, peeled,
　seeded, and chopped
Pinch of saffron
Pinch of powdered ginger
Salt and freshly ground
　pepper, to taste

Heat the oil in a saucepan and sauté the onions until they are translucent. Add the garlic and cook the mixture another minute or two. Stir in the tomatoes, saffron, and ginger, season with salt and pepper, and simmer the sauce for 15 minutes. Serve at room temperature with the Rabbit Terrine.

SALMON TERRINE

Makes 8 to 10 servings

This dish may be prepared a day in advance and chilled to be served cold. If it is to be served hot, it is best prepared the same day.

2 pounds skinless salmon
   fillet
3 to 4 egg whites (3 ounces)
1 quart heavy cream
1½ teaspoons salt
10 grinds of the pepper mill
¼ teaspoon freshly grated
   nutmeg

1. Place the bowl and paddle of a heavy-duty electric mixer in the freezer. Butter a 6-cup porcelain, earthenware, or enamel terrine mold.

2. Make sure that the salmon is completely free of bones (they can be removed with needle-nose pliers). Cut the salmon into 1-inch pieces and purée them using a food processor fitted with the steel blade. Transfer the salmon purée to the chilled mixing bowl. With the mixer at low speed, beat in the egg whites, cream, salt, pepper, and nutmeg. (Poach a small amount of the mixture in simmering water and taste for seasoning. If the terrine is to be served cold, the amount of salt, pepper, and nutmeg should be increased slightly.)

3. Pour the mixture into the buttered mold and smooth the top. Butter one side of a piece of wax paper that is slightly larger than the top of the mold, and place it on top of the salmon, buttered side down. Cover the wax paper with aluminum foil; do not allow the foil to come too far down the sides of the mold or water may seep in.

4. Preheat oven to 350°. Place the mold in a roasting pan and pour in enough boiling water to come halfway up the sides of the mold. Bake the terrine for about 1½ hours, or until a meat thermometer inserted in the center registers 160°.

5. Remove the mold from the bain-marie and pour off any excess juices. Serve the salmon directly from the terrine in slices, hot or cold.

⁂ Any fish or vegetable mousse or terrine, especially served cold, is likely to be very mild in flavor. A tangy mustard or dill sauce, or a spunky coulis, will bring it to life. Check the index for recipes for these and other sauces.

GALANTINE OF VEAL AND PORK

Makes 16 servings

Jane Grigson, a marvelous cookbook writer, is the affable British counterpart of our own Julia Child. Her *Art of Making Sausages, Pâtés, and Other Charcuterie* is certainly the best English-language volume on the subject. She taught her first cooking class at The Perfect Pan in 1983 when Anne Otterson convinced her to come to San Diego for the UCSD Cancer Center Celebrity Cook-Off.

Jane says that in current times a galantine has come to mean cold poultry or veal, boned and stuffed and poached in cheesecloth. She recommends that the galantine rest a minimum of one day for all the flavors to mingle. We think this variation on the galantine theme is Anne's, but our files are a little vague on the subject.

1 pound slab bacon, rind removed
1 pound boneless pork
12 ounces boneless veal
⅓ cup Cognac
1½ teaspoons salt
½ teaspoon freshly ground pepper
¼ teaspoon each: ground ginger, cinnamon, ground cloves, and freshly grated nutmeg
2 large eggs
8 cups chicken broth
1 cup dry vermouth
2 egg whites
3 envelopes unflavored gelatin
½ cup cold water

1. Cover the bacon with cold water, bring it to a boil, reduce the heat, and simmer the bacon for 10 minutes to remove the salt and smoked flavor. Drain, rinse the bacon under cold water, and drain again.

2. Mince the bacon, pork, and veal, one at a time, using a food processor fitted with the steel blade. Transfer the batches to a mixing bowl. Stir in the Cognac, salt, pepper, and spices, blending thoroughly. Stir in the 2 whole eggs.

3. Place the mixture on the center of a 16-inch square of cheesecloth, bring up the ends, and press and squeeze the mixture into a firm ball. Tie the cheesecloth to hold the shape.

4. Place the wrapped ball (called a *galantine*) in a large saucepan. Add the chicken broth, cover the pan, and bring the mixture to a boil. Reduce the heat to very low, and simmer it gently about 2½ hours, or until the meat is tender and the juices flow clear when the galantine is pierced.

5. Remove the galantine to a rack placed over a bowl and let it drain for 30 minutes. Add the vermouth to the poaching broth, bring it to a vigorous boil, and boil until the liquid is reduced to 6 cups. Cool the broth mixture slightly, cover, and refrigerate overnight. Wrap the galantine in a clean kitchen

towel, place it in a bowl, and cover it with a light weight. Refrigerate the galantine overnight.

6. The next day, skim the fat from the broth mixture and discard the fat. In a large bowl, whisk together the egg whites and 1 cup of the broth until foamy. Bring the remaining broth to a boil and gradually pour it into the egg white mixture, stirring constantly. Return the mixture to the saucepan and bring it just to the boiling point. Reduce the heat to very low, and simmer the broth gently. The egg whites will rise to the top, trapping any sediment with them. Let the broth simmer for 10 to 15 minutes.

7. Gently strain the broth through cheesecloth into a clean bowl, without disturbing the egg white cap. Place 6 cups of the clarified broth in a clean saucepan and heat it to simmering. Stir the gelatin into the ½ cup cold water and let it soften for 5 minutes. Stir the softened gelatin into the simmering broth, stirring until it is completely dissolved.

8. Place the saucepan in a bowl of water and ice, and stir the mixture until it begins to jell. Pour this aspic into a clean jellyroll pan (15½ × 10½ inches), and refrigerate until firm, about 1½ hours.

9. To serve, remove the towel and cheesecloth from the galantine. Place it on a serving platter and cut a few thin slices. Cut the aspic into ¼-inch cubes and arrange them around the galantine. The galantine will keep, well wrapped in aluminum foil and refrigerated, about one week.

ASPIC

Pâté shrinks as it bakes. When the fat is poured off, there's a gap between the pâté and the mold, or the crust the pâté has been wrapped in. A glistening layer of aspic is used to fill up the space and to keep the pâté moist.

If you are using stock as a jellied consommé, as a molded aspic for eggs or fish fillet, or as a glaze for pâté, it must be greatly reduced through boiling, until the natural gelatin in the stock is sufficiently concentrated to jell the chilled stock. Adding a veal knuckle to the stock helps, since the knuckle is rich in gelatin. Calves' feet and chicken feet, if you can find them (check in Oriental groceries), are great. If there is not enough natural gelatin in the stock to set it, the only solution is to add commercially produced unflavored gelatin. As a liner for pâté, you will need about 1 envelope for each 1½ cups of stock.

1 rib celery, cut into 1-inch pieces
1 leek, white part only, cut in 1-inch pieces
1 carrot, peeled and cut in 1-inch pieces
One of the following:
  For brown stock: ¼ pound lean ground beef
  For chicken stock: ¼ pound lean ground chicken
  For fish stock: ¼ pound lean fish
6 cups rich chicken or veal stock, preferably home-made (pages 316, 317)
3 egg whites (4 or 5 if the stock is very cloudy), slightly whisked
3 crumbled eggshells

1. Using a food processor fitted with the steel blade, finely chop separately the celery, leek, and carrot, and the beef, chicken, or fish. Set the mixture aside.

2. Bring the stock to a boil, reduce the heat to low, and simmer the stock gently. In order, whisk in the vegetable-meat mixture, the egg whites, and the eggshells, whisking until the stock turns milky. Gently simmer the stock for 25 to 30 minutes, without disturbing it, until the egg whites rise to the top in a foamy scum that traps any solid particles in the stock. Do not allow the stock to boil during this phase.

3. Line a fine-mesh strainer with cheesecloth. Very carefully, ladle the stock through the strainer into a clean saucepan, taking care not to disturb the egg whites. (Do not pour the egg whites through the strainer.) This process is best accomplished with two people, with one using a fine-mesh skimmer to hold back the egg whites.

4. To coat pâté in aspic, first remove any solidified surface fat from the chilled pâté. Place the pâté in a clean terrine mold with a chilled layer of aspic on the bottom, and pipe or spoon in cool or room-temperature aspic around it to completely cover the pâté. Refrigerate the pâté for at least six

hours, or overnight, to set. You can decorate the
pâté by placing garnishes in pretty designs in the
aspic itself, or by decorating the top of the aspic
after you unmold it with slices of fruits and vegetables in pleasing patterns. To unmold, quickly
plunge the bottom and sides of the mold in hot
water, place it over a serving platter, and turn it
upside-down. Additional aspic, chilled and cut into
small dice, can be placed around the unmolded pâté
as a garnish.

🐌 A quick test to make sure that aspic has enough gelatin to set is to place a salad
plate in the freezer and chill it for an hour or more. Pour a thin layer of the cooled
aspic on the frozen plate. If the aspic becomes thick within two to three minutes, it
has enough natural gelatin.

S P R E A D S A N D R E L I S H E S

Every culture enjoys finger foods or little snacks
during the cocktail hour or to tide one over till the
next real meal. The classic English tea serves much
the same purpose, with its scones, tea sandwiches,
and little sweets. Rillettes (poultry, meat, or fish
spreads) are the vogue in France. Served with pâtés,
cheeses, and crusty French bread, along with a glass
of Bordeaux or Burgundy wine, they make a splendid little pick-me-up.

Meaty spreads and pâtés benefit from an onion
relish, tangy mustard, or cornichons, the French
version of a briny gherkin. We've given you several
relish recipes to give you the idea of the sort of flavor
that best compliments charcuterie. We also like
hearts of palm in a tangy vinaigrette, pickled beans,
or pickled watermelon rind or pumpkin.

CHICKEN LIVER SPREAD

Makes 2 cups

Another recipe inspired by Paula Wolfert.

8 large chicken livers
1¼ teaspoons fine sea salt
Milk
¼ teaspoon freshly ground
   pepper
⅛ teaspoon ground coriander
¼ teaspoon *quatre épices*
   (page 131)
¼ teaspoon dried chervil
2 tablespoons unsalted
   butter
½ tablespoon chopped onion
   or shallot
¼ teaspoon chopped garlic
1½ tablespoons brandy
2 tablespoons Madeira or
   Port
Pinch of sugar
6 tablespoons unsalted
   butter, cut into bits
⅔ cup heavy cream, chilled

1. Trim the livers of any connective tissue. Sprinkle them with ½ teaspoon of the sea salt, and soak them for several hours in milk to cover. Drain the livers, discarding the milk, and rinse them under cold water.

2. Combine the remaining salt with the pepper, coriander, *quatre épices,* and chervil. Add the livers and marinate them in the refrigerator for a few hours, turning them from time to time.

3. Heat 1 tablespoon of the butter in a heavy skillet, and cook the onions or shallots and garlic over medium heat until they are soft but not brown. Add the remaining tablespoon of butter and, when it starts to foam, add the livers in a single layer. Cook them gently for a few minutes over medium heat until they are firm but still pink inside. Transfer the livers, onions or shallots, garlic, and pan drippings to the work bowl of a food processor fitted with the steel blade.

4. To deglaze the skillet, add the brandy and Madeira or Port and turn the heat up to high, stirring up the browned bits. Carefully ignite the brandy, using a long kitchen match held over — not in — the liquid. When the flames die down (meaning all the alcohol has been burned off), let the liquid cool a bit, and pour it into the work bowl of the processor with the liver mixture. Add the sugar, and process the mixture for 1 minute, or until it is puréed. Add the 6 tablespoons butter, bit by bit, and purée the mixture until well blended. Rub it through a fine sieve, then let it rest.

5. In a chilled bowl set over ice, whip the cream until it forms stiff peaks. Fold it into the liver purée. Taste for seasoning and adjust as necessary. Pack the spread into a serving terrine or crock,

cover, and refrigerate. Let the spread mellow for a day or two. It will keep, refrigerated, for three to four days. Serve it on crackers or toasted French bread rounds.

PAULA WOLFERT'S SALMON RILLETTES

Makes 12 or more servings

Paula Wolfert uses fresh and smoked salmon in this recipe, but a fish such as trout, combined with smoked trout, could be substituted. This recipe should be made two days in advance of serving, to allow the flavors to mellow.

8 ounces fresh, skinless salmon fillet
Salt and freshly ground white pepper, to taste
9 tablespoons unsalted butter, firm but not cold
1 large shallot, finely chopped
2 tablespoons dry white wine
4 ounces smoked salmon, cut into ½-inch pieces
1 egg yolk
1 tablespoon fresh lemon juice
2 tablespoons olive oil
Freshly grated nutmeg, to taste
Clarified butter (page 239)

1. Cut the fresh salmon into 4 pieces. Sprinkle them with salt and white pepper, and let them stand in a colander for 20 minutes.

2. Meanwhile, melt 2 tablespoons of the butter in a medium saucepan and slowly cook the shallots until they are soft but not brown. Add the drained salmon pieces and the wine, cover the mixture with wax paper and a heavy lid, and cook it over low heat for 5 minutes, turning the pieces midway. Uncover the saucepan and let the salmon cool. Remove any brownish-gray flesh that may remain on the salmon. Use a fork to flake the cooked salmon, then mix it well with the cooked shallot.

3. Cut the remaining 7 tablespoons of butter into small pieces and place them in the work bowl of a food processor fitted with the steel blade. Add the flaked salmon and the smoked salmon and chop, using 2 or 3 on/off pulses. With the machine running, quickly add the egg yolk, lemon juice, and olive oil. The mixture should have a slightly gritty texture. Add the nutmeg, and season with salt and white pepper.

4. Scrape the mixture into a 1¾- or 2-cup earthenware or stoneware pot, and chill it thoroughly. Cover it with a layer of cool, clarified butter. The mixture will keep, refrigerated, three to four days.

PORK RILLETTES

Makes 12 or more servings

Rillettes are to the French what guacamole is to Mexicans — a great make-ahead spread served any time. It is super on crackers, slices of French bread, or toasted breads of any sort. The classic version is shredded pork, but it's been updated in two variations that follow. Serve rillettes with sprightly cornichons, different varieties of olives, pickled beans, eggplant, and hearts of palm for a festive, interesting array of cocktail munchies. Rillettes are generally potted in small soufflé ramekins or other small pots or crocks. It is definitely a simple, peasant food, and the container should reflect this.

1½ pounds lean pork
12 ounces fatback
3 teaspoons salt
½ teaspoon freshly ground
   pepper
¼ teaspoon freshly grated
   nutmeg
1 bay leaf
½ teaspoon dried thyme

1. Cut the pork and fatback into 2- to 3-inch pieces and place them in a heavy pan with enough water to cover by 1 inch. Add the remaining ingredients. Bring the mixture to a boil, reduce the heat to very low, and simmer, covered, until the fat is completely rendered, about 4 hours. (Skim the mixture several times early in the cooking process.) Remove the cover and continue simmering until all the water has evaporated, about 1 hour more, leaving the pork chunks suspended in clear fat.

2. Remove the pan from the heat and refrigerate to solidify the fat. Pour off any remaining liquid, and remove the bay leaf.

3. Let the fat soften at room temperature until you can pull out the chunks of pork. Place them in another bowl and shred them, using two forks or your fingers. Add the fat to the shredded pork, stirring it with a wooden spoon until it is smooth. Taste for seasoning, keeping in mind that the spices will be muted when the rillettes are cold.

4. Spoon the mixture into small crocks or ramekins, smooth the tops, and cover them tightly with plastic wrap. Refrigerate for at least one day before serving. The rillettes will keep, refrigerated, for ten days, or for five to six months sealed with an additional layer of melted fat.

DUCK RILLETTES

Makes 6 to 8 servings

Rabbit can be substituted for the duck meat in this spread, or use turkey thigh, which is cheaper and more readily available.

1 pound lean duck meat
1 pound lean pork
13 ounces lean pork fat
1 cup white wine
1 cup or more water
2 teaspoons salt
2 tablespoons freshly ground pepper
1 teaspoon freshly grated nutmeg
1 bay leaf
1 teaspoon dried thyme

1. Cut the duck, pork, and pork fat into 2- to 3-inch pieces, and place them in a heavy pan with the wine and enough water to cover by 1 inch. Add the remaining ingredients. Bring the mixture to a boil, reduce the heat to very low, and simmer, covered, until the fat is completely rendered (about 4 to 6 hours). Remove the cover and continue simmering until all the water has evaporated, about 1 hour more, leaving the meat suspended in clear fat.

2. Remove the pan from the heat and refrigerate to solidify the fat. Pour off any remaining liquid, and remove the bay leaf.

3. Let the fat soften at room temperature until you can pull out the chunks of duck and pork. Place them in another bowl and shred them, using two forks or your fingers. Add the fat to the shredded mixture, stirring it with a wooden spoon until it is smooth. Taste for seasoning, keeping in mind that the spices will be muted when the rillettes are cold.

4. Spoon the mixture into small crocks or ramekins, smooth the tops, and cover them tightly with plastic wrap. Refrigerate for at least one day before serving. The rillettes will keep, refrigerated, for ten days, or for five to six months sealed with an additional layer of melted fat.

TAPENADE

Makes about 1 cup

Several of our guest cooking teachers have shared their own variations on the classic theme of tapenade, a mayonnaise-like olive spread. Inspired by them, in particular by Paula Wolfert's excellent version, we've created our own. Paula suggests serving tapenade on slices of country-style bread, spread with olive oil, sprinkled with *herbes de Provence*, and toasted in a hot oven. It's a delicious way to use day-old French bread.

18 pitted oil-cured ripe
   olives (or dried salted
   olives, marinated overnight in olive oil)
1 clove garlic
2 tablespoons capers,
   drained
1 tablespoon Dijon-style
   mustard
1 tin (2 ounces) anchovy
   fillets, drained
½ cup chopped fresh parsley
1½ tablespoons fresh basil
   (or 2 teaspoons dried)
1 egg yolk
⅔ cup extra-virgin olive oil
2 tablespoons fresh lemon
   juice
Dash of cayenne pepper

Using a food processor fitted with the steel blade, purée the olives, garlic, capers, mustard, anchovies, parsley, and basil. Add the egg yolk and process to blend thoroughly. With the machine running, pour the olive oil through the feed tube in a slow, steady stream. The tapenade should have the consistency of a firm mayonnaise. Add the lemon juice and cayenne, and adjust the seasoning. Spoon the mixture into a serving dish, and refrigerate. It will keep, refrigerated, up to one week.

TART ONION RELISH DIANA KENNEDY

Makes 2 cups

This is one of those recipes that we love to play with. Change the type of vinegar and you get a whole new flavor. If you're using the tarragon vinegar, add 2 sun-dried tomatoes, coarsely chopped, for a zippy flavor. Or substitute raspberry vinegar for a sweet-sour flavor, and stir in some cranberries. Balsamic vinegar makes for a more mellow flavor. Serve this condiment with pâté, sausages, curry, or roast or grilled meats and poultry. It will keep, refrigerated, for a week.

1 large red onion, thinly
   sliced
10 whole black peppercorns
¼ teaspoon oregano
2 cloves garlic, sliced
½ teaspoon salt
¾ cup tarragon vinegar
   (approximately)

In a wide-mouth 16-ounce glass jar, combine the onions, peppercorns, oregano, garlic, and salt. Pour on enough vinegar to cover, put the lid of the jar on loosely, and let the mixture stand in a cool place for at least two days before using. After that, refrigerate the relish. It will keep for several months.

JERRIE STROM'S RED ONION RELISH

Makes about 2 cups

Pâté and cold meats such as turkey or ham go particularly well with this tasty relish. It's simple to make and will keep for weeks. It's also wonderful with grilled meat or fish.

1 tablespoon dark soy sauce
2 tablespoons cider vinegar
2 tablespoons sugar
1 pound red onions
1 large clove garlic
2 tablespoons vegetable oil
¼ teaspoon salt

1. Combine the soy sauce, vinegar, and sugar in a small bowl and stir until the sugar is dissolved and the sauce is smooth. Set it aside.
2. Trim the root ends from the onions and peel them. Cut each onion into 1-inch wedges and separate the layers. Slightly flatten the garlic with the flat side of a knife or cleaver to loosen the skin. Remove the skin.
3. Heat a heavy skillet or sauté pan over high heat. Add the oil and swirl the pan to coat the

bottom. Heat the oil for 30 seconds, then add the garlic. Fry it a few seconds, pressing and stirring it with a wooden spoon to flavor the oil. Remove the garlic from the pan, scatter in the onions, and cook them for 2 to 3 minutes, stirring constantly. When they are glistening with oil and translucent, sprinkle in the salt and stir the mixture well. Pour in the sauce and let it sizzle a few seconds. Stir the onions briskly and pour them into a serving dish to cool. Refrigerate the relish, covered, until well chilled.

TOMATO RELISH

Makes about 4 cups

Jim Hill devised this recipe and the Red Pepper Confit that follows.

¼ cup virgin olive oil
3 medium onions, sliced
3 cloves garlic, minced
8 tomatoes, peeled, seeded, and chopped
½ cup sherry wine vinegar
¼ cup sugar
3 to 4 pickled tabasco or Capsicum peppers, seeded and minced
1 cup dry white wine
3 sprigs fresh parsley
2 bay leaves
3 sprigs fresh thyme
1 bunch fresh basil

1. In a large sauté pan, heat the olive oil until almost smoking. Reduce the heat to medium, and cook the onions and garlic for 2 to 3 minutes until they are limp but not browned. Add the tomatoes and continue simmering for 15 minutes, stirring frequently.

2. Add the remaining ingredients. Reduce the heat and simmer 30 minutes longer.

3. Remove the herbs and adjust the seasoning. Refrigerate overnight or longer. Serve with country-style pâtés and sausages. It will keep, refrigerated, for one week.

RED PEPPER CONFIT

Makes about 2 cups

¼ cup olive oil
8 red bell peppers, cored,
    seeded, and julienne-cut
⅓ cup raspberry vinegar
¼ cup sugar
½ cup dry white wine

1. In a large sauté pan, heat the olive oil until almost smoking. Add the red peppers and cook over medium heat, stirring frequently, for 15 minutes, or until they are cooked through but not browned.

2. Reduce the heat to low and add the remaining ingredients. Simmer for another 20 minutes, stirring occasionally.

3. Remove the confit from the pan. Refrigerate overnight or longer. Serve with pâtés and sausages. It will keep, refrigerated, for one week.

5

PIRET'S BISTRO

ENTRÉES

PASTA

ACCOMPANIMENTS

ENTRÉES

Boiled Beef with Vegetables · Flemish Beef Stew · Calf's Liver with Mustard Sauce · Hungarian Rolled Stuffed Cabbage Leaves · Pork Chops in Tarragon Mustard Sauce · Anne Otterson's Braised Pork in Bourbon · Veal Stew · Veal Shanks Trieste-Style · Eggplant Stew with Lamb and Pine Nuts · Rabbit with Prune Sauce · Lemon-Soy Swordfish Steaks with Avocado Butter · Scampi alla Fresca · Fish Fillets Baked in Parchment · Chicken Breasts Stuffed with Boursin · Roasted Chicken · Marinated Sautéed Chicken Breasts · Sautéed Chicken Breasts with Raspberry Vinegar · Garlic Chicken Provençal · Chicken in Red Wine Sauce · Chicken with Cabbage · Chicken Glasgow · Ben Patterson's Chicken Curry

PASTA

Basic Egg Pasta · Spinach Pasta · Tomato Pasta · Beet Pasta · Carrot Pasta · Food Processor Pasta · Tagliarini with Prosciutto and Green Peas · Tortellini with Cream Sauce · "Combed" Pasta with Sausage and Porcini Cream Sauce · Spinach Lasagne with Cheese and Basil Stuffing

TOMATO SAUCES · Basic Tomato Sauce · Fresh Tomato Sauce · Cold Tomato Purée · Tomato Sauce with Bacon · Italian Meat Sauce

ACCOMPANIMENTS

Celery Root and Carrot Sauté · George Munger's Carrots · Chayote Don Javier · Gratin of Zucchini · Jacques Pépin's Broccoli with Garlic · "Those Tomatoes" · Baked Stuffed Tomatoes · Turnips Stuffed with Roquefort · Roasted Red Onions and Sweet Peppers · Herbed New Potatoes · Pommes Byron · Potato Nests · Potato Skins Stuffed with Leeks and Three Cheeses · Potato Skins Doreg · Wild Rice Steamed with Mushrooms

WHEN WE OPENED PIRET'S IN 1979, our main intent was to create a fabulous marketplace for take-home foods and hard-to-find quality ingredients for the home cook. Piret's included a small informal bistro where our patrons could taste the foods that we offered for carry-out. Our bistro entrées were by and large reminiscent of the country dishes we had served at Lunch at The Perfect Pan. At Piret's, we began with a seating capacity for about 30 and were mobbed with people waiting for tables. Carry-out customers could scarcely get in the door, and once in, found it all but impossible to get close enough to the food cases to be served. Gradually we added more and more tables. Today Piret's six bistros seat from 70 to 120 guests each.

Our current menus and daily *plats du jour* are very similar in style to the kinds of dishes we offered in the early days — earthy, country foods, with smatterings of *nouvelle* and adaptations of classic dishes using the fresh ingredients available in Southern California. We continue to update our cuisine so our patrons can sample dishes using techniques and ingredients in vogue. Our chefs call these creations "state of the art" dishes.

The recipes in this chapter are typical of the entrées and accompaniments on Piret's menu. In making our selections, we have emphasized both ease of preparation and advance preparation. Many of the entrées, in fact, improve in flavor when made ahead and reheated, and some involve long, slow cooking, freeing the cook for other things.

Because The Perfect Pan and Piret's grew like Topsy, with recipes from the school finding their way to our restaurants, you'll find dishes in this section attributed to teachers who have taught with us over the years. Many of these recipes have undergone considerable alteration at the hands of various chefs.

It is our hope that among our bistro recipes you will find dishes that will become part of your own repertoire for day-to-day cooking and for entertaining.

E   N   T   R   É   E   S

BOILED BEEF WITH VEGETABLES

Makes 6 to 8 servings

This familiar dish is a perennial favorite, for good reason: it is easy and inexpensive to prepare and tastes great. The flavor improves if you allow the stew to rest for a day or so before serving. We like to serve it with our own fresh Cornichon or Caper Sauce and homemade Horseradish Sauce (recipes follow). Crusty country bread is a must. As always, remove the fat that has risen to the top of the dish before reheating.

2 pounds beef bones
1 pound beef rump or
    round, cut into 1½-inch
    cubes
1 teaspoon salt
Freshly ground pepper to
    taste
Bouquet garni (see below)
2 cups mixed coarsely
    chopped vegetables
    (onion, celery, white
    turnip, parsnip)
2 leeks, white part only,
    sliced
2 carrots, peeled and
    quartered
2 potatoes, peeled and
    quartered

1. Place the beef bones and cubes in a heavy soup kettle with enough water to cover. Add the salt, pepper, and bouquet garni. Bring the mixture to a boil, skimming the foam as it rises. Reduce the heat and simmer the mixture, covered, about 3 hours, or until the meat is almost tender. Discard the bouquet garni and beef bones. Taste the broth and adjust the seasoning. Refrigerate the meat and broth overnight.

2. When ready to serve, remove the accumulated fat from the top and reheat the meat and broth. Add the chopped vegetables, leeks, carrots, and potatoes, and simmer the mixture about 30 minutes, or until the vegetables are tender.

3. To serve, ladle the meat and vegetables into large soup plates and spoon over a little broth. Top each serving with one of the sauces below or with mustard, and accompany each serving with an additional cup of broth.

Cornichon or Caper Sauce
Makes about 2 cups

2 tablespoons butter
3 tablespoons unbleached,
    all-purpose flour
2 cups strained broth from
    the boiled beef
3 tablespoons diced
    cornichons or 2
    tablespoons capers
2 teaspoons white wine
    vinegar
Salt and freshly ground
    pepper, to taste
1 tablespoon chopped fresh
    dill or parsley

Melt the butter in a small saucepan over medium heat and stir in the flour. Cook this roux for 1 to 2 minutes, stirring constantly. Whisk in the broth and cook the sauce until it is creamy and smooth. Stir in the cornichons or capers and the white wine vinegar. Season the sauce with salt and pepper, then add the dill or parsley.

Horseradish Sauce
Makes about 1½ cups

¼ cup freshly grated
    horseradish or drained
    prepared horseradish
1 teaspoon sugar
½ teaspoon Dijon-style
    mustard
¼ teaspoon salt
1 to 1½ cups sour cream

Whisk together all the ingredients, blending them well. Refrigerate the sauce until ready to serve.

There are several ways to assemble a bouquet garni, which generally includes two sprigs of fresh thyme, one dried bay leaf, two sprigs of fresh parsley, one sprig of fresh rosemary, and a rib of celery:

- Cut a 5-inch square of cheesecloth, place the herbs and celery inside, and tie with heavy kitchen twine.
- Use a premade cheesecloth bag which has a pull string to enclose the bouquet. These are available at specialty cookware shops.
- Take two ribs of celery, about 4 inches long, and place the herbs inside the hollow of one rib. Top it with the other rib and tie them together with heavy kitchen twine.

FLEMISH BEEF STEW

Makes 6 servings

We were first introduced to this delicious and incredibly simple stew by Maurice Moore-Betty, the respected New York teacher and author. Since then, we have used it countless times at Lunch at The Perfect Pan, at Piret's, and in our home. The last time George and I served it was on a skiing trip in Utah. We invited about a dozen friends to dinner and made a huge pot of stew, which we served with crusty French bread and a heavenly Burgundy. The evening was a huge success.

This dish gets only better with time and reheats beautifully. You'll love it for supper on a cold winter night and for large groups. Serve it with buttered baby carrots and broccoli for a pretty color and texture contrast.

½ pound lean bacon in one piece, cut in ¼-inch cubes

4 tablespoons butter

6 large yellow onions, thinly sliced

1 cup unbleached, all-purpose flour

1 tablespoon plus 1 teaspoon salt

1½ teaspoons freshly ground pepper

4 pounds boneless beef chuck, cut in 1½-inch cubes

1 bay leaf, crushed

3 to 4 fresh thyme leaves (or a pinch of dried)

2 slices white bread

1 tablespoon Dijon-style mustard

2 12-ounce bottles dark beer

1. In a heavy frying or sauté pan, cook the bacon cubes until brown and crispy (about 20 minutes). Remove the bacon from the pan and pour off all but a few tablespoons of the bacon fat. Add the butter to the bacon fat and heat it over medium-high heat until the butter is hot and frothing but not burning. Add the onions and cook until they are translucent and golden, about 10 minutes. Remove the onions from the pan and reserve.

2. Stir together the flour, 1 tablespoon of the salt and 1 teaspoon of the pepper, and dredge the beef cubes in the mixture, taking care to shake off any excess. Quickly sear the meat in the skillet. In a heavy, flameproof 4-quart casserole (preferably enameled cast iron, which makes a nice serving dish as well), spread the bacon cubes in a layer. Add the browned meat cubes, and layer the cooked onions on top. Sprinkle on the bay leaf, the thyme, and the remaining 1 teaspoon salt and ½ teaspoon pepper.

3. Preheat oven to 325°. Spread one side of each bread slice with the mustard and place the slices over the beef, mustard side down. Pour the beer over the bread. Bring the mixture to a boil over high heat to boil off the alcohol. Cover the casserole and place it in the oven. Bake for about 40 minutes.

4. Stir the bread into the beef and continue to bake the casserole for another 1½ hours, or until the beef is tender.

CALF'S LIVER WITH MUSTARD SAUCE

Makes 4 servings

This is a great dish for people who love liver. The sauce is very quickly put together and makes a luscious mustard coating for the quickly sautéed slices of liver.

1 egg yolk
½ teaspoon potato flour
½ teaspoon dry mustard
2 teaspoons Dijon-style
   mustard
2 tablespoons half-and-half
4 thick slices calf's liver
½ cup Cognac or good
   brandy
4 tablespoons unsalted
   butter
2 teaspoons minced shallots
1 teaspoon minced garlic
1 teaspoon tomato paste
1 teaspoon glace de viande
   (page 315)
2½ cups heavy cream
1 tablespoon chopped fresh
   tarragon (or 2 tablespoons
   dried)

1. In a small bowl, whisk together the egg yolk, potato flour, mustards, and half-and-half, blending them thoroughly. Set the mixture aside.

2. Rinse the slices of liver and dry them with paper towels (see note). Brush the liver with a little of the brandy and let it stand a few minutes to marinate.

3. In a large, heavy sauté pan that will hold the liver in a single layer, heat 3 tablespoons of the butter until it becomes brown and fragrant, but do not let it burn. Quickly brown the liver slices on each side, lower the heat, and cook the liver to the desired degree of doneness.

4. Heat the remaining brandy in a separate pan and carefully ignite it with a long kitchen match. Pour the flaming brandy over the liver in the sauté pan. When the flames die down, transfer the liver to a warm platter and hold in a 180° oven while preparing the sauce.

5. Add the remaining butter to the sauté pan and briefly cook the shallots and garlic until they are just tender. Stir in the tomato paste and glace de viande. Very slowly, over low heat, stir in the cream.

6. Remove the pan from the heat and stir in the reserved mustard–egg yolk mixture. Add the tarragon and gently reheat the sauce. Spoon the sauce over the liver, and serve immediately.

NOTE

To remove any bitterness, marinate the liver in milk for several hours in the refrigerator. Dry with paper towels and proceed as directed.

HUNGARIAN ROLLED STUFFED CABBAGE LEAVES

Makes 6 servings

The Perfect Pan's first employee, Judy Miller, served these cabbage rolls when she was a guest chef at Lunch at The Perfect Pan. She developed the recipe while she was married to a Hungarian baron — in Kansas City!

12 large cabbage leaves

VEGETABLE SAUCE

2 tablespoons butter
1 cup sliced carrots
1 cup chopped onion
   (1 medium onion)
¼ teaspoon freshly ground
   pepper
1 bay leaf
¼ teaspoon dried thyme
1 tablespoon brown sugar
1 can (1 pound) Italian
   plum tomatoes, drained
1 cup brown stock (page
   313)

FILLING

1½ pounds lean ground beef
1 egg
1 teaspoon Worcestershire
   sauce
3 cloves garlic, minced
1 tablespoon minced fresh
   parsley
1 teaspoon salt
¼ teaspoon freshly ground
   pepper
1 cup fresh white bread
   crumbs

1 cup sour cream
1 tablespoon dill seed

1. Cook the cabbage leaves for 5 minutes in 1 inch of boiling water in an ovenproof, covered 12-inch skillet. Drain, and reserve the cabbage. Discard the cooking liquid.

2. *To prepare the vegetable sauce:* Melt the butter in the same skillet and cook the carrots and onions for 3 minutes. Add the pepper, bay leaf, thyme, brown sugar, tomatoes, and beef stock, mixing them well. Simmer the mixture gently while you prepare the filling.

3. *To prepare the filling:* In a large bowl, thoroughly combine the ground beef, egg, Worcestershire sauce, garlic, parsley, salt, pepper, and bread crumbs.

FINAL ASSEMBLY

1. Divide the filling mixture into 12 portions. Place one portion on each cabbage leaf. Roll each leaf, tucking in the sides to completely enclose the filling.

2. Preheat oven to 350°. Place the stuffed leaves, seam-side down, on the vegetable sauce in the skillet. Cover the skillet and transfer it to the oven. Bake the cabbage rolls for about 45 minutes.

3. Remove the cabbage rolls from the skillet and arrange them on a serving platter. Reduce the oven temperature to 180° and place the platter of cabbage rolls back in the oven to keep them warm.

4. Purée the vegetable mixture and cooking juices from the skillet, using a blender or food processor fitted with the steel blade. Reheat the purée in a saucepan.

5. To serve, top each serving of cabbage rolls

with dollops of sour cream and sprinkle with dill seed. Pass the vegetable sauce separately in a sauceboat.

PORK CHOPS IN TARRAGON MUSTARD SAUCE

Makes 6 servings

Jacques Pépin prepares this homey recipe with Dijon-style mustard. Our own Jack Monaco, who prepares a variation on Pépin's theme, says the tomato paste gives it a barbecue flavor, while the cornichons add piquancy. Tarragon mustard is available in specialty food stores.

6 pork chops (1½ inches thick)
½ teaspoon salt
½ teaspoon freshly ground pepper
3 tablespoons butter
1 cup minced onion (1 medium onion)
3 cloves garlic, minced
2 tablespoons chopped fresh chives
1 tablespoon chopped fresh parsley
½ teaspoon dried tarragon
½ cup dry vermouth
2 tablespoons tomato paste
2 tablespoons tarragon mustard
½ cup brown sauce (page 324)
12 cornichons, cut into fans (or spicy green olives), for garnish

1. Season the chops on both sides with the salt and pepper. Melt the butter in a large skillet and cook the chops in a single layer over high heat until one side is golden (about 7 minutes). Turn the chops, lower the heat to medium, cover the pan, and cook the other side for about 8 minutes, or until a meat thermometer inserted in the chops registers 160°.

2. Remove the pork chops from the skillet and keep them warm in a 180° oven. To the drippings in the skillet, add the onions, garlic, chives, parsley, and tarragon, and cook the mixture for 5 minutes, stirring to deglaze the pan. Add the vermouth, raise the heat, and boil the mixture until there is very little liquid left.

3. Add the tomato paste, tarragon mustard, and brown sauce to the skillet, bring the mixture to a boil, and simmer it for about 3 minutes. Season the sauce with salt and pepper.

4. To serve, place 1 pork chop on each warmed dinner plate. Top with the sauce and garnish with cornichon fans, or scatter spicy green olives over the top.

ANNE OTTERSON'S BRAISED PORK IN BOURBON

Makes 6 servings

4-pound pork roast
½ cup Dijon-style mustard
⅔ cup brown sugar
½ cup peanut oil
⅔ cup bourbon
2 cups rich chicken stock,
    preferably homemade
    (page 317)
½ teaspoon salt
¼ teaspoon freshly ground
    pepper
½ teaspoon dried thyme
¼ teaspoon dried sage
1 tablespoon chopped fresh
    parsley
1 tablespoon unbleached,
    all-purpose flour
1 tablespoon butter

1. Using your fingers, rub the mustard all over the pork, then roll the roast in the brown sugar. Heat the oil in a heavy, flameproof casserole over medium-high heat and brown the roast on all sides, taking care not to burn the sugar.

2. Preheat oven to 350°. Pour the bourbon over the pork and carefully ignite the bourbon with a long kitchen match. Add 1 cup of the chicken stock, and the salt, pepper, thyme, sage, and parsley. Insert a meat thermometer in the roast. Cover the casserole, transfer it to the oven, and braise the pork for 1½ to 2 hours, or until the meat thermometer registers 150°.

3. Remove the roast to a serving platter and keep it warm. Pour the remaining stock into the casserole and boil it over high heat, scraping up the browned bits to deglaze the pan. Strain the liquid into a saucepan and skim off as much fat as possible. With your fingers, quickly work the flour and butter together to form a *beurre manié*. Whisk it into the hot sauce, a bit at a time, and cook the sauce over medium heat until it is smooth and thickened. Serve the sauce with the roast.

VEAL STEW

Makes 16 servings

There's no need to panic when a crowd of people is coming for dinner. Set up a buffet and plan on a "fork dinner." This veal stew fits right in: it's a savory, satisfying main course that can be prepared ahead and reheated, then kept hot on the serving table. When the guest list is shorter, cut the recipe in half. Or, better still, prepare the larger quantity, but with only 16 boiling onions. Serve half the stew with the onions, which don't freeze well, and freeze the other half. To reheat, peel another 16 small white onions and boil them until tender. Add them to the thawed stew and simmer it for about 20 minutes.

At the Four Seasons restaurant in New York, this stew includes pitted, halved ripe olives, added just before serving.

15 medium tomatoes, peeled, seeded, and chopped
32 small white boiling onions
½ cup olive oil
12 pounds boneless veal, well trimmed of fat and cubed
3 medium onions, chopped
9 cloves garlic, chopped
1 cup tomato sauce
2 tablespoons tomato paste
Bouquet garni (page 163)
1½ cups rich veal stock, preferably homemade (page 316)
3 cups dry white wine
Salt and freshly ground pepper, to taste
Chopped fresh parsley, for garnish

1. Peel the tomatoes and boiling onions (see below.)

2. Heat the olive oil in a large skillet and brown the veal cubes in batches without crowding the pan, so the veal browns rather than steams. Transfer the browned cubes to a 15-quart casserole or low-sided stockpot.

3. Pour the oil out of the skillet and add the chopped onions. Cook the onions for 5 minutes, stirring up any browned bits. Add the cooked onions to the casserole along with the garlic, tomatoes, tomato sauce, tomato paste, and bouquet garni. Cook the mixture over medium heat for 5 minutes.

4. Add the boiling onions to the casserole along with the stock and wine, and season with salt and pepper. Simmer the stew, covered, over low heat about 1 hour, or until the veal is tender. Remove the bouquet garni and serve the stew garnished with parsley.

❧ To peel tomatoes and small boiling onions, trim the ends of the onions and remove the stem plug from the tomatoes with a sharp knife. Drop them into boiling water for a few seconds. Drain and cool. The skins will then slip off easily.

VEAL SHANKS TRIESTE-STYLE

Makes 6 servings

One of our favorite traveling teachers is Biba Caggiano, a native of Bologna who now lives in Sacramento. A slender woman barely over five feet tall, with a tussle of auburn curls framing twinkling eyes and effervescent smile, her whole being exudes enthusiasm and energy. Even the most timid novice leaves her classes with a confident "can do" attitude.

2 tablespoons butter
2 tablespoons olive oil
3 large onions, thinly sliced
6 veal shanks, sliced 2
   inches thick
Unbleached, all-purpose
   flour, for dredging
Salt and freshly ground
   pepper, to taste
1 cup dry white wine
1 cup rich chicken stock,
   preferably homemade
   (page 317)
3 tablespoons chopped fresh
   parsley
2 cloves garlic, chopped
3 anchovy fillets, drained
   and mashed to a paste
2 tablespoons tomato paste
Grated zest of 2 lemons

1. Melt the butter with the olive oil in a large, heavy casserole. When the butter foams, add the onions and sauté over medium heat until they turn a pale yellow. Remove the onions from the casserole with a slotted spoon and set them aside.

2. Dredge the veal shanks in flour, shaking off the excess. In the fat remaining in the casserole, brown the shanks a few at a time over medium heat, turning them to brown on all sides. Season the veal with salt and pepper.

3. Return the onions to the casserole, add the wine, and simmer until the wine is reduced by half. Add the chicken broth, and simmer the shanks very gently, covered, for 1½ hours, or until the meat falls from the bone.

4. Using a slotted spoon, remove the veal from the liquid and keep the veal warm. Stir in the parsley, garlic, anchovies, tomato paste, and lemon zest. Boil the sauce, uncovered, for about 10 minutes to thicken it, if necessary. If the sauce is too thick, stir in 1 or 2 tablespoons more of chicken broth. Taste the sauce and adjust the seasoning. Arrange the meat and sauce on a warmed platter, and serve immediately.

EGGPLANT STEW WITH LAMB AND PINE NUTS

Makes 6 servings

If you have leftover lamb, this is a great way to use it. We serve this dish very simply with a green salad and crusty French bread.

1 medium eggplant, pared and sliced

2 tablespoons virgin olive oil

1 pound lean cooked lamb, cut in ½-inch cubes

2 teaspoons minced garlic

1 tablespoon dried oregano

¼ teaspoon freshly grated nutmeg

1 green or red bell pepper, diced

3 tomatoes, peeled, seeded, and diced

1 tablespoon fresh lemon juice

4 tablespoons chopped fresh parsley (approximately)

Salt and freshly ground pepper, to taste

2 tablespoons pine nuts (approximately)

1. Sprinkle the eggplant liberally with salt and let it stand for 30 minutes in a colander. Pat the eggplant dry with paper towels.

2. Heat the olive oil in a heavy skillet over medium-high heat and brown the cooked lamb cubes quickly. Remove the lamb from the skillet and set it aside. To the same skillet, add the garlic, oregano, nutmeg, and eggplant. Simmer the mixture over low heat for 8 to 10 minutes, or until the eggplant is soft.

3. Stir in the bell pepper and tomatoes, and simmer the mixture for 2 to 3 minutes more. Return the lamb cubes to the skillet to heat them. Sprinkle in the lemon juice and 2 tablespoons of the parsley. Season with salt and pepper, and top with the remaining parsley and the pine nuts. Serve immediately.

RABBIT WITH PRUNE SAUCE

Makes 4 to 6 servings

Rabbit is a great favorite and quite common all over Europe. Yet it is a rarity in most parts of the United States. Some supermarkets sell rabbit, but often it must be ordered ahead. If you can't get rabbit, use 6 Cornish game hens, cut in half, as a substitute. Serve this dish with noodles or rice, and bread to soak up the sauce.

1 rabbit (about 4 pounds), cut into 12 serving pieces, liver and kidneys reserved
½ teaspoon salt
¼ teaspoon freshly ground pepper
4 tablespoons unsalted butter
½ cup unbleached, all-purpose flour
1½ cups dry vermouth
2½ cups rich chicken stock, preferably homemade (page 317)
3 cloves garlic, crushed
18 small boiling onions, peeled
¼ cup red wine vinegar
3 tablespoons sugar
⅓ cup water
2 cups pitted dried prunes

1. Season the rabbit pieces with the salt and pepper. Melt the butter in a large sauté pan and brown the rabbit pieces on all sides. Sprinkle the flour over the rabbit and cook for another minute or two. Remove the rabbit from the pan. Pour in 1 cup of the vermouth and all of the chicken stock, cooking them over high heat and stirring up the brown bits to deglaze the pan.

2. Using a food processor fitted with the steel blade, or a blender, purée the garlic with the rabbit liver and kidneys, and add the purée to the skillet along with the rabbit pieces. Stir in the remaining ½ cup of vermouth, and simmer the mixture for 15 minutes, covered. Add the onions, cover, and simmer 15 minutes longer.

3. Combine the vinegar and sugar in a small, heavy saucepan, stirring to dissolve the sugar. Bring the mixture to a rolling boil and let it cook until the sugar begins to turn a caramel color. Watch it carefully so that it does not scorch. Carefully add the water to the caramelized mixture, watching for spatters as it bubbles up, and stir to thin the caramel.

4. Stir the caramel into the skillet with the rabbit. Add the prunes, simmer the mixture for 10 minutes, and serve.

LEMON-SOY SWORDFISH STEAKS WITH AVOCADO BUTTER

Makes 8 servings

George has prepared this grilled fish both indoors and outdoors. It's a simple, very flavorful preparation, now a standard at Piret's.

Grayfish (shark) is much less expensive than swordfish and a good substitute in this dish. A nice first course would be ceviche. Or garnish the fish with ceviche — a great combination and not at all confusing to the palate. For other flavored butters that go well with grilled fish, see page 334.

MARINADE

⅓ cup soy sauce
1 teaspoon grated lemon zest
¼ cup fresh lemon juice
    (about 2 lemons)
1 clove garlic, crushed
2 teaspoons Dijon-style
    mustard
½ cup vegetable oil

8 swordfish steaks
    (6 ounces each)
Lemon or lime wedges and
    chopped fresh parsley, for
    garnish
Avocado Butter
    (recipe follows)

1. Whisk together all the marinade ingredients. Place the fish in a shallow glass or porcelain baking dish and pour on the marinade, piercing the fish with a fork to assure penetration. Turn the fish and pierce it again. Let the fish marinate, covered in the refrigerator, for at least 1 hour. It can marinate up to 6 hours, if necessary.

2. Grill the fish over hot coals or under the broiler for 5 to 6 minutes on each side, brushing the fish often with the marinade. Figure 10 minutes' total cooking time for each inch of thickness of the fish steaks. Serve the fish garnished with lemon or lime wedges and chopped parsley, and topped with Avocado Butter.

Avocado Butter
Makes about 1½ cups

½ cup butter, softened
½ cup ripe mashed avocado
5 tablespoons fresh lemon or
    lime juice
2 tablespoons chopped fresh
    parsley
2 cloves garlic, minced
Salt, to taste

Whip the butter in a small mixing bowl until it is soft and creamy. Beat in the remaining ingredients. Refrigerate the butter until ready to serve. This is a good accompaniment to any barbecued fish.

SCAMPI ALLA FRESCA

Makes 4 servings

Jack Monaco created this dish for Lunch at The Perfect Pan, and it has been a favorite of ours ever since. The garlic butter is divine, with just the right balance of garlic, scallions, lemon, salt, and pepper.

This dish must be made just before serving; however, ahead of time you may clean and devein the shrimp, clarify the butter, slice the scallions — in other words, do all the basic preparation. Cooking the shrimp takes only minutes. Be sure to serve plenty of crusty French bread to soak up the garlic butter.

1 pound large shrimp (15 or fewer to a pound)
8 sprigs fresh parsley
⅓ cup clarified butter (page 239)
3 tablespoons minced garlic
6 scallions, thinly sliced
Juice of 1 lemon (about 2 tablespoons)
3 ounces dry vermouth or dry white wine
Salt and freshly ground pepper, to taste
Lemon slices, for garnish

1. Shell and devein the shrimp. Rinse, and set them aside. Reserve a few nice sprigs of parsley for garnish, and mince the rest.

2. Heat the clarified butter in a large sauté pan over medium heat. Lightly sauté the garlic for 1 to 2 minutes, being careful not to let it brown. Add the shrimp, scallions, lemon juice, and vermouth or wine, and cook the mixture until the shrimp turn white and firm, a minute or two on each side, being careful not to overcook. They should be just white with a hint of translucency. At the last minute, add the minced parsley and season with salt and pepper.

3. Serve the scampi on individual shells or small gratin dishes, garnished with a slice or two of lemon and a fresh parsley sprig.

FISH FILLETS BAKED IN PARCHMENT

Makes 4 to 6 servings

At Piret's, our fish is always cooked fresh on the premises, with all preparation done ahead. Although aluminum foil will work as well as parchment for baking *en papillote,* we prefer parchment for its visual appeal. Cooking fish in parchment has many advantages. For one, the juices from the fish combined with whatever flavorings you may be using remain in the package, making it virtually impossible to dry out the fish.

We use tomatoes, mushrooms, *crème fraîche,* and olive oil in this Anne Otterson recipe; however, if you are dieting, you may use carrots, celery, and leek cut in julienne, perhaps some fresh herbs, and a bit of white wine. Combined with steamed snow peas and braised lettuce or leeks, this makes a satisfying yet low-calorie menu.

The recipe will serve 6 to 8 as a first course, made in smaller packets.

½ pound mushrooms, cleaned and quartered

4 tablespoons extra-virgin olive oil

1 pound tomatoes, peeled, seeded, and chopped

1 cup *crème fraîche* (see below)

1 tablespoon Moutarde de Meaux or other coarse-grained mustard

Salt and freshly ground pepper, to taste

1½ pounds fish fillets (such as sole, halibut, or sea bass), sliced ½-inch thick

1. Put a few mushrooms at a time in a clean dishtowel and twist the towel to squeeze excess moisture from the mushrooms. Sauté the mushrooms briefly in the oil. Add the tomatoes and cook until the mixture is nearly dry. Stir together the *crème fraîche,* mustard, salt, and pepper, and stir it into the tomato mixture.

2. Preheat oven to 500°. Place each fish fillet on a square of parchment paper or aluminum foil large enough to wrap generously. Divide the sauce among the fish packages, spreading the sauce over each fillet. Seal the fillet in the wrapper, making neat packages and leaving some room for expansion. Bake the packages for 3 to 5 minutes, or until they puff. Let them rest, unopened, for 2 to 3 minutes.

3. Serve the packages unopened, giving your guests the full benefit of the fragrance as they cut them open.

❧ CRÈME FRAÎCHE is similar to sour cream. It has a thick, rich texture and a delightful tang. Dollops of *crème fraîche* are wonderful on warm fruit compotes and tarts, and the cream has many uses in main-dish cooking. It's easy to make and so versatile that it's a good idea to have some on hand all the time. If you can find cream that has not been ultrapasteurized, the *crème fraîche* will have a lighter flavor.

To make 1 cup of crème fraîche

In a glass or earthenware bowl or jar, thoroughly stir 2 tablespoons buttermilk or 1 tablespoon plain yogurt into 1 cup of heavy cream, using a wooden spoon. Cover the container and let it stand in a warm place to allow the cream to set. This will take from 5 to 8 hours, depending on the quality of the cream and the temperature of the room. Refrigerate the cream to allow it to thicken, preferably over-night. Refrigerated in a covered container, the *crème fraîche* should keep up to two weeks, depending on the freshness of the dairy products used.

CHICKEN BREASTS STUFFED WITH BOURSIN

Makes 4 servings

Boursin cheese is readily available at specialty cheese shops, and supermarkets, but we have included a recipe you can make at home and season as you like. It is basically a cream cheese or farmer cheese base with various flavorings. If you like a sweet flavor with poultry, you may wish to substitute pineapple, oranges, peaches, or prunes and raisins for the customary herbs. The Boursin is easier to cut if it is very cold.

Boning chicken breasts is a snap, and if you don't have a boning knife, a sharp 4-inch paring knife will do. Lois Stanton, former director of our cooking school, introduced this recipe to us in one of her poultry-boning classes.

2 whole chicken breasts
8 tablespoons (approximately) Boursin cheese with herbs, cut in 1-inch cubes
1 egg, beaten
Unbleached, all-purpose flour for dredging
3 teaspoons vegetable oil
3 teaspoons butter

1. Buy boned chicken breasts, or bone them yourself (see below). Pull away the skin. Pull off the small, cylindrical fillet in the thick part of the chicken breast and lay it over the thinner part. Flatten the breast slightly with the broad side of a cleaver or a meat pounder.

2. Place a cube of cheese in the center of the chicken breast and fold or roll the chicken around it, tucking in the sides to completely enclose the cheese. Fasten it closed with a toothpick, if necessary. Repeat with each breast.

3. Dip the chicken rolls into beaten egg, then dredge in flour. Brown them on all sides in a mixture of the butter and oil. The chicken breasts are cooked when the juice runs clear when they are pierced with a fork. Serve immediately.

NOTE

Boursin cheese with garlic or pepper can be substituted for the cheese with herbs.

⁊ To bone a chicken breast half, separate the rib bones from the breast meat with your fingers, pulling the meat away. You may use a sharp boning knife to cut away any connective tissue, but this is a job that can be done almost entirely with your fingers. Pull away the narrow strip of cartilage, if any, and the keel bone. If the wishbone is attached, cut down to it, cut along its length, and work it free with your fingers.

Boursin-Style Cheese Spread

Makes 2 cups

1 teaspoon minced fresh
  basil
1 teaspoon minced fresh
  thyme
1 teaspoon minced fresh
  oregano
1 clove garlic, minced
1 cup minced fresh parsley
2 packages (8 ounces each)
  cream cheese or farmer
  cheese, softened
1 to 2 tablespoons heavy
  cream

1. Beat the basil, thyme, oregano, garlic, and parsley into the softened cream cheese. Stir in just enough of the cream to make the mixture spreadable. Refrigerate it several hours or overnight, to allow the flavors to combine. The spread will keep, refrigerated, up to a week. Serve whatever is left over from the chicken recipe on crackers, toast rounds, or in raw celery sticks.

NOTE

Do not substitute dried herbs for fresh in this recipe. They just don't have the right flavor. However, other fresh herbs, such as tarragon or marjoram, may be used.

ROASTED CHICKEN

Makes 4 servings

Serve this dish with Wild Rice Steamed with Mushrooms (page 215) and George Munger's Carrots (page 204).

1 chicken (2½ to 3 pounds)
4 cloves garlic, peeled
Juice of 1 lemon
2 teaspoons kosher-style salt
1 teaspoon freshly ground
  pepper
½ teaspoon crushed dried
  oregano
½ teaspoon marjoram
¼ teaspoon dried basil
¼ teaspoon dried thyme
1 tablespoon virgin olive oil

1. Clean the chicken, removing any large pieces of fat.
2. Mash together the garlic, lemon juice, kosher-style salt, pepper, herbs, and olive oil. Rub about 1 tablespoon of the garlic mixture inside the chicken. Rub the rest of the mixture into the chicken skin. (Another way to season the breast portion is to loosen the skin from the flesh, using your hand and being careful not to break the skin. Rub some of the seasoning mixture over the meat, under the skin.)
3. Preheat oven to 400°. Truss the chicken if it is

to be roasted on a rack. If you are using a vertical roaster, tuck the wings behind the back but do not truss. Roast the chicken for 1 hour, without basting. Let the chicken rest for 10 minutes, then cut into serving pieces.

MARINATED SAUTÉED CHICKEN BREASTS

Makes 6 servings

Nadia Frigeri, our cooking school's Italian cuisine specialist, calls this recipe "Petti di Pollo alla Montelliana," or Chicken Breasts Montello-Style. The marinade makes the chicken very flavorful. If you are serving this for company, you might want to debone the breasts before marinating, which will reduce overall cooking time to 15 to 20 minutes.

6 chicken breast halves
1 cup dry white wine
2 cloves garlic, minced
1 tablespoon minced fresh marjoram (or ½ teaspoon dried)
1 tablespoon minced fresh parsley
1 tablespoon minced fresh basil (or ½ teaspoon dried)
3 tablespoons butter
3 tablespoons virgin olive oil
2 medium tomatoes, peeled, seeded, and chopped
½ teaspoon salt
¼ teaspoon freshly ground pepper
2 tablespoons instant-blending flour (Wondra)

1. Place the chicken breasts in a shallow bowl. Combine the wine, garlic, marjoram, parsley, and basil, and pour the mixture over the chicken. Marinate the chicken for 2 hours, turning it several times. Drain the chicken, reserving the marinade. Dry the chicken with paper towels.

2. Melt the butter with the olive oil in a 12-inch skillet, and sauté the chicken for 3 minutes on each side. Add the marinade, tomatoes, salt, and pepper. Cook the chicken over medium heat, uncovered, for 20 to 30 minutes, or until tender.

3. Remove the chicken from the pan and keep it warm. Add the flour to the sauce remaining in the pan and cook it over medium heat, stirring often, for 5 minutes. (You may use unbleached all-purpose flour, but mix it with a little cold water to make a smooth paste, and then whisk it into the juices.) Serve the chicken on pasta or rice, topped with the sauce.

SAUTÉED CHICKEN BREASTS WITH RASPBERRY VINEGAR

Makes 3 to 4 servings

The raspberry vinegar in this recipe adds just a slight aura of pink and a hint of acid that is refreshing and interesting. Lightly sautéed green vegetables, such as broccoli, or a julienne of zucchini, snow peas, or asparagus, would be a lovely side dish. We like an austere salad with this sort of entrée — perhaps sliced tomatoes with watercress or red onions drizzled with a light vinaigrette. Ice cream with a fresh-fruit purée or one of the new chocolate toppings will make a quick, satisfying dinner. You can bone and slice the chicken breasts ahead and store them in the refrigerator layered in wax paper.

6 chicken breast halves
Salt and freshly ground
   pepper, to taste
1 tablespoon vegetable oil
3 tablespoons butter
1 tablespoon chopped
   shallots or white part of
   scallion
1 to 2 tablespoons raspberry
   vinegar (page 70)
2 to 3 tablespoons water

1. Bone and skin the chicken breasts (page 176). Holding the knife blade parallel to the cutting surface and flattening the chicken slightly with the palm of your hand, carefully slice each breast in half horizontally, making 12 thin fillets in all. Using the flat side of the knife, pound the fillets to flatten them slightly. (A butcher can do this for you, but you will pay dearly for it.*) Sprinkle each piece with salt and pepper.

2. Heat the oil and butter in a heavy sauté pan, and cook the breasts over medium-high heat for a few minutes on each side, just until they become opaque. Remove the chicken from the pan and keep it warm.

3. In the same pan, sauté the shallots or scallion for a few seconds. Add the raspberry vinegar and the water, stirring to loosen all the browned bits. Let the liquid bubble for a minute, then return the chicken to the pan and cook it a few minutes more, turning the pieces once to coat them with the sauce. Serve the chicken immediately, topped with the sauce from the pan.

---

* Our butcher, Ron Kiefer, does not charge for boning chicken breasts.

GARLIC CHICKEN PROVENÇAL

Makes 6 to 8 servings

Sealing a cooking vessel with a ribbon of flour-and-water paste is a classic technique to keep all the steam — and flavors and juices — inside the pot. The garlic bakes to mellow sweetness in this recipe, a Suzy Eisenman Sunday night dinner favorite.

When you serve the dish, include a few cloves of the cooked garlic with each portion. Instruct your guests to squeeze the garlic — it will pop out of the skins — and spread it on the bread.

2 frying chickens (3 pounds each)

Salt and freshly ground pepper, to taste

3 bouquets garnis (page 163)

1 lemon, cut in half

½ cup virgin olive oil

2 teaspoons crushed anise seeds

4 tablespoons dry white wine

3 whole heads of garlic, unpeeled

½ cup unbleached, all-purpose flour

Water

1. Remove any excess fat from the chickens and rub them inside and out with salt and pepper. Place one bouquet garni inside each chicken and rub the chickens all over with the cut lemon halves. Truss the chickens and place them in a casserole that will hold them both snugly.

2. Combine the olive oil, anise, wine, and garlic with the remaining bouquet garni, and season with salt and pepper. Pour the mixture over the chickens.

3. Preheat oven to 350°. Cover the casserole and seal it with a ribbon of flour-and-water paste: Mix the flour with enough of the water to form a paste. Cut a strip of cloth 2 inches wide and about 3 feet long. Submerge the cloth strip in the paste and smear the paste over both sides of the cloth with your fingers. Wrap the cloth around the edge where the lid of the casserole meets the pot, sealing them together. Make certain to seal around the handle. Place the sealed casserole in the oven and bake for 1 hour and 15 minutes.

4. To serve, bring the sealed casserole to the table. Using a pair of scissors, cut through the cloth and break the seal. Carefully remove the lid, tilting the top toward you and allowing the steam to escape away from you.

CHICKEN IN RED WINE SAUCE

Makes 6 servings

This is the classic *coq au vin* as we prepare it at Piret's. It's a robust stew with loads of flavor from the salt pork, garlic, Cognac, and red wine. Be very careful to cook the sauce sufficiently to get rid of the raw flour taste. Should the sauce thicken too much, add a little more wine, Cognac, or chicken stock.

This dish can get a little "muddy" looking because of the red wine, so we like to serve it with yellow and green vegetables to brighten up the presentation.

½ cup unsalted butter
¼ cup virgin olive oil
¼ pound salt pork, blanched and cut into small dice
18 small white boiling onions, peeled
18 small whole mushrooms
1 cup unbleached, all-purpose flour
1 teaspoon salt
1 teaspoon freshly ground pepper
6 chicken breast halves
6 chicken thighs
2 cloves garlic, mashed
2 sprigs fresh thyme (or ½ teaspoon dried)
2 bay leaves
4 sprigs fresh parsley
¼ to ⅓ cup chicken broth, wine, or water
½ cup Cognac, warmed
2 cups dry red wine
1 tablespoon sugar
¼ cup instant-blending flour (Wondra)
Chopped fresh parsley, for garnish

1. Heat the butter, olive oil, and salt pork in a large skillet over medium heat. When the pork begins to turn a golden color, add the onions and cook them for 2 minutes. Add the mushrooms and cook until they brown. With a slotted spoon, remove the salt pork, onions, and mushrooms to a strainer to drain.

2. Preheat oven to 375°. Combine the flour and ½ teaspoon each of the salt and pepper. Dredge the chicken pieces in the flour mixture and brown them in the skillet, skin-side down, for about 5 minutes. Turn and cook them for 5 more minutes. Using tongs, transfer the chicken to a 6-quart casserole. Sprinkle the chicken with the remaining salt and pepper, and add the garlic, thyme, bay leaves, and parsley. Bake the chicken, covered, for 30 minutes, or until it is tender.

3. Remove the chicken pieces from the casserole and place them on a warm platter. Cover with aluminum foil to keep the chicken warm. Protecting your hands with mitts, carefully pour the juices from the casserole into a skillet. Add the ¼ to ⅓ cup chicken broth to the casserole, and deglaze the casserole over high heat, scraping up any browned bits, and pour the deglazing liquid into the skillet.

4. Return the chicken pieces to the casserole, along with the salt pork, onions, and mushrooms. Add the warmed Cognac to the skillet and carefully ignite it with a long kitchen match. Cook the mixture over high heat for 2 minutes, then add the wine

and the sugar. Boil the sauce until it is reduced by half. Add the flour, whisking until smooth. (You may use all-purpose flour, but blend it with a little cold water to make a smooth paste, then whisk it into the sauce.) Cook the sauce until it loses its raw flour taste, 3 to 5 minutes.

5. Strain the sauce over the chicken in the casserole. Garnish with chopped parsley, and serve.

CHICKEN WITH CABBAGE

Makes 4 servings

You can't get much closer to country roots than this. The whole dish may be made in advance up to the baking step, then refrigerated for several hours. Serve it with baked, parsleyed, or roasted potatoes.

4 slices bacon, minced
6 boneless, skinless chicken
   breast halves
1 cabbage, cut into 8
   wedges
1 cup sliced mushrooms
2 cloves garlic, minced
1 onion, finely chopped
1 bay leaf
½ cup dry white wine
1 cup rich chicken stock,
   preferably homemade
   (page 317)
1 tablespoon dried thyme
½ cup minced fresh parsley
Salt and freshly ground
   pepper, to taste

1. In a large skillet, sauté the bacon until crisp. Set it on paper towels to drain.

2. Slice the chicken crosswise. Sauté the chicken slices in the bacon fat remaining in the skillet until nicely browned. Transfer the chicken to a casserole and arrange the cabbage wedges over it.

3. Preheat oven to 400°. In the same skillet, slightly sauté the mushrooms, garlic, and onion. Sprinkle them over the cabbage. Add the bacon and the bay leaf, wine, chicken stock, thyme, parsley, salt, and pepper to the casserole. Bake the chicken, covered, for 45 minutes.

3. Remove the vegetables and chicken to a warmed serving platter. Pour the casserole liquids into a small saucepan and reduce the liquids over high heat until thickened. (If the sauce does not thicken to your liking, whisk in a little flour and water mixed into a paste. Cook until the raw flour taste is gone, 3 to 5 minutes.) Pour the sauce over the chicken and serve immediately.

CHICKEN GLASGOW

Makes 6 servings

Bill Glasgow, a writer, editor, superlative gardener, great cook, and dear friend of many years, created this dish for Lunch at The Perfect Pan. We serve it family style from French clay casseroles. It's a marvelous country dish and will work beautifully for large groups by simple multiplication of ingredients.

3 small turnips, peeled and quartered

6 carrots, peeled and cut 1-inch thick

3 small potatoes, peeled and quartered

3 medium parsnips, peeled and cut 1-inch thick

6 chicken breast halves, boned, skins left on (page 176)

6 sprigs fresh thyme (or 1 tablespoon dried)

½ cup unsalted butter

½ teaspoon salt

¼ teaspoon freshly ground pepper

1. Preheat oven to 300°. Distribute half the turnips, carrots, potatoes, and parsnips in the bottom of a clay or earthenware casserole. Place the chicken, skin side up, over the vegetables. Tuck the thyme in and around the chicken. Dot with the butter and season with the salt and pepper. Top with the remaining vegetables and cover the casserole.

2. Bake the chicken for 2 hours. Remove the casserole from the oven and let it stand for 15 minutes. Serve from the casserole at the table.

BEN PATTERSON'S CHICKEN CURRY

Makes 6 to 8 servings

When Ben Patterson first introduced his curry at Lunch at The Perfect Pan, he served it with lots and lots of condiments: jalapeño jelly, ginger preserves, sunflower seeds, toasted coconut, chopped peanuts, currants, sieved hard-cooked eggs, chopped cilantro, chopped green bell pepper, and one or more chutneys. He called it a "12-boy curry."

The curry itself was served to guests at the table, with condiment trays set up on a buffet. Many guests began with three or four condiment selections and then returned again and again to sample all the different flavors.

3 pounds boneless, skinless chicken breasts (about 4 whole breasts)
2 cups rich chicken stock, preferably homemade (page 317)
4 tablespoons butter
2 cups coarsely chopped white onion (2 medium onions)
2 tablespoons curry powder
1 cup canned coconut milk
1 teaspoon salt
½ teaspoon freshly ground pepper
3 tablespoons minced crystallized ginger
1 teaspoon turmeric
½ teaspoon ground cloves
1 tablespoon crushed dried mint
1 tablespoon cornstarch
2 tablespoons water
¼ cup fresh lime juice
½ cup heavy cream

1. Place the chicken breasts in a large saucepan with the stock. Bring it to a boil, reduce the heat to very low, and simmer the chicken, covered, about 20 to 30 minutes, or until it is cooked through but still moist and tender. Remove the chicken from the broth and let it cool. Strain the broth, and reserve 1 cup. (Save the rest for another recipe.) Cut the chicken into 1-inch cubes.

2. Melt the butter in a large, flameproof casserole, and cook the onion for 5 minutes. Stir in the curry powder, coconut milk, and reserved 1 cup of chicken broth. Add the salt, pepper, ginger, turmeric, cloves, and mint, and cook the sauce, covered, over low heat for 30 minutes.

3. Add the cubed chicken and continue cooking for 10 minutes. Dissolve the cornstarch in the water in a small bowl. Stir in ½ cup of the sauce. Stir the mixture back into the chicken, and cook, stirring, until it is slightly thickened.

4. Just before serving, stir in the lime juice and then the cream. Serve the curry on hot rice, with a variety of condiments.

P A S T A

Americans have always had a love affair with Italian cuisine, and it's little wonder: from north to south, Italian cooking is delicious. At the heart of the cuisine is wholesome pasta, which when properly cooked to al dente rivals any food anywhere. Pasta is a versatile staple, which may be served hot in main dishes or cold in salads, and combinations of sauces, fillings, and styles of pasta are endless. Easy and fast to prepare, pasta dishes are ideal for everyday cooking.

Making fresh pasta at home is a fun project with the new equipment now available. But when time is short, there are many excellent dry pastas on the market, and fresh pasta shops are now a familiar part of the American landscape.

Pasta can be rolled and cut by hand, but it's a process that takes time, patience, and practice. Since so many excellent books on Italian cooking already have described the technique in detail, we're omitting it here. Instead, we suggest you use a pasta machine, which gives consistently good results and is so quick that you can have a whole bunch of pasta ready in minutes. And pasta cut and rolled by machine is finer in texture and thinner — making it, we think, a superior product. (If you still want to get into the spirit of the thing and try your hand — and biceps — at hand rolling, we suggest you check the instructions in Giuliano Bugialli's, Marcella Hazan's, or Biba Caggiano's excellent books.) If you have a pasta machine that mixes and extrudes pasta, we suggest you follow the manufacturer's recipes, because they have been written in proportions that suit the engineering capabilities of the specific machine.

The Basic Egg Pasta recipe can be cut into fettuccine, spaghetti, cannelloni, and other egg-based pastas. (None of the pasta-based dishes in this book require pasta made of just flour and water, so we are not including a recipe for it.) Pasta-making is very akin to bread- or pastry-making. We can give you general proportions for flour and eggs, but such factors as weather, additions of vegetables, and the way you plan to use the pasta in a dish make a huge difference. Only experience can tell you exactly how the proportions really work for the desired result. Pastas flavored with vegetables have different degrees of moisture, so you have to count on adding an extra ½ to 1 cup of flour. They also require a little more drying time — five minutes or so — before being cut.

When cooking pasta, remember it gets rubbery if it overcooks. Some cooks suggest as little as five seconds' cooking time for fresh pasta, while commercial dry pasta can take up to 20 minutes. You have to taste a strand to see if it is ready. When it is, stop the cooking immediately. Most Italian cooks strain pasta, put it back in the pan, and add a tablespoon or two of olive or vegetable oil to keep the pasta from sticking together and to give it a nice sheen. You may then toss it with sauce or mound it on a platter with the sauce on top. It is now stylish to have two sauces on the plate — say, a pesto and a tomato sauce — which makes a colorful presentation.

Another popular presentation idea is to change the color of the pasta itself by adding a vegetable purée or other color agent. We include recipes for Spinach Pasta (green), Tomato Pasta (rosy pink), Carrot Pasta (light orange), and Beet Pasta (darker pink). We've also seen black pasta (actually a charcoal gray), made with squid ink, and a gray-rose pasta using Burgundy wine.

BASIC EGG PASTA

Makes 6 servings (about 1 pound)

One problem with writing pasta recipes is that flour varies so much in moisture content. Humidity also plays a role, and even eggs can vary. We find in testing with large eggs that the following proportions work well. You'll need to do your own testing to come up with a result that works best with the flour and eggs sold in your area.

2 cups unbleached,
  all-purpose flour
3 large eggs
2 tablespoons olive oil
Pinch of salt

1. Put the flour in a bowl, or on a board or flat work surface, and make a well in the center. Place the eggs, olive oil, and salt in the well and stir to mix them slightly. Using a fork, gently mix the eggs and oil with the flour, and gradually stir in bits of flour little by little from the inside of the well. When the liquids are incorporated and the dough becomes stiff enough to form a ball, knead it for at least 10 minutes, or until it becomes smooth and elastic. Let the dough rest, covered with a damp towel, for 20 to 30 minutes.

2. Cut the dough into three portions (the general rule is to cut pasta dough into as many portions as there are eggs in the dough). Keep two of the portions covered with a damp towel. Pat the third portion into a flat disc. Set the pasta machine at its widest setting (number 1 on most machines), and roll the disc of dough through the machine. Sprinkle the dough with flour, wipe off any excess, and fold the dough in thirds. Repeat the rolling and folding process until the dough is very smooth and elastic. This further kneads the dough.

3. Change the machine to the number 2 setting and put the pasta through the rollers. It will get thinner and longer, and to keep it easy to handle, you can cut it into shorter strips. Change the setting to the next width and roll again. Continue reducing the space between the rollers until the dough is the desired thickness. As you roll the pasta, dust it with flour, brushing off any excess, to keep the dough from sticking.

4. Suspend a dowel between two chairs, or use a

pasta-drying rack, and hang the pasta strips to dry to a leathery texture before cutting them into noodles or lasagne. Skip this drying step if you are using the pasta for ravioli or any type of stuffed pasta.

5. Put the partially dried dough through the cutting rollers to make thin or wide noodles. Noodles can be draped over the dowel or drying rack. Or twirl the noodles in small piles, sprinkle them with a little flour, and let them dry for a few hours before cooking them. The noodles also may be packed into plastic freezer bags and frozen.

6. To cook, drop the noodles into a large pot of boiling, salted water (1 to 1½ teaspoons salt per quart of water), and boil them until tender. Fresh pasta cooks very quickly — 30 seconds to 1 minute — so watch it carefully, testing by tasting a piece, and remove it from the water when it is tender but still resists the bite (al dente). Drain the pasta, and toss it with olive oil, butter, or the sauce of your choice.

LASAGNE

Roll the dough and cut it into 4-inch squares or wide strips. Do not let the pasta dry any longer than it takes to bring 4 quarts of water to a boil. Have a bowl of cold water and clean towels ready. When the water boils, add 1 teaspoon salt and drop in the pasta, 4 pieces at a time. Cook the pasta until it is barely tender (it will cook further in the sauce during baking). Remove the pasta with a slotted spoon and rinse it at once in cold water. Place the pasta in a single layer on towels to dry. Continue in this manner until all of the pasta is cooked.

Spinach Pasta
Makes 6 to 8 servings (about 1½ pounds)

3 large eggs
¾ cup (1 10-ounce package) chopped, cooked fresh spinach, squeezed very dry
1 tablespoon olive oil

Stir together the eggs, spinach, oil, and salt before adding them to the flour well, and proceed as directed for Basic Egg Pasta.

Pinch of salt
3 cups unbleached,
    all-purpose flour

Tomato Pasta
Makes 6 to 8 servings (about 1½ pounds)

2 medium tomatoes, peeled,
    seeded, and coarsely
    chopped
3 to 3½ cups unbleached,
    all-purpose flour
3 large eggs
2 tablespoons olive oil
Pinch of salt

1. Place the tomatoes in a heavy, nonaluminum saucepan over low heat. Cook the tomatoes, stirring constantly, until they are pulpy and most of the juices have evaporated (about 10 minutes). Purée the tomato pulp, using a food mill or a food processor fitted with the steel blade. Push the tomato purée through a fine sieve to remove any solids.

2. Proceed as directed for Basic Egg Pasta, adding the tomato purée to the flour well along with the eggs, olive oil, and salt, and blending well. Allow 15 minutes' drying time before cutting the pasta.

Beet Pasta
Makes 6 to 8 servings (about 1½ pounds)

2 beets, cleaned, unpeeled
2½ to 3 cups unbleached,
    all-purpose flour
3 large eggs
2 tablespoons olive oil
⅛ to ¼ teaspoon salt

1. Place the beets in salted water, bring it to a boil, and cook the beets until they are tender enough to be easily pierced by a fork (45 to 90 minutes, depending on their size). Remove the beets from the water, and peel and coarsely chop them. Purée the beets using a food mill or a food processor fitted with the steel blade. Push the purée through a fine sieve to remove any large pieces.

2. Proceed as directed for Basic Egg Pasta, adding the beet purée to the flour well with the eggs, olive oil, and salt, and blending well. Allow 15 minutes' drying time before cutting the pasta.

Carrot Pasta
Makes 6 to 8 servings (about 1½ pounds)

2 large carrots, peeled and
   quartered
2½ to 3 cups unbleached,
   all-purpose flour
3 large eggs
2 tablespoons olive oil
⅛ to ¼ teaspoon salt

1. Cook the carrots in salted boiling water until tender enough to be pierced with a fork (about 20 minutes). Purée the carrots in a food processor fitted with the steel blade, or in a food mill. Push the purée through a fine sieve to remove any large pieces.

2. Proceed as directed for Basic Egg Pasta, adding the carrot purée to the flour well with the eggs, olive oil, and salt, and blending well. Allow 15 minutes' drying time before cutting the pasta.

FOOD PROCESSOR PASTA

Makes 6 to 8 servings (about 1½ pounds)

You can speed up the process of mixing the dough by doing it in your food processor, which works very well.

2 to 2½ cups unbleached,
   all-purpose flour
Pinch of salt
3 large eggs
2 tablespoons olive oil

1. Place the flour and salt in the bowl of a food processor fitted with the steel blade. Turn the machine on and off once.

2. Beat the eggs slightly in a small bowl. With the machine running, pour the eggs through the feed tube and process for about 12 seconds, or until the mixture resembles coarse meal. Add the oil and continue processing until the dough forms a ball.

3. Remove the dough, and divide it into three portions. Cover the dough with a damp towel to prevent it from drying out, and let it rest for 10 minutes. Roll the dough and cut it as directed for Basic Egg Pasta (page 187).

TAGLIARINI WITH PROSCIUTTO AND GREEN PEAS

Makes 4 to 6 servings

Tagliarini noodles are narrower than fettuccine. Either prepare pasta following the basic recipe, or, if you have a source for fresh pasta, buy 1 to 1½ pounds of tagliarini. Nadia Frigeri introduced us to this divine sauce.

Basic Egg Pasta (page 187), made with 3 cups flour and 4 eggs

2 tablespoons unsalted butter
⅓ cup finely chopped onion
1 cup fresh or frozen green peas
1 cup heavy cream
3 ounces prosciutto, cut in strips
Salt and freshly ground pepper, to taste
½ to ¾ cup freshly grated Parmesan cheese

1. Melt the butter in a heavy saucepan and sauté the onions over medium heat until they are translucent. Stir in the peas and the cream, and cook the sauce, covered, over low heat for 10 minutes, or until the peas are tender (about 4 minutes for frozen peas).

2. Add the prosciutto, and cook the sauce for 5 minutes more. Season it with salt and pepper (go easy on the salt; the prosciutto and cheese are salty).

3. Bring a large pot of salted water to a boil, and cook the pasta until it is al dente. Drain the pasta and toss it with the sauce. Top with the Parmesan cheese.

TORTELLINI WITH CREAM SAUCE

Makes 4 servings (8 first-course servings)

This is another of those recipes that looks formidable but actually is simple when you break it down into steps. The filling can be made a day ahead and refrigerated, though with a food processor it takes no more than 20 minutes. The tortellini themselves take some practice, but they, too, can be made ahead of time and frozen or refrigerated. The cream sauce is simplicity itself, and goes together in just about the time it takes to heat the cream. In fact, the cream sauce variation requires no cooking at all, just mixing.

Rumor has it that the man who invented tortellini did so because he was enamored of Botticelli's Venus and created the pasta shape to resemble her navel. That may be apocryphal, but it makes a good dinner-party story.

TO PREPARE THE FILLING

¾ pound pork loin
¼ pound prosciutto, minced
¼ pound mortadella, minced
2 eggs
½ teaspoon freshly grated nutmeg (or to taste)
Freshly ground pepper, to taste
¾ cup freshly grated Parmesan cheese
⅓ cup heavy cream (optional)

1. Dice the pork loin finely, removing all fat, and sauté it in a skillet until the meat loses its pink color. Remove the pork from the skillet with a slotted spoon and let it drain in a colander. Pour the fat from the skillet and sauté the prosciutto and mortadella in the skillet for several minutes. Drain them well, combine them with the pork in the work bowl of a food processor fitted with the steel blade, and mince finely. (The mixture can also be minced by hand or in a meat grinder.)

2. Beat together the eggs, nutmeg, and pepper. Stir in the minced meat mixture and the Parmesan cheese, blending thoroughly. If it seems dry, add enough cream to make it moist but not at all runny. Set the filling aside.

TO MAKE THE PASTA DOUGH

4 cups unbleached, all-purpose flour
5 eggs

Mound the flour on a work surface, make a well in the center, and break in the eggs. Using a fork, beat the eggs lightly, then incorporate the flour. When the dough becomes stiff enough to form a ball, knead it for at least 10 minutes, or until it is smooth and elastic (this can also be done in a food processor; see page 190). Wrap the dough in plastic wrap and let it rest 1 hour. Cut the dough into five portions.

Using a pasta machine, roll one portion at a time, keeping the remaining dough covered with a towel while you form the tortellini. (For more detailed instructions, see Basic Egg Pasta, page 187.)

TO FORM THE TORTELLINI

1. Sprinkle a towel with flour or bread crumbs and set it aside. Using a pasta cutter, cut the rolled dough into 2-inch squares or circles. Spoon about ½ teaspoon of the filling on each square. Do not overstuff. Fold the squares or circles in half to form triangles or semicircles that enclose the filling. Press the edges together firmly to seal. Put your finger on the long edge and bring the two corners of the triangle or semicircle around your finger, overlapping them. Press one end over the other to form a little circle. (This is easy to do but rather difficult to describe. Buy tortellini from a good pasta shop to see how they should look, then try forming one following our directions. Your first attempts may seem a little inelegant, but you'll get the hang of it with practice, and they'll taste just fine, no matter how they look.)

2. As the tortellini are formed, place them on the floured cloth, making sure they don't touch each other, or they'll stick together. Turn over the tortellini every couple of hours until they are completely dry. Refrigerate, uncovered, until ready to use. They also can be placed in a single layer on a cookie sheet, dusted with flour, and frozen. Once they're frozen solid, pack them in plastic freezer bags.

FINAL ASSEMBLY AND SAUCE

½ cup unsalted butter
1 cup heavy cream
2 egg yolks, lightly beaten
½ cup freshly grated
    Parmesan cheese

1. Bring a large pot of salted water to a boil, add 1 tablespoon oil and the tortellini, and boil the fresh pasta for about 2 to 3 minutes. (To cook frozen tortellini, drop them into the boiling water while they are still frozen, and cook for about 6 minutes.) Do not overcook; the tortellini should be al dente. Remove the pasta with a slotted spoon to a warm dish while you make the cream sauce.

2. *To make the cream sauce:* Melt the butter in a

medium saucepan until it foams. Add the cream, and cook it over medium-high heat, stirring, until the cream thickens. Beat the egg yolks. Spoon a little of the hot cream into the yolks, beating constantly, then, off the heat, beat the heated yolk mixture into the cream. Return the pan to very low heat and cook the sauce, whisking constantly, until it thickens. Do not let it boil, or it will curdle.

3. Pour the cream sauce over the tortellini, mixing very gently. Add the Parmesan cheese, and serve immediately. Pass additional freshly grated Parmesan at the table.

Cream sauce variation (adapted from Giuliano Bugialli)

Place ¾ cup unsalted butter in a skillet and place the skillet over the pot of boiling water you use for cooking the pasta. When the butter melts, toss the cooked pasta in it until coated. Stir in 2 cups heavy cream and 2 cups (8 ounces) freshly grated Parmesan cheese. Over very low heat, toss the pasta gently in the sauce and season it with freshly ground white pepper and nutmeg to taste. This sauce would work with any cooked pasta.

As a further variation, gently cook ½ to 1 teaspoon minced garlic or garlic purée in the butter before adding the pasta.

"COMBED" PASTA WITH SAUSAGE AND PORCINI CREAM SAUCE

Makes 4 servings

Garganelli is a specialty of Emilia-Romagna. In that region it is made with a special tool called a *pettine,* or "comb." When we tested this recipe (brought to us by Biba Caggiano) as a candidate for this book, the verdict was "absolutely superb." The sauce is great on other pasta, such as fettuccine.

Making the pasta is time-consuming and sounds complicated, but try it and you'll see it's easy. Put some Italian opera on the tape deck, sing along, sip some Chianti, and you'll be finished before the tenor's last big aria.

TO MAKE THE PASTA

2 cups unbleached,
   all-purpose flour
3 eggs

1. Mound the flour on a flat work surface, make a well in the center, and break in the eggs. Using a fork, beat the eggs lightly, then incorporate the flour. When the dough becomes stiff enough to form a ball, knead it for at least 10 minutes, or until it is smooth and elastic (this can also be done in a food processor; see page 190). Let the dough rest, covered with a towel, for 20 minutes. Cut the dough into three portions. Using a pasta machine, roll one portion at a time, keeping the remaining dough covered with a towel. (For more detailed instructions, see Basic Egg Pasta, page 187.)

2. Cut the pasta into 1½-inch squares with a fluted pastry wheel or a sharp knife. Put a clean, large-toothed comb on the work surface, with the teeth facing away from you. Place a pasta square over the comb, with one corner of the square pointed toward you. Place a pencil on this corner, with the pencil parallel to the long edge of the comb. Roll the pasta around the pencil, pressing it gently into the teeth of the comb as you roll it away from you, so the teeth of the comb make indentations on the pasta. Gently slide the pasta cylinder off the pencil, and place it on a tray lined with a kitchen towel. Repeat the forming step with the remaining pasta. The pasta can be cooked immediately or dried.

TO MAKE THE SAUCE

1 ounce dry porcini
   mushrooms
½ cup lukewarm water
2 sweet Italian-style sausages
   (4 to 5 ounces)
4 tablespoons butter
¾ cup dry white wine
1 cup heavy cream
1 tablespoon chopped fresh
   parsley
Pinch of powdered saffron
Salt and freshly ground
   pepper, to taste

1. Soak the mushrooms in the water for 20 minutes. Remove the mushrooms and place them in a colander to drain. Strain the soaking liquid through several layers of dampened cheesecloth, and set the liquid aside.

2. Remove the sausages from their casings and finely chop the meat. Melt the butter in a large skillet over medium heat, and when the butter begins to foam, add the chopped sausage. Cook the sausage over medium heat until it loses its raw color, breaking it up as it cooks. Increase the heat to high, add the wine, and cook, stirring constantly, until the wine evaporates.

3. Add the reserved mushroom-soaking liquid and the chopped mushrooms to the sausage, and simmer the mixture, uncovered, over medium heat until the water is nearly gone (about 15 to 20 minutes). Add the cream, parsley, and saffron, and season with salt and pepper. Simmer the sauce until it is fairly thick.

FINAL ASSEMBLY

¾ cup freshly grated Parmesan cheese

1. Bring a large pot of water to a boil. Add 1 tablespoon of salt and the pasta. Cook the pasta, uncovered, until it is al dente (a minute or less for very fresh pasta, longer for dried). Drain the pasta and add it to the skillet with the sauce.

2. Sprinkle the pasta with the Parmesan cheese, and mix it gently over low heat until the pasta is well coated with the sauce. Serve it immediately with additional Parmesan cheese.

SPINACH LASAGNE WITH CHEESE AND BASIL STUFFING

Makes 8 servings

Jerrie Strom brought us the recipe after an extended tour of Italy. Do try to use homemade tomato sauce, either the one below or one of the variations on page 198. If you're in a hurry, or if your produce department's tomatoes look sickly pink instead of ripe red, use canned tomatoes — but taste the sauce before you add salt, because canned tomatoes can be very salty. In either case, the sauce can be made a day in advance.

TO PREPARE THE PASTA

1 recipe Spinach Pasta (page 188)

1. Using a pasta machine, roll the pasta dough to the next-to-narrowest setting. Dry the pasta to a leathery texture and cut it into 3-inch strips or 4-inch squares.

2. Cook the pasta in salted boiling water for about 30 seconds, or until it is barely al dente. Immediately transfer the cooked pasta to a bowl of cold water that has a little olive oil in it, to stop the

cooking. Remove the cooled pasta with a slotted spoon and let it rest in a single layer between dampened cotton kitchen towels.

TO PREPARE THE TOMATO SAUCE

¼ cup olive oil
3 cloves garlic, chopped
2 pounds fresh tomatoes, peeled, seeded, and chopped (or 2 cans, 1 pound each, whole tomatoes, chopped)
Salt and freshly ground pepper, to taste

1. Heat the olive oil in a nonaluminum saucepan over medium heat, and sauté the garlic for 1 minute, or until it is light golden. Add the tomatoes, lower the heat, and simmer the mixture, covered, for 15 minutes. (If using dried basil, simmer it with the sauce.) Season with salt and pepper.

2. Purée the sauce, using a food mill, blender, or food processor fitted with the steel blade. Return it to the saucepan and cook over medium heat for 15 minutes. Taste the sauce again and adjust the salt and pepper. Transfer the sauce to a bowl to cool completely (about 1 hour).

TO PREPARE THE CHEESE STUFFING

15 ounces ricotta cheese
4 tablespoons freshly grated Parmesan cheese
8 ounces mozzarella cheese
20 fresh basil leaves (or 2 teaspoons dried)

Combine the ricotta and Parmesan cheeses in a bowl, and sprinkle them with salt and pepper. Coarsely grate the mozzarella cheese and put it in a separate bowl.

FINAL ASSEMBLY

1. Preheat oven to 375°. Heavily oil a glass, porcelain, or enamel-coated gratin pan (13 by 9 inches). Line the pan completely with pasta, leaving a 1-inch overhang on the sides. Cover the pasta with about a quarter of the tomato sauce, and sprinkle on some of the fresh basil leaves, if you're using them. Add a second layer of pasta, trying not to overlap the pasta strips or squares. Layer with a third of the cheese filling. Top it with a third layer of pasta, and with a third of the grated mozzarella.

2. Continue adding layers of pasta and alternating the tomato sauce and cheese fillings in the same order, ending with a layer of mozzarella. Cover the cheese with a layer of pasta and fold the overhanging pasta ends over the top. Pour on the last of the

tomato sauce and sprinkle fresh basil leaves on the top. Bake the lasagne for about 25 minutes, or until the sauce bubbles and the lasagne is heated through. Allow the pasta to rest at least 15 minutes before serving.

TOMATO SAUCE VARIATIONS

Mushroom

Sauté 1 pound thinly sliced mushrooms in 3 table-spoons butter and add them to the sauce.

Herb

Add ½ cup minced fresh Italian parsley to the sauce, or 1 teaspoon dried oregano, thyme, or marjoram (or 1 tablespoon of the fresh herb).

Sausage

Slice 1 pound hot Italian sausage and cook it in a skillet with ¼ cup water until the water evaporates and the sausage browns in its own fat. Layer the drained sausage with the cheese and sauce.

TOMATO SAUCES

In our cooking school classes, teachers have presented dishes using tomato concassé, tomato frappé, tomato coulis, plain old tomato sauce, and tomato purée. We've put together a collection of the best of them.

The first is a basic recipe by Jacques Pépin that can serve as a foundation for pasta sauces, and which can be used in any recipe that calls for tomato sauce. The two that follow use only fresh tomatoes, either uncooked or slightly cooked. These sauces have a nice garden quality, as opposed to the deep tomato flavor achieved by adding tomato paste (as in the first sauce) or by combining fresh tomatoes, stewed tomatoes, and tomato paste. The lighter, fresher sauce is favored by *nouvelle cuisine* chefs and is used as a garnish on soups or in combination with sauces cooked in the *nouvelle* style. It is also excellent with poached or light fish preparations. One word of caution, however — you really need excellent quality, ripe tomatoes for these sauces to have any flavor. The final two sauces are traditional and versatile for use with almost all pasta.

BASIC TOMATO SAUCE

Makes about 6 cups

1 tablespoon butter
2 tablespoons olive oil
2 medium onions, diced
　(about 1 cup)
2 carrots, peeled and diced
　(about 1 cup)
2 leeks, white and tender
　green only, diced
2 ribs celery, diced
2 to 3 cloves garlic, un-
　peeled and crushed
1 can (6 ounces) tomato
　paste
3 tablespoons unbleached,
　all-purpose flour
4 cups brown stock
　(page 313)
2 cups water
1 teaspoon salt
8 to 10 whole peppercorns,
　crushed
1 teaspoon sugar
1 bay leaf, crushed
¼ cup coarsely chopped
　fresh parsley
1 teaspoon fresh thyme (or
　½ teaspoon dried)
1 teaspoon fresh oregano (or
　½ teaspoon dried)
1 teaspoon fresh tarragon
　(or ½ teaspoon dried)
1 tablespoon olive oil
6 medium tomatoes (about
　1¼ pounds), coarsely
　chopped

1. Heat the butter and the 2 tablespoons oil in an enameled cast-iron sauté pan or 4-quart Dutch oven. When the mixture foams, add the onions, carrots, leeks, celery, and garlic. Sauté the mixture about 5 to 6 minutes, or until the onions are translucent. Stir in the tomato paste, flour, brown stock, water, salt, and peppercorns.

2. Bring the mixture to a boil, stirring occasionally. Reduce the heat to a simmer and add the sugar, bay leaf, parsley, thyme, oregano, and tarragon. Cook the mixture, uncovered, for 45 minutes. Remove any scum or foam with a skimmer.

3. Heat the 1 tablespoon olive oil in a small skillet and sauté the chopped tomatoes until most of their liquid has evaporated (about 10 minutes).

4. Add the cooked tomatoes to the sauce and simmer gently for 25 minutes to blend the flavors. Strain the sauce through a chinoise, pressing out all of the flavorful juices. (The sauce may be frozen in 1-cup containers for future use.)

NOTE

When you are ready to use the sauce, you can enrich it with butter, cooked ground beef, fried bacon, fresh herbs, or freshly grated Parmesan cheese. If you like your sauce chunky, peel, seed, and chop 1 tomato, sauté it for a few minutes in olive oil, and add to the sauce.

FRESH TOMATO SAUCE

Makes 3 cups

You can change the personality of this sauce by substituting basil, tarragon, or chervil for the thyme and adding 2 tablespoons of freshly grated Parmesan or other hard cheese. This sauce has a nice fresh tomato flavor because it does not contain any tomato paste. Be sure to use ripe, quality tomatoes, or the sauce will be flat in flavor. You may also substitute fresh Italian plum tomatoes when they are available. Serve the sauce over baked or broiled fish or omelets.

1 teaspoon olive oil
3 tablespoons chopped
  shallots
4 cloves garlic, minced
  (about 2 teaspoons)
8 large tomatoes, peeled,
  seeded, and diced
1 teaspoon chopped fresh
  thyme (or ½ teaspoon
  dried)
1 teaspoon sugar (optional)
1 teaspoon salt
½ teaspoon freshly ground
  pepper
1 bay leaf
2 tablespoons minced fresh
  chives
2 tablespoons minced fresh
  parsley

1. Heat the olive oil in a medium, nonaluminum saucepan, and sauté the shallots and garlic until they are limp (about 5 minutes). Stir in the tomatoes, thyme, sugar (if used), salt, pepper, and bay leaf. Bring the mixture to a boil, reduce the heat to low, and simmer the sauce, uncovered, for 20 to 25 minutes. (This is a coarse sauce. If you want a smooth texture, purée it.)

2. Stir in the chives and parsley.

COLD TOMATO PURÉE

Makes about 2 cups

This sauce has a nice bite and perks up cold vegetable pâtés and fish mousses, which tend to be bland.

1 ¼ pounds tomatoes, peeled and seeded
1 clove garlic, peeled
1 ½ tablespoons fresh lemon juice
1 large yellow onion, peeled and quartered
4 to 6 tablespoons fresh basil (or 2 tablespoons dried)
¼ cup olive oil
½ to 1 serrano or jalapeño chili pepper
Salt and freshly ground pepper, to taste

Combine the tomatoes, garlic, lemon juice, onions, basil, olive oil, and chili peppers in the work bowl of a food processor fitted with the steel blade (remove the seeds from the chilies if you want the sauce less hot). Process the mixture to a coarse purée. Taste it for seasoning and add salt and pepper to taste.

TOMATO SAUCE WITH BACON

Makes about 4 cups

3 to 4 tablespoons olive oil
1 small onion, chopped
¼ pound pancetta (Italian bacon), diced small (see note)
1 can (28 ounces) Italian plum tomatoes

1. Heat the olive oil in a saucepan and sauté the onions over medium heat until golden. Add the pancetta and sauté until it is lightly colored.

2. Put the tomatoes through a food mill to remove the seeds and add the tomatoes to the simmering bacon mixture. Simmer the sauce, covered, over low heat for 30 minutes, or until the sauce has thickened. Serve the sauce over pasta, topped with grated Parmesan cheese.

NOTE

Regular bacon may be substituted for pancetta, but blanch the bacon a couple of minutes in boiling water before adding it to the onions.

ITALIAN MEAT SAUCE

Makes 10 cups

This is a very thick sauce, delicious in lasagne or over spaghetti. The flavor actually is better the second day, so if you have time, make the sauce in advance and refrigerate it to allow the flavors to blend. The sauce also can be frozen.

1 pound hot Italian sausage, casings removed
1 pound lean ground beef
1 large onion, chopped
1 cup red wine
5 tomatoes (about 1½ pounds), peeled, seeded, and diced
1 can (15 ounces) tomato purée
1 can (6 ounces) tomato paste
2 teaspoons salt (or to taste)
1 teaspoon freshly ground pepper
½ teaspoon ground fennel seed
4½ tablespoons chopped fresh basil (or 1½ tablespoons dried)
1 tablespoon dried oregano
2 bay leaves
2 tablespoons garlic purée (about 12 cloves)
2 cups sliced mushrooms (optional)
1 cup water

1. Brown the sausage and ground beef in a large kettle, crumbling them as they cook. When the beef loses most of its color, pour off the fat and stir in the onions. Cook the mixture until the meat is no longer pink. Stir in the wine and simmer until the liquid is reduced by half. Stir in the tomatoes, tomato purée, tomato paste, salt, pepper, fennel, basil, oregano, bay leaves, garlic, and mushrooms (if using them). Add the water, and simmer the sauce, covered, for about 1 hour.

2. Remove the bay leaves. At this point the sauce can be refrigerated for up to three days, or frozen for three months.

ACCOMPANIMENTS

Not so very long ago, it seems, the vegetable world was a severely limited one, containing only mashed potatoes, canned beans, and frozen corn or peas. Nowadays there is a wealth of vegetables available in supermarkets year round, and there is little reason for anyone to use any canned produce, except stewed tomatoes, tomato sauce, and tomato paste because modern agribusiness has all but ruined the tomato for human consumption.

The French have always been marvelously exuberant with vegetable side dishes, which are often more complicated to cook than the entrée. They are especially inventive with parts of vegetables we throw out, such as using the root of celery in salads or cooking fennel like a vegetable instead of thinking of it as just an herb. We throw the whites of leeks into our stockpot; the French turn them into delicious gratins. We spend hours eradicating dandelions from our lawns; they pick them for the evening salad. We think of nasturtium as a pretty spring blossom; they think of it as an edible garnish.

Space limits our offering of vegetable side dishes, but we hope these will inspire you to experiment. There are only so many ways you can prepare meat but endless ways you can bring excitement to meals with vegetables.

New York's Maurice Moore-Betty is masterful with vegetables. His vegetable dishes are colorful and crisp, a delight to the eye and the palate. His trick is to blanch each vegetable group individually to a crispy stage; he then plunges them quickly into water with ice cubes to preserve color. Two things are very important in this process: the vegetables must not be overcooked, and they should stay in the ice water only a few seconds so they don't get waterlogged. He drains the vegetables on paper towels. At this point the vegetables may be held in individual airtight containers. When ready to serve, quickly sauté the vegetables in a little butter.

CELERY ROOT AND CARROT SAUTÉ

Makes 6 to 8 servings

Suzy Eisenman created this recipe while testing another for us. For a more elegant presentation, and to shorten cooking time, cut the celery root and carrots into julienne strips.

This dish is superb with braised shoulder of veal or lamb.

2 celery roots (1 pound each)
2 bunches carrots
2 tablespoons unsalted butter
2 tablespoons virgin olive oil
2 tablespoons fresh lemon juice
1 tablespoon anise seeds, crushed (optional)
Salt and freshly ground pepper, to taste
2 tablespoons minced fresh parsley

1. Wash and peel the celery root and carrots, and cut them into 1½-inch dice.

2. Melt the butter and olive oil in a skillet over medium heat. Sauté the celery root and carrots for 8 to 10 minutes. Add the lemon juice and anise and season with salt and pepper. Cover the pan and simmer the mixture over lowest heat about 5 to 7 minutes, or until the vegetables are fork-tender. Garnish them with the parsley just before serving.

GEORGE MUNGER'S CARROTS

Makes 6 servings

This carrot dish was developed by George and Ben Patterson. Since carrots are always available fresh and go with virtually anything, we think of this side dish as a good friend and standby. It is easy, fast, and delicious, and it's a godsend for crowds. Use the thin slicing blade of the food processor or a mandolin for quick slicing.

8 tablespoons unsalted butter
3 cups thinly sliced carrots (about 6 large carrots)
1 tablespoon sugar
1 tablespoon chopped fresh dill

1. Melt the butter in a large skillet or low-sided sauté pan and add the carrots, tossing to coat them with the butter. Cover the pan, and simmer the carrots over medium heat for 10 minutes.

2. Uncover the pan, sprinkle on the sugar, and raise the heat to high. Sauté the carrots for 5 minutes, tossing them constantly. Sprinkle with the dill and serve immediately.

CHAYOTE DON JAVIER

Makes 6 servings

"Don Javier" is F. J. Sauza, president of Tequila Sauza, S.A. He grows chayote squash at his La Jolla home and shares them and his recipes with friends, among them Ben Patterson. Chayote is divine with grilled or barbecued poultry.

3 pounds chayote squash
  (see note)
4 tablespoons butter, melted
2 tablespoons fresh lime
  juice
1 teaspoon salt
½ teaspoon Tabasco
3 tablespoons chopped cilantro (fresh coriander)

1. Peel the chayote and cut it into 1-inch cubes, including the edible seeds. Put the cubes in a large saucepan with boiling water to cover, and boil the squash for 5 minutes. Drain it well.

2. In a warm serving bowl, combine the butter, lime juice, salt, Tabasco, and cilantro, and toss gently with the chayote.

NOTE

To make it easier to remove the sticky chayote juice from your hands, rub them lightly with oil before peeling the squash. Afterward rub your hands with the lime peel, then wash with warm, soapy water.

GRATIN OF ZUCCHINI

Makes 6 servings

We've adapted this Jacques Pépin recipe for leeks, eggplant, and all sorts of moist yet firm vegetables. It's a great side dish for roasted meats.

2½ pounds zucchini,
  unpeeled, cut in
  2-inch chunks
4 large eggs
½ cup unbleached,
  all-purpose flour
1 cup heavy cream
1 cup freshly grated Swiss
  cheese
Salt and freshly ground
  white pepper, to taste

1. Place the zucchini in a saucepan with just enough water to cover. Bring it to a boil, reduce the heat, and simmer until the zucchini is barely tender. Drain in a colander.

2. Purée the zucchini, using a food processor fitted with the steel blade, or a food mill. Whisk together the eggs, flour, and cream until smooth, and stir into the zucchini with the cheese, salt, and pepper, blending the mixture thoroughly.

3. Preheat oven to 350°. Butter a ½-quart gratin dish and pour the zucchini mixture into it. Place on

a baking sheet and bake the gratin for 45 minutes.
(If the gratin is not browned enough on the top, run
it under a broiler for 1 minute.) Allow the zucchini
to rest for 10 to 15 minutes before serving.

JACQUES PÉPIN'S BROCCOLI WITH GARLIC

Makes 6 servings

For variety, garnish the broccoli with crumbled feta cheese instead of olives. This
dish may be chilled and served as a salad. Serve it with a hearty meat entrée — it
can easily overpower a bland or delicate dish.

2 bunches broccoli (about 3
  pounds total)
1 can (2 ounces) anchovy
  fillets, drained
4 large cloves garlic, finely
  chopped
5 tablespoons virgin olive oil
Freshly ground pepper, to
  taste
¾ cup oil-cured, pitted ripe
  olives, for garnish

1. Cut the florets from the broccoli. Peel the
stems and cut them into 1-inch pieces. Bring ½
inch of salted water to a boil in a large, shallow
saucepan. Add the broccoli and cook it, covered,
over high heat for 3 to 4 minutes. Drain and set it
aside.

2. Mash the anchovy fillets into a purée using a
mortar and pestle. Combine the purée with the
garlic and olive oil in a small saucepan and cook the
mixture for about 10 seconds. Combine the purée
with the broccoli, toss, and season with pepper (it
shouldn't need additional salt). Garnish the broccoli
with the olives, and serve lukewarm.

"THOSE TOMATOES"

Makes 6 servings

This dish was first prepared by Professor Travis Bogard at his Berkeley home, and
Ben Patterson adapted it for Lunch at The Perfect Pan. I can well imagine why he
called it "Those Tomatoes," having often watched Ben peel an entire gross of
slippery little cherry tomatoes. The effort is surely worth it, and the final preparation is simple. You can blanch and peel the tomatoes ahead and bake them just
before serving.

These tomatoes are a delicious and colorful accompaniment to sautéed and grilled
fish and chicken entrées. They also make a nice counterpoint to steak au poivre.

48 cherry tomatoes
½ cup dry vermouth
1 teaspoon salt
½ teaspoon freshly ground
   pepper
1 teaspoon garlic powder

1. Using a basket, immerse the tomatoes in boiling water for 3 to 4 seconds, and drain. Peel the tomatoes by removing the stem and cutting a small cross at the stem end. The peels should slide off easily.

2. Preheat oven to 350°. Place the tomatoes in one layer in a shallow baking dish. Sprinkle them with the vermouth, salt, pepper, and garlic powder, and bake them, uncovered, for 10 minutes. (They also may be baked at higher temperatures, along with other parts of the meal. Just vary the time.) The tomatoes should be cooked through but still retain their shape and texture. Serve immediately.

BAKED STUFFED TOMATOES

Makes 9 servings

Stuffed tomatoes go wonderfully well with roasted and sautéed meats, such as chicken, pork chops, beef or veal roast, and steak.

9 ripe medium tomatoes
2 cups fresh whole-wheat or
   rye bread crumbs
2 cloves garlic, minced
1 to 2 tablespoons capers,
   drained, rinsed, and
   finely chopped
3 tablespoons chopped fresh
   parsley
3 tablespoons minced
   fresh herbs: cilantro
   (fresh coriander), basil, or
   tarragon
4 tablespoons freshly grated
   Parmesan cheese
3 tablespoons virgin olive oil
Salt and freshly ground
   pepper, to taste

1. Cut the tomatoes in half crosswise. Gently squeeze or scoop out the seeds and discard them. Sprinkle the tomatoes with salt and let them drain, cut-side down, in a colander for 30 minutes.

2. Stir together the bread crumbs, garlic, capers, parsley, herbs, and Parmesan cheese. Sprinkle the mixture with the olive oil, tossing to blend well. Season with salt and pepper.

3. Preheat oven to 375°. Brush the bottom of a shallow baking dish with olive oil. Stuff the tomato halves with the bread-crumb mixture and place them in the dish in a single layer. Bake them for about 30 minutes, or until the filling is crispy and brown and the tomatoes are tender. Serve immediately.

TURNIPS STUFFED WITH ROQUEFORT

Makes 4 servings

Stuffed turnips are delicious with roast beef or poultry. Make them in advance, then tuck them around the roast in the last 15 or 20 minutes of roasting time to take on flavor from the pan juices. Another time, try using a chèvre instead of Roquefort. Anne Otterson brought us the recipe after one of her frequent trips to Europe.

1 pound turnips, peeled and quartered
2 ounces Roquefort cheese
2 tablespoons butter
2 tablespoons minced shallots
3 medium mushrooms, minced
1 teaspoon fresh thyme (or ¼ teaspoon dried)
Salt and freshly ground pepper, to taste
½ cup heavy cream
2 tablespoons chopped fresh chives

1. Boil the quartered turnips in salted water about 10 minutes, or until they are just tender. Drain them in a colander.

2. When the turnips are cool enough to handle, trim them into rounds with a paring knife and slice off the top third of each round to form lids. Scoop out the pulp from the bottoms to form small cups. Reserve the scooped-out turnip pulp. Set the turnip cups and lids aside, and keep them warm.

3. Using a food processor fitted with the steel blade, or a food mill, purée the reserved turnip pulp and the Roquefort. Set the purée aside.

4. Melt the butter in a small saucepan and cook the shallots and mushrooms for 2 to 3 minutes. Add the turnip-cheese purée, the thyme, and salt and pepper, and cook for another minute. Stir in the cream and cook the sauce over medium-high heat until it is quite thick (about 8 to 10 minutes).

5. Spoon the sauce into the turnip cups and top them with the lids. Brush the tops of the turnip lids with a little of the sauce and sprinkle them with the chives. Serve warm.

To peel bell peppers and chilies: Using a long fork, hold the pepper over an open flame, turning it to char the entire surface. Or place the pepper under the broiler until it blisters, turning it occasionally so that it is evenly charred. Place it in a plastic bag, and let it sweat for 15 minutes. Peel it under cool running water, and slice it into strips.

ROASTED RED ONIONS AND SWEET PEPPERS

Makes 8 servings

Jerrie Strom, founding chairman of the San Diego Center for the American Institute of Wine and Food, and fellow "foodie," brought us this great idea for a side dish. The sauce also makes a wonderful dip for raw vegetables.

6 red onions
2 cups dry white wine
    (approximately)
6 red bell peppers
6 green bell peppers
4 tablespoons unsalted
    butter
¼ cup virgin olive oil
1 clove garlic, finely
    chopped
6 anchovy fillets in oil
Freshly ground pepper,
    to taste

1. Trim the root ends and the papery skins from the onions, leaving the onions whole. Place the onions in a roasting pan that will hold them snugly in a single layer. Pour enough white wine over them to come up their sides about 1 inch. Tightly cover the pan with foil.

2. Preheat oven to 350°. Place the peppers directly on the oven rack and place the pan of onions in the oven also. Roast the peppers and onions about 1 hour, or until the peppers are browned and blistered but not charred and the onions are tender when pierced with a fork.

3. Remove the peppers from the oven and place them in plastic bags to "sweat." When the peppers are cool enough to handle, rub them with a towel, and the skins should slip off easily. Cut the peppers in half, remove the seeds and stems, and cut the peppers into ½-inch-wide strips, or larger pieces. Cut the onions into quarters.

4. Melt the butter and olive oil together in a terra cotta pot or saucepan over very low heat. Do not let the butter sizzle. Add the garlic. Drain the anchovies and add them to the pot, mashing them with a fork. Season with pepper. (The sauce should not need additional salt, because the anchovies are salty.) Whisk the sauce about 2 minutes, or until it forms a smooth emulsion. Keep it warm.

5. To serve, mix the onions with the peppers and arrange them on a serving platter. Spoon the sauce over all.

HERBED NEW POTATOES

Makes 4 servings

Herb-flecked potatoes make a pretty garnish for a platter of roast meat or poultry, and these are very quick and easy to prepare. The potatoes can stand 5 or 10 minutes after cooking, with the pan partially covered. The style of cooking was brought to us by Paula Wolfert.

1½ pounds small new potatoes (about 8 to 10 potatoes)
1 cup rich chicken stock, preferably homemade (page 317)
3 tablespoons unsalted butter
Kosher-style salt, to taste
Fresh herbs:
  for beef: 1 tablespoon each, thyme and oregano
  for lamb: 2 tablespoons dill or rosemary
  for chicken: 2 tablespoons thyme or tarragon

1. Scrub the potatoes and arrange them in a heavy skillet in a tight, single layer. Add the chicken stock, cover the skillet, and cook the potatoes over high heat for about 20 minutes, or until the liquid has almost evaporated. Lower the heat, add the butter, and cook the potatoes, covered, for 10 minutes, shaking the pan often.

2. Test the potatoes for doneness. They should be tender, but not mushy. Sprinkle the potatoes with the salt and herbs, and serve.

POMMES BYRON

Makes 6 servings

When nothing will do but a big, fluffy baked potato, consider these — favorites with us for years. You'll end up with leftover baked potato shells, happy-hour mainstays in Southern California when they're baked until crispy, topped with grated cheese, and served with sour cream and crumbled bacon. The Pommes Byron can be prepared ahead of serving, to finish baking with the main course.

8 large baking potatoes
½ cup unsalted butter
1 cup heavy cream
½ cup sliced fresh chives
¼ cup sour cream
1 egg

1. Preheat oven to 450°. Bake the potatoes for 1 hour, or until they are tender. Let the potatoes cool slightly, slice them in half, scoop out the pulp, and reserve 6 of the half shells, setting aside the rest for other recipes. Reduce the oven temperature to 350°.

2. In a small saucepan, heat the butter and cream

½ cup freshly grated
   Parmesan cheese
½ cup freshly grated
   Gruyère cheese
½ cup chopped fresh parsley
½ teaspoon salt
¼ teaspoon freshly ground
   white pepper
¼ teaspoon freshly grated
   nutmeg
¼ teaspoon paprika

until the butter is melted. Using a hand mixer, beat the potato pulp with half of the butter-cream mixture until it is smooth. Thoroughly beat in the chives, sour cream, egg, Parmesan and Gruyère cheeses, parsley, salt, white pepper, and nutmeg. Slowly add enough of the remaining butter-cream mixture until the potatoes have the texture of thick whipped cream (add more cream if the potatoes seem dry).

3. Using a pastry bag fitted with a large fluted tip, pipe the potato cream into the 6 potato shells, mounding it up high, and sprinkle them with the paprika. (They may be refrigerated at this point, tightly covered with plastic wrap, for up to two days.)

4. Place the potatoes on a baking sheet and bake at 350° for 30 minutes (about 15 minutes longer if they've been taken right out of the refrigerator). They should be golden brown. Serve immediately.

POTATO NESTS

Makes 6 large or 10 small nests

Crisp nests of fried potato make delicious baskets for serving cooked vegetables, creamed or unsauced. The larger baskets can also hold beef Stroganoff, chicken in velouté sauce, seafood Newburg, and leftovers bound with a béchamel.

Use peanut oil when frying the baskets, because it can take a high frying heat without smoking. You will need a wire potato-nest basket form, available at any good cookware shop or well-stocked housewares department. You don't need a deep-fryer; any pan with sides high enough to cover the basket and keep the oil from splattering will do. A Chinese wok is good for this purpose.

1 pound White Rose
   potatoes, peeled
Peanut oil, for deep-frying
Cooked vegetables for filling
   (such as peas and carrots,
   baby onions, Brussels
   sprouts, or broccoli
   florets)

1. Using a mandolin, or by hand, cut the potatoes into fine matchstick or julienne. The potatoes may also be shredded using a food processor fitted with the coarse shredding blade, or by hand. However, more starch is extracted from the potatoes when they are shredded, often making it more difficult to remove the nest after frying. In either case, do not rinse the potatoes, because the surface starch helps bind the potatoes during frying.

2. In a saucepan deep enough to accommodate the potato-nest basket, heat the oil to 360°. Dip the empty basket quickly in and out of the hot oil.

3. Line the outer basket with about ½ cup of the potatoes, and put the inner basket in place. Carefully dip it into the hot oil. When the potato nest begins to brown, loosen the inner basket and continue cooking until the potatoes are golden. Release the nest with the tip of a small knife, if necessary, and remove it gently. Drain the nest on brown grocery bags (they are more absorbent and less expensive than paper towels). You can also remove the nest from the basket by whamming it upside-down against the counter onto the bag. Repeat until all the potatoes are used.

4. Fill the potato nests with vegetables cooked to crisp-tender and sauced or buttered, and serve immediately.

NOTE

The nests may be made several hours in advance. To reheat, bake the nests on a cookie sheet at 400° for 5 to 7 minutes, or until they are nicely crisped.

For an elegant special-occasion breakfast

Make the nests the day before and store on cookie sheets in a dry place. Fill reheated nests with creamy scrambled eggs, top with a dollop of *crème fraîche* or sour cream and the best caviar you can afford. Or top with crisscrossed slices of smoked salmon. Serve with a whole baked ham, muffins, and a large platter of fresh fruit.

⁂ When deep-frying, it is a good idea to keep a box of baking soda handy in case the oil should accidentally catch fire. Baking soda will put out a cooking fire, whereas water may actually cause it to spread. For deep-frying vegetables, the oil should be at 360°. If the oil temperature is too low, too much oil will be absorbed in the food, making it soggy instead of crisp. If the oil is too hot, you risk a very real fire hazard.

POTATO SKINS STUFFED WITH LEEKS AND THREE CHEESES

Makes 8 servings

This is an Anne Otterson creation, hearty enough to be an entrée. Serve it with a small portion of roasted meat or grilled sausages, and a crisp salad.

4 large Russet potatoes,
    baked
3 leeks
1 tablespoon butter
½ cup heavy cream
½ cup milk
4 eggs, beaten
½ cup freshly grated Gouda
    cheese
½ cup freshly grated Havarti
    or Doux de Montagne
    cheese
Salt and freshly ground
    pepper, to taste
Freshly grated nutmeg,
    to taste
½ cup freshly grated
    Parmesan cheese

1. Preheat broiler. Cut the baked potatoes in half and scoop out the pulp, leaving a ¼-inch shell. Mash the pulp and set it aside. Place the potato shells under the broiler for 3 to 5 minutes to crisp them slightly.

2. Thoroughly wash the leeks and chop them coarsely, including the tender green. Put the leeks and the butter in a small saucepan with about 1 inch of water, bring the mixture to a boil, reduce the heat, and cook the leeks, covered, about 8 to 10 minutes, or until they are very tender. Make sure the water doesn't completely boil away. Thoroughly drain the leeks and purée them using a food processor fitted with the steel blade.

3. Gently heat the cream and milk in a small saucepan. Do not let them boil.

4. Beat together the leeks, potato pulp, and heated milk and cream. Beat in the eggs, then stir in the grated Gouda and Havarti or Doux de Montagne. Season the mixture with salt, pepper, and nutmeg.

5. Preheat oven to 350°. Spoon the cheese mixture into the potato shells, mounding the filling, and top with the grated Parmesan cheese. (The potatoes may be refrigerated at this point.) Place the filled potato shells in a baking dish and bake for 20 to 25 minutes, or until the filling is puffy and the top is bubbly. (If the potatoes have been refrigerated, increase the baking time by 15 or 20 minutes.) Serve immediately.

POTATO SKINS DOREG

Makes 12 servings

Potato Skins Doreg are a Saturday night treat at the famed Golden Door spa in northern San Diego County. Spa chef Michel Stroot gave us this recipe. Save the cooked potato pulp for another, more fattening, occasion.

6 Russet baking potatoes
Vegetable oil
Fresh or dried herbs (see note)
Freshly ground pepper

1. Preheat oven to 400°. Scrub the potatoes thoroughly and pierce them in several places with a long fork. Sprinkle a small amount of oil on each potato and rub it into the skins so the entire surface is filmed with oil. Bake the potatoes for 1¼ hours, or until tender. Remove the potatoes from the oven.

2. Reduce the oven temperature to 375°. When the potatoes are cool enough to handle, cut them in half lengthwise and scoop out most of the potato pulp. Sprinkle the potato shells with a few drops of oil and season them lightly with fresh or dried herbs of your choice, and freshly ground pepper. Bake the shells for 40 minutes or until they are nice and crisp.

NOTE

Combinations of herbs, such as thyme and rosemary, oregano and parsley, parsley and dill (particularly good with fish), or parsley and sage, are delicious on these potato shells. They're also good simply with plain black pepper — freshly ground, of course.

WILD RICE STEAMED WITH MUSHROOMS

Makes 6 to 8 servings

This recipe is an adaptation of one by Maurice Moore-Betty.

1 pound mushrooms, sliced
½ cup unsalted butter
8 ounces wild rice
1½ cups rich chicken stock,
   preferably homemade
   (page 317)
½ cup dry vermouth

1. In a medium saucepan with a tight-fitting lid, sauté the mushrooms in the butter until golden. Add the rice and stir to coat it evenly with the butter. Pour in the chicken stock and vermouth. Bring the mixture to a boil, cover, and turn off the heat. Let it stand undisturbed for 1 hour.

2. Stir the rice lightly, add water just to the level of the top of the rice, and bring it back to a boil. Reduce the heat to the lowest setting and steam the rice, tightly covered, for 30 minutes. Fluff it with a fork before serving.

6

ENTRÉES FOR ENTERTAINING

Sole with Caviar Beurre Blanc · Striped Bass with Mushrooms · Salmon with Moutarde de Meaux and Tomato Beurre Blanc · Salmon Steaks with Caper Beurre Blanc · Diana Kennedy's Pompano with Green Sauce · Seafood Lasagne · Fettuccine with Scallop Sauce · Nadia Frigeri's Spinach Ravioli with Meat Filling and Cream Sauce · Green Cannelloni with Ricotta Filling · Poulet Suprême Maurice · Stuffed Chicken Breasts with Watercress Sauce · Roasted Chicken with Red Wine Vinegar Sauce · Filets Mignons with Roquefort Sauce · Fillet of Beef with Capers · Braised Stuffed Flank Steak · Rolled Flank Steak with Mushrooms · Nadia Frigeri's Veal Scallops with Lemon Juice · Anne Otterson's Veal with Mustard Sauce · Veal with Green Peppercorn Sauce · Perfect Pan Rack of Lamb · Roast Lamb with Onion Sauce · Crown Roast of Pork with Apple and Sausage Stuffing · Choucroute Garnie · Strom and Jenkins' Mexican Stew · Arrington's Irish Chili · Feijoada Completa

WHETHER THE GUEST LIST IS LARGE or small, whenever we entertain, the accent is in equal measure on good food and lively company. We enjoy sit-down dinner parties for six to twelve, and we think it's fun to include guests who have not met before but we suspect will enjoy one another's company. Out of these little dinners, many long-term friendships have formed. In contrast to this intimate approach are big affairs like the annual George Munger Cook-Off, which is a moveable feast of dishes prepared and presented by about a hundred guests. Each dish — we try to have no more than fifty — is rated by judges and is eligible for an award in its category. The top food award for culinary expression is the Grand Prize, but the Gladys Schwartz Award gets the big action. Gladys Schwartz, named for her maker, is a handmade cloth doll, about five feet tall, which I found at a senior citizens' center crafts shop. The winner gets to take Gladys home for one year.

The Gladys Schwartz doll has been awarded to ambitious entrants for the most improved dish and other notable feats. In recent years, she has been awarded for "excess," which can mean anything from lavish ingredients to gaudy presentations. At the Fourteenth Annual George Munger Cook-Off in 1984, Gladys went home with Lorenzo and Olga Gunn, who presented their ham hocks and collard greens with a performance by break dancers. The Gunns narrowly beat Frank and Linnea Arrington, who had a forty-piece marching band present their root beer floats. (Head Judge in Perpetuity Al Jacoby observed that the cook-off was, after all, a contest in food preparation, and root beer floats were inadequate in cooking technique.) Frank and Linnea are formidable competitors in the Gladys Schwartz category. One year they presented a soufflé-like savoury aloft in a hot-air balloon bearing the message "Arrington's Soufflés Rise Higher." Another time, they presented a curry from atop a trained Indian elephant.

Whatever the presentations, the cook-off is always a fabulous event. Though the demands of business now prevent us from holding it annually, we still always look forward to the next one. A number of award-winning recipes from the cook-offs appear in this book.

As hosts for any event, we always try to convey a sense of effortlessness, even though considerable organization has gone into the planning. We have some advantages in that we have Piret's catering staff to call on, and for the cook-offs, Piret's managers keep kitchen schedules moving and guests apprised of their presentation time. Without this help, the cook-offs would be chaos instead of fun. Still, with or without help, the success of any sort of party is based on advance planning.

When planning your menu, organize the courses or foods so that most of them can be made ahead of time or require very little last-minute attention, especially if you are doing all of the cooking yourself. And don't tackle a dish you are unfamiliar with, or a whole group of extremely complicated dishes. Instead, make one course the headliner of the menu, with all others in supporting roles. The calmer and more organized the cook is, the better the food and the party.

Watching our cooking teachers organize themselves for class has provided helpful guides to enjoying cooking for company. First, and most important, organize in advance. Our teachers break down each recipe step by step, premeasuring each ingredient on a separate tray according to when it will be used. This ensures that you won't have to find and measure an ingredient or figure out what you are doing at a critical cooking point. It also eliminates nasty surprises, like finding midway into the recipe that you are missing an ingredient.

Anne Willan, founder of La Varenne, the famous cooking school in Paris, and Julia Child are superb teachers and impressively organized cooks. We like to follow their example when entertaining. On separate sheets of paper, they organize the whole menu recipe by recipe and step by step. The whole meal is mapped out on a flow chart so that while one dish is baking, they can be working on another one or two simultaneously. Anne and Julia tape their flow charts in sequence on the refrigerator, cupboard doors, and walls, for easy reference.

For a buffet, dishes must be selected carefully. Avoid any that will dry out if it sits out too long or that can't be kept at the ideal serving temperature. For a large buffet, have several serving stations. Depending on the number of dishes and guests, you might consider a salad area, a separate table for the entrées, and another for desserts. This will keep guests from lining up to get to the food. Or you might have one buffet for cold foods, another for hot dishes. Try to put out small portions of each dish, with back-ups ready in the kitchen. Large portions of hot food will tend to get cold, and cold foods warm. The presentation of your buffet will lose its charm with disheveled platters and bowls. Reserve replenishments will keep your buffet as attractive at the end of the meal as it was in the beginning.

Diana Hewett, for many years manager of the Perfect Pan shops, and Jerrie Strom have inspired me to think creatively about table decor and centerpieces. Both of them use everything from heirloom quilts to designer bedsheets to cover tables, and centerpieces range from collectibles to fresh greens and produce. Jerrie teaches a class we call Sensuous Tables, where she puts together a dozen examples of party themes, from casual to elegant to festively ethnic. Through Jerrie, students learn to see everyday objects in a new and creative way.

We like to put lots of bouquets of fresh flowers around the house. This is a simple and relatively inexpensive way of achieving a festive air. And we think music adds to the mood. We vary it according to the occasion, the guests, or the particular part of the evening: perhaps chamber music as guests arrive, quiet piano or violin concertos during dinner, and jazz with coffee and after-dinner drinks.

In this chapter, you will find a wide range of entrées for entertaining. Some of the dishes are very simple, while others require advance planning. We've purposely chosen entrées that either cook for a long time — which means that you have little last-minute fussing in the kitchen — or that can be accomplished quickly at the last minute. Many of the dishes, such as Arrington's Irish Chili, the Seafood Lasagne, and the Feijoada Completa, are great for serving a crowd and work well in a buffet setting. Other dishes, including the Filets Mignons in Roquefort Sauce and the Stuffed Chicken Breasts with Watercress Sauce, are perfect for a small sit-down dinner.

SOLE WITH CAVIAR BEURRE BLANC

Makes 6 to 8 servings

George taught this recipe in one of his caviar classes. The caviar beurre blanc would be great on other fish, including snapper or bass. Try it with salmon, using salmon roe instead of black caviar. This dish is a last-minute preparation — beurre blanc cannot sit around for long — however, the fish takes but a minute or two to cook, so make the sauce first and keep it warm. For more information on beurre blanc, see page 329.

TO MAKE THE BEURRE BLANC

¼ cup dry white wine
¼ cup white wine vinegar
1½ tablespoons shallots, minced
1 cup unsalted butter, firm but not cold, cut into 16 pieces
¼ teaspoon kosher-style salt
Scant ¼ teaspoon freshly ground white pepper
1 jar (2 ounces) black caviar, drained

1. In a nonaluminum saucepan, combine the wine, white wine vinegar, and shallots. Bring them to a boil, lower the heat, and cook, uncovered, until the liquid is reduced to 3 tablespoons (about 5 minutes).

2. Quickly raise the heat to high and bring the reduction to a fast boil. Add the pieces of butter all at once and whisk vigorously so the butter melts evenly. Continue whisking over medium-high heat as the mixture thickens into a creamy sauce. When just two or three small lumps of butter are not yet incorporated into the sauce, quickly pour the contents of the saucepan into a small bowl. Stir the sauce until it is smooth, and season it with the kosher-style salt and white pepper. (Undersalt the sauce because the caviar is also salty.)

3. Gently stir in 1 to 2 tablespoons of the caviar. Set the sauce aside in a warm place (makes about 1 cup).

TO PREPARE THE SOLE

6 to 8 sole fillets
½ cup unsalted butter
Freshly ground white pepper, to taste
Juice of 1 to 2 lemons

1. Cut the sole fillets in half lengthwise. Melt the ½ cup butter in a skillet and sauté the fillets for 1 to 2 minutes on each side. Sprinkle the fish with white pepper and drizzle with the lemon juice.

2. Spoon about 4 tablespoons of the sauce onto each warmed dinner plate and place one fillet on top. Garnish each fillet with a small dollop of caviar, and serve immediately.

STRIPED BASS WITH MUSHROOMS

Makes 6 servings

Paula Wolfert makes this dish using oysters. Since I'm allergic to oysters but love bass, we've preserved the idea of the dish, substituting mushrooms. Chanterelle and shiitake mushrooms are available at many specialty shops.

3 ounces dried shiitake or chanterelle mushrooms

2 cups warm water or fish stock (page 318)

2 tablespoons diced carrot

2 tablespoons diced celery

2 tablespoons coarsely chopped leek, white part only

1 cup water

4 striped bass fillets (8 ounces each), skin left on

Salt and freshly ground white pepper, to taste

2 tablespoons minced shallots

1 teaspoon minced fresh parsley

½ cup dry white wine

1 cup *crème fraîche*

¼ teaspoon each: ground cumin, coriander, turmeric, and ginger

1 medium carrot, julienne-cut

Parsley sprigs, for garnish

1. Soak the dried mushrooms in the warm water or fish stock for 1 hour. Drain them well, and strain the soaking liquid through a double layer of dampened cheesecloth. Reserve the liquid. Slice the mushrooms and set them aside.

2. Combine the diced carrot and celery and the leek in a small saucepan and add the 1 cup water. Bring the mixture to a boil, reduce the heat, and simmer the vegetables for 10 minutes. Strain the liquid into a clean saucepan and discard the vegetables. Reduce the liquid over high heat to ⅓ cup, and keep it hot.

3. Preheat oven to 425°. Butter a deep, ovenproof skillet or flameproof casserole wide enough to hold the fish in a single layer. Season the fish with salt and white pepper. Scatter the shallots and chopped parsley into the skillet and arrange the fish over them, skin-side up. Pour on the wine, the reduced vegetable-cooking liquid, and ⅓ cup of the reserved mushroom-soaking liquid. Bake the fish for 7 to 10 minutes, or until the fish is barely translucent in the center (err on the side of undercooking). When the fish is done, remove it to a warmed platter and cover it with a sheet of aluminum foil. (It will continue to cook slightly as it stands.)

4. Over high heat, rapidly reduce the liquid in the skillet to ¼ cup. Whisk in the *crème fraîche*, bring the sauce to a boil, and cook it over medium heat, whisking constantly, for 1 minute, or until the sauce coats the back of a spoon. Strain the sauce into a clean saucepan and stir in the cumin, coriander, turmeric, and ginger. Gently reheat the sauce and add the sliced mushrooms. Taste for seasoning, and adjust if necessary. If the sauce is too thick, thin

it with a few spoonfuls of mushroom-soaking liquid; if it is too thin, reduce it by boiling.

5. While the sauce finishes heating, drop the carrots into boiling water to blanch for 1 minute, then drain them.

6. To serve, place the fish fillets on warmed individual serving plates and spoon on the sauce. Garnish with the blanched carrots and a few sprigs of parsley. Serve immediately.

SALMON WITH MOUTARDE DE MEAUX AND TOMATO BEURRE BLANC

Makes 4 servings

Brown-speckled, mustardy *crème fraîche* coats fish fillets in this dish from Paula Wolfert, who learned it from Georges Blanc. Other fish, such as swordfish or halibut, may be substituted for the salmon. If thicker fillets are used, the fish should be broiled on one side, turned halfway through the cooking time, coated with more *crème fraîche*, and broiled until done. Figure 10 minutes' total cooking time for each inch of thickness of the fish. For more information on beurre blanc, see page 329.

TO MAKE THE BEURRE BLANC

1 pound ripe tomatoes
2 tablespoons fruity olive oil
Salt, to taste
½ teaspoon freshly ground pepper
⅛ teaspoon crumbled dried thyme leaves
1 tablespoon minced shallots
2 tablespoons dry white wine
2 tablespoons white wine vinegar
¼ cup *crème fraîche*
8 tablespoons unsalted butter, cut into large pats

1. Remove the stem plugs from the tomatoes. Drop them into boiling water for 10 seconds to loosen the skins. Drain and peel the tomatoes. Remove the seeds, and cut the tomatoes into small dice. Heat the olive oil in a small skillet, add the tomato cubes, and cook them over medium-high heat, stirring, until they are thick and well reduced (about 7 or 8 minutes). Season the sauce with salt, and add the pepper and thyme.

2. In a medium, nonaluminum saucepan, bring the shallots, wine, and white wine vinegar to a boil, and boil until the mixture is reduced by half. Lower the heat slightly, whisk in the *crème fraîche,* and cook the mixture over high heat until it is reduced by half. Lower the heat slightly again, and whisk in the butter, a piece at a time. When all of the butter has

been added and the mixture is thick and foamy, pour it into the tomato purée, straining it if you wish to eliminate the texture of the shallots. Adjust the seasoning, and set the sauce in a warm place (a double boiler set over hot water works well), until ready to serve.

TO PREPARE THE SALMON

1 salmon fillet (about 1 pound), skin left on
1½ tablespoons unsalted butter
1 teaspoon salt (approximately)
½ cup *crème fraîche* or heavy cream
2 tablespoons Moutarde de Meaux

1. Place the salmon skin-side down on a cutting board and cut the fish into 4 scallops, cutting at about a 30° angle. Discard the skin. Run your hand over the surface of the fish to make sure no small bones remain. Thinly slice any salmon trimmings and reserve them.

2. Coat a heavy baking sheet with the butter. Arrange the salmon scallops equal distances apart on the baking sheet. Add any extra pieces of salmon to the scallops, dividing it up equally among them so the scallops will cook at the same rate. Sprinkle each fillet with about ¼ teaspoon salt.

3. In a small mixing bowl, combine the *crème fraîche* with the mustard, blending them well. Coat the top of each salmon fillet with the mixture.

4. Broil the fish 4 inches from the heat source for 3 to 5 minutes, or until the creamy topping is glazed and spotted brown. To serve, spoon about ⅓ cup of the tomato beurre blanc on each of four warmed dinner plates, and carefully top each with a salmon fillet. Serve immediately.

SALMON STEAKS WITH CAPER BEURRE BLANC

Makes 6 servings

Jack Monaco has taught this marvelous recipe many times at The Perfect Pan. He and George have also cooked it on television. It's simple but elegant. For more information on beurre blanc, see page 329.

TO MAKE THE BEURRE BLANC

4 tablespoons dry white
    wine
4 tablespoons white wine
    vinegar
1½ tablespoons minced
    shallots
¾ pound unsalted butter, at
    room temperature, cut
    into chunks
⅓ cup capers, drained
¼ teaspoon kosher-style salt
¼ teaspoon freshly ground
    white pepper

Combine the wine, white wine vinegar, and shallots in a small, nonaluminum saucepan. Bring the mixture to a boil, lower the heat, and cook the mixture until it is reduced to about 3 tablespoons. Quickly raise the heat to medium-high and bring the reduction to a boil. Remove the pan from the heat and whisk in the butter one piece at a time, allowing each piece to emulsify before whisking in the next. You may have to move the pan on and off the heat to keep the sauce hot enough to emulsify the butter but not so hot that the butter melts and becomes oily. When all the butter has been added, whisk the sauce until it is thick and creamy. Stir in the capers, and season with the kosher-style salt and white pepper. Keep the sauce warm in a double boiler or thermos bottle.

TO PREPARE THE SALMON

6 salmon steaks
Salt and freshly ground
    pepper, to taste
1 tablespoon unsalted butter
¼ cup heavy cream
    (approximately)
1 red onion, thinly sliced
6 cloves garlic, minced
6 bay leaves
Pinch of dried thyme

1. Preheat oven to 400°. Lightly salt and pepper the salmon. Use the 1 tablespoon butter to thoroughly grease an ovenproof baking dish large enough to hold the fish in a single layer without touching. Pour enough of the cream into the dish to barely cover the fish, and top each steak with a few onion slices, some garlic, a bay leaf, and a pinch of thyme. Bake the fish for 5 to 10 minutes, or until the fish is opaque and tests done when pierced with a fork or skewer. (Alternatively, you may cook the fish under the broiler for 10 to 12 minutes, to give the cream topping a golden-brown color.)

2. To serve, spoon some of the beurre blanc onto each warmed dinner plate and center a salmon steak

on the sauce. Top, if desired, with a little more sauce, and serve immediately.

DIANA KENNEDY'S POMPANO WITH GREEN SAUCE

Makes 4 servings

Diana Kennedy has become a dear and close friend to many of us in San Diego over the years. A scholar of the first order and a remarkable cook, her humor, good fellowship, and extraordinary common sense make us look forward to her every visit. Because her ingredients and cooking methods are not easily accessible, we've not included many of her recipes here — but I strongly recommend her wonderful books if you are interested in learning Mexican cuisine, and for exceptionally fine reading.

This recipe has been successfully prepared with striped bass. A 4-pound bass is about right for this amount of sauce, and takes between 1 and 1½ hours to cook.

2 pompano (about 1¼ pounds each)
¼ teaspoon peppercorns
¼ teaspoon cumin seeds
½ teaspoon salt
Juice of 1 large lime

GREEN SAUCE

2 cloves garlic
½ green (bell) pepper
1 serrano chili
3 sprigs cilantro (fresh coriander)
3 sprigs fresh parsley
6 scallions
1 pound green (unripe) tomatoes
⅛ teaspoon dried oregano
1 tablespoon champagne wine vinegar
⅓ cup water
¼ teaspoon salt

6 tablespoons virgin or extra-virgin olive oil

1. Clean the fish, leaving the heads and tails on. Using a mortar and pestle, grind together the peppercorns, cumin seeds, and salt. Add the lime juice to the ground seasonings.

2. Prick the fish all over with a coarse-tined fork and rub in the seasonings mixture. Place the fish in an ovenproof dish and set it aside to macerate for at least an hour.

3. *To make the green sauce:* Roughly chop the garlic, green pepper, serrano chili, cilantro, parsley, scallions, and tomatoes. Using a blender or food processor fitted with the steel blade, purée the chopped ingredients with the oregano, vinegar, water, and salt until the sauce is smooth.

4. Preheat oven to 300°. Brush 2 tablespoons of the olive oil on the undersides of the fish, then cover the fish with the remainder of the oil and the sauce. Cover the dish with aluminum foil, and bake the fish for 20 minutes. Carefully turn the fish over, re-cover, and bake for an additional 15 to 20 minutes, basting occasionally. Serve immediately.

SEAFOOD LASAGNE

Makes 8 to 10 servings

Serve this delicious dish with crusty French bread and champagne or a Fumé Blanc. Jack Monaco taught this recipe in 1983 and we've enjoyed it many times since.

PASTA

3½ cups unbleached,
   all-purpose flour
4 to 5 eggs
1 tablespoon vegetable oil
1 teaspoon salt

CHEESE FILLING

2 cups ricotta cheese
4 egg yolks
3 tablespoons freshly grated
   Parmesan cheese
Scant ⅛ teaspoon freshly
   grated nutmeg
1 teaspoon salt
½ teaspoon freshly ground
   pepper
½ teaspoon sugar
4 tablespoons minced
   scallions or chives

SEAFOOD FILLING

½ pound sea scallops
½ pound salmon fillet
½ pound medium shrimp
   (25 to 30 per pound),
   shelled
Court bouillon (page 319) or
   water, to cover

SAUCE

2 tablespoons butter
2 tablespoons unbleached,
   all-purpose flour
2 cups heavy cream
2 cups reserved court
   bouillon

TO MAKE THE PASTA

1. Mound the flour on a flat work surface, and make a well in the center. Place the eggs, oil, and salt in the well and gently mix them with the flour using a fork. When the dough becomes stiff enough to form a ball, knead it for at least 10 minutes, or until it becomes smooth and elastic. Let the dough rest, covered with a towel, for 20 minutes.

2. Using a pasta machine, roll the dough to the next-to-narrowest setting. Dry the pasta to a leathery texture (about 10 minutes) and cut it into 3-inch strips or 4-inch squares. (For more detailed instructions, see page 187.)

3. Cook the pasta in salted boiling water for about 30 seconds, or until it is barely al dente. Immediately transfer the cooked pasta to a bowl of cold water that has a little olive oil in it, to stop the cooking. Remove the cooled pasta with a slotted spoon and let it rest in a single layer between dampened cotton kitchen towels.

TO PREPARE THE FILLINGS AND SAUCE

1. Combine the ricotta, egg yolks, Parmesan, nutmeg, salt, pepper, sugar, and scallions in a bowl and blend them thoroughly. Set the filling aside.

2. Remove any connective tissue from the scallops, cut them in half horizontally, and then into quarters. Poach the scallops, salmon, and shrimp very lightly, about 3 to 5 minutes, in enough court bouillon or water to cover. Lift the seafood out of the liquid with a slotted spoon and let it cool in a colander. Strain the liquid through a double layer of dampened cheesecloth, and reserve 2 cups.

3. Melt the butter in a saucepan over medium

heat. Whisk in the 2 tablespoons flour and cook the roux for 3 to 4 minutes. Whisk in the cream and bring the sauce to a boil to thicken. Add the 2 cups of reserved poaching liquid and cook the sauce over medium heat until it is reduced to 3 cups.

FINAL ASSEMBLY

4 hard-cooked eggs, sliced
¾ cup freshly grated
    Parmesan cheese
8 ounces mozzarella cheese,
    thinly sliced

1. Preheat oven to 350°. Butter a 9 × 12 inch lasagne pan. Spoon in a layer of the sauce, and cover it with a single layer of the cooked pasta. Do not overlap the pasta. Add layers, in order, of the poached seafood, sliced hard-cooked eggs, cheese filling, sauce, and pasta. Repeat in the same order, ending with a layer of the sauce. Sprinkle on the Parmesan cheese and spread the mozzarella slices over the top.

2. Bake the lasagne for 45 minutes. Let set for 15 minutes to firm up before serving.

FETTUCCINE WITH SCALLOP SAUCE

Makes 6 to 8 servings

Whole bay scallops are called for in this recipe, but you also could use larger sea scallops, sliced. Be sure to trim and clean them thoroughly.

TO MAKE THE PASTA

3 cups unbleached,
    all-purpose flour
4 eggs
Pinch of salt
1 teaspoon virgin or extra-
    virgin olive oil

1. Mound the flour on a flat work surface and make a well in the center. Place the eggs, salt, and olive oil in the well and mix them with the flour, using a fork. When the dough becomes stiff enough to form a ball, knead it for at least 10 minutes, until it becomes smooth and elastic. Let the dough rest, covered with a towel, for 20 minutes.

2. Using a pasta machine, roll the dough to the next-to-narrowest setting, cut fettuccine noodles, and let the pasta dry (for more detailed instructions, see page 187).

TO MAKE THE SCALLOP SAUCE

4 tablespoons unsalted
  butter
2 small carrots, minced
  (about 1 cup)
1 bunch scallions, minced
  (about ¾ cup)
½ cup minced fresh parsley
1½ cups dry white wine
2 tomatoes, peeled, seeded,
  and minced
Salt and freshly ground
  pepper, to taste
¾ pound bay or sea scallops
¾ cup heavy cream
3 teaspoons fresh tarragon
  (or 1 teaspoon dried)
3 teaspoons fresh thyme (or
  1 teaspoon dried)

1. Melt the butter in a saucepan over medium heat. Add the carrots, scallions, and parsley, and sauté until the vegetables are limp. Stir in the wine and tomatoes, reduce the heat to low, and simmer the sauce gently for 10 to 12 minutes. Season the sauce with salt and pepper. Add the scallops and cook them about 2 minutes, or until they are no longer translucent. Remove the scallops from the sauce with a slotted spoon and set them aside.

2. Stir the cream into the sauce over medium heat. Add the tarragon and thyme, and cook the sauce until it is reduced by half (about 10 minutes).

FINAL ASSEMBLY

1. Bring a large pan of salted water to a boil and cook the pasta until al dente (2 to 3 minutes for fresh pasta; follow package directions for packaged pasta). Drain the fettuccine well and keep it warm.

2. Return the scallops to the sauce and toss them gently to heat them through. Spoon the sauce over the cooked pasta and serve immediately.

NADIA FRIGERI'S SPINACH RAVIOLI WITH MEAT FILLING AND CREAM SAUCE

Makes 6 to 8 servings

Spinach ravioli are also good topped with a light tomato or meat sauce.

TO MAKE THE PASTA DOUGH

3 cups unbleached,
  all-purpose flour
3 large eggs
¾ cup chopped cooked
  spinach, squeezed very
  dry

Mound the flour on a flat work surface. Make a well in the center and break the eggs into it. Stir in the spinach, oil, and salt. Using a fork, beat the eggs slightly, then start incorporating the flour to make a dough. Knead the dough about 10 minutes, wrap it

1 tablespoon olive oil
Pinch of salt

in plastic wrap, and let it rest for 1 hour. (For more detailed instructions for making and rolling pasta dough, see page 187.)

TO FILL THE PASTA

½ pound boneless veal or chicken (or ¼ pound each)
¼ pound prosciutto, trimmed of excess fat
¼ pound mortadella (or more prosciutto)
4 tablespoons unsalted butter
1 cup dry white wine
2 eggs, beaten
½ cup freshly grated Parmesan cheese
Salt and freshly ground pepper, to taste
Freshly grated nutmeg, to taste

1. Using a meat grinder or food processor fitted with the steel blade, or by hand, finely mince the veal or chicken, prosciutto, and mortadella. Melt the butter in a saucepan over medium heat and sauté the ground meats until they are a light golden color. Add the wine, reduce the heat to low, and cook the mixture, covered, until the liquid is reduced to about ¼ cup. Remove the saucepan from the heat and stir in the eggs and Parmesan cheese, and season with salt, pepper, and nutmeg. Set the filling aside to cool.

2. Cut the pasta dough into three pieces. Cover two pieces with a towel so they don't dry out while you roll out and fill the first piece of dough. Roll the dough to the next-to-last narrowest setting on the pasta machine.

3. Using a pasta-cutting wheel, cut the pasta into 2-inch squares. Put 1 teaspoon of the meat filling in the center of each square, fold the square in half, and press the edges together to seal the ravioli. Repeat with remaining squares. Place the raviolis on trays dusted with flour until ready to cook. (They may be lightly dusted with flour at this point and frozen. Cook the unthawed raviolis in a large pot of rapidly boiling water.) Repeat the rolling and filling step with the remaining two pieces of pasta dough.

4. Bring a large pot of salted water to a boil over high heat. Add the raviolis and cook to the al dente stage (about 2 to 3 minutes). When they start to pop to the surface of the boiling water, taste one for doneness. Drain the raviolis and set them aside.

TO MAKE THE SAUCE

1 cup unsalted butter
1 cup heavy cream
2 cups freshly grated
   Parmesan cheese
2 teaspoons crushed dried
   rosemary

Melt the butter in a wide skillet and stir in the cream. Bring the cream to a boil over moderately low heat. Sprinkle in the Parmesan cheese and rosemary. Lightly toss the cooked ravioli in the sauce, heating them for about 2 minutes. Serve the raviolis immediately.

🍂 Pasta-cutting wheels are available with a straight or fluted cutting edge. Also available at specialty shops are ravioli molds and presses, which come in square and round shapes. With the mold, which is a rectangular plaque, you place a sheet of pasta in the mold, add the filling, and top it with another sheet of pasta. Pass a rolling pin over the top of the plaque to cut the raviolis into uniform pieces.

GREEN CANNELLONI WITH RICOTTA FILLING

Makes 8 servings

Cannelloni are the Italian version of crêpes. This is our variation of a cannelloni dish prepared by Giuliano Bugialli.

TO MAKE THE PASTA

3½ cups unbleached,
   all-purpose flour
2 extra-large eggs
1 heaping tablespoon
   minced cooked spinach,
   squeezed dry (about ½
   pound fresh spinach)
2 teaspoons vegetable oil
Pinch of salt

2 tablespoons vegetable oil
1 teaspoon salt

1. Place the flour in a mound on a flat work surface and make a well in the center. Place the eggs, spinach, 2 teaspoons oil, and a pinch of salt in the well, mix the liquids with a fork, then begin to mix in the flour, stirring it in a bit at a time from the inside of the flour mound. Knead the dough for 5 minutes. Wrap it in plastic wrap and let it rest 1 hour.

2. Cut the dough into two pieces, and roll each with a pasta machine, starting at the widest setting. Dust the pasta with flour, shaking off the excess, if it starts to stick. Roll the pasta to the next-to-narrowest setting, and cut the strips of pasta into 6-inch squares or rounds. Let them dry for 1 hour. (For more detailed instructions, see page 187.)

3. Bring a large pot of water containing the 2

tablespoons oil and 1 teaspoon salt to a rolling boil. Cook the pasta squares for several minutes, a few at a time, until they are pliable but still firm. Remove them from the water with a slotted spoon, and plunge them briefly into cold water to which a few tablespoons of oil have been added. Layer the cooked pasta between dampened towels.

TO PREPARE THE FILLING

¼ cup minced fresh parsley
16 ounces ricotta cheese
2 cups (8 ounces) freshly
   grated Parmesan cheese
2 whole eggs
2 egg yolks
Salt and freshly ground
   pepper, to taste
Freshly grated nutmeg,
   to taste

Combine the parsley, ricotta and Parmesan cheeses, eggs, and egg yolks, stirring to mix them well. Season the filling with salt, pepper, and nutmeg. Refrigerate, tightly covered, until needed.

TO PREPARE THE BÉCHAMEL

3 tablespoons butter
¼ cup unbleached,
   all-purpose flour
1½ cups milk
Salt, to taste

Melt the butter in a saucepan over medium heat. Whisk in the flour and cook the roux for 2 minutes. Do not let it brown. Whisk in the milk all at once and cook the sauce over medium heat, whisking constantly, until it is smooth and thick (about 5 to 10 minutes). Season it with salt, but lightly — the cheese will also add a salty taste. Remove the pan from the heat and set the béchamel aside, covered, until needed.

FINAL ASSEMBLY

2 cups freshly grated
   Parmesan cheese
   (optional)

1. Place a piece of pasta on a work surface and spread 3 tablespoons of the filling along one side. Roll the pasta, enclosing the filling. Repeat with the remaining pasta and filling.

2. Preheat oven to 375°. Place the cannelloni in two well-buttered 13½ × 8¾ inch baking dishes. Spoon the béchamel over the cannelloni and, if desired, sprinkle 1 cup of the Parmesan cheese over each dish. Bake the cannelloni for 20 minutes. If you used the additional Parmesan cheese, run the

dishes under the broiler until the top is browned and bubbly. Let the cannelloni stand 10 minutes before serving.

POULET SUPRÊME MAURICE

Makes 6 servings

Servings are very generous in this terrific dish devised by Maurice Moore-Betty, so plan on serving the chicken with a simple side dish.

½ pound fresh mushrooms
½ cup fresh whole-wheat bread crumbs
1 tablespoon minced fresh tarragon (or 1 teaspoon dried)
3 tablespoons minced fresh parsley
Salt and freshly ground pepper, to taste
½ cup minced cooked ham
¾ cup dry Marsala
6 tablespoons butter, melted
6 whole chicken breasts, boned, skin left on
Unbleached, all-purpose flour, seasoned with salt and freshly ground pepper
½ cup rich chicken stock, preferably homemade (page 317)
Watercress and chopped fresh parsley, for garnish

1. Wipe the mushrooms with a damp cloth and chop them finely. Combine them with the bread crumbs, tarragon, parsley, salt, pepper, and ham. Moisten the mixture with about ½ cup of the Marsala and 3 tablespoons of the melted butter — enough to make the filling moist but not soggy.

2. Brush the chicken with some of the melted butter and dust with salt and pepper. Place the small fillets on the thinner part of the meat (where the ribs were). Place about 1 tablespoon of the filling mixture on each breast. Fold each side of the breast to the center (the shape will resemble a closed fist).

3. Preheat oven to 450°. Place the breasts, seam-side down, in a well-buttered flameproof baking dish, brush them with melted butter, and dust them with the seasoned flour. Bake the chicken breasts for 30 minutes, basting occasionally with the pan juices.

4. Remove the chicken to a serving platter and reduce the oven temperature to 180°. Cover the chicken with aluminum foil and put it back in the low oven to keep warm while you finish the sauce.

5. Deglaze the baking dish with the chicken stock and remaining ¼ cup of Marsala, and boil it over high heat until it is reduced by half. Adjust the seasoning, and spoon the sauce over the chicken breasts. Garnish with watercress and parsley.

STUFFED CHICKEN BREASTS WITH WATERCRESS SAUCE

Makes 8 servings

An Anne Otterson recipe in the *nouvelle* style.

VEGETABLE STUFFING

2½ tablespoons butter
1 medium carrot, peeled and minced
½ medium onion, peeled and minced
2 medium mushrooms, minced
1 large (¾ ounce) truffle, minced (optional)
¼ teaspoon dried thyme
Salt and freshly ground pepper, to taste

8 boneless, skinless chicken breast halves
Salt and freshly ground pepper, to taste
2 teaspoons butter
1 leek, white part only, finely sliced
1 teaspoon minced shallot
½ cup tightly packed watercress, stems removed
2 tablespoons Port
1 cup rich chicken stock, preferably homemade (page 317)
1 cup *crème fraîche* or heavy cream
2 egg yolks
3 tablespoons cold water

1. *To prepare the stuffing:* Heat the butter in a small saucepan, and cook the carrots over medium heat for 3 minutes. Stir in the onions and cook for 3 minutes more. Stir in the mushrooms and the truffle, if used, and cook the mixture 3 minutes longer, stirring frequently to prevent sticking. Add the thyme and season with salt and pepper. Let the stuffing cool so you can handle it easily when stuffing the chicken.

2. Using a sharp knife, cut a pocket in each chicken breast, being careful not to cut them all the way through. Lightly salt and pepper each pocket, and stuff them with the vegetable mixture. To enclose the stuffing, close the pocket in each chicken breast with a 4-inch bamboo skewer.

3. Heat the 2 teaspoons butter in a large skillet and cook the leeks and shallots over medium heat for 10 minutes, stirring frequently. Do not let the leeks brown. Stir in the watercress, Port, chicken stock, and *crème fraîche* or cream, and simmer the mixture over medium heat for another 10 minutes.

4. Place the chicken breasts in the cream sauce and simmer them over low heat for 10 to 15 minutes, turning them once, until they are barely cooked through. They will continue to cook while resting. Remove them from the skillet with a slotted spoon, and arrange them on an ovenproof serving platter. Keep the chicken warm in a 180° oven while you finish the sauce.

5. Pour the cream sauce into a blender and process until smooth. Transfer the sauce to a small saucepan, bring it almost to a boil, reduce the heat to low, and keep the sauce very hot but not boiling.

6. Beat the egg yolks and cold water until

foamy, then whisk them into the sauce. Heat the sauce but do not let it boil or it will curdle. When it is thickened and smooth, pour it over the chicken breasts, and serve immediately.

ROASTED CHICKEN WITH RED WINE VINEGAR SAUCE

Makes 3 to 4 servings

Roasted *coq au vin* may be a good description for this recipe from Anne Otterson, who learned it from Jacques Pépin. The subtle vinegar flavor in the sauce gives this dish its special character.

1 frying chicken (about 3
    pounds)
½ cup unsalted butter
Salt and freshly ground
    pepper, to taste
½ cup red wine vinegar
½ cup water

3 cloves garlic, minced
⅓ cup red wine vinegar
1 tablespoon tomato paste
Salt and freshly ground
    pepper, to taste
¼ cup cold unsalted butter,
    cut into bits

1 tablespoon chopped fresh
    parsley
2 teaspoons chopped fresh
    tarragon

1. Preheat oven to 400°. Truss the chicken and rub the skin with the ½ cup butter. Season the chicken well with salt and pepper. Roast the chicken on a rack in a roasting pan, breast-side down, for 30 minutes.

2. Turn the chicken over and add the ½ cup vinegar and the water to the pan. (Do not pour the vinegar and water over the chicken, or the skin will turn murky brown.) Reduce the oven temperature to 375° and roast the chicken on its back for another 30 minutes, or until the juices run clear when the thickest part of the thigh is pierced with a skewer. Remove the chicken to a warmed platter while preparing the sauce.

3. Pour the roasting-pan juices into a saucepan. Add the garlic and cook it over medium heat for 1 minute, taking care not to burn the garlic. Pour the ⅓ cup vinegar into the roasting pan and deglaze the pan over medium heat, scraping up any browned bits. Add the liquid to the saucepan along with the tomato paste, salt, and plenty of pepper — the sauce should be peppery. Remove the pan from the heat, and whisk in the ¼ cup butter, bit by bit.

4. Carve the chicken, sprinkle on the chopped parsley and tarragon, and serve with the sauce.

FILETS MIGNONS WITH ROQUEFORT SAUCE

Makes 4 servings

André Daguin, owner/chef of Mapotel de France in Auch, taught Jack Monaco this exceptional filet mignon entrée when they cooked a series of special dinners at Piret's in 1980. Jack serves it with his green bean salad (page 19).

2 ounces Roquefort cheese, mashed

4 tablespoons unsalted butter

1 tablespoon oil (preferably grape seed oil)

4 filets mignons (1¼ inch thick), each barded and tied with string (see note)

Salt and freshly ground white pepper, to taste

1½ cups rich veal stock, preferably homemade (page 316), reduced to ½ cup

1 tablespoon pine nuts

1 tablespoon chopped walnuts

1 tablespoon slivered almonds

1. In a small mixing bowl, work the Roquefort and the butter together using a wooden spoon, until they form a smooth, creamy paste. Divide the mixture into 4 or 5 chunks.

2. Meanwhile, heat the oil in a large, heavy skillet over high heat until the oil is nearly smoking. Lower the heat to medium-high, and sauté the beef on one side for 3 minutes. Turn the filets, sprinkle the browned sides with salt and white pepper, and sauté 3 minutes longer for rare meat. Transfer the filets to a warmed serving platter, partially cover, and keep warm.

3. Pour the fat from the skillet, add the reduced veal stock, and deglaze the skillet over high heat, scraping up the browned bits. Simmer the stock for 1 minute and whisk in the butter-Roquefort mixture, a piece at a time, allowing each piece to emulsify completely before adding the next. You may need to move the skillet on and off the heat to keep the sauce hot enough to emulsify the butter but not so hot that it melts and becomes oily (see note).

4. When the sauce coats the back of a metal spoon, spoon it over the beef. Sprinkle on the nuts, and serve immediately.

NOTE

To bard the filets, wrap the sides of the steaks with bacon or thinly sliced salt pork or fresh pork, and tie the fat in place with kitchen twine or fasten with toothpicks. Remove the fat before serving. Barding keeps the lean filets from drying out during high-heat cooking.

This sauce is similar to a beurre blanc. For more information, see page 329.

FILLET OF BEEF WITH CAPERS

Makes 2 servings

This quick reduction sauce of shallots cooked in vinegar, enriched with demi-glace and cream and spiked with capers, has been a favorite at our cooking school and when Piret's caters. It was originally brought to us by Paula Wolfert. It's a quick way to sauce simply sautéed meat and is a foundation technique for many similar dishes.

3 tablespoons clarified butter (see below)

12 ounces (trimmed weight) beef fillet, cut into 6 rounds (¾ inch thick)

Salt and freshly ground pepper, to taste

3 tablespoons unsalted butter

2 tablespoons minced shallots

2 tablespoons red wine vinegar

3 tablespoons demi-glace (page 315), flavored with 1 tablespoon tomato paste

3 tablespoons heavy cream

⅓ cup small capers, drained on paper towels

1 tablespoon chopped fresh parsley

1 tablespoon chopped fresh tarragon

1. Heat the clarified butter in a heavy 12-inch skillet until it is very hot but not smoking. Sear the meat 1 minute on each side, then remove it to a platter and season with salt and pepper. Keep the steaks warm in a 180° oven. Wipe the fat from the pan with paper towels.

2. Add 1 tablespoon of the fresh butter to the skillet, lower the heat, and cook the shallots, stirring often, for 1 minute. Add the vinegar and deglaze the skillet over high heat, scraping up the browned bits. Boil the mixture down to a glaze. Stir in the demi-glace, then the cream, and reduce the mixture over high heat to about ⅔ cup. Add any meat juices that have accumulated around the beef on the platter. Remove the skillet from the heat and whisk in the remaining 2 tablespoons of butter and the capers. Taste the sauce and adjust the seasoning with salt and pepper.

3. Reheat the meat for an instant in the hot sauce. Place 3 pieces of meat on each of two warmed dinner plates, spoon over the sauce, and scatter the parsley and tarragon on top. Serve immediately.

CLARIFIED BUTTER: Butter burns more readily than oil during frying and sautéing because it contains milk solids. Clarifying the butter removes the milk solids, reducing this hazard. Some foods, such as crêpes, are far superior when fried in butter rather than margarine or oil.

With some sauces — hollandaise, for example — you have a choice of clarifying or not clarifying. Some chefs insist that only clarified butter be used, because the water content in the milk solids tends to thin out the sauce somewhat. Others, including Jacques Pépin, prefer to use whole butter, because the water in the milk solids will make the emulsion less temperature sensitive, giving you more control over it.

Another reason to clarify butter is that in some sauces and preparations the milk solids will impart an unattractive residue (almost a scum), detracting from the visual appeal of the dish. Drawn butter is a synonym for clarified butter. You are drawing the butter fat out of the milk solids when you clarify it.

Generally speaking, we prefer to use unsalted butter in cooking. However, salt tends to act as a preservative in butter, so unsalted butter is more perishable and will begin to go rancid very quickly. Clarified salted butter will be fine in your refrigerator for many weeks; if you are clarifying unsalted butter, make only what you can use in a week's time.

To make clarified butter — Melt the butter over low heat, and skim off the foam that rises to the top. The remainder will separate into two parts: a clear yellow liquid, and a white residue, which sinks to the bottom of the pan. Drain off the clear yellow (clarified) butter into a bowl. Discard the white residue.

BRAISED STUFFED FLANK STEAK

Makes 6 servings

Flank steaks, once rather neglected by American cooks, have become popular in recent years. Unfortunately, as their popularity has risen, so has their price. A good way to stretch this flavorful cut is by stuffing it. The stuffed steak is braised to tenderness and served with a flavorful sauce. A similar version of this recipe was once taught at our school by Jacques Pépin; however, over the years some minor changes have slipped in. We think stuffed flank steak makes an excellent buffet entrée for entertaining and is certainly as grand as a galantine for sit-down dinner parties.

1 flank steak (2½ pounds, trimmed weight) (see note)

1. Trim the steak of all fat. To prepare the steak for stuffing, have the butcher cut a pocket horizontally through the steak, or do it yourself, using a sharp boning knife and being careful not to pierce the meat with the tip of the knife. If you do poke a hole in the side, use a bit of steak from the edge to patch it.

STUFFING

¼ cup vegetable oil

3 tablespoons unsalted
butter

3 cups ½-inch white bread
cubes

1 pound lean ground beef

¼-inch-thick slice of
prosciutto, diced

1 egg

¾ cup chopped onion (1
medium onion)

½ rib celery, chopped

¾ cup grated carrot

1 tablespoon chopped fresh
parsley

2 cloves garlic, minced

1½ teaspoons salt

½ teaspoon freshly ground
pepper

¼ teaspoon crushed dried
thyme or savory

FOR BRAISING

2 tablespoons butter

1 tablespoon vegetable oil

¾ cup finely diced carrot

1 onion, chopped

2 bay leaves

1 tomato, coarsely chopped

1 teaspoon dried thyme

2 cups rich brown stock
(page 313)

1 cup dry red wine

2 tablespoons cornstarch,
mixed with ¼ cup cold
water

Salt and freshly ground
pepper, to taste

NOTE

2. *To prepare the stuffing:* Heat the oil and butter in a skillet over medium heat, and cook the bread cubes until they are browned on all sides. Combine the ground beef, prosciutto, egg, onions, celery, carrots, parsley, garlic, salt, pepper, and thyme in a large bowl. Stir in the bread cubes, lightly tossing the stuffing only until the ingredients are blended (overmixing will make the stuffing mushy).

3. Fill the flank steak with the stuffing mixture. Bring the lower edge of the opening up against the stuffing, then bring the top edge down to form a neat loaf. Season the meat liberally with pepper and lightly with salt. Tie it closed with strings placed about 2 inches apart.

4. *To braise the meat:* Heat the butter and oil in a large, deep, flameproof casserole with a cover. Brown the meat on all sides. Add the carrots, onions, bay leaves, tomato, and thyme, and cook the mixture over medium heat, uncovered, for 5 minutes. Add the brown stock and wine, bring the liquid to a boil, and lower the heat to a bare simmer. Braise the meat, covered, either on top of the stove or in a 400° oven for 1 hour and 10 minutes.

5. When the meat is tender, remove it from the casserole, place it on a serving platter, and remove the strings. Keep the meat warm, covered, in a 180° oven while you make the sauce.

6. Stir the cornstarch-water mixture into the cooking juices in the casserole and bring the liquid to a boil. Cook, stirring often to bring up any browned bits, until the sauce thickens slightly. Season it with salt and pepper. The sauce may be served as is, or you may strain it, pressing the solids to release all their flavor. Slice the meat and serve it with the sauce.

We've found flank steaks ranging from 1¼ pounds to 2½ pounds (trimmed weight). To serve six, you'll need about 2½ pounds of trimmed flank steak. If your butcher has the heavier steak, proceed as directed above, cutting a pocket in the meat. If the butcher only has smaller steaks, buy two, and instead of cutting a pocket, spread half of the filling over each steak and roll each one separately, starting from the long end. Tie the rolls with string and braise as directed.

ROLLED FLANK STEAK WITH MUSHROOMS

Makes 8 servings

We've used shiitake mushrooms, which have a wonderful flavor, in this flank steak roll. This recipe takes some time to prepare, but it's worth every minute — "incredibly delicious" is how our tester described it.

TO PREPARE THE STUFFING

1 ounce dried shiitake
   mushrooms
1 cup rich chicken stock,
   preferably homemade
   (page 317), warmed
4 tablespoons butter
3 cloves garlic, minced
3 shallots, minced
1½ pounds fresh
   mushrooms, sliced
¼ cup Cognac
2 tablespoons fresh lemon
   juice
½ cup minced fresh parsley
1½ cups fresh bread crumbs
Salt and freshly ground
   pepper, to taste
Dash of cayenne pepper
¼ teaspoon dried sage
½ teaspoon dried thyme
½ to ¾ cup freshly grated
   Parmesan cheese

1. Soak the dried mushrooms in the warm chicken stock for 1 hour. Strain the mushrooms and soaking liquid through a double layer of dampened cheesecloth and set the liquid aside. Chop the mushrooms and set them aside.

2. Melt the butter in a skillet and sauté the garlic, shallots, and sliced fresh mushrooms until most of the liquid evaporates. Add the Cognac and lemon juice and cook for 1 to 2 minutes longer. Add the shiitake mushrooms, parsley, bread crumbs, salt, pepper, cayenne pepper, sage, thyme, and the mushroom-soaking liquid. Taste for seasoning and adjust if necessary. Thoroughly blend in the Parmesan cheese.

TO PREPARE THE STEAK

2 flank steaks (2 to 2¼
    pounds each, trimmed
    weight)
3 tablespoons butter
3 cloves garlic, peeled and
    halved
6 cups rich chicken stock,
    preferably homemade
    (page 317)
1 cup dry white wine
1 tablespoon tomato paste

¼ cup Madeira
¼ cup heavy cream or *créme
    fraîche*

1. Trim any fat or connective tissue from the flank steaks. Place them on a work surface, with narrow ends facing you. Spread half the mushroom filling on each steak, leaving a 1-inch border on the long sides. Roll the steaks, tucking in the filling as you roll. Tie the rolled steaks with butcher's twine at 2-inch intervals, tucking in any filling that squeezes out.

2. Melt the butter in a large skillet and sauté the garlic for 1 minute. Remove the garlic and add the flank steaks, browning them on all sides. Remove the flank steaks to a roasting pan that will hold them without crowding.

3. Preheat oven to 350°. Add the chicken stock, wine, and tomato paste to the skillet and bring them to a boil, scraping up the browned bits. Over high heat, reduce the mixture to 3 cups. Pour the liquid over the flank steak rolls, place the roasting pan in the oven, and roast the meat for 30 minutes. Turn the rolls, and roast them an additional 30 minutes.

4. Reduce the oven to 180°. Remove the rolls to a platter and keep them warm in the low oven. Strain the pan juices into a saucepan and reduce them by half over high heat. Stir in the Madeira and cream. Adjust the seasoning and cook the sauce gently for 1 minute. Slice the rolled steaks and spoon some sauce over each serving. Serve the remaining sauce separately.

NADIA FRIGERI'S VEAL SCALLOPS WITH LEMON JUICE

Makes 6 servings

Veal and lemon seem to have a natural affinity for each other. If you want to give this dish a bit of extra zing, add the zest of the lemon along with the juice.

1 pound boneless veal top
  sirloin or loin, cut into 6
  scallops
½ cup unbleached,
  all-purpose flour
Salt and freshly ground
  pepper, to taste
6 tablespoons butter
Juice of 1 lemon
3 tablespoons minced fresh
  parsley

1. Pound the veal scallops with a mallet until they are very thin. Dredge each piece lightly with flour and sprinkle with salt and pepper.

2. Melt 4 tablespoons of the butter in a large skillet. When the butter foams, add the veal and cook it over high heat for 1 minute on each side. Remove the veal to a warmed serving platter and cover with aluminum foil.

3. Add the lemon juice and the remaining 2 tablespoons of butter to the skillet, and deglaze the skillet over high heat, scraping up any browned bits. Stir in the parsley, taste the sauce, and adjust the seasoning. Spoon the sauce over the veal, and serve immediately.

ANNE OTTERSON'S VEAL WITH MUSTARD SAUCE

Makes 4 servings

Wrapping a lean veal roast in a latticework of fat will ensure a juicy, moist roast: the fat melts and bastes the meat during cooking.

1 boneless veal rump or
  round roast (2 to 3
  pounds)
4 tablespoons Dijon-style
  mustard
1 pound thinly sliced pork
  fat
½ cup dry white wine
½ cup heavy cream
Salt and freshly ground
  white pepper, to taste

1. Preheat oven to 325°. Spread 2 tablespoons of the mustard over the veal. Cut the pork fat into ½-inch strips. Cover the roast with the strips in a lattice design, enclosing the sides with bigger slices. Tie the roast with butcher's twine to secure the fat strips and place it in a shallow, flameproof roasting pan. Roast the veal for 1¼ hours, basting it frequently.

2. Remove the roast from the oven and increase

the oven temperature to 400°. Transfer the roast to a warmed platter.

3. Add the wine to the roasting pan and deglaze the pan over high heat, scraping up the browned bits. Pour the pan juices into a glass measuring cup through a strainer lined with a double layer of dampened cheesecloth. Remove as much of the surface fat as possible. Set the juices aside.

4. Remove the string and pork fat from the veal roast and return it to the roasting pan. Stir together the remaining 2 tablespoons of mustard with 4 tablespoons of the cream. Spoon the mixture over the roast, return it to the oven, and roast the veal an additional 15 minutes.

5. While the veal cooks, bring the reserved pan juices to a boil and reduce them slightly. Stir the remaining cream into the juices, and season the sauce with salt and white pepper.

6. Remove the veal from the roasting pan and let it rest for 10 minutes on a warmed serving platter. Meanwhile, pour any additional pan juices into the sauce. Slice the veal and serve it with the sauce.

VEAL WITH GREEN PEPPERCORN SAUCE

Makes 4 servings

Green peppercorns add an elegant touch to any menu, and this sauce can be used for chicken, turkey, duck, and rabbit as well as for veal. Sauté the meat or poultry longer for duck breast or rabbit, and proceed as directed for the sauce.

3 tablespoons clarified unsalted butter (page 239)
4 scallops veal loin (each 1 inch thick)
2 tablespoons minced shallots
¼ cup Armagnac
2 tablespoons fresh lemon juice

1. Heat the butter in a heavy skillet, and sauté the veal scallops until they are golden brown on both sides, turning them once. Transfer them to a warmed platter and keep them warm in a 180° oven while you prepare the sauce.

2. Sauté the shallots in the fat left in the pan, until they are limp but not brown. Blend in the Armagnac and lemon juice. Lower the heat and boil

½ cup heavy cream
2 teaspoons green pepper-
    corns, rinsed and drained
1 teaspoon fresh tarragon (or
    ¼ teaspoon dried)
Salt and freshly ground
    white pepper, to taste

the sauce, scraping up the browned bits, until the liquids are reduced by half.

3. Stir the cream into the reduced sauce. Mash 1 teaspoon of the peppercorns and stir the mashed and whole peppercorns and the tarragon into the sauce, continuing to boil it until it is syrupy. Season the sauce with salt and white pepper, pour it over the veal, and serve immediately.

PERFECT PAN RACK OF LAMB

Makes 6 to 8 servings

The mustard used at The Perfect Pan to make this lamb is *moutarde au vinaigre de vin et champagne,* mustard with wine vinegar and champagne. Successful variations have been made with green-peppercorn mustard, hot mustards, grainy mustards, and even plain old yellow hot dog mustard.

3 English muffins
8 cloves garlic, peeled
Zest of 1 lemon
½ cup fresh parsley
½ cup unsalted butter
¼ cup champagne mustard
¼ teaspoon freshly ground
    pepper
2 racks of lamb (see note)

1. Quarter the muffins and mince them using a food processor fitted with the steel blade. Transfer the crumbs to a bowl and set them aside.

2. Combine the garlic, lemon zest, and parsley in the work bowl of the processor, and mince. Add the butter, mustard, and pepper, and process to blend. Add the reserved bread crumbs, and process until smooth.

3. Preheat oven to 375°. Place the racks of lamb, bone-side down, in a baking pan, and coat the top sides evenly with the mustard mixture. Roast them for about 45 minutes (time varies with weight of the racks), or until a meat thermometer inserted in the lamb registers 130°, for rare. The end chops will be more well done than center chops. Allow the meat to rest for 10 minutes.

4. To serve, cut the ribs into chops, being careful not to dislodge the mustard coating. Serve 2 chops per person.

NOTE

Have the butcher French the rib ends and remove the chine bone and the top layer of fat.

ROAST LAMB WITH ONION SAUCE

Makes 6 servings

A creamy onion purée combines with enriched white sauce to coat slices of roast lamb in this Anne Otterson recipe from our first Diplôme cooking class series in 1979. It's great for buffets, or any dinner when you want to have the main course prepared in advance.

1 leg of lamb (6 to 7 pounds), boned (net weight 3½ to 4 pounds)
1 teaspoon salt
½ teaspoon freshly ground pepper
2 cloves garlic, slivered

ONION PURÉE

8 tablespoons unsalted butter
6 tablespoons raw long-grain white rice
3 medium onions, sliced
½ teaspoon salt
¼ teaspoon freshly ground white pepper

WHITE SAUCE

2 tablespoons unsalted butter
1 tablespoon unbleached, all-purpose flour
¼ cup rich chicken stock, preferably homemade (page 317)
1 tablespoon fresh lemon juice
½ cup heavy cream
2 egg yolks, slightly beaten

1 cup rich chicken stock
3 to 4 tablespoons unsalted butter

1. Preheat oven to 350°. Trim the fat from the lamb and rub the meat with the salt and pepper. Pierce the lamb at regular intervals with the tip of a small knife, and insert the garlic slivers. Place the lamb in a roasting pan, and roast the lamb 50 to 60 minutes (figure 15 minutes per pound; a meat thermometer will register 140° for rare, 145° for medium-rare, and 165° for well done).

2. *To prepare the onion purée:* Melt the 8 tablespoons butter in a saucepan and stir in the rice, onions, salt, and pepper. Cook the mixture, covered, over medium heat for 25 minutes. Purée the sauce, using a food processor fitted with the steel blade, or a blender. Set the purée aside.

3. *To prepare the white sauce:* Melt the 2 tablespoons butter in a saucepan, whisk in the flour, and cook this roux until it bubbles thoroughly. Whisk in the chicken stock and lemon juice. Combine the cream with the beaten egg yolks and slowly pour this into the sauce while whisking vigorously. Add the onion purée, adjust the seasoning, and remove it from the heat.

4. Remove the roast from the oven and increase the oven temperature to 400°. Let the meat stand 15 to 20 minutes, then slice it into serving portions. Spread some sauce over each slice, and arrange them, overlapping, in an ovenproof serving dish.

5. Add the 1 cup of chicken stock to the roasting pan, and deglaze the pan over high heat, stirring to bring up the browned bits. (If preparing the dish in advance, set these juices aside and reheat just before serving time.) Swirl in the 3 to 4 tablespoons of butter.

¼ cup dry bread crumbs
¼ cup chopped fresh parsley
¼ cup melted butter

6. Sprinkle the bread crumbs and parsley over the sliced meat, then drizzle on the pan juices and butter. Reheat the meat in the 400° oven for 15 minutes, and serve.

NOTE

This dish may be cooked ahead and refrigerated, covered. Bring it to room temperature before reheating.

CROWN ROAST OF PORK WITH APPLE AND SAUSAGE STUFFING

Makes 8 to 10 servings

A crown roast of pork makes a spectacular main course. The roast is made up of two pork loins, trimmed and tied to form a circle. The rib bones stick up like points of a crown. The roast makes an ideal container for savory stuffings, such as the two below. We like a crown roast as an alternative to turkey at Christmas and Thanksgiving. Fortunately, so does Anne Otterson, who first brought us this marvelous recipe. Instead of the apple and sausage stuffing, she sometimes uses a delicious cranberry stuffing, which we've included below.

1 crown roast of pork (see note)

STUFFING

1 cup raisins
¾ cup butter
1 medium onion, chopped
½ cup chopped celery
3 cups chopped, peeled apples (pippins or other cooking varieties)
½ teaspoon cinnamon
½ teaspoon mace
½ teaspoon dried sage
½ teaspoon dried thyme
½ teaspoon freshly grated nutmeg
1 teaspoon salt
¼ teaspoon freshly ground pepper
6 cups fresh bread crumbs
1 pound pork sausage

1. Preheat oven to 350°. Wrap the rib ends of the roast in aluminum foil to keep them from burning. Place the pork in a roasting pan and roast about 1 hour. (The total cooking time for the roast will be about 2 hours [figure 15 minutes per pound] but the stuffing will be added to the roast for the last hour of cooking.) Meanwhile, prepare the stuffing.

2. Pour enough simmering water over the raisins to barely cover them. Let them stand until plump. Drain, and reserve the raisins.

3. Melt the butter in a skillet, and lightly sauté the onions and celery. Add the apples and cook the mixture for a few minutes more.

4. Stir together the cinnamon, mace, sage, thyme, nutmeg, salt, pepper, and bread crumbs, blending them thoroughly.

5. Combine the raisins, the apple mixture, and the bread crumb mixture, and crumble in the sausage. Blend the stuffing lightly but thoroughly.

6. Remove the crown roast from the oven an

hour before it is done, and spoon the stuffing into the center. (Any extra stuffing can be placed in a covered casserole and baked for 30 minutes.) Return the roast to the oven to finish cooking for 1 hour, basting the meat and stuffing a few times with the pan juices. The roast is done when a meat thermometer inserted into the thickest part registers 165°. To serve, slice between the ribs to make wedges of meat and stuffing.

NOTE

Have the butcher prepare the crown roast from two loins, totaling about 8 pounds. The fat and meat should be trimmed from the rib tips, and the chine bone removed to make the roast easier to carve.

Cranberry Stuffing

This stuffing is also delicious in turkey, or cooked in a casserole and served with roast duck. (Do not stuff the duck; the dressing will be too greasy.)

½ cup butter
3 tablespoons grated onion
1½ cups fresh cranberries, chopped
4 tablespoons brown sugar
4 cups fresh bread crumbs
¾ teaspoon salt
½ teaspoon mace
½ teaspoon dried thyme
⅛ teaspoon freshly ground pepper
Zest of 1 orange

1. Melt the butter in a skillet and sauté the onion until it is limp but not browned. Stir in the cranberries and brown sugar.
2. Thoroughly blend the bread crumbs with the salt, mace, thyme, pepper, and orange zest. Add the bread crumb mixture to the skillet, and cook the stuffing for about 5 minutes before spooning it into the roast.

CHOUCROUTE GARNIE

Makes 6 servings

Choucroute Garnie is a great gastronomic tradition from Alsace. At Lunch at The Perfect Pan, Ben Patterson and George fooled around with lots of versions, making it at various times with champagne, white wine, or some combination of both. Their latest coup, offered here, uses Bombay gin and white wine. Ben also uses juniper berries, which accentuate the flavor of the gin.

This delicious dish reheats splendidly and serves multitudes inexpensively. The boiled potatoes are a mild touch that we highly recommend as a counterpoint to the spicy sausages, salty bacon, and smoked ham. Alternatively you can bake the potatoes, if you want a bit of color and want to bother. Halve the raw potatoes and then cut them into thirds lengthwise. Bake them in about ¼ inch of oil until golden brown. They will be crispy on the outside, yet mild and mellow on the inside.

3 pounds sauerkraut
1 pound bacon, in 1 piece
½ cup lard
1½ cups chopped yellow onions (2 medium onions)
1 tablespoon chopped garlic
2 tart green apples, unpeeled, cored and chopped
1½ cups rich chicken stock, preferably homemade (page 317)
1 cup dry white wine
½ cup Bombay gin
12 juniper berries
½ teaspoon salt
Bouquet garni (page 163)
6 small garlic pork sausages
6 ¼-inch slices smoked ham (precooked)
½ cup chopped fresh parsley

6 red or small white potatoes, boiled

1. Drain the sauerkraut, soak it in cold water for 15 minutes, then drain and squeeze out the excess water. Blanch the bacon in boiling water to cover for 10 minutes. Drain, and set it aside.

2. Preheat oven to 325°. Melt the lard in a heavy, flameproof 4-quart casserole. Add the onions and garlic and cook them over medium heat for 5 minutes. Add the apples and sauerkraut and braise them, covered, over very low heat for 10 minutes. Stir in the chicken stock, wine, gin, juniper berries, and salt, and push the bouquet garni down into the sauerkraut. Place the bacon on top, cover the pan, and bring the mixture to a boil. Place the covered casserole on the middle shelf of the oven and bake it for 3 hours.

3. Prick the sausages in several places with a fork and add them to the casserole, pushing them into the sauerkraut. Continue to bake the casserole, covered, for 30 minutes. Place the ham slices on the sauerkraut and bake, covered, another 15 minutes (total baking time, 3 hours and 45 minutes).

4. Transfer the sauerkraut to a deep, warmed platter. Discard the bouquet garni. Slice the bacon in 6 pieces and arrange them around the edge, alternating with the ham. Mound the sausages in the center, sprinkle on the chopped parsley, and serve with the boiled potatoes.

STROM AND JENKINS' MEXICAN STEW

Makes 20 servings

Jerrie Strom and Fran Jenkins are best friends and often collaborate when teaching at The Perfect Pan. Both are well versed in classic French cooking techniques, but their real love is Mexican and Chinese cooking. They serve this stew with Green Chili and Cheese Corn Bread.

½ pound salt pork or bacon
2 pounds boneless cooked ham
2 pounds beef brisket
2 pounds veal, in one piece
1 broiler chicken (2½ to 3 pounds), cut up
3 quarts water
8 small carrots
3 turnips, cut in 2-inch cubes
3 tomatoes, cut up
1 pound green beans, tied together in bunches
2 Anaheim chilies, chopped
4 pattypan squash, cut into 2-inch cubes
2 apples, peeled and cut into 2-inch chunks
2 pears, peeled and cut into 2-inch chunks
4 ears corn, broken into quarters (or kernels scraped from the cob)
1 can (1¼ pounds) garbanzo beans, drained (see note)
2 sweet potatoes, peeled and cut into 2-inch cubes (see note)
6 boiling potatoes, peeled and cut into 2-inch cubes
4 Chorizo sausages, casings removed, cut up
1 head cabbage, cut into wedges

1. Place the salt pork in cold water to cover, bring it to a boil, reduce the heat, and simmer for 10 minutes to remove excess salt (not necessary if you're using bacon). In an 8-quart Dutch oven or stockpot, combine the salt pork, ham, brisket, veal, and chicken. Add the 3 quarts of water, and bring the liquid to a boil over high heat. When it has begun to boil, reduce the heat to medium. Skim the surface, cover the pot, and simmer the mixture over low heat for 2 hours.

2. Scatter over the meats the carrots, turnips, tomatoes, green beans, Anaheim chilies, squash, apples, pears, corn, garbanzos, sweet potatoes, and boiling potatoes. Cover, and simmer the stew, without stirring, for 1 hour.

3. Meanwhile, place the Chorizos and cabbage in another pot, cover them with water, and simmer over medium heat, uncovered, for 1 hour. Add this mixture to the stew.

4. Melt the butter in a sauté pan and brown the onion and garlic over medium heat until translucent. Add the coriander seeds, caraway seeds, oregano, cinnamon, salt, and pepper. Add this mixture to the stew.

5. Simmer the stew for 15 to 20 minutes, skimming several times, to allow the flavors to blend. Taste for seasoning, and add salt if needed.

6. Remove the vegetables and fruits from the pot with a slotted spoon, and arrange them in separate groups on a large serving platter. Remove the meats from the pot, slice them into serving pieces, and group them separately on another serving platter. Strain the broth into a soup tureen through a fine

3 tablespoons butter

2 onions, sliced

2 cloves garlic, minced

½ teaspoon crushed
coriander seeds

1 tablespoon caraway seeds

1 tablespoon dried oregano

½ teaspoon cinnamon

2 teaspoons salt

1 teaspoon freshly ground
pepper

2 avocados

2 limes, cut in wedges, for
garnish

Fresh tomato salsa (optional;
see below)

---

wire-mesh sieve. To serve, place a slice of avocado in each bowl, then fill the bowls with the broth. Garnish the meats with lime wedges and salsa, and serve with Green Chili and Cheese Corn Bread (recipe follows).

NOTE

Dried beans may be substituted for the canned garbanzos: soak 1 pound dried garbanzos overnight in water to cover, drain, and cook according to package directions.

Fresh pumpkin may be substituted for the sweet potatoes.

TOMATO SALSA

Chop a ripe but firm tomato and add to it some chopped onion, chopped cilantro (fresh coriander), chopped poblano or serrano chili, and salt and pepper to taste. If the salsa does not have enough natural liquid, add a small amount of water. Allow the salsa to rest for 30 minutes to an hour so the flavors can mingle.

Green Chili and Cheese Corn Bread
Makes one 10-inch-round loaf

4 long green fresh chilies (or
canned jalapeño peppers)

3 eggs

2 cups buttermilk, plain
yogurt, or sour cream

⅓ cup corn oil

2 cups whole-grain cornmeal

1 teaspoon baking soda

1 teaspoon salt

1 to 2 cups freshly grated
sharp Cheddar cheese

1. Roast the chilies under the broiler, or spear each chili with a fork and hold it over the flame of a gas burner (it helps to rub them with oil first). Turn the chilies so the skin blisters and chars slightly and evenly. Wrap the roasted chilies in a damp towel, plastic bag, or a water-sprinkled brown paper bag, and leave them for 15 to 20 minutes before peeling them. The number of chilies used in the bread may be increased or decreased, according to taste. Halve the peeled chilies, seed them, and chop them.

2. Mix together the eggs, buttermilk, and oil. In another bowl, stir together the cornmeal, baking soda, and salt, pressing out the lumps. Stir the dry mixture into the egg mixture. Stir in the chopped chilies and all but ¼ cup of the Cheddar cheese.

3. Preheat oven to 450°. Oil a 10-inch cast-iron skillet and heat it in the oven. Pour the batter into the hot skillet, and top with the reserved cheese. Bake the bread for 25 to 30 minutes, or until it is set and slightly brown on top. Remove the pan from the oven and allow the bread to cool slightly. Cut into wedges, and serve.

ARRINGTON'S IRISH CHILI

Makes about 20 servings

Frank Arrington is one of George's oldest friends and a consistent winner of the Gladys Schwartz Award for excess at the George Munger Cook-Off. Frank is Irish, but having lived all his life within minutes of the Mexican border, he has a taste for fiery dishes.

The blend of chili powders in this recipe and their proportions can be widely varied according to your own taste and how spicy you like your foods. The long cooking melds the flavors. If you make the chili a day ahead, cook it for two hours, then refrigerate. Reheating it before serving will complete the cooking. Serve the chili with cooked pinto, pink, or kidney beans, and bowls of chopped onion and grated Cheddar cheese. Allow your guests to choose their own proportion of each type of bean to suit their own taste. Purists add only a few beans, always on top of the chili, never mixed in.

4 tablespoons lard, oil, or shortening
6 pounds extra-lean beef chuck, cut into ¼-inch cubes
2 pounds extra-lean pork loin, cut into ¼-inch cubes
3 large onions, finely chopped
4 ribs celery, finely chopped
10 cloves garlic, finely chopped

1. In an 8-quart or larger Dutch oven, melt the lard over medium heat. Brown the beef and pork cubes in the fat. Transfer the browned meat to a large, low-sided stockpot or Dutch oven, and reserve the fat in the pan.

2. Sauté the onions, celery, and garlic in the remaining fat until the vegetables are soft and golden but not brown. Add them to the meat. Stir in the tomato sauce, beef stock, and bourbon.

3. Pour the beer into a bowl and add the cumin, oregano, nutmeg, sugar, cocoa, chili powders, chili quebrado, mace, salt, and pepper. Stir the season-

1 can (6 ounces) tomato
  sauce
3 cups rich brown stock
  (page 313)
6 to 12 ounces high-quality
  bourbon whiskey
1 bottle (12 ounces) dark
  beer
3 tablespoons cumin
1 tablespoon dried oregano
1 teaspoon freshly grated
  nutmeg
1 tablespoon sugar
1 tablespoon unsweetened
  cocoa
3 heaping tablespoons New
  Mexico chili powder
3 heaping tablespoons
  Pasilla chili powder
3 heaping tablespoons
  crushed chili quebrado
1 teaspoon mace
Salt and freshly ground
  pepper, to taste
Chopped cilantro (fresh
  coriander), for garnish

ings into the meat mixture, and simmer the chili uncovered for 2½ to 3 hours. If more liquid is needed to maintain consistency, add either water, beer, or bourbon.

FEIJOADA COMPLETA

Makes 6 servings

When Ben Patterson was our chef for Lunch at The Perfect Pan, he brought not only his vast repertoire of French dishes but a wealth of ethnic specialties from his travels to South America and Mexico. He served these dishes and his superb chicken curry (page 184) buffet-style, giving the occasion a festive, party air.

Feijoada Completa is Brazil's national dish. It includes separate presentation platters and bowls of fresh and smoked meats and sausages, black beans, rice, collard greens or kale, uncooked farina or tapioca, sliced oranges, sliced onions, and piquant sauces. In Brazil, this ritualistic meal is washed down with a sugar cane brandy or a punch made with the brandy, lemon juice, and sugar; we always served beer. If you have a huge group, add a braised pork loin to your fresh meat selection and any sausages to your liking. Since all the elements of this feast are easy to make, you can increase the amount you cook at will, while allowing greater cooking time for the extra volume.

The farina or tapioca is sprinkled over the top of the foods on each guest's plate, and the orange slices act as a palate freshener. The sauces can be anything from a variety of mustards and horseradishes to fiery salsas made with chilies.

1 pound dried black beans
8 cups hot water
½ pound salt pork
1 whole smoked tongue (2 to 3 pounds)
½ pound beef chuck
6 small garlic sausages
2½ teaspoons salt
1 teaspoon freshly ground pepper
4 cloves garlic, minced
3 oranges
3 tablespoons sugar
2 large white onions
2 tablespoons Tabasco
2 tablespoons olive oil
1 tablespoon white wine vinegar
2 packages (10 ounces each) frozen collard greens
1½ cups raw white rice
2¾ cups cold water
1 tablespoon butter
1 tablespoon garlic vinegar
½ cup uncooked farina or tapioca (or 1 cup dry-roasted peanuts, minced)

1. Carefully wash the beans and combine them with the hot water in a heavy 6-quart stockpot. Boil them for 2 minutes, cover the pot, and set the beans aside for about 2 hours.

2. Cut the salt pork into 6 slices and add it to the beans. Bring the beans back to a boil, then reduce the heat to low and cover the pot. From this point, the total cooking time will be about 2½ hours.

3. Skin the tongue and cut the meat crosswise into 1-inch slices. Add them to the beans at the 30-minute mark. Cut the beef chuck into 6 pieces and add it to the pot at the 1-hour mark. Prick the sausages with a fork and add them after 1½ hours.

4. At the 2-hour mark, test the beans for tenderness, cooking longer if necessary. Transfer 1 cup of the beans to a small bowl, mash them, and return them to the pot. Add 2 teaspoons of the salt, and the pepper and minced garlic, and simmer for 30 minutes.

5. Peel the oranges and cut them crosswise into ¼-inch-thick slices. Remove seeds, arrange slices in a serving bowl, and sprinkle with the sugar.

6. Slice the onions crosswise in ¼-inch-thick slices and arrange them in another serving bowl. Combine the Tabasco, remaining ½ teaspoon salt, olive oil, and white wine vinegar, and drizzle this over the sliced onions.

7. Combine the rice, cold water, butter, and garlic vinegar in a small saucepan. Bring to a boil, stirring occasionally, then reduce the heat to low, cover the pan, and steam the rice for 20 minutes. Meanwhile, cook the frozen collard greens according to package directions. Transfer the rice and the cooked greens to separate serving bowls. Place the farina or peanuts in another small serving bowl.

8. Using a slotted spoon, remove the meats from the bean pot and arrange them on a serving platter. Put the beans in a serving bowl. Set all the separate serving dishes on the buffet.

7

PÂTISSERIE

TARTS

CAKES, PASTRIES &
COOKIES

CREAM & FRUIT DESSERTS

ICE CREAMS & SORBETS

DESSERT SAUCES &
SWEET TOPPINGS

🍂 TARTS

Kiwi Tart and Variations · Apple Tart with Calvados · Country Tart with Apples · Lemon Curd Tart · Ricotta and Almond Tart · Montrachet Tart

🍂 CAKES, PASTRIES, AND COOKIES

Génoise · Chocolate Génoise · Gâteau Grand Marnier · Alice Medrich's Gâteau du Prieur · Strawberry Mousse Cake · Orange Brownie Cake · Mixed-Fruit Cake with Vanilla Sauce · Zuccotto Frigeri · Rum Babas · Savarin · Pâte à Choux · Paris-Brest Cake · Madeleines · Tuiles · Jenny Saar's White Chocolate Chip Cookies · Tommies · Cigars

🍂 CREAM AND FRUIT DESSERTS

Piret's Chocolate Mousse · Lemon Bavarian Cream · Orange Cream with Chopped Nuts · Pears with Melba Sauce · Baked Sliced Apples · Baked Peaches with Warm Lemon Sauce

🍂 ICE CREAMS AND SORBETS

Modern Kansas Farm Vanilla Ice Cream · Lorenzo and Olga's Vanilla Mint Ice Cream · Praline Ice Cream · Hugh Carpenter's Grand Marnier Mocha Ice Cream · Peach Ice Cream · Strawberry Sorbet · Anne Otterson's Pineapple Sorbet in Cookie Cups · Carrot Sorbet with Dill · Cucumber Sorbet

🍂 DESSERT SAUCES AND SWEET TOPPINGS

Crème Anglaise · Zabaglione · Sweet *Crème Fraîche* Sauce · Strawberry Sauce Supreme · Brandied Peach Sauce · Almond Nut Brittle · Hot Fudge Sauce · Chocolate Sauce

GEORGE IS A SWEETS JUNKIE, and he is not alone. Nearly every dessert class we offer at The Perfect Pan School of Cooking is an instant sellout, especially if the desserts are chocolate. Personally, I prefer simpler fare — beautiful fruit tarts, luscious zabaglione and Bavarian creams, and homemade ice cream. These are by no means less sinfully rich than chocolate génoise cakes slathered with buttercreams, Grand Marnier, and Cognac, but they tend not to overwhelm after a multicourse dinner. This chapter reflects both of our tastes in desserts.

We begin with several recipes for fruit tarts. Tarts can be made with pâte brisée, pâte sucrée, or puff pastry. Once you've mastered these pastry crusts (you'll find the recipes and techniques in chapters 4 and 8), and experimented with pastry creams, you're on the road to a veritable pastry shop full of fruit tarts. Use whatever fruit is fresh, in season, and beautifully ripe. Flavor the pastry cream with liqueurs, citrus zest, extracts, ground nuts — whatever suits your fancy. When making a fruit tart, fully prebake the pastry shell until it is golden brown, and brush it with sieved heated fruit preserves in a flavor and color that will complement the filling. Then spread on your pastry cream and top it with fruit. Leftover puff pastry from other recipes can be used to make a special top crust for an otherwise ordinary fruit pie. Score it to create a decorative effect.

The grand génoise cakes we offer here seem

daunting at first, but broken down into steps they're actually very manageable. The building blocks — plain or chocolate génoise, chocolate biscuit, chocolate truffle cream, chocolate buttercream, simple syrup, and fruit glazes — are simple to make, and all can be prepared well in advance of serving time. Once you have mastered the basics, let your imagination take over. Try your own combinations: maybe layers of génoise moistened with Framboise and layered with sieved raspberry jam and chocolate buttercream; or génoise sprinkled with Grand Marnier and layered with orange-flavored buttercream and chocolate biscuit spread thinly with apricot preserves; or génoise sprinkled with Kirschwasser and layered with drained tart cherries. For those of you who prefer simpler, homey desserts, we also include a variety of delicious custard and fruit desserts.

Homemade ice creams and sorbets are easy and fun to make. A wide variety of electric ice cream–making equipment is now available, ranging in price from inexpensive to moderately expensive. If you are thinking about investing in a home ice cream maker, take storage into consideration: if the equipment is easily accessible and visible, it will tend to be used; but "out of sight, out of mind" is an adage of considerable truth when it comes to kitchen appliances. We highly recommend Mable and Gar Hoffman's book *Ice Cream,* which includes a comprehensive guide to equipment.

T A R T S

KIWI TART

Makes one 8- to 10-inch tart

1 Pâte Brisée or Pâte Sucrée shell (pages 338, 340), fully baked

PASTRY CREAM

2 cups milk
2 tablespoons vanilla
5 egg yolks
¾ cup sugar
½ teaspoon unflavored gelatin
½ cup unbleached, all-purpose flour

1. *To make the pastry cream:* Place the milk and vanilla in a heavy saucepan and warm them over medium heat. In a medium bowl, whisk together the egg yolks, sugar, and gelatin until the mixture falls from the whisk in an undulating ribbon. Beat in the flour. Whisk the hot milk into the egg mixture, then pour the combination back into the saucepan. Bring it to a boil, whisking so it does not scorch, until it is thick. Take it off the heat and stir until it cools. Cover with plastic wrap and set it aside to cool completely.

2. In a small saucepan, stir together the sugar

1 cup sugar
½ cup water

1 jar (8 ounces) apricot
  preserves
4 kiwi fruit

and water over medium-high heat until the sugar dissolves. Continue to cook the syrup over medium heat until it begins to turn golden. Remove the pan from the heat. Brush this caramel over the bottom of the prepared pastry shell to glaze it.

3. Melt the preserves with a little water in a small saucepan over medium heat. Strain the melted preserves through a fine sieve to remove the lumps, and set the strained preserves aside. Peel and slice the kiwis, and set them aside.

4. Spread the pastry cream over the glazed tart shell, and arrange the kiwi slices in a circular pattern on the top. Brush on the sieved glaze.

VARIATIONS

- Substitute sliced strawberries for the kiwis. Glaze with melted currant jelly.
- Substitute whole raspberries, blueberries, and strawberries for the kiwis, and arrange them over the pastry cream in alternating concentric circles. Glaze with melted currant jelly.
- Substitute sliced bananas for the kiwis. Toss them with lemon juice or lime juice to prevent darkening before arranging them over the pastry cream. Sprinkle on shaved coconut and sprinkle with rum.
- Substitute sliced peaches for the kiwis. Arrange the slices pinwheel fashion on the pastry cream. Glaze with sieved apricot preserves.
- Substitute different colored grapes for the kiwis. Arrange the different colors on the pastry cream either in alternating concentric circles or in wedges of one color. Glaze with melted jelly made from Zinfandel grapes.
- Sprinkle crumbled Amaretto cookies over the fruit instead of glazing it.
- Flavor the pastry cream with orange liqueur and tiny strips of orange zest. Peel an orange, cutting away all the white pith. Cut between the membranes to remove the segments, holding the orange over a bowl to catch the juices. Combine the juice and equal amounts of orange marmalade

and apricot preserves and heat to melt the glaze. Arrange the orange segments on the pastry cream, and glaze. (For a prettier result, sieve the glaze. Stir the bits of peel from the glaze into the pastry cream before filling the tart.)

APPLE TART WITH CALVADOS

Makes one 8- to 10-inch tart

1 Pâte Brisée shell (page 338), unbaked
8 medium pippin apples
½ teaspoon freshly grated nutmeg
2 tablespoons Calvados (apple brandy)
1 teaspoon almond extract
3 tablespoons sugar

½ cup toasted ground almonds
¼ cup sugar (or to taste)
1 tablespoon Calvados or Cognac
½ cup apricot preserves

1. Peel, core, and slice 6 of the apples. Place them in a saucepan with about ½ inch of water and the nutmeg, Calvados, almond extract, and sugar, and simmer over low heat until the apples are soft. Increase the heat to evaporate the excess liquid, stirring the mixture to keep it from scorching. The filling will resemble applesauce. Set the filling aside to cool.

2. Peel and core the remaining apples and cut them in half lengthwise. Place one half on a board cut-side down, and thinly slice it lengthwise, holding the slices together.

3. Preheat oven to 425°. Sprinkle the ground almonds over the bottom of the pastry shell. Spread the apple filling into the crust. Place a sliced apple half on the filling and fan it out in a circular pattern. Repeat with the remaining sliced apple halves, covering the filling with concentric circles of apple slices. Sprinkle the apples with sugar to taste. Bake the tart for about 25 minutes.

4. Cool the tart and brush it with the Calvados or Cognac. Prepare the apricot glaze by melting the preserves over medium-low heat in a small saucepan. Strain the heated preserves through a fine sieve to remove the lumps. Brush the glaze over the top of the tart, and serve.

COUNTRY TART WITH APPLES

Makes one 12-inch tart

If you've been making pastry and have some left over, turn it into this quick apple tart. The finished tart, with its concentric circles of baked apple slices, looks very elegant but is super-simple to prepare. The trick is to keep from stretching the dough when you roll it out. If you do stretch the dough, it will shrink as it bakes into a less-than-beautiful shape. Also, the dough should be kept chilled so the fat doesn't melt and make the pastry greasy. It's best to work on a chilled marble slab, which keeps the pastry cold. The rolling technique, which comes from Paula Wolfert, makes the most of the "puff" in the puff pastry. If you're using our Pâte Brisée, just roll it in a circle, taking care to work from the center outward.

Sliced pears, peaches, nectarines, or plums, or a combination of fruit, also work well for this tart.

8 ounces Classic Puff Pastry
(page 342) or 1 recipe
Pâte Brisée (page 338)
3 or 4 firm, tart apples
¼ cup sugar
3 tablespoons unsalted
butter
Confectioners' sugar

1. On a lightly floured surface, roll the pastry to a 7-inch square. Cut a 7-inch round. Spread the pastry trimmings on the pastry circle, pressing them into the circle. Turn it over and roll the pastry into a 10-inch circle, rolling outward from the center. Lift the pastry occasionally and give the work surface another light dusting of flour to keep the pastry from sticking. If the dough starts to warm up (it will resist rolling or begin to spring back), chill it a few minutes, covered loosely with plastic wrap, and then finish rolling. Let the pastry rest in the refrigerator for 15 minutes.

2. Spray a 12-inch pizza pan or tart pan with water. (This will help keep the pastry from shrinking.) Starting about 3 inches in from the edge of the pastry, roll straight out to the edge of the circle. Pivot the circle a quarter turn and repeat. Complete the circle by pivoting and rolling twice more. Then, beginning in the center of the circle, repeat this rolling process. Keep rolling, spoke fashion, until the pastry is in a rough 14-inch circle. Roll the pastry onto the rolling pin, transfer it to the dampened pan, and pat the pastry into place. Neatly trim the overhanging pastry. Cover the pan with plastic wrap and chill.

3. Peel and core the apples, and slice them,

crosswise, about ¼-inch thick. Prick the pastry over its entire surface, and sprinkle on 2 tablespoons of the sugar. Beginning about ¾ inch from the edge, place the apple slices in concentric circles, overlapping them slightly. Sprinkle the remaining sugar over the apples and dot with the butter. Refrigerate it, tightly covered with plastic wrap, until ready to bake.

4. Place a heavy baking sheet or brick tile on the lowest rack of the oven, and preheat the oven to 475°. Slide the tart onto the preheated baking sheet or tile, and bake it for 15 minutes. Cover the edges with foil if they brown too quickly. After 15 minutes, sprinkle on some confectioners' sugar, move the tart to the top oven rack, and bake it an additional 5 minutes, or until the top is spotted brown.

LEMON CURD TART

Makes one 8- to 10-inch tart

Our lemon tarts are made in individual 4-inch sizes. You can use this recipe for either variation.

TO PREPARE THE PASTRY SHELL

1⅔ cups unbleached, all-purpose flour
⅓ cup pulverized almonds
⅓ cup sugar
Pinch of salt
¾ cup unsalted butter, cut into bits
1 large egg, beaten
1 egg yolk
1 tablespoon light rum

1. Combine the flour, almonds, sugar, and salt in the work bowl of a food processor fitted with the steel blade. In a separate bowl, stir together the butter, beaten egg, egg yolk, and rum. With the processor running, add the butter mixture to the flour mixture. Stop processing the moment the dough is blended. Form the dough into a ball, wrap it in plastic wrap, and chill it at least one hour.

2. Roll the pastry to a 12- to 14-inch circle, and use it to line a tart pan with a removable bottom. Pierce the pastry all over with a fork and refrigerate it for 10 minutes.

3. Preheat oven to 400°. Place the tart pan on a baking sheet, and bake the pastry shell for 15 minutes. Refrigerate until needed.

TO FILL THE PASTRY SHELL

Zest of 2 lemons, grated
6 tablespoons unsalted
    butter, softened
4 eggs
⅔ cup sugar

1 whole lemon, unpeeled

1. Place the lemon zest, butter, eggs, and sugar in a heavy, enameled saucepan, stirring to blend them well. Cook the mixture over low heat, whisking constantly, until it is slightly thickened. Cool the filling by setting the pan in cold water. When the filling is cool, spread it into the pastry and chill.

2. Slice the unpeeled lemon very thinly and place the slices in a decorative pattern over the tart (use 1 slice for each individual tart).

RICOTTA AND ALMOND TART

Makes one 8- to 10-inch tart

Ricotta and almonds have a special affinity. They combine particularly well in this tart, where ricotta mellows the sweet almond flavors.

1 Pâte Sucrée shell (page
    340), unbaked

4 eggs
½ cup sugar
1 pound ricotta cheese
3 tablespoons Amaretto
    liqueur
6 ounces Amaretto cookies

1. Beat the eggs with the sugar until the mixture is fluffy. Add the ricotta cheese and continue beating until the mixture is smooth. Thoroughly blend in the Amaretto. Set the filling mixture aside.

2. Preheat oven to 350°. Crumble the cookies and spread half of the crumbs over the bottom of the prepared pastry shell. Pour in the filling, and sprinkle the remaining crumbs over the filling. Bake the tart for about 40 minutes, or until it is golden brown. Serve it at room temperature.

MONTRACHET TART

Makes 8 to 10 servings

Dan Belajack and Jack Monaco came up with this savory cheesecake-tart for one of Tawfiq Khoury's spectacular dinner parties. We have also served it as a dessert, but some guests are put off by the fact that it is not sweet. You might serve it with Cognac or Armagnac after dessert, or like the cheese course the French serve before a sweet dessert.

TO PREPARE THE PASTRY SHELL

½ cup unbleached, all-purpose flour

6 tablespoons unsalted butter, chilled

2 tablespoons shortening, chilled

Scant ⅛ teaspoon salt

Scant ⅛ teaspoon sugar

4 tablespoons cold water

1. Place the flour, butter, shortening, salt, and sugar in a bowl. Mix the ingredients together with your fingertips until the mixture is crumbly. Using a fork, stir in the cold water, mixing thoroughly. Refrigerate the pastry, covered, for 2 hours.

2. Roll out the pastry to a 14-inch circle. Place it in a 12-inch tart pan with a removable bottom, pressing the pastry in against the sides and trimming any overhanging edges. Refrigerate the pastry-lined pan for 1 hour.

3. Preheat oven to 350°. Line the pastry with parchment paper or aluminum foil and place pie weights or dried beans on top. Bake the pastry for 30 minutes, or until it is golden brown around the sides and slightly pale in the center. Remove the weights and paper and set the pastry aside. Leave the oven on.

TO FILL THE PASTRY SHELL

1 log (13 ounces) Montrachet (goat cheese), softened

2 packages (8 ounces each) cream cheese, softened

3 large eggs

½ teaspoon chopped fresh rosemary

¾ pound pine nuts, lightly toasted

1 papaya (or sweet citrus fruit), sliced, for garnish

1. Using a food processor fitted with the plastic blade, or by hand, cream together the Montrachet and cream cheeses. Add the eggs, one at a time, blending thoroughly after each addition. Stir in the rosemary.

2. Fill the pie shell with the cheese mixture and top with the pine nuts. Bake the tart at 350° for 25 minutes. Allow the tart to cool, cut it into 8 to 10 wedges, and serve garnished with the fruit slices.

CAKES, PASTRIES, AND COOKIES

GÉNOISE

Makes two 9-inch layers

Some baking notes: Most recipes call for a single layer of génoise to be cut into thinner layers. An easy way to do this is to use a slicing knife with a serrated edge. Place the genoise on a flat work surface. Place the knife parallel to the work surface. With a sawing motion, cut through the layer, keeping the knife parallel to the work surface to cut an even layer. Note that all dry ingredients should be measured *before* sifting, unless the directions specify otherwise.

Génoise is a sponge cake leavened entirely with eggs. The trick is to beat and heat the egg-and-sugar mixture so that it increases greatly in volume without cooking the eggs. You may substitute cake flour, which has about two-thirds of the gluten or protein of unbleached, all-purpose flour. Do not, however, use bread flour, which has about double the gluten content of cake flour.

6 large eggs
1 cup sugar
1 cup cake or unbleached, all-purpose flour, sifted
½ cup clarified unsalted butter (page 239), melted
1 teaspoon vanilla

1. Butter and flour two 9-inch cake pans. Place the eggs and sugar in a mixing bowl, and stir them briefly, just to combine. Place the bowl over a saucepan of simmering water (do not let the bowl touch the water, and do not let the water boil). Whisk the mixture until the sugar is dissolved and it is warm to the touch. Remove the bowl from the heat and beat the mixture with an electric mixer on high speed for 2 minutes, then lower the speed to medium and beat the mixture until it forms a mousselike consistency. It should nearly triple in volume and be pale yellow.

2. Lightly fold in the flour in three batches. With the last addition, lightly fold in the clarified butter and vanilla.

3. Preheat oven to 350°. Pour the batter into the prepared pans and bake the cakes for 25 to 30 minutes, or until the cakes pull away from the sides of

the pans. Cool the cakes for 5 minutes, and turn the layers out onto a rack.

NOTE

Instead of vanilla, you may use 1 teaspoon grated orange zest plus 1 tablespoon orange juice, or 1 teaspoon grated lemon zest plus 1 tablespoon lemon juice. The cake also may be baked without any fat (i.e., butter) at all, resulting in a slightly less moist cake that will dry out faster. Génoise may be frozen, tightly wrapped in plastic wrap.

If you do not need layers, you may bake the cake in an 11 × 16 inch jellyroll pan.

CHOCOLATE GÉNOISE

Makes one 8-inch layer

Alice Medrich, the founder of Cocolat in Berkeley, taught at The Perfect Pan in 1980. Her cakes are dense with chocolate — nirvana to the chocoholic. Alice uses this génoise for her spectacular Gâteau Grand Marnier (page 268). When any recipe calls for a layer of chocolate génoise, this is the one we recommend. And please, use the very best cocoa you can afford; it makes all the difference.

4 large eggs
⅔ cup sugar
½ cup unbleached,
   all-purpose flour
½ cup unsweetened cocoa
3 tablespoons clarified
   unsalted butter
   (page 239), melted
1 teaspoon vanilla

1. Butter and flour an 8-inch-round cake pan. Place the eggs and sugar in a mixing bowl, and stir them briefly, just to combine. Place the bowl over a saucepan of simmering water (do not let the bowl touch the water, and do not allow the water to boil). Whisk the mixture until the sugar is dissolved and it is warm to the touch. Remove the bowl from the heat and beat the mixture with an electric mixer on high speed until it has cooled, tripled in volume, and resembles softly whipped cream.

2. Sift together the flour and cocoa, and then sift them, a little at a time, over the beaten eggs, folding them quickly but gently. Just before the folding is completed, scoop about 1 cup of the batter into the clarified butter and add the vanilla. Blend thoroughly, then fold the mixture back into the chocolate batter.

3. Preheat oven to 350°. Turn the batter into the prepared pan and bake it for 45 to 60 minutes, or until the cake shrinks slightly from the edges of the pan and the top springs back firmly when depressed with your finger. Turn the cake out onto a rack, invert the layer right-side up, and cool it completely.

Chocolate Buttercream
Makes about 1½ to 2 cups

½ cup sugar
¼ cup water
⅛ (scant) teaspoon cream of tartar
1 egg
12 tablespoons unsalted butter
8 ounces semisweet chocolate
4 tablespoons water

1. Combine the sugar, ¼ cup water, and cream of tartar in a very small saucepan. Cover and bring the mixture to a boil, reduce the heat, and simmer it, covered, for 2 to 3 minutes. Uncover the pan and use a pastry brush dipped in water to wash down any sugar crystals that remain on the sides of the pan. Cook the syrup until a candy thermometer registers 242°.

2. Beat the egg with an electric mixer at high speed until the egg is light colored and thick. When the syrup reaches 242°, pour it in a thin stream into the egg, beating the mixture constantly, until the mixture is cool. Beat in the butter, bit by bit, beating the mixture until it is smooth and spreadable.

3. Combine the chocolate and 4 tablespoons water in a small bowl placed over a pan of barely simmering water. Stir the mixture frequently until the chocolate is melted and smooth. Cool it slightly, and stir it into the buttercream.

Simple Syrup
Makes about 1½ cups

2 cups sugar
1 cup water
¼ teaspoon cream of tartar

Combine the sugar, water, and cream of tartar in a small saucepan. Cover the pan and bring the mixture to a simmer. Simmer it, covered, for 2 minutes, then cool the syrup, uncovered. Store it in a covered jar until needed.

GÂTEAU GRAND MARNIER

Makes 6 to 8 servings

Our variation of Anne Otterson's variation of Helen McCully's Grand Marnier Torte!

1 recipe Chocolate Génoise
   (page 266)
⅓ cup Simple Syrup (page 267)
⅓ cup Grand Marnier
Apricot preserves
1 recipe Chocolate Buttercream (page 267)

1 to 2 ounces semisweet chocolate, melted

1. Slice the cooled génoise into three layers. Place the top layer, cut-side up, on a stiff 8-inch cardboard circle. Stir together the syrup and Grand Marnier. With a pastry brush, moisten the génoise with the syrup mixture. Spread a thin layer of apricot preserves over the génoise, and spread on a layer of the buttercream.

2. Brush the second génoise layer with the syrup and place it, moist-side down, on top of the first layer. Brush the génoise with more syrup, and spread on more preserves and chocolate buttercream. Repeat the step with the third génoise layer, so the smooth side of the last layer is up. This time, spread buttercream over the top and sides of the cake.

3. Spoon the melted chocolate into a paper cone or small pastry bag fitted with a small, plain tip, and decorate the cake as you wish.

ALICE MEDRICH'S GÂTEAU DU PRIEUR

Makes 8 to 10 servings

1 recipe Chocolate Buttercream (page 267)
1 teaspoon or more instant espresso or coffee powder, dissolved in an equal amount of water
4 ounces semisweet chocolate, chopped
2 tablespoons water
1 recipe Chocolate Génoise
   (page 266)

1. Stir together ¾ cup of the buttercream and the dissolved instant coffee. Taste the cream and add more coffee if you want a stronger flavor. Set aside.

2. Combine the chopped chocolate and 2 tablespoons water in a bowl set over simmering water. When the chocolate melts, stir it into the remaining buttercream (without the coffee).

3. Slice the génoise into four very thin layers. Place the top layer on a stiff 8-inch piece of cardboard, cut-side up. Stir together the syrup and Cognac. With a pastry brush, moisten the génoise

½ cup Simple Syrup
(page 267)
4 to 6 tablespoons Cognac

1 to 2 ounces semisweet
chocolate, melted

with a little of the syrup mixture. Spread on a thin layer of the coffee-flavored buttercream.

4. Brush a second layer of génoise with the syrup mixture and place it on top of the first, moist-side down. Brush on more syrup, and spread on a layer of plain chocolate buttercream.

5. Repeat with a third layer of génoise, spreading it with the coffee-flavored buttercream. Stir any remaining coffee buttercream into the plain chocolate buttercream. Brush the cut side of the last génoise layer with syrup, and place it, moist-side down, on top of the cake. Brush it with more syrup. Spread the buttercream over the top and sides of the cake.

6. Decorate the cake as you wish with the melted chocolate piped through a paper cone, or with buttercream forced through a pastry bag with a decorating tip.

STRAWBERRY MOUSSE CAKE

Makes 8 to 10 servings

There's much more to génoise than chocolate buttercream, as this cake composed of layers of génoise and strawberry mousse demonstrates. To make this dessert even easier, prepare the génoise and mousse a few days before serving. The génoise can be frozen, tightly wrapped, and the mousse keeps up to a week, refrigerated. The assembled cake can be frozen in the pan for up to four days. If you plan to store the cake, it's a good idea to moisten the génoise layers with Simple Syrup (page 267) mixed with Kirschwasser or some other spirit.

STRAWBERRY MOUSSE

1 cup strawberries, hulled
½ cup confectioners' sugar, sifted
2 tablespoons Kirschwasser
1½ tablespoons unflavored gelatin, softened in 3 tablespoons cold water
1 cup heavy cream

1. Reserve 4 of the prettiest strawberries and purée the rest in a blender or food processor fitted with the steel blade. Stir in the confectioners' sugar and Kirschwasser. Pour ½ cup of the puréed berries into a saucepan, add the softened gelatin, and heat the mixture over medium heat stirring constantly, until the gelatin is dissolved. Stir together the rest of the strawberry purée and the gelatin mixture, and cool the mixture to room temperature.

2. Whip the cream until it forms stiff peaks, and

1 layer of Génoise (page 265), split into 3 layers

fold it gently into the strawberry mixture. Refrigerate the mousse until it is slightly set (about 10 minutes).

3. Butter and sugar a 9-inch-round cake pan. Slice the reserved strawberries and arrange them in a star pattern, cut-side down, in the bottom of the pan.

4. Carefully pour a third of the mousse into the pan without disturbing the berries. Place one layer of the génoise on the mousse, and press it lightly to remove any air bubbles. Repeat this layering twice with more mousse and génoise. Refrigerate the dessert for 3 to 4 hours, or freeze it. To serve, unmold the dessert onto a pretty plate.

NOTE

If you want to garnish the cake after unmolding it, whip 1 cup heavy cream with ½ teaspoon vanilla and 2 teaspoons sugar, until stiff. Spread the cream over the sides of the cake and pipe a shell border around the top, using a pastry bag fitted with a star tip.

ORANGE BROWNIE CAKE

Makes 10 to 12 servings

With apologies to the ubiquitous Reine de Saba, flourless chocolate cakes are not our favorites. This one, however, is an exception — more like a brownie than a fudgy torte. It's best made a day before serving.

TO PREPARE THE CAKE

½ cup unsalted butter
⅔ cup sugar
3 eggs
¼ cup dry bread crumbs
1 cup slivered almonds (see note)
Zest of 1 orange
4 ounces semisweet chocolate, melted
1 tablespoon Grand Marnier

1. Butter and flour an 8-inch-round cake pan. Line the pan with wax paper or parchment paper, and butter the paper.

2. Cream together the butter and all but 2 tablespoons of the sugar until light and fluffy. Beat in the eggs, one at a time, with an electric mixer on high speed, beating the mixture well after each addition.

3. Combine the bread crumbs, almonds, orange zest, and remaining 2 tablespoons sugar in the work bowl of a food processor fitted with the steel blade,

and process to finely grind the nuts. (The sugar helps to keep the nuts from forming butter.)

4. With the mixer on low speed, add the nut mixture to the egg mixture, along with the melted chocolate, to form a smooth batter. Fold in the Grand Marnier.

5. Preheat oven to 375°. Pour the batter into the prepared pan and bake it for 25 to 30 minutes. (A toothpick test won't work with this moist cake; instead, check after 25 minutes: it should have a dry, cracking crust and the cake should feel a bit firm when you press it with your finger.) Remove the cake from the oven and let it cool in the pan until it pulls away from the sides. Invert the cake onto a plate, pull off the paper, and let the cake cool completely. It will sink down to about ½-inch thickness.

TO GLAZE THE CAKE

2 ounces unsweetened chocolate
2 ounces semisweet chocolate
¼ cup unsalted butter
2 teaspoons honey
2 teaspoons Grand Marnier

1. Combine all the glaze ingredients in a double boiler and cook over low heat until the chocolate melts. Stir the glaze to blend it thoroughly.

2. Place the cake on a rack over a pan to catch the drips. Brush any crumbs from the cake. Spoon the glaze over the cake, using a thin spatula to evenly coat the sides, but working the glaze as little as possible on the top, to keep the surface smooth. (Or place the cooled cake on a plate with a rim, and pour the glaze over the cake; transferring the glazed cake from a rack to a plate can be tricky.)

NOTE

Slivered almonds are commonly sold in 2½-ounce packages, containing about ¾ cup. The remaining slivered almonds can be used to garnish the cake: Grind them with a little sugar in the food processor, and sprinkle them over the glaze. Or cool the cake on a cardboard circle, and glaze as directed above. Holding the cake in one hand, fill your other hand with ground almonds, and press them into the sides of the cake.

VARIATIONS

· Substitute hazelnuts or walnuts for the almonds.
· Use Framboise (raspberry liqueur) instead of

Grand Marnier in the cake and glaze, and substitute strained, puréed raspberries for the honey in the glaze.

- Use half bittersweet and half semisweet chocolate for a denser, less sweet cake.
- Instead of glazing the cake, dust the top with confectioners' sugar, and decorate with strips of candied orange zest.

MIXED-FRUIT CAKE WITH VANILLA SAUCE

Serves 6 to 8

Think of this as nearly instant fruit coffee cake. As the seasons change, the combination of fruit in the filling can change, too. The sauce improves with a few hours' refrigeration to allow the flavors to blend. This concoction came to us by way of Virginia Thomas.

Zest of 1 lemon
⅓ cup sugar
4 cups mixed fruit (see note)
¼ cup Cognac
1 teaspoon fresh lemon juice
½ cup unbleached,
  all-purpose flour
⅓ cup sugar
¼ teaspoon salt
3 large eggs
1 cup milk (approximately)
2 tablespoons vanilla
Cinnamon, to taste
1 tablespoon confectioners'
  sugar

VANILLA SAUCE

3 tablespoons confectioners'
  sugar
1 teaspoon vanilla
1 vanilla bean
1 cup sour cream

NOTE

1. Mince the lemon zest and sugar, using a food processor fitted with the steel blade. Add the zest mixture to the fruits and pour the Cognac and lemon juice over them. Let them stand for at least ½ hour. Drain the fruit and reserve the juice.

2. Combine the flour, sugar, salt, and eggs in the work bowl of the food processor. Add enough milk to the reserved Cognac and juice to make 1¼ cups, and add it and the vanilla to the flour mixture. Process to a smooth batter.

3. Preheat oven to 375°. Distribute the fruit over the bottom of a buttered quiche pan. Pour the batter over the fruit, and sprinkle it with cinnamon and the confectioners' sugar. Bake the cake for 1 hour, or until it is puffy and brown. Serve it warm or at room temperature with the vanilla sauce.

4. *To make the vanilla sauce:* Combine the confectioners' sugar, vanilla, the seeds scraped from the vanilla bean, and the sour cream, and beat until smooth.

Good fruit choices are unpeeled sliced apples, pitted cherries, peeled and pitted peaches and plums, and whole blueberries.

ZUCCOTTO FRIGERI

Makes 6 to 8 servings

Another example of génoise-based dessert, this is a sort of chocolate-nut trifle. Decorate with whipped cream or a buttercream icing, if you wish, or leave it plain with a dusting of confectioners' sugar.

1 layer of Génoise (page 265)
2 tablespoons brandy
2 tablespoons Cointreau or other liqueur
2 tablespoons Maraschino liqueur

FILLING

2 ounces almonds
2 ounces hazelnuts or filberts
5 ounces semisweet chocolate (squares or chips)
3 cups heavy cream
½ cup sugar

Confectioners' sugar or grated chocolate, for garnish

1. Line a 2-quart bowl with plastic wrap, leaving 5 to 6 inches overhanging the sides of the bowl. Slice the génoise in half horizontally. Set aside one layer. Cut the other into triangles, and place them in the bowl with the narrow points at the bottom, so that they completely line the bowl.

2. Combine the brandy, Cointreau, and Maraschino liqueur, and sprinkle about 4 tablespoons of the mixture over the cake lining. Set it aside.

3. Preheat oven to 400°. Drop the almonds into boiling water, blanch them for 20 to 30 seconds, and drain. When the almonds are cool enough to handle, squeeze them between your thumb and forefinger to remove the skins. Spread the almonds on a baking sheet and toast them in the oven until they are golden (about 3 to 5 minutes). Watch them carefully so they don't burn; they'll continue to cook after they're removed from the oven.

4. Spread the hazelnuts or filberts on the baking sheet and toast them in the oven for about 5 minutes. Rub the hazelnuts vigorously between kitchen towels to remove the skins. Coarsely chop the almonds and hazelnuts, and set them aside.

5. Coarsely chop the chocolate, if you're using squares. Melt 3 ounces of the chocolate in a small bowl set over hot water. Set it aside.

6. Whip the heavy cream with the ½ cup of sugar until it forms stiff peaks. Fold the nuts and remaining chopped chocolate (or chips) into the whipped cream. Divide the cream mixture into two equal parts. Spoon half of the cream mixture into the cake-lined bowl, spreading it up the sides to form a cavity in the center.

7. Fold the melted chocolate into the remaining

cream mixture, and spoon it into the cavity. Place the remaining sponge circle over the cream filling. If the cake is too wide for the bowl, trim the circle, and scatter the trimmings over the filling before covering it with the cake circle. Sprinkle the cake circle with the remaining liqueur mixture.

8. Fold the overhanging plastic wrap over the cake and refrigerate it for several hours or overnight. When ready to serve, invert the mold onto a serving platter and remove the plastic wrap. Sprinkle the cake with confectioners' sugar and/or grated chocolate.

RUM BABAS

Makes 8 babas

The basic formulas for babas and savarins (page 274) are similar. Babas are baked in little bucket-shaped molds called darioles, while savarins are baked in a ring-shaped pan called a savarin. Both cakes are soaked liberally in a sugar syrup spiked with rum or other spirits and flavorings such as orange zest. They're related to the Alsatian kugelhopf, with its rich, eggy yeast dough, and are mixed much the same way, with the dough lifted from the bowl or work surface and slammed down again. Messy but effective.

Both babas and savarins may be baked up to one week before serving and kept in an airtight container, or they may be frozen. The drier they are, the more syrup they will absorb. On serving day, make the syrup and soak the cakes in it. This is a very spongy dough and will soak up an extraordinary amount of syrup, but if there's any left over, refrigerate it in a jar; it will keep indefinitely. Use the syrup to poach fruit or moisten cake layers. Like all pastries, these cakes should be served at room temperature, to bring out their full flavor. These babas are very boozy and you may want to cut down somewhat on the amount of rum, if this is not to your taste. Once the babas have been soaked and filled, they should be served the same day. If you fill them hours before they are served, store them in the refrigerator and bring them to cool room temperature before serving.

DOUGH

1 package dry yeast
3 tablespoons lukewarm water

1. For this recipe, you will need eight dariole molds. Butter the molds, chill them in the freezer, and butter again. Set them aside in a cool place.

1 tablespoon sugar

3 large eggs, beaten

1¾ cups unbleached,
   all-purpose flour

½ cup unsalted butter,
   softened

1 teaspoon salt

½ cup rum

¼ cup water

RUM SYRUP

2½ cups sugar

1 quart water

2 tablespoons dark rum

CREAM FILLING

2 cups heavy cream

⅓ cup confectioners' sugar

2 tablespoons dark rum

⅓ cup heated, strained
   apricot preserves,
   for glaze

Sliced fresh fruit, for garnish
   (optional)

2. Sprinkle the yeast over the lukewarm water and let it stand about 5 minutes, or until the yeast is dissolved. Stir in the sugar, then the eggs. Add the flour all at once, and beat the mixture with a wooden spoon, slapping it against the side of the bowl until you can lift a very thick but smooth sheet that is quite elastic. (You may have to add another egg, depending on the moisture of the flour and the size of the egg.) Another way to mix the dough is to turn it out onto a work surface and, with your hand, lift up the dough and slap it back onto the counter. Continue this lifting and slapping, scraping up the dough from the counter every now and then with a pastry scraper, until the dough no longer sticks to the counter and is thick, smooth, and elastic.

3. Return the dough to a clean bowl. Mix the butter and salt and drop little spoonfuls of it around the edge of the bowl, letting it rest on the dough. (This way the yeast has time to grow without being in contact with the salt, and the dough and butter reach the same temperature, which makes them easier to combine.) Set the dough aside in a warm place to rise.

4. When the dough has doubled in bulk (about 45 minutes to 1 hour), beat it with a wooden spoon to incorporate the butter. (You may use the same slapping and lifting technique you used in step 2, incorporating the ingredients well, but don't work the dough to death.) Pinch off the balls of dough to fill the molds about one-third full, drawing the batter away from the center with your finger so it doesn't rise too high in the middle when baked. You want the dough to rise just to the top of the mold — no higher. Place the molds on a baking sheet, cover them with a cloth, and let them rise in a warm place about 1 hour, or until the dough just reaches the tops of the molds.

5. Preheat oven to 400°. Bake the babas for 20 minutes, or until they begin to shrink from the sides of the molds. Unmold the babas and let them cool completely.

6. *To prepare the rum syrup:* Heat the sugar with

the water over low heat until the sugar dissolves. Boil the mixture 2 to 3 minutes, or until it is clear. Stir in the rum. Cool the rum syrup to about 120°.

7. Soak the babas one at a time in the syrup, spooning the syrup over the baba so it absorbs as much syrup as possible. Do not soak so long that the baba begins to fall apart. Using a slotted spoon, carefully transfer the baba to a rack placed over a pan to catch the drippings. Repeat until all eight babas have been soaked. Let them drain.

8. When ready to serve, whip the cream with the sugar and rum. Heat the apricot preserves and strain them through a fine sieve. Cut the babas in half lengthwise, and pipe in the whipped cream with a pastry bag fitted with a fairly large tip. Brush the babas with the apricot glaze. Garnish the serving plate with sliced fruit, such as strawberries.

SAVARIN

Makes 8 to 10 servings

DOUGH

1 package dry yeast
¼ cup warm water
2 tablespoons sugar
4 large eggs
2¼ cups unbleached,
    all-purpose flour
½ teaspoon salt
9 tablespoons unsalted
    butter, softened

1 recipe rum syrup
    (page 275), plus juice and
    zest of ½ lemon
1 recipe cream filling
    (page 275–76)
Sliced fresh fruit or berries
⅓ cup apricot preserves, for
    glaze

1. Make the dough using the method for Rum Babas (page 274). Thoroughly butter a 5-cup savarin mold. Spoon in the dough, cover it with a cloth, and let it rise in a warm place until the dough has risen to the top of the mold (about 30 to 35 minutes).

2. Preheat oven to 400°. Bake the savarin for 20 to 25 minutes, or until it is browned and shrinks from the sides of the pan. Remove it from the pan and cool it on a rack.

3. Soak the savarin in the rum syrup–lemon mixture, following the instructions for the babas.

4. When ready to serve, whip the cream with the sugar and rum, and heat and strain the apricot preserves. Slice the savarin in half horizontally, and fill with whipped cream and fresh fruit. Top with the other half and brush with the apricot glaze.

PÂTE À CHOUX

Makes 12 cream puffs

Pâte à choux, also called cream-puff paste, is the basic dough for cream puffs, gougères, Paris-Brest Cake (page 279), and éclairs. Made from a roux-like paste called panade (flour, water, and butter) and beaten eggs, the paste can be used to make sweet or savory dishes. Recipes can vary rather widely in proportions of flour, fat, and eggs, but in general the greater the amount of egg in the paste, the lighter the result; and the more eggs you use, the less fat (butter) is needed. Recipes richest in fat are best used for small choux pastries.

Pâte à choux is ordinarily used immediately, but it may be refrigerated and brought to a warm temperature by beating it vigorously over heat for a minute or two. Be careful when reheating it: if the eggs get too hot and cook, the pastry won't puff. Be sure to bake puffs thoroughly, or they'll collapse when they cool. After baking larger puffs and éclairs, cut a small hole in the side near the top to allow steam to escape (this will help keep them from becoming soggy) and return them to the turned-off oven for a few minutes, to dry.

1 cup water
6 tablespoons unsalted butter
¼ teaspoon salt
5 ounces (about 1 cup) unbleached, all-purpose flour
5 large eggs
2 teaspoons sugar (optional for sweetened choux paste)

1. Bring the water, butter, and salt to a boil in a porcelain-covered cast-iron pan or other heavy saucepan. Remove the pan from the heat, and stir in the flour all at once. (For sweet pastry, add the sugar.) Beat the mixture vigorously with a wooden spoon to blend it well. Return the pan to the heat and beat the mixture over medium-high heat until it leaves the sides of the pan and forms a ball. Remove the pan from the heat.

2. Scrape the panade into a clean bowl, and allow it to cool. Using an electric mixer on medium speed, or working by hand with a wooden spoon, beat in 1 egg at a time, making certain that the egg is thoroughly incorporated before adding the next one. The choux is ready to use when it is glistening, velvety, and about the consistency of thick mayonnaise.

3. Spoon the mixture into a pastry bag fitted with a plain tip, and pipe out puffs on a lightly greased baking sheet. They may be made dime-size, 1 inch, or 3 inches in diameter. Dime-size puffs are used to garnish consommé and other soups. One-inch puffs may be filled with savory mixtures for

hors d'oeuvres. Larger puffs may be filled with a fish or vegetables in cream sauce, sweetened whipped cream, or flavored pastry cream.

4. Preheat oven to 425°. Bake dime-size puffs for 10 minutes, 1-inch puffs for 20 minutes. Three-inch puffs should bake for 20 minutes at 425°, then bake an additional 10 to 15 minutes at 375°. The puffs may then be slit and returned to the turned-off oven for another 10 minutes, to let them dry.

SAVORIES

Savory choux paste

Omit the sugar and add a dash of freshly ground pepper and nutmeg to the pan with the butter and water, and increase the salt slightly.

Gougères

To savory choux paste, omit the sugar and add 2 ounces of finely diced or grated Gruyère cheese. Other types of hard cheese may be substituted. Bake small puffs. Fill them with cheese sauce or one of the savory sauces from chapter 8.

Cheese Sauce
Makes about 2 cups

2 tablespoons unbleached, all-purpose flour
2 tablespoons butter
2 cups milk
Salt and freshly ground pepper, to taste
⅔ cup freshly grated Gruyère cheese

In a small, heavy saucepan, melt the butter and stir in the flour. Cook this roux for 2 minutes to eliminate the raw flour taste. Whisk in the milk all at once, and cook the sauce, stirring often, until it thickens. Stir in the cheese, and continue stirring until it melts. Spoon a little of the sauce into each cheese puff.

SWEETS

Éclairs

Fit a pastry bag with a large plain tip and fill it with the sweetened choux paste. Pipe out fingers of paste about 5 inches long. Preheat oven to 425° and bake the pastry 30 to 35 minutes, or until golden. Cut a slit near the top of each and return them to the turned-off oven to dry, if desired. Pipe pastry cream (page 280) or vanilla-flavored whipped cream into the puff, and frost with a favorite icing.

Cream puffs   Using two small spoons or a pastry bag with a large plain tip, drop rounds of sweetened choux paste on a lightly buttered baking sheet and bake as directed above for savory puffs. The cooled puffs can be filled and iced in the same manner as éclairs.

PARIS-BREST CAKE

Makes 8 to 10 servings

The classic Paris-Brest is a choux pastry ring, filled with nougat-flavored pastry cream redolent of caramel and almonds. The pastry cream, nougatine, choux pastry ring, and whipped cream all can be made in advance, and the cake constructed just before serving. Additionally, the cake can stand for several hours, refrigerated, before serving. Individual-size cakes can be made by piping smaller rounds of choux paste.

Nougatine is a staple in the pastry kitchen. It's useful for flavoring pastry cream to use in cream puffs, éclairs, and génoise-based cakes, for flavoring buttercream frostings, and for ice cream. The powder keeps indefinitely in an airtight container. Other types of nuts, such as hazelnuts, alone or in combination with almonds, may be used.

TO PREPARE THE CAKE

1 recipe Pâte à Choux
(page 277)
1 large egg, beaten
1 tablespoon thinly sliced
almonds

1. Butter and flour a cookie sheet and trace a 10-inch circle in the flour. Place the pâte à choux dough in a pastry bag with a large plain tip, and pipe a ring of dough on the baking sheet, following the traced circle. Pipe another ring inside and against the first one. Pipe a third ring on top of the first two, in the seam where they join.

2. Preheat oven to 400°. Brush the dough with the beaten egg and let it dry for 10 minutes. Sprinkle on the almonds. Bake the cake for 50 minutes. During the last 5 minutes of baking, prop the oven door open a little so the steam can escape.

3. Remove the cake from the oven and let it cool in a warm place. If the cake cools too fast, it will soften. When the cake is cool, slice it horizontally, about one-third of the way from the top. The layers will be hollow.

TO PREPARE THE NOUGATINE

¾ cup sugar
3 tablespoons water
½ cup unskinned, sliced
   almonds

1. Lightly oil a baking sheet and set it aside. Dissolve the sugar in the water in a heavy saucepan over medium heat, stirring until it melts. Stop stirring, and watch the sugar carefully, because it will very quickly turn from sugar to caramel to a blackened mess. When the caramel is golden, quickly stir in the almonds. Pour the caramel mixture onto the baking sheet and spread it with an oiled spatula. Set it aside to cool.

2. When the nougatine is completely cool, break it into pieces, and pulverize it to a coarse powder, using a blender or a food processor fitted with the steel blade. Set it aside.

TO PREPARE THE PASTRY CREAM

4 egg yolks
⅓ cup sugar
1 teaspoon vanilla
2 tablespoons cornstarch
1¼ cups milk

1. In a small bowl, whisk together the egg yolks, sugar, and vanilla, beating the mixture vigorously until it is thick and light and forms an undulating ribbon when dropped from the whisk. Whisk in the cornstarch, mixing it until well blended.

2. Bring the milk to a boil in a heavy saucepan. Pour a ladleful of hot milk into the yolk mixture, whisking it until smooth. Pour the heated egg mixture back into the saucepan, and bring it to a boil over medium heat, stirring constantly to avoid scorching. (The cornstarch stabilizes the cream so the eggs won't curdle when it boils.)

3. Pour the pastry cream into a bowl, stir to cool it and release steam, and cover the cooled cream with plastic wrap, pressing the wrap right onto the surface of the cream. Chill.

FINAL ASSEMBLY

2 cups heavy cream
3 tablespoons confectioners'
sugar
2 tablespoons dark rum

1. Stir the nougatine powder into the pastry cream, and spoon the mixture into the bottom cake layer, filling it half to three-quarters full.

2. Whip the 2 cups heavy cream. When it starts to thicken, beat in 2 tablespoons of the confectioners' sugar and the rum. Whip the cream until it forms stiff peaks.

3. Using a pastry bag fitted with a fluted tip, pipe the whipped cream over the nougatine layer so it comes about an inch above the rim. Replace the top cake layer, sprinkle on the remaining confectioners' sugar, using a sieve, and serve.

NOTE

For individual cakes, pipe single rings of choux paste about 3 inches wide on buttered and floured baking sheets, and proceed as directed above. Bake the rings a shorter period, about 20 to 30 minutes, or until they are golden brown.

MADELEINES

Makes 24 to 30 small cookies

Legend has it that a cook named Madeleine Palmier invented the recipe for madeleines (but not palmiers, we gather) while she was in the service of King Stanislaus of Poland. It is said that she passed it along to the Debouzie-Bray family in Poland. From there its popularity grew by — what else? — word of mouth. Madeleines are baked in a tin plaque usually containing 12 individual fan-shaped molds.

1 cup superfine sugar
4 large eggs, at room
    temperature
2 cups unbleached,
    all-purpose flour
1 cup unsalted butter,
    melted
1 teaspoon vanilla or zest of
    1 lemon

1. Grease 2 madeleine molds with shortening, and set them aside.

2. Whisk together the sugar and eggs in a heatproof mixing bowl. Place the bowl over a pan of simmering water, and whisk the mixture until it is very warm to the touch (see note).

3. Remove the bowl from the heat and beat the eggs with an electric mixer on high speed for 2 minutes, then on medium speed for 5 minutes. Gradually stir in the flour, then the butter and vanilla or lemon zest.

4. Preheat oven to 350°. Spoon the batter into the prepared molds to barely fill them. Bake the cookies for about 15 minutes, or until they are golden. Immediately unmold the cookies onto racks to cool completely. They will keep up to one week in airtight containers.

For chocolate madeleines

Follow the above recipe, but melt 3 ounces of unsweetened chocolate with the butter.

NOTE

Professional cooks will submerge the bowl right into the simmering water so the egg mixture is beneath the level of the water. That's risky; unless you're very skilled, you take a chance of scrambling the eggs. It's also quick: with a metal bowl in the water, the beating takes about 2 minutes, or 3 to 4 minutes in a ceramic bowl. With the bowl over the water, figure on twice that time.

TUILES

Makes 5 dozen small cookies

Tuiles are named for roof tiles, which these thin, crispy cookies resemble. Although French by heritage, they're much the same shape as the red tiles found on so many Spanish-inspired homes in the American Southwest.

The cookies are formed by draping them over a rolling pin while they are still hot from the oven. You must work quickly so they don't harden before you mold them. In very humid weather, you may find that the tuile cookies are not as crisp as they should be; in that case, place them in a low-temperature oven for a few minutes to remove excess moisture. They are terrific at tea time and with ice cream, sorbet, sweet mousse, or fresh-fruit compote.

¾ cup sugar

5 tablespoons unbleached, all-purpose flour

Grated zest of 1 orange

3 egg whites, at room temperature

5 tablespoons unsalted butter, melted

2 cups blanched almonds, thinly sliced

1. Stir together the sugar, flour, and orange zest. Stir in the egg whites. Slowly stir in the melted butter, then the almonds. Refrigerate the batter for 30 minutes.

2. Lightly oil a baking sheet. Drop the dough by teaspoonfuls about 3 inches apart. Dip a fork in water, and use the fork to flatten each cookie to ⅛ inch thick.

3. Preheat oven to 350°. Bake the cookies for 8 to 10 minutes, or until the edges turn brown. Immediately remove the cookies from the baking sheet with a spatula and drape them over a rolling pin that has been very lightly oiled. As the cookies cool and harden, remove them to racks to cool completely. Store them in airtight containers in a cool place.

NOTE

If the cookies harden before you can remove them all from the baking sheets, return them to the oven for a minute or so to soften.

JENNY SAAR'S WHITE CHOCOLATE CHIP COOKIES

Makes about 5 dozen cookies

1 cup unsalted butter
1¾ cups sugar
2 large eggs
2 teaspoons brandy or
    vanilla
1 ounce unsweetened baking
    chocolate
¼ cup sour cream
2 cups unbleached,
    all-purpose flour
¾ cup unsweetened cocoa
½ teaspoon baking soda
¼ teaspoon baking powder
½ teaspoon salt
12 ounces white chocolate,
    chopped (about 2 cups)
1 cup chopped Brazil nuts
    or almonds

1. Using an electric mixer, beat the butter and sugar together until light and fluffy. Beat in the eggs, one at a time. Beat in the brandy or vanilla. Melt the chocolate in a dish over hot water. Stir the melted chocolate and sour cream into the creamed mixture.

2. Sift together the flour, cocoa, baking soda, baking powder, and salt. Stir the dry ingredients gradually into the melted chocolate mixture to form a batter. Stir in the white chocolate and nuts.

3. Preheat oven to 350°. Drop the batter by tea-spoonfuls onto buttered baking sheets. Bake the cookies for about 10 minutes. Remove the cookies from the baking pans and cool them completely on a rack.

TOMMIES

Makes about 3 dozen cookies

Our tester says he gained five pounds while he tested this cookie recipe.

¾ cup hazelnuts
½ cup sugar
½ cup pastry or cake flour
½ teaspoon salt
¼ cup unsalted butter
4 ounces semisweet
    chocolate
¼ cup honey

1. Preheat oven to 350°. Roast the shelled hazelnuts for 10 minutes, or until the skins darken. When they are cool enough to handle, rub the hazelnuts in a towel to remove the skins. Set the hazelnuts aside to cool.

2. When the hazelnuts are cool, grind them with 4 tablespoons of the sugar. Sift together the flour and salt, and add them to the nut-sugar mixture. Pour the mixture onto a clean surface and make a well in the center. Add the butter, cut into bits, and the remaining 4 tablespoons of sugar, and work the mixture to a paste, gradually drawing in the dry

ingredients. Knead the dough until it is pliable. Chill it for 30 minutes wrapped in plastic wrap.

3. Preheat oven again to 350°. Roll the dough ¼ inch thick and cut it into 2-inch rounds with a cookie cutter. Place the cookies on a lightly greased baking sheet and bake them for 7 to 10 minutes, or until they are firm. Remove them from the baking sheet with a spatula and cool the cookies on a rack.

4. Using a double boiler, melt the chocolate over, but not in, simmering water. Spread half the cookies with a smooth coating of chocolate. Spread the remaining cookies with honey, and place a chocolate-covered cookie on top, chocolate-side up. Store the cookies in an airtight container at room temperature.

CIGARS

Makes about 3 dozen cookies

⅔ cup unsalted butter, at room temperature
2 cups confectioners' sugar
6 large egg whites
1¼ cups pastry or cake flour
1 tablespoon heavy cream
1 teaspoon vanilla

1. Cream the butter, and beat in the confectioners' sugar using an electric mixer. Slowly beat in the egg whites. When the mixture is smooth, stir in the flour, mixing it well. Beat in the cream and vanilla.

2. Pour the batter into a pastry bag fitted with a plain tip, and pipe dollops of the batter 5 inches apart on a lightly buttered baking sheet. Spread the batter evenly, forming circles about 4 inches in diameter.

3. Preheat oven to 350°. Bake the cookies for 4 to 5 minutes. Remove them immediately with a spatula to a work surface dusted with sugar, and roll them into cigar-shaped cylinders. If the cookies cool and harden before all are formed, return them to the oven for a few seconds to soften.

NOTE

If you're new at making shaped cookies, work with just a few at a time. These can also be shaped into fortune cookies or cone shapes to hold ice cream, sorbet, or mousse. Store the cookies in an airtight container.

CREAM AND FRUIT DESSERTS

PIRET'S CHOCOLATE MOUSSE

Makes 8 servings

½ pound top-quality
  semisweet chocolate
10 egg yolks
½ cup sugar
¼ cup Grand Marnier
2 cups heavy cream
1½ teaspoons vanilla

1. Chop the chocolate and melt it in a metal bowl over hot water, stirring occasionally.

2. Beat the egg yolks and sugar until the mixture is fluffy and light. Wipe the underside of the bowl containing the chocolate so that no water drips into the mousse. Using an electric mixer on slow speed, beat the chocolate into the egg-sugar mixture a little at a time until just combined, working quickly so the chocolate does not harden. Beat the mixture on medium speed for 2 minutes. Reduce the speed to slow and blend in the Grand Marnier. Set the mixture aside.

3. Using chilled bowl and beaters, whip the cream until it forms very stiff peaks, incorporating the vanilla as you beat.

4. Using a whisk, fold half of the whipped cream into the chocolate mixture, blending completely to lighten it. Using a chopping motion with a spatula, fold in the remaining whipped cream to create a marbelized coloration.

5. Refrigerate the mousse at least overnight (don't skip this step, or the mousse won't have the proper consistency), and spoon into dessert bowls to serve. The mousse will keep, refrigerated, for two to three days.

❧ When whipping cream, place the utensils — bowl and mixing beaters — in the freezer to chill thoroughly. This helps keep the cream temperature lower during whipping. If the cream gets too warm, you can end up with butter instead of whipped cream.

LEMON BAVARIAN CREAM

Makes 8 to 12 servings

Roberta Silberman won in the dessert category in the 1973 George Munger Cook-Off with this fine recipe. We've used it countless times since in the cooking school and at catered dinners. Melba Sauce is also delicious with poached pears (page 289) or other fruit, or spooned over ice cream or pound cake.

2 envelopes unflavored
   gelatin
½ cup cold water
2 packages (8 ounces each)
   cream cheese, softened
1 cup sugar
¾ cup fresh lemon juice
3 teaspoons lemon zest
1½ cups half-and-half
2 cups heavy cream,
   whipped
Fresh mint leaves and thin
   lemon slices, for garnish

MELBA SAUCE

1 package (1 pound) frozen
   raspberries, thawed (or 1
   pound fresh berries)
2 tablespoons raspberry jam
1 teaspoon Kirschwasser or
   Framboise

1. Soften the gelatin in the cold water in a small saucepan. Stir the mixture over low heat until it is completely dissolved. Using an electric mixer, whip the cream cheese until it is fluffy and light. Add the sugar, lemon juice, and zest, and beat until the mixture is smooth. Stir in the half-and-half and the gelatin, and refrigerate the mixture until it is slightly thickened (about 30 minutes).

2. Fold the whipped cream into the thickened gelatin and pour the mixture into a 2½-quart ring mold, Charlotte mold, or bowl. Refrigerate the mold until the mixture is firm.

3. To unmold, dip the bottom of the mold in warm water. Place a plate over the top of the mold and invert it. Garnish with fresh mint leaves and thin slices of lemon.

4. *To make the Melba Sauce:* Purée the raspberries, using a blender or a food processor fitted with the steel blade. Add the jam and liqueur, and purée again. Strain the sauce through a fine sieve to remove the seeds. Spoon the sauce around the Lemon Bavarian Cream and pour the remainder into a creamer or gravy boat so guests can help themselves.

ORANGE CREAM WITH CHOPPED NUTS

Makes 6 servings

A deliciously simple dessert, this can be made well ahead of time. We like to intensify the flavor with about ¼ cup of Grand Marnier, and when our orange trees are in bloom, we garnish the plate with a small sprig of orange blossoms, which have an intensely fragrant aroma.

We think the sweet and flavorful navel orange is best in this recipe. Whatever orange variety you use, taste its juice for sweetness, and vary the amount of sugar accordingly. Some markets in our area now carry blood oranges from Italy, which make a wonderful variation on this dish. Lemons, limes, grapefruit, persimmon, and raspberries also work very well. If you use a pulp-type fruit, add liquid in the form of a liqueur, water, or lemon juice, or the syrup will be too thick.

3 large oranges
¾ cup sugar
1 cup water
Pinch of salt
⅓ cup unsalted pistachio nuts
2 cups heavy cream
½ cup blanched almonds, finely chopped

1. Wash and dry the oranges and cut them in half crosswise. Squeeze the orange juice into a saucepan. Scrape out and discard the pulp, and reserve the shells. Stir the sugar into the juice, bring it to a boil, and cook until the orange syrup thickens. Set it aside to cool.

2. In another saucepan, bring the water and salt to a boil. Drop in the pistachio nuts, blanch them for 1 to 2 minutes, and drain them thoroughly. When the nuts are cool enough to handle, rub them between towels to remove the skins, and finely chop the nuts.

3. Using chilled bowl and beaters, whip the cream until it forms stiff peaks. Gently fold the orange syrup into the whipped cream, along with the almonds. Spoon the mixture into the reserved orange shells, and sprinkle the chopped pistachio nuts on top. Refrigerate until serving time.

PEARS WITH MELBA SAUCE

Makes 6 servings

Escoffier created Melba Sauce to honor opera star Nellie Melba after her performance in *Lohengrin*. The classic preparation is to serve it with poached peaches, but we like this sauce as well with poached pears or figs. Use 12 to 18 figs, and if they are perfectly ripe, there's no need to poach them; otherwise, poach them as you would the pears.

6 firm ripe pears, peeled and cored, stems intact
3 cups water
½ cup sugar
1 vanilla bean (or ½ teaspoon vanilla extract)

1 recipe Melba Sauce (page 287)

1. To poach the pears, bring the water and sugar to a boil in a medium saucepan, stirring to dissolve the sugar. Add the vanilla, and the pears in a single layer. Reduce the heat so that the water is at a bare simmer, and poach the pears until they are just tender when pierced with the tip of a knife. Remove them to a rack to cool. If using a vanilla bean, dry it and store it for further use.
2. To serve, spoon a little of the Melba Sauce into a serving dish. Stand the pears in the sauce and spoon on a little more.

BAKED SLICED APPLES

Makes 8 to 10 servings

Paula Wolfert brought us this lovely, easy dessert, which she learned from Paris chef Jacques Cagna.

8 to 12 Granny Smith apples or other cooking apples (about 2½ pounds)
1 cup unsalted butter, softened
1 cup sugar (approximately)

1. Quarter, peel, and core the apples. Slice them about ¼ inch thick, lengthwise, and place them in a single overlapping pattern in an 11 × 13 inch glass or porcelain baking dish, completely covering the bottom. Brush the slices lavishly with butter and sprinkle them generously with sugar (figure about 2 tablespoons for every apple).
2. Preheat oven to 425°. Bake the apples on the lowest rack for about 30 minutes, or until the sugar caramelizes. For a crispier caramel top, run the dish under a broiler for a few minutes.

BAKED PEACHES WITH WARM LEMON SAUCE

Makes 8 servings

Baked fruit with a simple sauce makes a quick, homey dessert. This is a Patty McDonald recipe.

8 peaches, halved and pitted
Juice of 2 lemons
4 tablespoons honey
4 tablespoons unsalted
   butter
8 tablespoons Grand Marnier
6 whole cloves
Pinch of freshly grated
   nutmeg

LEMON SAUCE

¾ cup sugar
½ cup unsalted butter
1 large egg
Juice and zest of 2 lemons
1 teaspoon freshly grated
   nutmeg
½ cup boiling water

1. Sprinkle the peaches with the lemon juice and place them in a baking dish. Combine the honey, butter, Grand Marnier, cloves, and 3 grates of nutmeg in a saucepan, and cook them over medium heat until the butter melts.

2. Preheat oven to 400°. Pour the butter over the peaches and bake them for 30 minutes. Let the peaches cool slightly.

3. *To make the lemon sauce:* In a small saucepan, beat together the sugar and butter until light and fluffy. Stir in the egg, lemon juice and zest, and 1 teaspoon nutmeg. Slowly stir in the boiling water, whisking the mixture constantly, and cook the sauce over low heat until it thickens. Do not let it boil.

4. To serve, spoon some of the warm sauce into a serving dish. Place 2 peach halves on the sauce, and spoon a little more of the sauce over them. If desired, garnish with sprigs of mint.

ICE CREAMS AND SORBETS

Ice creams and sorbets have been around since ancient times and are believed to have originated in
China and the Far East. Universally loved as a summer sweet, in France ice creams and sorbets are
known under the family name of *glaces*. Ice creams
are made with milk or cream and egg yolks — a
basic custard base; sorbets have a simple sugar syrup
as their base. To these are added various flavorings.
In the case of ice cream, the flavoring might be
vanilla, chocolate, fresh fruit pulps, ginger, or liqueurs; for sorbets, liqueurs, wine, fruit, or vegetable pulp might be added. The following are tips to
keep in mind in making ice cream and sorbet at
home:

- If you are adding a liqueur to an ice cream or
  sorbet mixture, ⅓ to ½ cup per quart of liquid is
  a good guideline.
- When you are making an ice cream custard, it is
  imperative that it not come to a boil, or it will
  curdle. To lessen the danger of curdling or
  scrambling the egg yolks when they are added to
  heated milk or cream, stir a ladleful of the milk
  or cream into the egg yolks to warm them
  slightly before adding them.
- The cream mixture, custard, or syrup should always be cool, even chilled, before pouring it into
  the canister, or you'll have butter clots in the ice
  cream.
- When making a syrup for a caramelized nut brittle, stir the sugar and water to blend, then bring
  it to a boil over medium heat without further
  stirring, which will crystallize the sugar. Once
  the syrup comes to a rolling boil, cover the pan
  for a few minutes to allow the steam to wash any
  sugar crystals down from the sides of the pan.
  When the syrup reaches 248° on a candy thermometer, remove the pan from the heat and stir

in the nuts. Continue stirring until the nuts are coated with syrup and appear dry and white. Let the nuts cool, and chop, grind, or pulverize them.

· Approximately 1½ cups of rock salt are needed for a 2-quart freezer. Too much salt makes the ice cream freeze too quickly, making it grainy.

· Increase the salt amount when the ice cream mixture is above average in sugar or contains alcohol, since these will inhibit freezing; decrease the salt amount slightly when the ice cream mixture is low in sugar or high in butterfat.

· As a general rule, most ice creams will take 20 to 40 minutes to freeze with an ice cream maker. If it takes less than 20 minutes, you used too much rock salt; if it takes longer than 45 minutes, there was too little salt. Sorbet takes longer to freeze than ice cream because of its high sugar content. Count on about 45 minutes.

· When the ice cream is finished, it should be smooth and creamy but stiff and clinging to the dasher. It is usually softer than commercial ice cream.

· Ice cream can be kept in the freezer three to four weeks in a closed container. Sorbets do not keep as long, and they should be served within two weeks.

· If molding the ice cream, pack it tightly to eliminate any air pockets. To unmold, dip the mold in warm water for 10 seconds, slip a knife around the edges, and invert the mold immediately. Refreeze the unmolded ice cream for 15 minutes to harden the outside, then decorate with chantilly cream, or serve with a sauce.

Homemade ice cream is so good it really doesn't need to be topped with anything, but the toppings we include in this chapter are irresistible. For large picnics, we sometimes make two or three ice creams and a sampling of sauces for an ice cream extravaganza.

Ices or sorbets are commonly used in France as a palate cleanser after the main course, a practice becoming increasingly common for formal dinners here in the States. Sorbets function best as a palate cleanser when they have a very clean, clear flavor, more tart than sweet. At the end of this section, you'll find two sorbets created for this purpose.

MODERN KANSAS FARM VANILLA ICE CREAM

Makes 3 quarts

Lois Stanton's favorite vanilla ice cream is one she remembers from her childhood on a Kansas farm. The original was slightly grainy with a lingering milky aftertaste, "whetting your appetite for more ice cream," she says. However, since most of us are more accustomed to highly emulsified, creamy commercial ice creams, she modernized the recipe for a more contemporary texture and flavor. Recipes for the authentic version, and Marcella Hazan's Scotch whiskey–espresso coffee topping, appear below.

4 cups whole milk
2 cups sugar
½ teaspoon salt
4 tablespoons unbleached, all-purpose flour
4 egg yolks
2 tablespoons vanilla
4 egg whites
2 cups heavy cream

1. In a medium saucepan, combine the milk, sugar, salt, flour, and egg yolks. Cook the mixture over medium heat, stirring constantly, for 15 to 20 minutes, or until the custard is very slightly thickened. Do not let the mixture boil or the egg yolks may scramble.

2. Cool the mixture over a bowl of ice water, stirring occasionally. Stir the vanilla into the custard.

3. Beat the egg whites to a soft peak stage. Whip the heavy cream lightly. Stir the egg whites and the whipped cream into the cooled custard, and blend thoroughly. Chill.

4. Freeze the mixture in an ice cream freezer, following the manufacturer's instructions.

Authentic Kansas Farm Vanilla Ice Cream

Follow the directions above, using 5 cups whole milk, 1 cup sugar, ¼ teaspoon salt, 2 tablespoons unbleached, all-purpose flour, 2 egg yolks, ¾ teaspoon vanilla, 2 egg whites, and 1 cup heavy cream. Chill. If you want to be really authentic, Lois suggests you freeze the ice cream in an old-fashioned, hand-crank oak bucket freezer.

Marcella Hazan's Scotch-Espresso Topping

While testing the ice cream one evening over a glass of Scotch, Lois's husband, Bill, remarked that Scotch went rather well with vanilla ice cream, reminding Lois of Marcella Hazan's delicious topping: over a scoop or two of vanilla ice cream, pour one jigger of Scotch whiskey, and sprinkle with fresh, finely ground espresso coffee beans or instant espresso coffee powder.

LORENZO AND OLGA'S VANILLA MINT ICE CREAM

Makes 3 quarts

Lorenzo Gunn was the first to demonstrate the true meaning of "excess" at the George Munger Cook-Off in 1978. He had scavenged up an antique sidewalk ice cream cart, and he and his wife, Olga, who wore a thirties garden-party dress topped with a prettier-than-spring straw hat bedecked with flowers, rolled it into our living room to dish up this incredibly rich dessert. The following year, their ice cream won the Grand Prize at the Celebrities Cook for Cancer Cook-Off, where one of the judges, James Beard, insisted it was the best ice cream he had ever eaten.

6 vanilla beans
1 ¼ cups sugar
1 quart half-and-half
1 tablespoon cornstarch
1 ½ quarts heavy cream
2 egg yolks, beaten
1 tablespoon vanilla
2 tablespoons mint extract
   (not peppermint)

1. Slice the vanilla beans in half lengthwise and scrape out the seeds. Pulverize the seeds in a mortar or spice grinder. Reserve both the beans and seeds.

2. Place the sugar and half-and-half in a medium saucepan and warm over very low heat, stirring constantly. Stir in the cornstarch. Add the vanilla seeds and beans to the half-and-half mixture. Stir in the heavy cream, then the egg yolks. As the mixture warms, it will begin to thicken slightly. Continue to stir, pressing the vanilla beans against the sides of the pan, over very low heat just until the mixture begins to steam. Do not let it simmer, or it will turn into a custard, which you do not want.

3. Remove the pan from the heat, and take out the vanilla beans, leaving the seeds. Add the vanilla

and mint extract a little at a time, until it suits your taste. Set the pan aside and cool to room temperature.

4. Freeze the mixture in an ice cream freezer, following the manufacturer's instructions.

PRALINE ICE CREAM

Makes 1 quart

Ice cream made with egg yolk and cream is usually called French ice cream and the mixture is close to a basic crème Anglaise (custard cream). The addition of coffee to the basic mixture makes it mocha ice cream, the addition of chocolate makes it chocolate ice cream, and so on. In this recipe, the custard is flavored with praline. An ice cream maker is needed for this ice cream: it emulsifies the mixture, making it light, smooth, and voluminous. This is a Jacques Pépin concoction, and very, very good.

Praline is a nougatine (caramelized sugar and nuts) ground to a paste. The cold mixture is usually crushed and reduced to a paste by machine, in the process of which some of the essential oils from the almonds are extracted. A food processor does not achieve the exact effect but produces a reasonable facsimile. Praline can be used to flavor custards and buttercreams as well.

TO PREPARE THE PRALINE

½ cup unskinned hazelnuts
½ cup unskinned almonds
¾ cup sugar
3 tablespoons water
1½ teaspoons almond or
    peanut oil

1. Preheat oven to 350°. Place the hazelnuts and almonds on a tray and roast them in the oven until golden brown. Check them after 15 minutes, and every 5 minutes thereafter, to be sure they don't scorch.

2. Place the sugar in a small, heavy saucepan and mix in the water, stirring just once to avoid crystallization. Boil the syrup over medium-high heat until it turns golden brown. Cover the pan for a few minutes to allow the steam to wash any sugar crystals down from the sides of the pan. Add the roasted nuts and shake to mix them well. Pour the mixture onto a lightly oiled baking sheet. Let the nougatine cool until it becomes brittle.

3. Break the nougatine into large pieces. Using a food processor fitted with the steel blade, process

the nougatine to coarse crumbs. Set aside ¼ of the coarse crumbs to use as a garnish.

4. Process the remaining nougatine to a crumbly, soft powder. Add the oil and blend the mixture another 2 to 3 minutes, stopping the machine every 20 to 30 seconds, until the mixture looks pasty and slightly wet. Set it aside. (At this point the praline can be refrigerated in a jar with a tight-fitting lid, and kept for months.)

TO MAKE THE ICE CREAM

3 cups milk
8 egg yolks
1 cup sugar
1 teaspoon vanilla
1 cup heavy cream, chilled

1. Bring the milk to a boil in a medium, heavy saucepan. While the milk heats, whisk together the egg yolks, sugar, and vanilla until the mixture is light, smooth, and pale colored and falls from the whisk in an undulating ribbon. Warm the egg mixture with a ladleful of the hot milk, then whisk it into the remaining milk. Cook the mixture over medium heat, stirring constantly, until it thickens slightly. Do not let it boil, or it will curdle. The custard should register about 170° on a candy thermometer.

2. Pour the chilled cream into a clean, chilled bowl and strain the cooked custard through a fine sieve into the cream, stirring constantly. The cream will quickly cool the custard, eliminating any further danger of the sauce's curdling. Whisk in the praline paste and cool the mixture to room temperature. Chill it thoroughly.

3. Freeze the mixture in an ice cream freezer, following the manufacturer's instructions. Serve the ice cream topped with the reserved crumbled nougatine.

HUGH CARPENTER'S GRAND MARNIER MOCHA ICE CREAM

Makes 2 quarts

9 egg yolks
1 cup sugar
4 cups heavy cream
1 pound best-quality
  European semisweet
  chocolate
½ cup strong, freshly
  brewed mocha coffee,
  plus 2 tablespoons coffee
  grounds from the pot
½ cup Grand Marnier

1. Beat the egg yolks and sugar with a whisk until they are thick and lemon colored and the mixture falls from the whisk in an undulating ribbon. In a medium saucepan, scald 3 cups of the heavy cream until bubbles form on the edges of the pan. Stir the hot cream into the egg mixture. Stir very quickly with the whisk so the eggs do not cook.

2. Pour the cream mixture back into the saucepan. Heat the mixture over high heat for 1 or 2 minutes, whisking constantly. (If you beat the mixture furiously, it will thicken without curdling the egg yolks. Or cook the custard in the top of a double boiler, whisking constantly, until the mixture thickens.)

3. When the custard has thickened, pour it into a clean bowl and place the bowl in a pan of cool water. Stir the custard periodically until it is cool.

4. In a double boiler over medium-high heat, combine the chocolate, coffee, and coffee grounds, and heat until the chocolate melts completely. Stir the chocolate mixture into the cool (but not cold) custard, and stir to blend thoroughly. Set aside to cool to room temperature. When the mixture is cool, add the Grand Marnier and the remaining 1 cup heavy cream, and stir to blend. Chill.

5. Freeze the mixture in an ice cream freezer, following the manufacturer's instructions.

PEACH ICE CREAM

Makes 1 quart

2 cups milk
1 cup sugar
6 egg yolks
1 cup heavy cream
4 peaches, peeled and
    chopped or puréed
¼ teaspoon almond extract

1. In a medium saucepan, stir together the milk and ½ cup of the sugar. Bring them to a boil and remove the saucepan from the heat. Beat the egg yolks with the remaining ½ cup of sugar until they are thick and lemon colored. Carefully whisk some of the hot milk into the yolk mixture, then pour it back into the remaining milk. Cook the custard over low heat, stirring constantly, until it registers 185° on a candy thermometer or lightly coats the back of a spoon.

2. Remove the pan from the heat and stir in the cream, the chopped or puréed peaches, and the almond extract. Chill.

3. Freeze the mixture in an ice cream freezer, following the manufacturer's instructions.

STRAWBERRY SORBET

Makes 1 quart

Dessert sorbets are excellent with delicate cookies, such as Madeleines (page 282) or Tuiles (page 283).

3 cups sugar
2 cups water
2½ pints fresh strawberries
    or frozen, unsweetened
    strawberries
1 tablespoon fresh lemon
    juice

1. Dissolve the sugar in the water, and bring it to a rolling boil over medium-high heat, stirring constantly until the sugar is dissolved. Remove the pan from the heat, pour the syrup into a bowl, and let it cool.

2. Hull and wash the berries. Using a blender or a food processor fitted with the steel blade, purée the berries (yields about 1½ cups). Stir in the lemon juice and 2 cups of the sugar syrup. Save any remaining sugar syrup for other recipes.

3. Freeze the mixture in an ice cream freezer for about 45 minutes, following the manufacturer's instructions.

ANNE OTTERSON'S PINEAPPLE SORBET IN COOKIE CUPS

Makes 8 cups

Little cookie cups, called *coupelles,* are delicious containers for sorbet, ice cream, or pudding. They're easier to make than you may think, although they require exact baking time and temperature, and quick work. The filled cookie cups can be made several days ahead and frozen, tightly wrapped. The sugar veil should be added just before serving.

TO MAKE THE SORBET

1 pineapple (2 pounds)
⅓ cup superfine sugar
Juice of ½ lemon (about 1 tablespoon)
2 tablespoons Kirschwasser

Cut the leaves from the pineapple and set them aside. Peel the pineapple, quarter it lengthwise, and remove the core. Cut the pineapple into large chunks and place them in the work bowl of a food processor fitted with the steel blade. Add the superfine sugar, lemon juice, and Kirschwasser, and purée the mixture to a frothy liquid. Pour it into a freezer tray and freeze it until it is slushy and not quite frozen (about 1 to 2 hours).

TO MAKE THE COOKIE CUPS

4 tablespoons unsalted butter, softened
⅓ cup granulated sugar
Grated zest of 1 orange or lemon
2 egg whites
⅓ cup unbleached, all-purpose flour

1. Butter and flour two baking sheets. Mark four circles, each 6 inches in diameter, on each sheet. Lightly oil three or four small custard cups and set them aside.

2. Using an electric mixer or a whisk, beat together the butter, sugar, and orange or lemon zest until the mixture is pale and fluffy. Beat in the egg whites for 10 to 15 seconds, until just blended. Sift in the flour, rapidly folding it in with a rubber spatula.

3. Preheat oven to 425°. Place a small dollop (1 to 2 tablespoons) of the batter in the center of each circle marked on one of the baking sheets. Spread the batter to fill the circles, getting it as thin as possible without breaking the surface (less than ⅛ inch thick). Place the baking sheet on the lowest rack of the oven and bake the cookies about 5 minutes, or until they are light brown.

4. As soon as the cookies are done, set the baking sheet on the open oven door so the cookies will stay warm and pliable. With a spatula, scrape one cookie off the baking sheet and place it upside-down into one of the oiled cups. Press it into the cup with your fingers. It will crisp in seconds. Remove it from the cup and let it cool completely on a rack. Working very quickly, repeat the molding steps with the remaining cookies. If they get too crisp to remove from the baking sheet, return them to the oven for a few seconds to soften.

5. Close the oven door and wait a few minutes for the temperature to return to 425°. Bake and mold the second sheet of cookies in the same manner.

TO MAKE THE SUGAR VEIL

½ cup water
Juice of ½ lemon
1 cup granulated sugar

1. When the sorbet has frozen to a slushy but not quite firm consistency, pipe or spoon it into the cookie cups. Return them to the freezer while you prepare the sugar veil.

2. Combine the water, lemon juice, and sugar in a small, heavy saucepan and bring them to a boil. Cover the pan for a few minutes to allow steam to wash any sugar crystals down from the sides of the pan. Cook the syrup, without stirring it, until the water evaporates and the sugar begins to caramelize. Watch it carefully, because the caramel can turn from brown to black very quickly.

3. Place the pan in cold water to stop the cooking. As it cools, the caramel will thicken, so work quickly. Place a fork in the caramel and draw it over the top of the sorbet in a zigzag motion. Give the cookie cup a half turn and repeat the zigzag with the caramel, to form a grid pattern. The caramel strands will harden almost immediately into a lacy "veil." Garnish with the reserved pineapple leaves, and serve.

CARROT SORBET WITH DILL

Makes 1 quart

Whenever time permits, George and Jack Monaco like to experiment with new approaches to traditional foods and methods. In this instance, we needed an interesting palate cleanser. We already had a salad course in the menu, and a fruit sorbet seemed inappropriate with the menu and wines being featured. They came up with this very interesting combination of flavors, using carrots, orange juice, Scotch whiskey, and dill weed. The sorbet was served in green pepper halves.

⅔ cup sugar
⅔ cup water
1 pound carrots, peeled and
    sliced
¼ cup fresh lemon juice
2 tablespoons frozen orange
    juice concentrate
1 tablespoon Scotch whiskey
1 teaspoon fresh or dried dill
    weed
Pinch of salt

1. Combine the sugar and water in a small saucepan over medium-high heat, and stir until the sugar is dissolved. Thoroughly chill the syrup.

2. Cook the carrots in water to barely cover them. When they are tender, drain them thoroughly, and purée them, using a blender, food mill, or food processor fitted with the steel blade. Thoroughly chill the carrot purée.

3. Combine the syrup and carrot purée in the work bowl of a food processor fitted with the steel blade, or in a blender. Add the lemon juice, orange juice concentrate, Scotch, dill, and salt, and process to a smooth texture.

4. Freeze the mixture in an ice cream freezer, following the manufacturer's instructions. (The sorbet also can be frozen in ice-cube trays. When the edges are frozen, remove the mixture from the trays and beat it with an electric mixer. Return the sorbet to the trays and repeat this freezing and beating step twice. Finally, let it freeze solid.)

CUCUMBER SORBET

Makes 1 quart

⅔ cup sugar
⅔ cup water
4 hothouse cucumbers,
   sliced thick
½ cup cider vinegar
1 tablespoon apple cider
2 small shallots, finely
   minced
1½ ounces vodka
Salt, to taste

1. Combine the sugar and water in a small saucepan over medium-high heat, and stir until the sugar is dissolved. Remove the syrup from the heat and allow it to cool.

2. Blanch the cucumber slices in salted boiling water for about 1 minute, then plunge them into ice water to stop the cooking. Pat the cucumbers dry and place them in the work bowl of a food processor fitted with the steel blade, along with the vinegar, cider, shallots, vodka, and salt. Process the mixture to blend, and chill it thoroughly.

3. Stir the syrup into the chilled mixture. Place the mixture in the freezer until it is slushy. Beat the mixture until it is smooth but not melted, and return it to the freezer. When it turns slushy again, repeat the beating process once more, then freeze it solid (or use an ice cream freezer, following the manufacturer's instructions).

DESSERT SAUCES & SWEET TOPPINGS

In this section, we're including three basic recipes we think are so useful in their application they deserve to be called indispensable. Crème Anglaise is lovely with chocolate ice cream, molded fruit and chocolate mousses, fresh berries, and dense, unadorned chocolate cakes. Zabaglione travels well all by itself. If you want embellishments, fresh raspberries are terrific. The sweet *crème fraîche* is superb with citrus fruits, berries, cherries, or a mixture of all of these. Other dessert sauce recipes can be found in chapter 7.

The toppings we've included here are all great with ice cream, but they also go well with other desserts. Try them with génoise, pound cake, poached fruit, crêpes, and flan. See also Marcella Hazan's Scotch-Espresso Topping (page 294).

CRÈME ANGLAISE

Makes about 2 cups

1 vanilla bean (or 1½ tea-
    spoons vanilla extract)
2 cups milk
6 egg yolks
4 tablespoons sugar

1. If using a vanilla bean, split it and add it to the milk in a medium, heavy saucepan. Bring the milk to a boil, remove the pan from the heat, and let it stand for 5 minutes to allow the flavors to infuse.

2. Beat together the egg yolks and sugar until they are light and lemon colored. Remove the vanilla bean from the milk (it can be dried and used again), and whisk half of the milk into the yolk mixture. Pour it back into the remaining milk. Heat the mixture gently, stirring constantly, until the custard thickens and coats the spoon. If vanilla extract and/or liqueur is being used, it should be added at this point.

3. Strain the custard into a bowl and let it cool. The sauce will keep, refrigerated in a covered container, for two days. To prevent a skin from forming on the top, cover the sauce with plastic wrap, pressing it right down onto the surface of the sauce.

NOTE

For coffee-flavored Crème Anglaise, substitute 1 tablespoon instant coffee granules for the vanilla bean. Or you may use any quality liqueur to taste along with the vanilla bean. Grand Marnier (orange flavor), Kirschwasser (cherry), Calvados (apple), Poire William (pear), and Framboise (raspberry), are all good candidates, depending on how you are serving the sauce.

ZABAGLIONE

Makes 6 servings

George's first encounter with the very interesting Thomas Cara, a San Francisco merchant of espresso makers and cookware, became a lesson in making zabaglione. According to Cara, you use half an eggshell as your measure. His recipe is 1 whole egg, 6 egg yolks, 3 shells of sugar, 3 shells of good white wine, and 3 shells of Marsala.

6 egg yolks
6 tablespoons sugar
½ cup Marsala

1. Put the egg yolks and sugar in the top pan of a double boiler. Using a large wire whisk or an electric beater, beat the mixture until it is pale and creamy. Or use a zabaglione pan — a copper bowl with a long wooden handle.

2. Fit the pan with the egg mixture into the bottom of the double boiler filled with simmering water. Make sure that the water does not touch the top pot and does not boil. Beat the Marsala into the egg mixture, and continue beating. You must take care only to heat the eggs, not to cook them. The mixture will increase in volume as it heats. When it has doubled in volume and is soft and fluffy, it is done. Spoon the zabaglione into glasses and serve immediately.

NOTE The sauce may be served over peaches in individual glass bowls or dessert cups and decorated with candied violets. The general proportion for zabaglione is 1 egg yolk and 1 tablespoon sugar per serving, plus Marsala to taste. To serve 8, use 8 egg yolks, 8 tablespoons sugar, and 1 cup Marsala.

SWEET CRÈME FRAÎCHE SAUCE

Makes about 1 1/2 cups

When you have the season's best, perfectly ripe fruit — strawberries, pears, grapes, raspberries — it doesn't need much gilding. This not-too-sweet sauce is a perfect topping.

2 tablespoons brown sugar
1 tablespoon Kirschwasser
   (cherry brandy)
1 cup *crème fraîche* (page
   175)
¼ cup heavy cream,
   whipped

Stir together the brown sugar and Kirschwasser. Stir the mixture into the *crème fraîche*. Gently fold in the whipped cream, working lightly so the cream does not lose its thick consistency.

STRAWBERRY SAUCE SUPREME

Makes about 2 cups

Use either fresh or frozen strawberries.

2 tablespoons confectioners'
   sugar
2 tablespoons Crème de
   Cassis
1 cup strawberry purée
1 cup sliced strawberries

Stir the sugar and Crème de Cassis into the puréed berries. Carefully add the sliced strawberries. The sauce will keep, tightly covered and refrigerated, for three to four days.

BRANDIED PEACH SAUCE

Makes about 2 cups

2 peaches, peeled, pitted,
  and puréed
2 tablespoons sugar
1 tablespoon fresh lemon
  juice
3 tablespoons brandy

Combine the peach purée, sugar, and lemon juice in a small saucepan. Heat the mixture gently until the sugar dissolves and the sauce thickens slightly. Stir in the brandy. Serve the sauce warm. It will keep, tightly covered and refrigerated, for three to four days.

ALMOND NUT BRITTLE

Makes about 2 cups

1¼ cups sugar
¼ cup water
1½ cups blanched almonds

1. Combine the sugar and water in a small, heavy saucepan, and stir to dissolve the sugar. Bring the mixture to a boil over medium heat, without stirring (which can crystallize the sugar). Bring the syrup to a rolling boil. Cover the pan for a few minutes to allow the steam to wash any sugar crystals down from the sides of the pan.

2. When the syrup registers 248° on a candy thermometer (firm-ball stage), add the nuts. Remove the pan from the heat and stir the nuts until they are coated with the sugar. They will appear dry and white. Return the pan to medium heat and cook until the sugar dissolves and turns golden brown (about 7 to 10 minutes).

3. Pour the mixture onto a large, oiled baking sheet and cool it completely. For ice cream topping, grind the brittle to the desired consistency, using a food processor fitted with the steel blade. Store the brittle in an airtight jar.

HOT FUDGE SAUCE

Makes about 2 cups

4 ounces unsweetened
   chocolate
1½ cups sugar
3 tablespoons unsalted
   butter
1 cup heavy cream
1 teaspoon vanilla

1. Melt the chocolate in a bowl over (not in) simmering water or in a double boiler. Pour the melted chocolate into a small, heavy saucepan, and stir in the sugar, butter, and cream. Bring the sauce to a boil over medium heat, reduce the heat slightly, and continue cooking the sauce for 5 to 10 minutes more, or until it registers 238° on a candy thermometer (soft-ball stage).

2. Remove the pan from the heat and stir in the vanilla. The sauce will keep, tightly covered and refrigerated, for three to four days. Allow it to return to room temperature before serving, whisking to soften it; or it can be reheated and whisked over very low heat.

CHOCOLATE SAUCE

Makes about 2 cups

This easy chocolate sauce is particularly good with coffee ice cream or chilled poached pears or peaches.

1 pound sweet, dark chocolate, broken into chunks
1 cup heavy cream

Combine the chocolate and cream in a small, heavy saucepan. Heat the mixture over medium heat, stirring often, until the chocolate melts. Stir it to thoroughly blend the chocolate and cream. Serve the sauce hot.

NOTE

For variety, add 2 teaspoons of Amaretto, Kahlua, Cognac, Grand Marnier, or other liqueurs to the sauce.

8

THE PERFECT PAN SCHOOL OF COOKING

STOCKS

SAUCES

PASTRY

THE BASIC KITCHEN

STOCKS

Brown Stock · Demi-Glace and Glace de Viande · Veal Stock · Chicken
Stock · Fish Stock · Court Bouillon for Poached Fish

SAUCES

Velouté Sauce · Herb Sauce · Béchamel Sauce · Brown Sauce · Hollan-
daise Sauce · Béarnaise Sauce · Basic Mayonnaise · Green Mayonnaise ·
Mustard Mayonnaise · Tomato Mayonnaise · Curry Mayonnaise · Beurre
Blanc · Beurre Blanc Enriched with Eggs and Herbs · Tomato Beurre Blanc
· Herb Butter · Parsley Butter · Roquefort and Walnut Butter · Butter
Diablo

PASTRY

Pâte Brisée · Food Processor Pâte Brisée · Pâte Sucrée · Classic Puff Pastry
· Food Processor Puff Pastry · Palmiers · Piret's Croissants · Piret's Cinnamon Walnut Rolls

THE BASIC KITCHEN

THE PERFECT PAN SCHOOL OF COOKING offers about four hundred classes annually, covering every style of cooking, technique, and cuisine imaginable. We have a core of fifteen to twenty local teachers, each a specialist in a specific style of food preparation or cuisine. An equal number of regional, national, and international experts, including chefs and cookbook authors, make guest appearances at The Perfect Pan at least once each year and sometimes more often. The emphasis in our classes, which last anywhere from two to four hours, is on the techniques of proper food preparation. Lois Stanton, the director of The Perfect Pan School of Cooking, and her predecessor, Anne Otterson, both take the approach that a recipe is a guide or tool to learning a fundamental concept about proper food handling that will enable a student to execute any recipe using similar techniques or groups of ingredients.

This final chapter of our book covers basic information about stocks, sauces, and pastry making. Loosely based on a seventeen-week course we call "Le Premier Diplôme: The Fundamentals of Good Cooking," which allows students to approach these basics in an organized way, this chapter provides many tips about the pitfalls you might encounter in preparing recipes and how to avoid or correct them. We conclude with a section on the Basic Kitchen, which discusses cooking equipment.

We hope that as you use this chapter, you will get a feel for what it's like to attend a cooking class. If you haven't attended a professional cooking class, we encourage you to do so soon. You benefit enormously from the wealth of experience a teacher brings to each session, and seeing a technique, and understanding why it is used and how it works, takes the mystery out of cooking. Cooking classes are a valuable short cut to learning how to cook well. To find out about cooking schools in your area, contact the International Association of Cooking Schools, 1001 Connecticut Avenue NW, Suite 800, Washington, D.C. 20036.

S   T   O   C   K   S

Stocks are easy to prepare, requiring very little attention from the cook after the initial cooking has been completed. Stocks should be started in cold water and cooked very slowly, so the albumin in the bones will harden and come to the surface in the form of a gray scum, which should be skimmed off. Basic stock is the foundation for sauces, soups, or aspic. No salt should be added until you are preparing the final dish to be served, because as the stock is reduced, the flavor intensifies.

Brown stock, demi-glace, and glace de viande all are members of the same family. For brown stock, the bones and vegetables are first browned, giving the stock and resulting sauces a rich, dark color. Stock strained and then boiled down to concentrate its flavor becomes a thick, dark, syrupy sauce, called demi-glace; concentrated further, it becomes glace de viande, a much thicker syrup, very dark brown.

Ten pounds of bones will yield 3 quarts of brown stock, 6 cups of demi-glace, or 2½ cups of glace de viande. Ten pounds of bones may sound like a lot, but since stocks take quite a long time to make and produce only small quantities when reduced for demi-glace and glace de viande — which will probably last you for many months — we see no reason to make less at one time. Stock should be refrigerated no longer than two or three days, uncovered. If you wish to refrigerate stock for a longer period, boil it rapidly for 15 minutes every few days. Stock may be frozen for several weeks. Demi-glace also may be refrigerated or frozen. Glace de viande, which hardens when it cools, can be stored indefinitely in the refrigerator, loosely wrapped in wax paper or in an uncovered container. When it has cooled and solidified, glace de viande may be cut into small portions, 2 to 3 tablespoons each, and stored in plastic freezer bags; or form it into a cylinder, wrap tightly, and freeze. When you need some for a dish, slice off the right amount.

BROWN STOCK

Makes 3 quarts

10 pounds meat bones
   (about ⅓ each veal, beef,
   and chicken bones —
   wings add good flavor)
1 pound carrots, scraped and
   cut into thirds
1 pound yellow onions,
   peeled and quartered
2 cups water
2 large leeks, white part
   only, cut into thirds
2 ribs celery, halved
Bouquet garni (tied in
   cheesecloth):
   ½ teaspoon whole
   peppercorns
   2 bay leaves, crumbled
   1 sprig fresh thyme (or ½
   teaspoon dried)
½ onion, burned (see note)

1. Preheat oven to 450°. Use a cleaver to cut or crack the bones into 2- to 3-inch chunks (or have your butcher do it). Place the bones in a roasting pan and brown them in the oven for 45 minutes, turning them once to brown both sides. Add the carrots and onions to the bones and continue roasting for 30 minutes more. Remove the bones and vegetables from the pan, allowing the fat to drain away, and place the bones and vegetables in a 10- to 12-quart stockpot (large enough to hold them comfortably).

2. To deglaze the roasting pan, pour out all of the fat. Pour the water into the pan and heat it on the stovetop, using two burners if necessary. As the water bubbles, scrape the pan with a spatula to loosen the solidified juices. Pour this mixture over the roasted bones and vegetables in the stockpot and fill the pot with enough cold water to cover the bones by 3 to 4 inches. Over medium heat, slowly bring the mixture to a boil, reduce the heat, and gently simmer the stock for about 1 hour. Skim the stock often with a wire mesh skimmer to remove any scum that rises to the top. A well-skimmed stock will have a cleaner taste and no cloudiness.

3. When no more scum rises to the top, add the leeks, celery, bouquet garni, and burned onion. Simmer the stock over low heat for 8 to 10 hours. (We start the stock in the early evening and let it simmer overnight.) The surface should shimmer and an occasional bubble should break on the surface, but the stock should not boil during this cooking. As it cooks, some of the water will evaporate; add more to keep the bones completely covered.

4. When the stock is cooked, pour the liquid through a fine strainer into a clean stockpot, pressing the bones and vegetables to release all their juices.

5. Cool the stock and place it in the refrigerator, uncovered. The next day, remove the solidified fat that has risen to the top. Bring the stock to a boil and reduce it to about 3 quarts of liquid.

6. If you are not going to use the stock within the next few days, on every third day, boil the stock rapidly for 15 minutes. With this intermittent boiling, the stock will last about two weeks, refrigerated.

NOTE

The burned onion is optional, but it lends a rich color to the stock. To burn the onion, cut it in half crosswise, without peeling. Place the onion cut-side down in a cast-iron skillet without any fat, and brown the onion over medium-high heat until it has a nearly burned appearance.

Demi-Glace and Glace de Viande

Demi-glace and glace de viande are simply reductions of brown stock. For a demi-glace, you reduce the stock by boiling it down to half its original volume. At this point, it will be thick enough to coat a metal spoon. For glace de viande, continue to boil until it is about a sixth of the original volume and the liquid is very thick and syrupy. Many chefs and teachers recommend transferring the liquid to smaller and smaller saucepans during this process so you have greater control and less surface evaporation. At the glace de viande stage, you face the danger of reducing the liquid into scorched crystals. You must devote your full attention to the project during the reduction phase.

For storage purposes, it makes a great deal of sense to reduce stocks to the lowest possible volume, at which point you can freeze them for a very long time. Storing reduced stock in plastic wrap or in a tightly covered container will promote mold growth, but storing it uncovered in a frost-free refrigerator, which is designed to remove moisture to prevent frost from forming, will cause your reduced stock to become dehydrated. Hence, we recommend freezing as the preferred method for storing both demi-glace and glace de viande. However you wrap or store them, allow for some air circulation.

Store reduced stocks in small quantities: because they are concentrates, you'll need only a small amount for any recipe. For demi-glace, ½-cup to 1-cup portions are practical. Glace de viande should be frozen in 2- to 3-tablespoon cubes or scoops. Glace de viande will harden in the refrigerator, making it easy to cut into small portions.

VEAL STOCK

Makes 2 to 3 quarts

Veal stock is used as a base for sauces, soups, and stews and with braised and sautéed meats. Veal stock is more bland than brown stock and will blend with virtually any meat or poultry preparation. You can concentrate the flavor by reducing the stock. However, since veal stock does not have the depth of flavor of a brown stock, veal stock reductions are only practical for storage purposes and not as substitutions for demi-glace or glace de viande.

2 to 3 pounds cracked veal bones (see note)

1 to 2 pounds chicken backs and wings

4 quarts cold water

1 medium onion, unpeeled, cut into quarters

4 whole cloves

2 to 3 carrots, peeled and cut into 1-inch rounds

2 pounds leeks, white part only, cut into thirds

2 cloves garlic, unpeeled (optional)

Bouquet garni (tied in cheesecloth):
  2 sprigs fresh thyme (or 1 teaspoon dried)
  1 bay leaf, crushed
  ½ bunch fresh parsley

½ onion, burned (optional; page 314)

1. Have the butcher cut the veal bones into pieces 2 to 3 inches long. Cover the veal and chicken bones with enough cold water to cover them by at least 2 inches. Bring the mixture slowly to a boil, skimming it often.

2. When the water comes to a boil, reduce the heat to a simmer and continue skimming until no more scum rises to the surface. Stick the cloves into the onion quarters and add them to the stock with the carrots, leeks, garlic, and bouquet garni. Continue to simmer the stock gently, skimming as needed. At this point, you may want to add the burned onion for a nice golden color. Cook the stock at a bare simmer, uncovered, for 4 hours, skimming off any scum that appears.

3. Strain the stock through a sieve lined with a double layer of dampened cheesecloth into a large, clean pot, pressing the liquids from the bones, vegetables, and bouquet garni. Cool the stock and refrigerate.

4. Remove the coagulated fat and bring the stock to a boil. Taste for flavor concentration and reduce more by boiling, if necessary. The stock will keep, refrigerated, for several weeks if you boil it for 10 to 15 minutes on every third day. Or freeze it in small containers for future use.

NOTE

The hock, or lower hind leg, and the shank, or foreleg, are good bones to use. Some cooks suggest blanching the bones briefly to whiten them before making the stock.

CHICKEN STOCK

Makes about 5 quarts

Most people don't have 8 pounds of spare chicken parts lying around, unless they've just prepared a dinner party for twenty-five people. You can either purchase the chicken parts or keep a "stock cache" in the freezer. Every time you cut up a chicken, toss the back, neck, wing tips, and other bony parts into a heavy-duty freezer bag. After you've carved the meat from roast chicken, toss in the carcass. If your family doesn't like giblets, add them to the cache (except, of course, livers, which you can collect for pâté or mousse). When you've accumulated enough or when freezer space runs short, make stock. If you live near a kosher market, have a Chinese market nearby, or know a butcher who sells whole birds, get a few chicken feet to add to the stockpot. They're unlovely, we admit, but they add a rich, gelatinous quality to the stock. Be sure to soak the chicken feet for several hours in salted water, then rinse them thoroughly under cold running water.

8 pounds (approximately) bony chicken parts, fat removed (or 6 pounds chicken bones and 2 pounds cracked veal bones)

6 quarts cold water (approximately)

1 medium onion, unpeeled, cut into quarters

4 whole cloves

3 medium carrots, peeled and coarsely cut

2 leeks, white and 2 inches of green, coarsely cut

2 ribs celery with leaves, coarsely cut

Bouquet garni (tied in cheesecloth):
   ⅓ cup coarsely chopped fresh parsley
   1 large clove garlic, crushed
   1 bay leaf
   ½ teaspoon dried thyme
   10 whole peppercorns

1. Combine the chicken and cold water in a 10- or 12-quart stockpot. Be sure the water covers the chicken by at least 2 inches. If necessary, add more water. Bring the liquid to a simmer over medium heat, reduce the heat, and simmer the stock for 45 minutes to 1 hour, skimming off and discarding the foam and scum. Do not let it boil, or the finished stock will be cloudy. Skim it often.

2. Pierce each onion quarter with a whole clove, and add them to the stock with the carrots, leeks, celery, and bouquet garni. Simmer the stock, partially covered, for at least 3 hours, or until the stock is well flavored.

3. Turn off the heat and, with a slotted spoon or tongs, remove the chicken parts and vegetables. Strain the stock through a sieve lined with a double layer of dampened cheesecloth. Let the stock cool to room temperature.

4. Refrigerate the stock, uncovered, until it is chilled and the surface is covered with a layer of yellow fat. Sealed in this fat, the stock may be safely refrigerated for three or four days. After the fat has been removed, bring the stock to a rolling boil and check it for flavor. If you think it needs more flavor, reduce it to the desired strength by boiling. If you

wish to freeze the stock, remove the solidified fat as soon as it hardens, place portions of the stock in freezer containers, and freeze. It will keep for three or four months.

NOTE	For a more full-flavored stock, chop the vegetables and brown them with the chicken in a preheated 350° oven for about 15 minutes. Then cook the stock as directed above.

Concentrated Chicken Stock

Pour the strained and degreased stock into a stockpot and boil it for 2 hours, or until the liquid is reduced by half, skimming it occasionally. Pour the reduced stock into a clean pot. Simmer it again until the stock is reduced to 4 to 6 cups. At this point the stock will reduce very quickly, so place it in a sauté pan and reduce it to about 2 cups. The final reduction will be thick enough to coat a metal spoon.

Pour the reduced stock onto jellyroll pans and let it stand at room temperature until it is firm. Cut it into cubes or scoop out 1-tablespoon portions, and freeze them on a cookie sheet. Then put the portions into freezer bags to freeze indefinitely.

To reconstitute, dissolve 1 tablespoon of the concentrate in 1 cup boiling water.

FISH STOCK

Makes about 1 quart

Use the bones and head of snapper, bass, trout, or other similar fish for fish stock. Do not use cold-water fish with high oil content, such as salmon or shark. Fish stock is very fragile. If you are not using it immediately, boil it daily for a few minutes, or freeze it.

2 pounds raw fish bones, with some meat still attached
1 medium onion, peeled, stuck with 2 cloves
1 leek, white part only, cut into thirds
1 rib celery, halved

Combine all the ingredients and bring the mixture to a boil. Reduce the heat and simmer the stock over low heat for 15 or 20 minutes, skimming off the scum that rises to the surface. Strain the stock through a fine sieve.

Pinch of dried thyme
2 cups dry white wine or
    fresh lemon juice
1 quart cold water

COURT BOUILLON FOR POACHED FISH

Makes about 5 cups

Court bouillon is an aromatic poaching liquid for fish or shellfish. Seasonings can vary, but the basic principle remains the same: simmer together water, wine, and seasonings for about 30 minutes. Some sources say to cool the court bouillon, add the fish, then heat it to a simmer, but we find it's just as easy to start the fish in already simmering poaching liquid. The poaching liquid also may be used as a base for sauce, in the same manner as fish stock.

Fatter fishes such as salmon, halibut, cod, haddock, and snapper are especially well suited for poaching.

2 cups dry white wine
1 quart water
2 carrots, coarsely chopped
2 medium onions, sliced
2 shallots, coarsely chopped
3 sprigs fresh parsley
1 teaspoon salt
1 sprig fresh thyme (or ½ teaspoon dried thyme)
1 bay leaf
6 whole peppercorns

Combine all the ingredients in a skillet that will hold the fish in a single layer. Bring the mixture to a boil, reduce the heat, and simmer it until the vegetables are tender (about 30 minutes). At this point you may strain the court bouillon; for a more concentrated, rich sauce base, leave in the vegetables and strain the court bouillon after the fish is poached.

To poach fish:

1. Have the fish cleaned, scaled, and ready to cook. The fish will be easier to remove from the poaching liquid if it is placed on a grid or tied in cheesecloth.

2. Gently lower the fish into enough simmering court bouillon to nearly cover it. Cook the fish at a bare simmer (don't let it boil), covered, for 8 to 10 minutes per inch of thickness of the fish. Check after the shorter cooking time. The fish is done when it is nearly opaque yet somewhat translucent, and when a skewer pierces it easily. It will continue to cook after it is removed from the poaching liquid. Do not cook the fish until it flakes easily with a fork; at that

point, it is overdone. The fish should feel springy, not mushy, to the touch.

3. Remove the fish from the poaching liquid and let it cool until it can be handled (catch any juices on a platter under the fish and return them to the poaching liquid). Remove the skin and dark flesh close to the backbone, and serve the poached fish on a large platter.

NOTE

The poaching liquid can be reduced over high heat to form a sauce. (Add any liquid that accumulates on the serving platter around the poached fish.) To enrich the poaching liquid, boil it down to a glaze, and pour in about 1 cup heavy cream. Cook the cream to form a thick sauce. To season, stir in some mustard, mashed green peppercorns, or fresh herbs.

S   A   U   C   E   S

Recipes throughout this book are accompanied by sauce recipes. This section is a reference to help you if you want to change the sauce. It also will give you a little more perspective on the subject of sauces in general. While sauce recipes look simple, and often are, care and practice are required to execute them perfectly. A good sauce is delicately complex in flavor and aroma and lends distinction to the food it accompanies. It should have a velvety quality with a slight sheen. We encourage you to approach sauce-making in a structured fashion, practicing techniques until you feel comfortable with them.

The French organize sauces into families: roux-based, emulsified, and reduction sauces. Each family of sauces works with the same base ingredients and techniques, varying only the seasoning and aromatic ingredients to achieve a distinctive flavor for a "mother" sauce. Velouté is a roux-based sauce, for example, and mayonnaise and beurre blanc are emulsified sauces. The mother sauces are only a base on which to build; on their own they are quite bland.

Many sauce recipes call for nonaluminum pans because untreated aluminum can react with some substances, particularly acidic foods, and discolor the food. This does not occur with anodized aluminum pans, such as Calphalon, or with aluminum pans lined with stainless steel. Cast iron should be used in sauce-making only if it is coated with enamel.

ROUX-BASED SAUCES

Velouté, béchamel, and brown sauce all are sauces thickened with roux, a combination of flour and fat. The base or "mother" sauces can be, and usually are, flavored with herbs and other ingredients to make them interesting companions to meat, poultry, fish, or pasta.

There are two pitfalls to watch for in making roux-based sauces. First, you want to avoid having little lumps of flour in the sauce, which can be accomplished by stirring or whisking the sauce vigorously and continuously. Second, uncooked flour leaves an unpleasant aftertaste in a sauce. Most cookbooks recommend cooking the roux for 2 to 3 minutes; however, many French chefs insist that the roux be cooked for 10 minutes and as long as 15 minutes. While cooking the roux, you must give it your full attention, both to avoid lumps and to cook it thoroughly without scorching it. Experimentation and practice are definitely advised to achieve good results.

VELOUTÉ SAUCE

Makes 1 cup

1½ tablespoons unsalted
   butter
1½ tablespoons unbleached,
   all-purpose flour
1 cup concentrated stock
   (chicken, veal, or fish), at
   room temperature
Salt and freshly ground
   white pepper, to taste

1. Melt the butter in a heavy, nonaluminum saucepan. When the butter froths, stir in the flour with a wire whisk, whisking until the butter and flour are completely integrated. Reduce the heat and cook the roux, whisking constantly, until the raw flour flavor is completely gone.

2. When the roux is cooked, remove the pan from the heat. Pour in the stock all at once, and whisk rapidly until the stock and roux are thoroughly combined. Season the sauce with salt and white pepper.

3. Return the pan to medium heat and simmer the sauce for 20 to 25 minutes, skimming the surface as necessary. Strain the sauce through a fine-mesh chinoise (cone-shaped strainer) to remove any lumps.

4. If the sauce is not to be served immediately, spread a bit of butter on the top to prevent a skin from forming. It will hold for one to two hours.

NOTE

Tradition has it that adding hot stock to room-temperature roux (or vice versa) will prevent lumps from forming, but we have seen cooks add hot liquid to hot roux without any problems.

Velouté by itself is pretty uninteresting. Try adding egg yolks, cream, butter, herbs, white wine, or whatever flavor best suits the dish you are saucing.

HERB SAUCE

Makes 2 cups

Another example of a velouté, this sauce uses fish stock enriched with cream. It's delicious with grilled or poached fish. To serve it with roasted or poached poultry, substitute chicken stock for fish stock, and tarragon for dill.

5 tablespoons plus
 1½ teaspoons butter
4 tablespoons unbleached,
 all-purpose flour
2 cups fish stock (page 318)
Salt and freshly ground
 white pepper, to taste
Dash of cayenne pepper
2 tablespoons minced
 shallots
½ cup heavy cream
2 to 3 tablespoons fresh
 chives
1 tablespoon fresh dill
1½ teaspoons chervil

1. Melt 4 tablespoons of the butter in a small saucepan over medium heat. Whisk in the flour and cook the roux for 2 to 3 minutes, or until it loses its raw flavor. Whisk in the fish stock, and cook the sauce until it thickens, stirring often. Season with salt, white pepper, and cayenne pepper, and set the velouté aside.

2. Cook the shallots in the remaining butter in a saucepan over medium-high heat for 3 to 5 minutes. Be careful not to let the shallots brown.

3. Whisk the velouté into the shallot mixture, with the cream, chives, dill, and chervil, and cook the sauce over medium-high heat until the sauce is reduced to 2 cups. Taste it and adjust the seasoning.

BÉCHAMEL SAUCE

Makes 2 cups

Béchamel is the base for soufflés, and béchamel-based sauces are often used in baked gratin and Italian dishes.

2 cups milk
4 tablespoons unsalted
  butter
3 tablespoons unbleached,
  all-purpose flour
¼ teaspoon salt

1. Heat the milk until bubbles form around the edges, but do not let it boil.

2. In a heavy, enameled saucepan, whisk together the butter and flour, and whisk constantly over medium heat until the mixture bubbles. Let the mixture bubble for 2 minutes, but do not let the flour brown. Add the heated milk all at once, whisking constantly. Add the salt and cook the sauce over medium heat until it thickens.

3. If you are not going to use the sauce immediately, spread a bit of butter on the top to prevent a skin from forming. If the sauce cools completely, reheat it before using.

Brown Sauce

Use the same proportions and techniques described in Velouté Sauce, but use brown stock; and when cooking the roux, allow it to become dark in color before incorporating the brown stock.

You can also make a brown sauce by using the caramelized juices and cooking liquid that remain in the pan after roasting, braising, or sautéing meats. Pour off the fat and deglaze the pan by scraping up the bits of meat and caramelized juices while heating the pan on top of the stove. If you don't have enough liquid, you can add water or wine, bring it to a boil, and scrape the pan. While the liquid simmers, make a brown or white roux, allow it to cool slightly, then strain and quickly stir the pan juices into the roux. Cook until the sauce thickens. Wine, cream, or milk may be used to enrich the sauce. Season with salt and pepper.

EMULSIFIED SAUCES

An emulsion requires three basic ingredients: acid (lemon juice or vinegar), protein (egg yolk), and fat (butter or oil). Temperature is the key to cooked emulsions. Eggs will not thicken until they reach 140°, but they will begin to thicken very quickly if overheated or heated too quickly. Shirley Corriher, who explains the "hows" of cooking in her food-chemistry classes, recommends that eggs be cooked slowly over low heat. She also points out that failed sauces usually have too little liquid. If your sauce begins to curdle and separate (you'll see this around the sides of the pan), quickly take the pan off the heat, plunge it into a bowl of ice-cold water to stop the cooking, add an ice cube or a little cold water to the sauce, and beat it like crazy. Shirley also likes to add a little dry mustard or paprika to hollandaise and béarnaise, which helps coat the fat molecules and hold them in the emulsion.

Hollandaise and béarnaise are cooked emulsified sauces, while mayonnaise is cold. The principles of making a hollandaise and béarnaise are essentially the same, except that you use vinegar instead of lemon in béarnaise, and the sauce is flavored with herbs such as tarragon, scallions or shallots, peppercorns, and perhaps chervil.

In hot or cold emulsions, it is very important that the liquefied butter or oil be added to the egg yolks very slowly, especially in the beginning. Julia Child recommends starting with driblets and gradually working up to a slow, steady stream.

In sauces where egg yolk is a thickener, it is important to warm the yolks before they are added to a hot mixture. Otherwise, the yolks will scramble upon contact with hot liquid instead of thickening the sauce. To warm the yolks, spoon a little of the hot liquid into the yolks, whisking constantly. Then whisk the warmed yolk mixture into the hot liquid.

HOLLANDAISE SAUCE

Makes about 1 cup

3 egg yolks
2 tablespoons cold water
1 tablespoon fresh lemon
juice
Large pinch of salt
1 tablespoon unsalted
butter, chilled
¾ cup unsalted butter,
melted and kept very
warm
Salt and freshly ground
white pepper, to taste
Fresh lemon juice, to taste

1. In a small saucepan, beat the egg yolks until they are thick. Add the cold water, the 1 tablespoon lemon juice, and the salt, and beat the mixture for 1 minute more. Add the tablespoon of butter but do not beat it in. Place the saucepan over low heat, and whisk the mixture for 1 to 2 minutes, or until the sauce is the thickness of cream. (If the sauce begins to get lumpy, immediately stop the cooking by dipping the pan into ice cold water, and beat vigorously.) Continue cooking the sauce over low heat, stirring constantly, until it has thickened enough that you see the bottom of the pan between turns of the whisk. (If the egg yolks are very hot, use 1 tablespoon of cold butter or a small ice cube to cool them.) Remove the pan from the heat.

2. Add the melted butter by droplets until the sauce begins to thicken. Place the pan on low heat and add the butter in a thin stream, whisking constantly. Season the sauce with salt, pepper, and lemon juice.

NOTE

Hot emulsified sauces do not keep well and cannot be reheated. Keep the sauce warm in a bain-marie with lukewarm water (do not let the water boil), or use a wide-mouthed thermos.

BÉARNAISE SAUCE

Makes about 1 cup

½ cup white wine vinegar (or ¼ cup white wine vinegar flavored with tarragon or chervil, plus ¼ cup dry white wine)
1 tablespoon minced shallot
1 tablespoon chopped fresh tarragon (or ½ tablespoon dried)
½ teaspoon freshly ground white peppercorns
Salt, to taste

1. In a nonaluminum saucepan, bring the vinegar or vinegar mixture to a simmer. Add the shallots, tarragon, peppercorns, and salt, and continue simmering until the liquid is reduced to about 2 tablespoons.

2. Substitute this mixture for the lemon juice in the hollandaise recipe (page 326), and proceed as directed.

BASIC MAYONNAISE

Makes about 2 cups

Any of the mayonnaise variations would be good dips for small shrimp or vegetables. The tomato mayonnaise, in particular, is great with grilled meat.

3 egg yolks
1 teaspoon dry mustard
½ teaspoon salt
1 to 2 tablespoons fresh
   lemon juice
2 cups extra-virgin olive oil
   (or 1 cup olive oil plus 1
   cup vegetable oil)
Salt and freshly ground
   white pepper, to taste

1. Place the egg yolks, mustard, and salt in the work bowl of a food processor fitted with the steel or plastic blade. Process the mixture for 1 minute. With the machine running, add the lemon juice and 1 cup of the oil, in drips or a thin stream.

2. Taste the mayonnaise at this point for seasoning. Add enough of the remaining 1 cup of oil to obtain the desired texture. Season the mayonnaise with salt and white pepper.

NOTE

To prepare mayonnaise by hand, whisk together the egg yolks, mustard, salt, and lemon juice. Add the oil a drop at a time, whisking the mixture vigorously, until you have added about ¼ cup, then start adding the oil in a very thin stream, whisking as the mayonnaise takes on volume. The second cup of oil can be added a little more quickly — but not much.

Green Mayonnaise
Makes 2½ cups

¾ cup mixed fresh herbs
   (chervil, parsley, chives,
   basil, tarragon, etc.)
2 tablespoons vegetable oil
2 cups Basic Mayonnaise

Blanch the herbs for 1 minute in boiling water. Refresh them under cold running water, drain them thoroughly, then pat them dry with paper towels. Using a blender or food processor fitted with the steel blade, purée the herbs with the oil. Fold the herbs into the mayonnaise.

Mustard Mayonnaise
Makes 2 cups

3 teaspoons Dijon-style
   mustard
1½ cups Basic Mayonnaise
½ cup heavy cream

Whisk the mustard into the mayonnaise. Lightly whip the cream and fold it into the mayonnaise.

Tomato Mayonnaise
Makes about 1½ cups

2 fresh tomatoes, peeled,
seeded, and coarsely
chopped
1 teaspoon fresh basil,
minced (or ½ teaspoon
dried)
½ teaspoon sugar
2 tablespoons sour cream
1 cup Basic Mayonnaise

Combine the tomatoes, basil, and sugar in a small, heavy saucepan and cook them over medium heat until they form a thick paste. Cool the tomato mixture and fold in the sour cream. Stir the mixture into the mayonnaise.

Curry Mayonnaise
Makes 1¾ cups

2 tablespoons curry powder
1 teaspoon turmeric
1 tablespoon white wine
vinegar
1½ cups Basic Mayonnaise
2 teaspoons capers, drained
and crushed

Whisk together the curry powder, turmeric, wine vinegar, and mayonnaise. Stir in the capers.

BUTTER SAUCES

BEURRE BLANC

Makes about 1 cup

Beurre blanc is a classic white sauce "mounted" with butter. That is, the butter is beaten in bit by bit to form a liaison with the acidic wine and vinegar mixture. The object is to beat in the butter at a temperature hot enough that it softens and forms a silky texture, but not so hot that the butter melts and becomes oily. You may have to move the pan on and off the heat source to regulate the temperature. Once you're comfortable with the bit-by-bit process of making beurre blanc, you might like to try a quicker, high-heat method. We've added "rescue" instructions in case the sauce turns on you and curdles, melts, or otherwise falls apart.

As Shirley Corriher demonstrated clearly in a class at The Perfect Pan, the lecithin in milk solids is the emulsifier that makes beurre blanc work. Made with clarified butter, the sauce will not thicken.

Beurre blanc may be flavored with any number of ingredients — fresh basil, tomato coulis, herbs and other spices — the possibilities are limited only by your imagination. Beurre blanc sauces need to be used immediately, or kept in a warm place for a short time, since they are tricky to reheat. Another storing idea suggested by Shirley Corriher is to place the sauce in a wide-mouthed thermos where it will maintain its temperature for several hours.

¼ cup dry white wine
¼ cup white wine vinegar
1½ tablespoons finely
    chopped shallots
1 cup unsalted butter, firm
    but not cold, cut into 16
    pieces
¼ teaspoon kosher-style salt
Scant ¼ teaspoon freshly
    ground white pepper

LOW-HEAT METHOD

1. In a heavy, medium saucepan, combine the wine, vinegar, and shallots. Bring the mixture to a boil, lower the heat, and cook, uncovered, until it is reduced to about 3 tablespoons. Remove the saucepan from the heat.

2. Let the saucepan cool a while. It should be hot, but the shallot mixture should no longer be bubbling. (A good way to test the temperature, although one that takes some daring, is to touch the bottom inside of the pan with your finger; the pan should be just hot enough that your finger can withstand the heat for 2 seconds. You may just want to take a look at it and guess.) Quickly whisk in two pieces of the butter. When it is soft and creamy, return the saucepan to a very low heat. (Metals that hold heat well, such as stainless steel–lined aluminum, Calphalon, enameled cast iron, and copper, will require barely any additional heat.)

3. Whisking constantly, add the remaining pieces of butter, a few at a time. Add more butter only when the previous addition has been absorbed. When about half the butter has been added, whisk the remaining pieces into the sauce at a faster rate over low heat. The consistency of the mixture should be creamy and thick. Remove the pan from the heat whenever the butter appears to be melting rather than thickening and foaming. Season the sauce with the kosher-style salt and white pepper.

4. If a perfectly smooth sauce is desired, strain it into a lukewarm serving bowl. Otherwise, pour it directly into a bowl, and set the bowl in a pan of warm water until ready to serve.

HIGH-HEAT METHOD

1. In a heavy, medium saucepan, combine the wine, vinegar, and shallots. Bring the mixture to a boil, lower the heat, and cook, uncovered, until it is reduced to 3 tablespoons.

2. Quickly raise the heat and bring the reduction to a fast boil. Add the butter pieces all at once and whisk them vigorously so the butter melts evenly in the boiling reduction. Continue whisking over medium-high heat as the mixture thickens into a creamy sauce.

3. When just two or three small lumps of butter are not yet incorporated into the sauce, quickly pour the contents of the saucepan into a small serving bowl. Stir until the butter sauce is smooth. Season with the kosher-style salt and white pepper and serve as soon as possible.

⋙ If your sauce "turns," it can be saved. Combine 2 tablespoons of cold water and 1 tablespoon of firm butter in a clean saucepan and whisk them together over low heat for 30 seconds, or until well combined. Slowly whisk this mixture into the turned sauce. Whisk the sauce constantly over low heat for 1 minute. Beat in 3 to 4 tablespoons of fresh butter. When the sauce is smooth and thick, readjust the seasoning, and serve.

BEURRE BLANC ENRICHED WITH EGGS AND HERBS

Makes about 1 cup

This sauce works particularly well with poached or grilled fish fillets.

2 tablespoons finely chopped shallots
1 cup dry white wine
¾ cup unsalted butter, firm but not chilled, cut into pieces
3 tablespoons heavy cream
Salt and freshly ground pepper, to taste
1 tablespoon chopped fresh herbs (see note)
2 egg yolks
2 tablespoons cold water

1. In a medium saucepan, combine the shallots and wine. Boil the mixture, uncovered, until it is reduced to about 3 tablespoons. Whisk in the pieces of butter, one at a time, whisking constantly. When all of the butter has been added and the mixture has become a thick, foamy sauce, whisk in the cream. Season the sauce with salt, pepper, and herbs, and cook it a few minutes more, whisking it all the while.

2. In a small, heatproof bowl, whisk the egg yolks with the cold water until they are well combined. Set the bowl over simmering water and whisk the mixture for 3 to 4 minutes, or until it is light, foamy, and almost doubled in volume. Gently fold the egg mixture into the beurre blanc.

NOTE

Choose any fresh herbs that are available, such as basil, dill, cilantro, thyme, oregano, or rosemary. A combination of dill and chervil or cilantro, for example, is delicious with grilled fish.

TOMATO BEURRE BLANC

Makes about 1 cup

Tomato Beurre Blanc is delicious served with poached, grilled, or baked seafood or chicken. Try it with thin veal strips dredged in flour and quickly fried in butter. A beautiful garnish is a chiffonnade of basil.

2 tablespoons extra-virgin olive oil

1 pound tomatoes, peeled, seeded, and minced

Salt and freshly ground pepper, to taste

⅛ teaspoon crumbled dried thyme

1 tablespoon finely chopped shallots

2 tablespoons dry white wine

2 tablespoons white wine vinegar

1½ tablespoons *crème fraîche* (page 175)

½ cup unsalted butter, cut into 8 pieces

1. Heat the olive oil in a small skillet. Sauté the tomatoes over medium-high heat, stirring often, until the tomatoes form a thick, well-reduced sauce (about 7 to 8 minutes). Season the tomatoes with the salt, pepper, and thyme. Set them aside.

2. Combine the shallots, wine, and vinegar in a small saucepan. Bring the mixture to a boil and cook it over medium heat until it is reduced to a glaze of about 2 tablespoons.

3. Over medium-high heat, whisk in the *crème fraîche,* and quickly boil the mixture until it is reduced by half. Whisk in pieces of the butter, one at a time, whisking constantly. When all of the butter pieces have been added and the mixture has become a thick, foamy sauce, remove the pan from the heat. Stir the sauce into the tomatoes.

FLAVORED BUTTERS

Flavored butters are a beautiful match for the delicate flavors of baked or grilled fish. After the fish is cooked, top it with a pat of flavored butter; it will melt tantalizingly as you serve the fish. (As an example, see the recipe for Lemon-Soy Swordfish Steaks on page 173.) Herbed butters also are delicious on steamed vegetables and grilled steak.

Herb Butter
Makes 1 cup

2 cloves garlic
1 teaspoon onion
1 cup unsalted butter, softened
1 teaspoon caraway seed
1 teaspoon minced fresh basil (or ½ teaspoon dried)
½ teaspoon minced fresh oregano (or ¼ teaspoon dried)
¼ teaspoon cayenne pepper

1. Using a food processor fitted with the steel blade, mince the garlic by dropping it into the feed tube while the machine is running. Mince the onion in the same way. Remove the lid and add the butter, caraway seed, basil, oregano, and cayenne pepper, blending the ingredients thoroughly. (The mincing and mixing may be done by hand, as well.)

2. Store the butter, refrigerated, in a small earthenware crock, or form it into a fat cylinder, wrap it tightly in freezer-weight plastic wrap, and freeze. Cut pats of the butter as needed.

Parsley Butter
Makes 1 cup

1 teaspoon minced fresh parsley
1 teaspoon minced onion
2 cloves garlic, minced
4 tablespoons fresh lemon juice
1 cup unsalted butter
Freshly ground pepper, to taste

1. Using a food processor fitted with the steel blade, mince the parsley, onion, and garlic. Remove the lid and add the lemon juice, butter, and pepper. Blend the ingredients thoroughly.

2. Store the butter, refrigerated, in a small earthenware crock, or form it into a fat cylinder, wrap it tightly in freezer-weight plastic wrap, and freeze. Cut pats of the butter as needed.

Roquefort and Walnut Butter
Makes 1¾ cups

Serve a tablespoon of this butter on grilled meats, fish, or poultry. It's also wonderful on baked potatoes or toasted bread. Or try it with crisp celery and radishes.

1 cup shelled walnuts
6 tablespoons unsalted butter
6 ounces Roquefort cheese
1 tablespoon Cognac or Armagnac

1. Using a food processor fitted with the steel blade, finely chop the walnuts. Remove the nuts and set them aside. Cut the butter into pieces and process them to a smooth paste. Add the Roquefort cheese and process to blend it slightly with the butter. Transfer the mixture to a mixing bowl and stir in the chopped nuts and brandy, blending them well.

2. Store the butter in a small crock, or form it into a fat cylinder, wrap it tightly in freezer-weight plastic wrap, and freeze. Cut pats of the butter as needed.

Butter Diablo
Makes 1 cup

Mustard and peppercorns take this flavored butter out of the ordinary. Mireaux mustard is a dark, acidic mustard from Bordeaux; use any mustard with similar characteristics. Try Butter Diablo on grilled fish, particularly swordfish. It's also marvelous on grilled chicken, beef, or lamb.

1 cup unsalted butter, softened
1 teaspoon Dijon-style mustard
1 tablespoon Mireaux mustard
½ teaspoon prepared horseradish
2 teaspoons crushed dry green Madagascar peppercorns (or 2 teaspoons brine-packed green Madagascar peppercorns, rinsed and minced)
1 tablespoon minced garlic
⅛ teaspoon Worcestershire sauce

Whisk together the butter, mustards, horseradish, peppercorns, garlic, and Worcestershire sauce, until smooth and creamy. Or blend them together, using a food processor fitted with the steel blade. Refrigerate the butter until ready to use.

P A S T R Y

Pastry-making is similar to sauce-making in that there are "mother" doughs that can be used for a variety of applications. Space does not permit us to be comprehensive in either the base doughs presented or the ways of using them. What we have sought to do is to get you started in the very interesting and satisfying world of handling dessert doughs and baking.

In the beginning, pastry- and bread-making may seem like something of a gastronomic Catch-22. On the one hand, you are told that precision in measuring ingredients is everything. Then you are told that the proportion of, say, flour to liquid will vary wildly according to the type of flour used and the amount of humidity in the air on the day you happen to be baking. Hence, regardless of all the meticulous measuring and weighing you do, the final outcome is really based on experience and judgment. Bruce Healy points out, for example, that when 1 pound of flour is converted to cups, it can vary by as much as 1½ cups, depending on the amount of moisture in the flour and the manner in which you go about measuring it (loosely packed cups versus tight packing). When Julia Child taught classes in San Diego to benefit the University of California, San Diego, Medical Auxiliary, she found our unsalted butter exceptionally watery and pounded the blocks of butter between kitchen towels with a rolling pin to extract as much water as possible before making puff pastry. Our pastry chefs are used to working with our butter and automatically adjust for the extra moisture.

Most of our recipes call for unbleached, all-purpose flour, which has a protein content of about 10 percent and is designed to be used for breads, cakes, and pastries with equal success. The protein content in flour determines the elasticity or pliability of the dough.

The temperature of the room in which you are baking and the temperature of the ingredients are very important, and you should follow these instructions carefully. For example, if you are working with a recipe having a high butter content, the butter and the environment should be chilly; otherwise, the butter will begin to melt, separating the butterfat from the milk solids, and you'll have a real mess on your hands. Many recipes also tell you to work quickly and to take care not to overhandle or knead the dough. Overworking certain doughs will make them too elastic, and instead of a flaky product, you'll have a breadlike result.

Pastry recipes (by pastry we mean virtually all doughs and batters) generally call for sweet or unsalted butter. The reason is that you don't always know how much salt is in salted butter and you are much better off adding the salt yourself. (Salt tends to inhibit yeast growth, for example.) Sweet or unsalted butter has a shorter shelf life than salted butter, so use it within two weeks or freeze it. Before using, always taste sweet butter to make sure it is not rancid.

Throughout this book, and especially in this chapter, when a recipe calls for heavy cream, we mean whipping cream or a cream with a very high butterfat content. Always taste cream for freshness; it should taste sweet. Chilled cream, whipped in a chilled bowl with chilled beaters, achieves a higher volume than at room temperature.

When you are figuring your proportions of flour and liquid, think of eggs (if they are called for) as liquid. So, if we call for large eggs and you have small or medium eggs, you will have to increase the number of eggs to get both the desired liquid and protein content. Old eggs will be more watery than fresh eggs. One way to determine whether your eggs are fresh or old is to immerse one in water. If it sinks to the bottom, it's fresh; if it floats, it means that air has seeped in through the porous shell and that the egg has been around for a while.

We've selected recipes that are typical of Piret's

and that we think are both basic and approachable for a beginner. Obviously, some will be easier than others. If you are a beginner, we encourage you to consult other, more complete references on baking, such as Bruce Healy and Paul Bugat's *Mastering the Art of French Pastry*, Lenôtre's *Desserts and Pastries*, and Jacques Pépin's *La Technique* and *La Méthode*.

PÂTE BRISÉE

Makes two 8-inch pastry shells

Pâte brisée — basic pie dough — can be made using several techniques. The fat can be cut into the flour, using two knives, a pastry blender, or a food processor fitted with the steel blade. The butter should be thoroughly chilled, and you must work quickly so it doesn't melt and become greasy. The object is to make small bits of butter that are coated with flour. Liquids are mixed in quickly and lightly to form a light dough. Overworking this or any pastry dough makes it tough and heavy. Leftover pastry can be formed into a ball, wrapped in plastic wrap, and frozen.

   Another excellent pie pastry can be found with recipes for Charcuterie quiches (page 103). To make dessert tarts with pâte brisée, refer to chapter 7.

1 ½ cups unbleached, all-purpose flour
½ teaspoon salt
6 tablespoons unsalted butter, chilled
1 egg yolk
4 to 5 tablespoons cold water

1. Sift the flour and salt into a mixing bowl. Cut the chilled butter into ⅛-inch pats, and add them to the flour. Cut the butter into the flour just until the mixture is coarse and mealy.

2. Make a well in the mixture. Stir together the egg yolk and 2 tablespoons of the water, and, using a fork, stir them into the flour, working quickly to form a light dough. Add only enough additional water to make a dough that has a somewhat dry appearance but that holds together.

3. Turn the dough out onto a work surface. Using the heel of your hand, press the dough in a streak about 8 inches long. Gather the dough back into a ball, and wrap it in plastic wrap. Chill it at least 30 minutes.

4. On a lightly floured surface, roll the dough to the desired thickness, about ¼ inch thick for quiche, a bit thicker for pie. Work quickly as you roll the dough, and roll from the center to the edge.

5. Use the pastry to line tart shells or quiche rings. It should be fitted into the pans without stretching, because stretched pastry can shrink from the sides of the pan when it bakes. An easy way to transfer the pastry is to loosely roll it around the rolling pin, then unroll it over the pan. Use your floured thumb to press the dough into the sides of the pan, cut off any excess, and form an edge.

6. To prebake the pastry shell (called baking it "blind"), preheat the oven to 400°. Prick the pastry with a fork in several places to prevent shrinkage. Line the pastry with foil and fill it with pie weights, dried beans, or rice, and bake it for 10 minutes. Remove the weights and bake the crust another 2 to 5 minutes, or until it is light golden brown. Proceed as directed for either sweet or savory tarts.

FOOD PROCESSOR PÂTE BRISÉE

Makes two 8-inch pastry shells

2 cups unbleached,
   all-purpose flour
½ teaspoon salt
8 tablespoons unsalted
   butter, cut into pieces
   and frozen (see note)
2 tablespoons lard, cut into
   pieces and frozen
6 to 8 tablespoons ice water

1. Combine the flour and salt in the work bowl of a food processor fitted with the steel blade. Blend by using two on/off pulses. Drop in the pieces of frozen butter and lard, and pulse three to four times, then continue to process until the mixture becomes crumbly, resembling coarse meal.

2. With the machine running, add the ice water, one tablespoon at a time. When the mixture lumps together, remove it from the work bowl to a pastry board and quickly press the dough into a patty with your hands.

3. Wrap the dough in wax paper or plastic wrap and chill for 20 to 30 minutes. Roll and use as directed.

NOTE

The butter and lard must be frozen because of heat generated by the steel blade. Overly soft fats prevent the pastry from flaking. The lard makes the pastry richer and flakier. If you are making dessert pastry, add one tablespoon of sugar to the recipe.

PÂTE SUCRÉE

Makes two 8-inch pastry shells

Pâte sucrée is a sweetened, enriched version of pâte brisée. It is ideal for fruit tarts.

2 cups unbleached,
    all-purpose flour
¾ cup unsalted butter
⅓ cup sugar
1 large egg

Blend the flour, butter, and sugar, following the directions for Pâte Brisée (page 338). Stir in the egg. Turn the dough out onto a work surface. Using the heel of your hand, press the dough in a streak about 8 inches long. Gather the dough back into a ball, and wrap it in plastic wrap. Chill it at least 30 minutes, and proceed as directed for Pâte Brisée.

NOTE

If you are using the pâte sucrée for a fruit tart, glaze the crust with 1 beaten egg yolk.

P U F F   P A S T R Y

Puff pastry is one of those recipes that are daunting to contemplate. But the pastry is such a useful commodity in the kitchen that it's worth the trouble to at least try to make your own.

Basically, puff pastry is made from two mixtures: a dough made with a lot of flour and very little butter (called a *détrempe*), and a square made with a lot of butter and very little flour. These mixtures are rolled together, folded, rolled again, and chilled several times, so that the butter is eventually flattened into super-thin layers between thin layers of dough. When the pastry is baked, the butter melts and expands, steam forms, expanding the dough, and *voila!* The layers of dough are lifted and separated into a startlingly high, flaky puff, supremely buttery and tender.

This is the pastry used for vol-au-vents, feuilletées, tarts, palmiers, and an array of pastries. The rolling and folding procedure is used with a somewhat different dough to make croissants. Because it's so useful, we'll go into some detail in the directions for basic puff pastry. What follows are a classic recipe, a food processor version, and some ideas for using the dough. Our own croissant recipe, a mainstay of Piret's breakfast menu, is also included.

You'll notice that we specify weights of flour and other ingredients. There's just no other way to guarantee the correct proportions. If you're going to bake pastry, an accurate kitchen scale would be a worthwhile investment. However, the water content of butter and the amount of water and gluten in the flour vary with producers and location. You'll have to practice until you feel comfortable with ingredients from your region. Weather, too, is a factor. It is best to avoid making puff pastry on hot, muggy days. At Piret's, we have air-conditioned a portion of our bakery, even though San Diego's temperature is generally in the low seventies and our humidity is quite low. All ingredients should be very cold. Put the flour into the freezer for 30 minutes to chill it.

Another important thing to remember is to brush off any loose flour remaining on the dough after rolling. If you don't, your baked dough may have hard, tough flour nuggets in it or it may not flake properly.

Since puff pastry is time-consuming to make and it freezes beautifully, consider making several batches at a time, or one large recipe, and freeze some for future use. (Or do what we do: buy it from a specialty shop like Piret's and forget trying to make it yourself!)

CLASSIC PUFF PASTRY

Makes 2 pounds

1 pound unsalted butter,
  chilled
1 pound unbleached,
  all-purpose flour,
  chilled
1 teaspoon salt
1 cup ice water

1. Cut ¼ pound of the butter into small chunks. (Chill the remaining butter.) Measure out ¼ cup of the flour, and set it aside. Mound the remaining flour on a marble slab or counter (the cooler the better). Stir in the salt. Work the butter chunks into the flour with your fingertips, working quickly so the butter is evenly incorporated but not melted. It should have a coarse, mealy texture. Sprinkle on ¾ cup of the water, working the flour to form a soft dough. Add just enough remaining water to completely moisten the dough. Don't knead it, or too much gluten will form and the dough will be hard to roll. Form the dough into a ball and flatten it to a thick disc. Wrap it in plastic wrap and chill the dough for 15 minutes.

2. While the dough chills, put the remaining ¾ pound of the butter on a pastry board and sprinkle it with the reserved ¼ cup of flour. (It helps if they're the same cool, but not cold, temperature.) Pound the butter lightly into a square with a rolling pin; fold it in half and pound it again. The object is to make the butter pliable but not melted.

3. Pat the butter into a flat square. Roll the chilled dough into a circle, about ¼ inch thick. Place the butter square in the middle of the dough and bring up the dough over the butter, to enclose it completely. Seal the edges by pressing them firmly with your fingertips.

4. Roll the dough into a rectangle, and refrigerate it for 30 minutes. This chilling step is important; it keeps the butter from melting.

5. Roll the cold dough ⅜ inch thick. Fold the dough into thirds, as if it were a letter, with a fold facing you. Give the dough a quarter turn, so the folded edge is to your right. This completes one "turn." Roll it again and fold it into thirds. Press two fingertips into the dough. That lets you know

it's been rolled twice. Wrap the dough in plastic wrap and refrigerate it until thoroughly chilled (30 minutes or more).

6. Repeat this rolling, folding, and turning step two more times. Now it's had four turns. Press four fingertips into the dough, and wrap and chill it again. At this point the dough may be wrapped well and frozen (it will keep a few months), or refrigerated (up to a week).

7. To use the dough, let it thaw, then roll, fold, and turn it two more times (a total of six turns).

FOOD PROCESSOR PUFF PASTRY

Makes 2 pounds

Paula Wolfert first developed this method for Cuisinart's *Pleasures of Cooking* magazine. It works wonderfully well, but take care not to overwork the dough.

1 pound unbleached, all-purpose flour
1 ¼ teaspoons salt
1 ¼ pounds unsalted butter
⅔ cup cold water
1 tablespoon white wine vinegar

1. Set aside ½ cup of the flour. Combine the remaining flour and the salt in the work bowl of a food processor fitted with the steel blade. Cut ¼ pound of butter into 8 pieces and add it to the processor. Process the mixture for 2 seconds. Combine the water and vinegar. With the machine running, add the liquid to the processor, and process the dough for about 15 seconds. It should start to form a ball. Divide the dough in half and process each half for another 1 ½ minutes. Combine these two balls of dough, wrap in plastic wrap or wax paper, and freeze for 30 minutes.

2. Sprinkle some of the reserved flour on a cool work surface. Place the remaining butter on the surface and sprinkle on the reserved flour. Pound it together as directed for Classic Puff Pastry (page 342). Shape the butter mixture into a 6-inch square, wrap, and chill until both the butter and dough are cool and firm but flexible.

3. Roll, fold, and turn as directed for Classic Puff Pastry.

Here are some suggestions for using leftover scraps of puff pastry

Garnishes

Small puffs make a lovely garnish for soups. Baked puff pastry squares or rounds make very impressive "lids" or garnishes for stews or ragouts, or for first courses using lightly sauced vegetables, fish, or shellfish. Simply roll the dough to a thickness of about ¼ inch, cut the desired shape and size with a pastry cutter, and place the dough on a parchment-lined jellyroll pan. Brush the top with egg wash, taking care not to let it drip down the sides (it will glue the flaky pastry leaves together so they can't rise), and bake in a preheated 425° oven about 15 to 20 minutes, or until dark golden in color. Puff pastry should be quite dark in color to assure that all the "leaves" have opened up and are cooked.

Cheese or Sugar Twists

For cheese twists, use any grated hard cheeses and a spice such as freshly ground pepper, nutmeg, or coriander. If you want a sweet twist, use sugar with cinnamon and omit the cheese. Roll out the dough as thin as possible early in the day and let it stand in the refrigerator. Just before baking brush the top with a beaten whole egg, and sprinkle it liberally with the cheese or sugar mixture. Press the topping lightly into the dough with your hand or a spatula. Turn it over and repeat the process. Use a ruler with a metal edge to give you a straight line, and cut the dough with a very sharp knife into ¼-inch strips. Twist the strips and place them in a parchment-lined jellyroll pan, leaving about ¾ inch between each (remember, they will puff). Press down both ends of the strips so they will not untwist while baking (use a drop of water, if necessary, to make them stick to the paper). Preheat the oven to 425°, and bake the twists about 10 minutes, or until they are golden brown and crisp. Cool and cut them into whatever lengths you desire.

PALMIERS

Makes about 10 to 14 pastries

Palmiers are addictive, crunchy, cookie-like affairs, so named because they resemble palm leaves. They go wonderfully with a steaming cup of good coffee or café au lait.

1 recipe Classic Puff Pastry
 (page 342), with 4
 complete turns
½ cup granulated sugar

1. Sprinkle a cutting board or pastry marble with the granulated sugar. Roll the puff pastry into a rectangle about ⅛ inch thick. Fold the dough so the ends meet in the center.

2. Flatten the dough slightly by passing a rolling pin over it without pressing down. Fold the dough so the ends meet in the center. Fold in half lengthwise. Refrigerate the dough for several hours.

3. Slice the loaf into ⅜-inch slices and place them on a parchment-lined jellyroll pan, leaving a generous amount of space between each since they will expand during baking.

4. Preheat oven to 425°. Bake the palmiers about 20 minutes, or until they are golden brown. Turn the palmiers over to brown the other side for about 5 minutes. They are delicious warm or cold.

PIRET'S CROISSANTS

Makes about 24 to 30 croissants

Similar to puff pastry, croissant dough is softer and has a more "bready" flavor. But the rolling steps are similar to those of puff pastry. If you wish, prepare the crescents well ahead of baking and freeze them, well wrapped; they will keep for weeks. The croissant-making process at Piret's takes three days. The dough is made on day one and refrigerated overnight. Next day, it's formed into crescents and refrigerated. The next morning, the crescents are proofed (allowed to rise) and baked.

2 cups milk, slightly warmed to about 85°

2 ounces compressed cake yeast, crumbled

3 to 5 ounces sugar (about ½ cup)

2 pounds unbleached, all-purpose flour

½ ounce salt (about 1 tablespoon)

1 pound unsalted butter

1 egg, beaten

1. Combine the milk, yeast, and sugar in a mixing bowl. When the yeast is dissolved, add the flour, then the salt. Mix the dough thoroughly with your fingers, but not to the point where it becomes smooth and elastic. Cover the bowl with a damp towel and refrigerate overnight.

2. Pound the butter into a flat square. Roll the chilled dough to a rectangle twice the size of the butter square. Place the butter on one half of the dough and fold the rest of the dough over to completely enclose the butter. Pinch together the edges of the dough to seal.

3. Roll the dough, fold it into thirds, and turn, as directed for Classic Puff Pastry (page 342). Chill the dough at least one hour after each turn. Give the dough three complete turns. The dough may be frozen at this point.

4. With the folded edge facing you, roll the dough until it is 12 inches wide from the folded edge to the open edge. Turn the dough so the folded edge is to your right and roll the dough to about ⅛ inch thick. At this point it should be a long rectangle, 12 inches wide. Using a sharp knife and cutting straight down, cut the dough in half lengthwise, to form 2 long rectangles, each 6 inches wide. Trim the top and bottom edges. Then cut the dough strips into triangles, each 3 inches wide at the base.

5. Hold the two points of the base of one triangle and give it a pull. Holding the tip of the triangle

and the base, pull it again. This stretching will ensure that the croissant has nice long "legs." Roll up the triangle, base to tip, and curve the ends toward the center to form a crescent. Repeat with all the dough. Chill the crescents thoroughly. (All this chilling is important; it keeps the butter from melting and making the dough greasy.)

6. Arrange the crescents on baking sheets, allowing plenty of room for expansion. Let them rise in a warm spot until doubled (about 1½ to 2 hours).

7. Preheat oven to 380°. Brush each crescent with beaten egg, and bake them for 20 to 25 minutes, or until they are golden brown.

PIRET'S CINNAMON WALNUT ROLLS

Makes about 36 rolls

If you prefer, use any favorite pastry cream instead of the one recommended here.

20 ounces cold milk (about 2½ cups)

2 ounces compressed cake yeast

2¾ pounds unbleached, all-purpose flour

4 ounces sugar (about ⅓ cup)

1 ounce salt (about 2 tablespoons)

1½ pounds unsalted butter, chilled

1 recipe pastry cream (page 280)

Cinnamon sugar

Chopped walnuts

2 medium eggs, beaten, for glaze

1. Follow the directions in steps 1 through 3 of Piret's Croissants (page 346) for mixing, rolling, and turning the dough. Chill the dough at least an hour after each turn, and give the dough three complete turns. Chill the dough several hours before proceeding (it may be frozen at this point).

2. Roll the dough into a rectangle three times as long as it is wide. Fold it in half crosswise. Turn the dough so the folded edge is to your right and roll the dough to about ⅜ inch thick (about 18 by 36 inches).

3. Spread the dough with pastry cream. Sprinkle it generously with cinnamon sugar and chopped walnuts, leaving a 1-inch border along one long side. Paint the border with the beaten egg. Starting from the long side (not the one with the egg wash), roll the dough like a jellyroll, keeping it tight. Seal the egg-washed edge by pressing it firmly.

4. Cut the roll into 1-inch slices. (An easy way to cut slices without smashing down the roll with a

knife is to use strong thread. Cut about 10 inches of thread, hold an end in each hand, and slide the thread under the roll, about an inch from the end. Cross the ends of the thread over the top of the roll and pull the ends away from the roll. The thread will cut neatly through the pastry.)

5. Line five or six baking sheets with parchment paper and arrange the rolls on the paper. Let them rise in a warm place until almost doubled (about 45 minutes to 1 hour). They should be airy and springy.

6. Preheat oven to 375°. Brush the rolls thoroughly with beaten egg, and bake them about 20 to 25 minutes, or until they are golden brown and baked through.

NOTE

For raisin rolls, follow the same procedure as above, but after spreading the dough with pastry cream, sprinkle it with raisins that have been soaked in dark rum.

⁊ The key to a well-equipped basic kitchen is durability and utility. A few intelligently designed pots and pans in functional sizes are a lot more useful than cupboards full of flimsy ones that scorch the food or have plastic handles that fall off or are so short you risk burning yourself. Dull knives dull the joy of cooking. Drawers jumbled with gadgets that don't work are an aggravation no one needs. A good kitchen is a pared-down kitchen, thoughtfully organized to make cooking fun and cleanup a breeze. In our own kitchen, we have only a single cupboard door and only three drawers. Pots and pans hang above and next to the stovetop. Knives hang from four magnet bars near the butcher-block work center. Virtually everything is within arm's reach. It makes cooking a pleasure.

THE BASIC KITCHEN

A well-equipped kitchen should be functional for the style of cookery and number of people being served. The cook we have in mind likes to cook but doesn't have all day to spend in the kitchen. We like utensils that do double duty, are easily cleaned, and minimize time-consuming chores. We believe you are money ahead when you invest in quality, because most kitchen equipment will be with you for fifteen to twenty-five years, or even your lifetime. When patrons are buying cookware in our Perfect Pan shops, we try to find out how elaborately they cook on a day-to-day basis and we advise them to buy only what they need. Shun prepackaged sets: you always end up with pots you don't need and rarely use. Mix and match metals and cooking surfaces and always buy the heaviest possible pans. Are you messy or neat? Select items that will withstand the abuse you are likely to inflict on them.

COOKING METALS

Cookware is available in a wide selection of metals and surfaces. For general cooking, you want a variety of equipment that includes both highly conductive metals and nonreactive surfaces. Conductivity in metals used for cookware describes three specific characteristics: 1) how quickly the pan will heat to the desired temperature; 2) how well it maintains heat evenly during cooking; and 3) how quickly the pan cools when removed from the heat source. In sauce-making, for example, these considerations are critical.

Cast Iron and Steel

The least costly cooking metals are cast iron and steel. Cast iron is great for outdoor cooking, dry-pan sautéing, and high-heat uses. Steel is used in woks and crêpe pans for the same reasons. Cast iron and steel heat slowly and cool slowly but can withstand abusive heat. These metals rust with moisture and must be seasoned. To season a pan, scour it, dry it, and wipe the inside and outside with corn oil, using a paper towel. Pour ¼ to ½ inch of oil into the pan and place it in a 200° oven for several hours. Periodically oil the internal sides of the pan, using a pastry brush. Seasoned pans should be wiped clean with a paper towel after use. Use salt to remove food that has stuck to the pan. If the pan needs further scouring, do so and then reseason it. Steel and cast-iron pans often are coated with enamel to eliminate the need to season them and to make them nonreactive with acidic foods. Since they are attractive, enamel-clad pans can double as cooking and serving ware. However, the enamel heats at a different temperature than the metal, so these pans should never be heated without food in them and they cannot be used for high-heat applications.

Aluminum

Aluminum is an excellent conductor of heat and is relatively inexpensive. It is a soft metal and scratches easily; metal utensils and abrasives should not be used on it. Aluminum is reactive with acidic foods, and white sauces and eggs tend to become gray when cooked in an aluminum pan.

Anodized and Bonded Aluminum

Anodizing, first used for cookware by Calphalon, is a process that hardens the surface of aluminum, making it less reactive with foods and durable enough for metal utensils. Teflon, Tefal, and Silverstone are nonstick surfaces that have been bonded to the interior surface of aluminum pans. All Clad's Master Chef cookware features an aluminum exterior and nonreactive stainless steel interior.

Stainless Steel

Pure stainless steel is a poor conductor of heat. To counter the problem, manufacturers put a sandwich of aluminum or copper on the bottom. In better-quality pans, the conductive metal extends up the sides of the pan. Stainless steel cookware is beautiful and expensive.

Copper

Copper is the premier cooking metal and most expensive as well. Because it is so conductive, it is preferred by chefs. Except for copper bowls used for beating egg whites, and polenta and zabaglione pans, copper cookware is lined with tin or stainless steel. Food should not be cooked in an unlined copper pan. Tin has a low melting point and pans coated with it should not be heated without food in them; nor is it wise to use a tin-lined copper pan with very high heat. Copper pans may be retinned, however. Craftsmen who know how to re-tin are hard to find, and you may have to ship your pans out of town for re-tinning. But considering the expense of copper cookware and their utility, it is worth the time and effort.

COOKWARE

Saucepans

At least one pan should have a nonreactive surface, such as stainless steel, enamel, or anodized aluminum. Several should be heavy enough to simmer food evenly without scorching. One pan can be relatively lightweight, for boiling. The most functional sizes are 1½ quart, 2½ quart, 4½ quart, and 6 quart.

Fry Pans and Sauté Pans

These pans should be as heavy as possible. A 10-inch, slope-sided omelet pan is indispensable. For your basics, get a 12-inch sauté pan, which will handle a whole chicken or filets mignons for six. We like metal handles, which will allow you to use the pans in the oven or under a broiler.

Stockpot and Roaster

If you have no immediate plans to use these, postpone buying them until you need them. Since they are big pieces in which you are unlikely to be cooking acidic foods, aluminum is the best buy. Choose a 12- to 20-quart stockpot, and consider those with strainer inserts for cooking pasta and steaming shellfish or vegetables. We like a rectangular roaster, which will accommodate more food than an oval-shaped one.

Casserole or Dutch Oven

These do double duty as cooking vessels and serving pieces. A ceramic baker, most useful in an oval or rectangular shape, is less costly than porcelain, but porcelain is sturdier and a sounder investment in the long haul. An enameled cast-iron Dutch oven is useful for stewed dishes where you braise the meat on top of the stove, add other ingredients, and finish cooking in the oven.

BAKEWARE

Unless you are a serious baker, one cookie sheet, a jellyroll pan, two 9-inch cake pans, a 9- or 10-inch quiche pan, and a loaf pan should suffice. You can always add other items as you need them. Bakeware is made of aluminum, steel, and stainless steel. Stainless steel tends to be expensive, and the pans are lightweight and warp easily. Plain steel rusts, but if it is coated with a black wash or Teflon-type material, this problem is minimized. Whatever metal you choose, be sure it is heavy grade so the pans don't warp in the oven (because of their size and shape, jellyroll pans and cookie sheets often warp regardless of the weight). Loaf pans can also be made of glass. Soufflé and quiche pans are available in glass and porcelain. Metal quiche pans come with removable bottoms, which makes the quiche easier to remove from the pan. If you're using a porcelain quiche pan, serve directly from the pan at the table. When you are buying porcelain bakeware, be sure it really is porcelain and not ceramic. You can tell by the price (porcelain is more expensive) and very often by the color. Ceramic bakeware, which is not as highly fired as porcelain, tends to chip more quickly and it usually is an off-white color. Porcelain is pure white and has a very high gloss and a hard finish. It, too, however, can chip and break.

For a baker, an oven thermometer is a useful tool, because an oven that is off by 25° can cause very real problems.

KNIVES

You will save hours of frustration if you buy good knives. High-quality carbon steel stays sharp longest, but carbon steel will rust, stain, and leave black marks on foods. A good alternative is a combination of carbon steel and a nonstaining additive such as molybdenum. When knives are described to you as stainless steel, be sure the stainless steel content is minimal and the principal metal is carbon steel. Well-made knives are properly balanced, and the metal extends through the entire length of the handle. The handle should feel comfortable in your hand. For basics, you'll need a chef's knife for chopping and mincing, a slicing knife, a paring knife, and, most important, a sharpening steel to maintain the cutting blade. Never store knives in a drawer, where the edges will bang into each other, or wash them in a dishwasher. Use a magnetic knife bar, which takes very little space, or a wooden knife block. From time to time, depending on how well you care for them, knives must be professionally sharpened on a grinding wheel and their cutting edges renewed.

FOOD PROCESSOR AND MIXER

It is possible to get by without these time-savers, but most cooks find the financial investment eminently worthwhile. The food processor is especially valuable and now comes in a range of prices and sizes. In terms of customer service and reliability, as well as availability of add-on attachments, Cuisinart continues to be the leader in the field. If you are not a baker, a small hand mixer will suffice for most cooking purposes. For bakers, we recommend the KitchenAid.

SPICE GRINDER

A good pepper grinder is indispensable, and a mortar and pestle (made of porcelain, not wood, which picks up flavors) is great for cracking and grinding spices. We use a small electric coffee grinder as a spice grinder, which works very well. A word of caution, however: you must reserve this grinder just for spices, as coffee beans leave an oily residue.

KITCHEN UTENSILS AND COOKING ACCESSORIES

Stainless steel utensils will not rust or pick up telltale flavors. Select varying handle lengths for your cooking spoons, spatulas, and whisks to fit a variety of pots and bowls. You should have a range of sizes in bowls: some metal, some porcelain or glass. Your cutting board should be heavy hardwood. The optimum size will depend on your kitchen working surface; 15 by 14 inches is a reasonable size. Your rolling pin should be as heavy and long as you can manage. Amazingly, many people buy pot holders and aprons for their decorative value, giving little thought to function. Look for sturdy, durable materials and workmanship. Frills can be dangerous around an open flame, and cutesy pot holders filled with cotton will burn the hand that feeds you.

INDEX

I N D E X

A

Almond
    and Marscapone filling for Brie, 30
    nut brittle, 306
    and ricotta tart, 263
Appetizer(s). *See also* Spreads
    brie with Roquefort and herbs, 27
    calamari Belajack, 43
    carpaccio with caviar mayonnaise, 38
    coquilles Florentine, 32
    duck breast and cèpes salad, 44
    duck, roasted, salad, 45
    escargots Piret's, 41
    fettuccine with caviar, 36
    fettuccine with shrimp sauce, 35
    gravlax with mustard sauce and
        cucumber salad, 26
    noodle salad, pon-pon, 40
    pasta with cream sauce, 37
    pasta salad with smoked salmon and
        sun-dried tomatoes, 39
    scallops Vesuvio, 34
    shrimp, marinated, stuffed with chèvre,
        31
    shrimp scandia, 30
    wild mushroom walnut spread on garlic
        toast rounds, 28
Apple(s)
    baked sliced, 289
    country tart with, 261
    and sausage stuffing for crown roast of
        pork, 247
    tart with Calvados, 260
Apricot and ginger compote, Madeleine
    Kamman's, 17
Artichoke and chestnut soup, cream of, 56
Artichoke heart salad, 83

Aspic for pâté, 148
Avocado butter, lemon-soy swordfish steaks
    with, 173

B

Babas. *See also* Savarins
    about, 274
    rum, 274; syrup for, 275
Bain-marie, 133
Basic kitchen equipment, 349–53
Basic
    custard quiche, 104
    egg pasta (dough), 187
    mayonnaise, 328
    pie dough (pâte brisée), 338
    sausage, 123
    tomato sauce, 199
    vinaigrette, 73
Basil
    dressing, pasta salad with capers, and,
        96
    dressing, pea and snow pea salad with,
        84
    and tomatoes with garlic vinaigrette,
        Dee Biller's, 86
    vinaigrette, 75
Bass
    with caviar beurre blanc, 222
    sea, fillets baked in parchment, 174
    sea, fish soup, 47
    striped, with green sauce, 227
    striped with mushrooms, 223; with
        oysters, 223
Bavarian cream, lemon, 287
Beans. *See* Green beans, Lima beans, White
    beans
Béarnaise sauce, 327; about, 325

Béchamel sauce, 324
Beef
    boiled with vegetables, 162
    carpaccio with caviar mayonnaise, 38
    chili, Arrington's Irish, 252
    filets mignons with Roquefort sauce,
        237
    fillet of, with capers, 238
    fillet, steak au poivre, George Munger's,
        9
    flank steak, braised stuffed, 239
    flank steak rolled with mushrooms, 241
    ground, rolled stuffed cabbage leaves,
        Hungarian, 166
    stew, Flemish, 164
Beet pasta, 189
Beet salad, cold, with sour cream–orange
    dressing, 83
Bell peppers. See Peppers
Beurre blanc, 330
    about, 329–31
    caper, salmon steaks with, 226
    caviar, sole with, 222
    enriched with eggs and herbs, 332
    tomato, 333
    tomato, salmon with, 224
Blanching, 203
Blue cheese and walnut quiche, 107
Boudin blanc (white sausage), 128
Bouquet garni, 163
Bourbon, braised pork in, 168
Boursin-style cheese spread, chicken breasts
    stuffed with, 177
Brandied peach sauce, 306
Brazil's national dish (Feijoada completa), 253
Bread, corn bread, green chili and cheese,
    251
Brie
    with Gorgonzola–pine nut filling, 27
    with Marscapone and almond filling, 30
    with Robiolla and walnut filling, 30
    with Roquefort and herbs, 27
Broccoli
    with garlic, Jacques Pépin's, 206
    soup, cream of, 55
    vinaigrette, 80
Brown sauce, 324
Brown stock, 313

Brown stock reduction, demi-glace and glace
    de viande, 315
Brownie cake, orange, 270; variations, 272
Brussels sprouts vinaigrette, 80
Butter(s)
    clarified, 239
    diablo (mustard-peppercorn), 335
    flavored. See Flavored butters
    sauce (beurre blanc). See Beurre blanc
Buttercream, chocolate, 267

C

Cabbage
    chicken with, 182
    green, salad, 95
    leaves, rolled stuffed, Hungarian, 166
    pie (tourte au chou), 110
Cake
    (coffee), mixed-fruit with vanilla sauce,
        272
    gâteau du prieur, Alice Medrich's, 268
    gâteau Grand Marnier, 268
    orange brownie, 270; variations, 272
    Paris-Brest, 279
    sponge, chocolate génoise, 266
    sponge, génoise, 265
    strawberry mousse, 269
Calamari Belajack, 43
Calf's liver with mustard sauce, 165
Cannelloni, green, with ricotta filling, 232
Caper(s)
    beurre blanc, salmon steaks with, 226
    or cornichon sauce for boiled beef, 163
    pasta salad with, and basil dressing, 96
Carpaccio with caviar mayonnaise, 38
Carrot(s)
    and celery root sauté, 204
    George Munger's, 204
    -ginger salad, 84
    pasta, 190
    salad, Moroccan, Piret's, 88
    sorbet with dill, 301
Caul fat, 130
Cauliflower vinaigrette, 80
Caviar
    beurre blanc, sole with, 222
    fettuccine with, 36
    mayonnaise, for carpaccio, 38

Celery root and carrot sauté, 204
Cèpes. *See also* Wild mushrooms
    and duck breast salad, 44
Chanterelles. *See also* Wild mushrooms
    striped bass with, 223
Charcutier's cuisine, 101–2
Chayote (squash) Don Javier, 205
Cheddar cheese and potato soup, 52
Cheese. *See also* name of cheese
    gougères (cheese puffs), 278
    and green chili corn bread, 251
    and herb quiche, 106
    and mushroom quiche, 107
    pizza (five), 121
    sauce, savory topping, 278
    soup, potato and cheddar, 52
    spread, boursin-style, 177
    twists (puff pastry), 344
Cheesecake tart Montrachet (savory), 264
Chestnut and artichoke soup, cream of, 56
Chèvre. *See also* Goat cheese
    marinated shrimp stuffed with, 31
    quiche, 105
    salad with walnuts, 97
Chicken
    barbecued, ravigote dressing marinade
      for, 75
    curry vinaigrette for, 73
    liver spread, 150
    provençal, garlic, 180
    in red wine sauce, 181
    roasted, 177
    roasted, with red wine vinegar sauce,
      236
    salad, pon-pon noodle, 40
    salad with potatoes and beets, 92
    stock, 317; concentrated, 318
Chicken (breasts)
    about boning, 176
    with cabbage, 82
    curry, Ben Patterson's, 184
    Glasgow, with vegetables, 183
    marinated sautéed, 178
    poulet suprême Maurice, 234
    salad, summer, French, 91
    sautéed with raspberry vinegar, 179
    stuffed with boursin, 176
    stuffed with watercress sauce, 235

Chiffonnade cutting technique, 85
Chiffonnade vinaigrette, 73
Chili, Arrington's Irish, 252
Chili, green and cheese corn bread, 251
Chilies and bell peppers, peeling, 208
Chocolate
    buttercream, 267
    chip cookies, white, Jenny Saar's, 284
    génoise, 266
    madeleines, 282
    mousse, Piret's, 286
    sauce, 307
    sauce, hot fudge, 307
Choucroute garnie, 248
Choux paste
    for éclairs, 278
    savory, 278; gougères, 278
    pastry ring, 279
Chowder. *See* Soups
Cigars (cookies), 285
Cinnamon walnut rolls, Piret's, 347; raisin,
    348
Clam chowder, New England, 52
Clarified butter, 239
Classic puff pastry, 342
"Combed" pasta with sausage and porcini
    cream sauce, 194
Compote, apricot and ginger, 17
Confit, red pepper, 157
Consommé, tomato, 61
Cookies
    chocolate chip, white, 284
    cigars, 285
    madeleines, 282; chocolate, 282
    palmiers (puff pastry), 345
    tommies, 284
    tuiles, 283
Cook-off, George Munger, 219–21
Coq au vin. *See* Chicken in red wine sauce;
    Chicken, roasted, with red wine vinegar
    sauce
Coquilles Florentine, Bill Glasgow's, 32
Corn bread, green chili and cheese, 251
Cornichon or caper sauce for boiled beef,
    163
Coulis, tomato, rabbit terrine with, 144
Country pâté en croûte, 133
Country pâté, French, 136

Country tart with apples, 261; other fruit variations, 261
Court bouillon, 319
Couscous salad, 93
Cranberry stuffing for crown roast of pork, 248
Cream, orange with chopped nuts, 288
Cream-puff paste (pâte à choux), 277
Cream puffs, 279
Cream sauce
    for pasta, 37
    porcini, "combed" pasta with sausage and, 194
    tortellini with, 193; variation, 194
Cream soup
    artichoke and chestnut, 56
    broccoli, 55
    mushroom, 53
    scallop, 50
Creamy cucumbers with dill, 87
Creamy vinaigrette, 73
Crème
    Anglaise, 303; variations, 304
    fraîche, 175
    fraîche sauce, sweet, 305
Crêpes. See Cannelloni
Crépinettes (sausage), 124
Croissants, Piret's, 346
Croutons
    fried, 58
    oven-toasted, 58
Cucumber(s)
    with dill, creamy, 87
    and pepper, Mediterranean salad, 94
    salad, 27
    sorbet, 302
Curry
    chicken, Ben Patterson's, 184
    mayonnaise, 329
    vinaigrette (chicken or fruit), 73
Custard quiche, basic, 104

D
Demi-glace, 315
Dessert(s). See also Cakes, Cookies, Ice creams, Sorbets, Tarts
    apples, baked sliced, 289
    chocolate mousse, Piret's, 286
    éclairs, 278
    lemon Bavarian cream, 287
    orange cream with chopped nuts, 288
    peaches baked with warm lemon sauce, 290
    pears with Melba sauce, 289
    pears Rosemonde, Marc Meneau's, 13
Dessert sauce(s)
    about, 303
    brandied peach, 306
    chocolate, 307
    crème Anglaise, 303; variations, 304
    crème fraîche, sweet, 305
    hot fudge, 307
    lemon, warm, baked peaches with, 290
    Melba (raspberries), 287
    strawberry supreme, 305
    vanilla, mixed-fruit cake with, 272
    zabaglione, 304
Dessert topping(s)
    almond nut brittle, 307
    Scotch-Espresso, Marcella Hazan's, 294
Diablo butter (mustard-peppercorn), 335
Dill dressing, creamy cucumbers with, 87
Dill vinaigrette, sweet, 82
Dinner, ultimate potluck, 7
Dinner, wedding, 20
Dough. See Pizza dough, Pasta dough, Pastry dough
Dressing. See Salad dressing
Duck
    apricot and ginger compote for, 17
    breast and cèpes salad, 44
    pâté à l'orange, 138
    rillettes, 153
    salad, roasted, 45
    terrine with green peppercorns, 141
    terrine with raisins, 140

E
Éclairs, 278
Egg pasta, basic, 187
Eggplant. See also Gratin of zucchini
    stew with lamb and pine nuts, 171
    ratatouille, 89
Endive salad with walnuts and goat cheese, 79
Enoki mushrooms, three-mushroom pizza, 116
Entertaining, about, 219–21

Escargots Piret's, 41

᳘ F

Feijoada completa (Brazil's national dish), 253
Fennel sausage, fragrant, 127
Fettuccine
    with caviar, 36
    pasta with cream sauce, 37
    with scallop sauce, 229
    with shrimp sauce, 35
Filets mignons with Roquefort sauce, 237
Fillet of beef
    with capers, 238
    steak au poivre, George Munger's, 9
Fish. *See also* name of fish
    fillets baked in parchment, 174
    poached, court bouillon for, 319
    soup, 47
    soup, Mediterranean with garlic, 48
    stock, 318
Five-cheese pizza, 121
Flank steak, braised stuffed, 239
Flank steak rolled with mushrooms, 241
Flavored butter(s)
    avocado for grilled fish, 173
    diablo (mustard-peppercorn), 335
    garlic for scampi alla fresca, 174
    herb, 334
    parsley, 334
    Roquefort and walnut, 335
Flemish beef stew, 164
Florentine, coquilles, 32
Food processor
    pasta, 190
    pâte brisée, 339
    puff pastry, 343
French country pâté, 136
French summer salad, Anne Otterson's, 91
Fruit. *See also* name of fruit
    curry vinaigrette for, 73
    desserts. *See* Desserts
    mixed-fruit cake with vanilla sauce, 272
Frying, 212
Fudge sauce, hot, 307

᳘ G

Galantine. *See also* Pâtés, Terrines
    veal and pork, 146

Garlic
    butter for scampi alla fresca, 174
    chicken provençal, 180
    toast rounds, 28
    vinaigrette, 73
    vinaigrette, tomatoes and basil with, 86
Garnishes (puff pastry), 344
Gaspacho (cold), 59
Gâteau du prieur, Alice Medrich's, 268
Gâteau Grand Marnier, 268
Génoise, 265; variations, 266
Génoise-based cakes, 265–70, 273
Génoise, chocolate, 266
George Munger Cook-off, 219–21
Glace de viande, 315
Goat cheese. *See also* Chèvre
    Montrachet tart, 264
    and smoked salmon pizza, 115
    and walnuts, endive salad with, 79
Gorgonzola–pine nut filling for Brie, 27
Gougères (savory), 278
Grand Marnier gâteau, 268
Grand Marnier mocha ice cream, Hugh
    Carpenter's, 297
Gratin of zucchini, 205
Gravlax with mustard sauce and cucumber
    salad, 26
Green and red pepper salad, 88
Green bean(s)
    salad, Jack Monaco's, 19
    salad with shrimp and fresh tomato
        vinaigrette, 82
Green cabbage salad, 95
Green cannelloni with ricotta filling, 232
Green chili and cheese corn bread, 251
Green mayonnaise, 328
Green peppercorn sauce, veal with, 244
Green peppercorns, duck terrine with, 141
Green peppers. *See* Peppers
Green sauce, pompano with, Diana
    Kennedy's, 227
Ground beef. *See* Beef, ground

᳘ H

Halibut
    fillets baked in parchment, 174
    Mediterranean fish soup with garlic, 48
    with moutarde de meaux and tomato
        beurre blanc, 224

Herb(s)
about, 69
butter, 334
and cheese quiche, 106
fresh, lemon vinaigrette with, 74
how to keep fresh, 26
sauce, 323
vinaigrette, 73
vinegar, 70
Herbed new potatoes, 210
Hollandaise sauce, 326; about, 325
Horseradish sauce for boiled beef, 163
Hungarian rolled stuffed cabbage leaves, 166

&\ I

Ice Cream(s). *See also* Sorbets
about, 291–92
almond nut brittle topping for, 307
chocolate sauce for, 307
Grand Marnier mocha, 297
hot fudge sauce for, 307
peach, 298
praline, 295
vanilla mint, 294
vanilla, modern Kansas farm, 293;
authentic, 293
vanilla, Scotch-espresso topping for,
Marcella Hazan's, 294
Irish chili, Arrington's, 252
Italian meat sauce, 202

&\ K

Kansas farm vanilla ice cream, modern, 293;
authentic, 293
Kitchen equipment, basic, 349–53
Kiwi tart, 258; other fruit variations, 259
Klodniak, Becky's (cold shrimp buttermilk
soup), 62
Knives, 352

&\ L

Lamb
and pine nuts, eggplant stew with, 171
rack of, Perfect Pan, 245
roast, with onion sauce, 246
sausage, 126
sausage pizza, 117
Lasagne
Italian meat sauce for, 202

pasta, 188
seafood, 228
spinach, with cheese and basil stuffing,
196
Leeks. *See also* Gratin of zucchini
and sausage pie, 112
and three cheeses, potato skins stuffed
with, 213
Lemon
Bavarian cream, 287
curd tart, 262
sauce, warm, baked peaches with, 290
-soy swordfish steaks with avocado
butter, 173
vinaigrette with fresh herbs, 74
Lentil salad, Marie-Christine Forester's, 77
Lima beans vinaigrette, 76
Liver. *See also* Pâtés, Terrines
calf's, with mustard sauce, 165
chicken, spread, 150
rabbit, terrine, 142

&\ M

Madeleines (cookies), 282; chocolate, 282
Marinated sautéed chicken breasts, 178
Marinated shrimp stuffed with chèvre, 31
Marscapone and almond filling for Brie, 30
Marscapone cheese, substitute for, 116
Mayonnaise
basic, 328; hand preparation, 328
caviar, for carpaccio, 38
curry, 329
green, 328
mustard, 328
tomato, 329
Meatballs and spaghetti, Frank Munger's, 6
Meat sauce, Italian, 202
Mediterranean fish soup with garlic, 48
Mediterranean salad, 94
Melba sauce (raspberries) for lemon Bavarian
cream, 287
Mexican stew, Strom and Jenkins, 250
Minestrone alla Diana, 60
Mint vinaigrette, creamy, 82
Mocha Grand Marnier ice cream, Hugh
Carpenter's, 297
Montrachet tart (savory cheesecake), 264
Morels. *See* Wild mushrooms
Moroccan carrot salad, Piret's, 88

Mousse cake, strawberry, 269
Mousse, chocolate, Piret's, 286
Mushroom(s). *See also* Wild mushrooms
    and cheese quiche, 107
    duck breast and cèpes salad, 44
    flank steak rolled with, 241
    pizza, three-mushroom, 116
    pie, woodland torte, 111
    soup, cream of, 53
    striped bass with, 223
    wild rice steamed with, 215
Mussel soup Piret's, 51
Mustard(s)
    about, 69
    butter diablo, 335
    mayonnaise, 328
    moutarde de meaux and tomato beurre
        blanc, salmon with, 224
    sauce for calf's liver, 165
    sauce for gravlax, 27
    sauce for shrimp scandia, 30
    sauce, veal with, Anne Otterson's, 243
    varieties of, 69

&a N

New England Clam Chowder, 52
Noodle salad, Hugh Carpenter's pon-pon, 40
Nougatine for Paris-Brest cake, 280
Nouvelle cuisine, 11, 14
Nut brittle, almond, 306

&a O

Oils, about, 68; varieties, 68
Olive spread (tapenade), 154
Onion(s)
    burned, 314
    and orange salad with raspberry
        vinaigrette, 90
    red, and sweet peppers, roasted, 209
    relish, red, Jerrie Strom's, 155
    relish, tart, Diana Kennedy, 155
    sauce, lamb roast with, 246
    soup Piret's, 57
    tart, Piret's, 108
Orange
    brownie cake, 270; variations, 272
    cream with chopped nuts, 288
    and onion salad with raspberry
        vinaigrette, 90

—sour cream dressing, cold beet salad
        with, 83
    and watercress salad, 90
Oyster (or abalone) mushrooms, three-
    mushroom pizza, 116

&a P

Palmiers (puff pastry), 345
Panade. *See* Pâte à choux
Paris-Brest cake, 279
Parsley butter, 334
Pasta
    about preparing, 185–86
    beet, 189
    cannelloni, green, with ricotta filling,
        232
    carrot, 190
    "combed" with sausage and porcini
        cream sauce, 194
    with cream sauce, 37
    dough, basic egg, 187
    food processor, 190
    lasagne, 188
    lasagne with cheese and basil stuffing,
        196
    ratatouille with, 89
    ravioli, spinach with meat filling and
        cream sauce, 230
    salad with capers and basil dressing, 96
    salad with smoked salmon and sun-dried
        tomatoes, 39
    spaghetti and meatballs, Frank
        Munger's, 6
    spinach, 188
    spinach ravioli with meat filling and
        cream sauce, 230
    tagliarini with prosciutto and green
        peas, 191
    tomato, 189
    tortellini with cream sauce, 192
Pastry
    cream, 280
    dough (pâte brisée), 338; food processor,
        339
    -making, about, 336–38
    Piret's quiche, 103
    puff. *See* Puff pastry
    sweet, pâte sucrée, 340

Pâte (pastry)
brisée, 338; food processor, 339
à choux (cream-puff paste), 277
à choux, savory, 278; gougères, 278
sucrée (for tarts), 340
Pâté(s). *See also* Galantine, Terrines
about, 130–31
aspic for, 148
country, French, 136
en croûte, country, 133
duck à l'orange, 138
peppercorn, 132
Pea and snow pea salad with basil dressing, 84
Peach(es)
baked with warm lemon sauce, 290
ice cream, 298
soup with champagne (cold), 63
Pears with Melba sauce, 289
Pears Rosemonde, Marc Meneau's, 13
Pepper(s)
bell, and chilies, about peeling, 208
and cucumber, Mediterranean salad, 94
red, confit, 157
salad, red and green, 88
sauce, sweet red, scamorze pizza with, 120
sweet, and red onions, roasted, 209
Peppercorn pâté, 132
Peppercorns, green. *See* Green peppercorns
The Perfect Pan (kitchenware store and cook-ing school), 3–5, 10–11, 14–16, 311–12
Perfect Pan rack of lamb, 245
Pie. *See* Tarts
Pie dough, basic (pâte brisée), 338
Pineapple sorbet in cookie cups, Anne Otterson's, 299
sugar veil for, 300
Pine nut–Gorgonzola filling for Brie, 27
Piret's Enterprises, 17–21, 67, 101, 161–62
Pizza
about, 113–14
dough, Piret's, 114
five-cheese, 121
lamb sausage, 117
scamorze with sweet red pepper sauce, 120
smoked salmon and goat cheese, 115

three-mushroom, 116
verde with tomatillo sauce, 118
Poaching, fish, 319
Pommes Byron (potatoes), 210
Pompano with green sauce, Diana Kennedy's, 227
Porcini cream sauce, "combed" pasta with sausage and, 194
Porcini mushrooms. *See* Cèpes
Pork. *See also* Pâtés, Sausages, Terrines
in bourbon, braised, Anne Otterson's, 168
chili, Arrington's Irish, 252
chops in tarragon mustard sauce, 167
crown roast of, with apple and sausage stuffing, 247
rillettes, 152
sausage, 125
and veal, galantine of, 146
Potato(es)
and beets, chicken salad with, 92
and Cheddar cheese soup, 52
herbed new, 210
and mushroom pie (woodland torte), 111
nests, 211; fillings for, 212
pommes Byron, 210
skins Doreg, 214
skins stuffed with leeks and three cheeses, 213
Potluck dinner, ultimate, 7
Pots and pans for cooking and baking, 349–52
Poulet suprême Maurice, 234
Praline ice cream, 295
Provençal vinaigrette, 73
Prune sauce, rabbit with, 172
Puff pastry. *See also* Croissants
about, 340–41
cheese or sugar twists, 344
classic, 342
food processor, 343
for garnishes, 344
palmiers, 345
Purée, tomato, cold, 201

Q
Quatre épices, 131
Quiche
about, 102–3

basic custard, 104
blue cheese and walnut, 107
cabbage pie (tourte au chou), 110
cheese and herb, 106
chèvre, 105
leek and sausage pie, 112
Lorraine, 108
mushroom and cheese, 107
onion tart, Piret's, 108
pastry, Piret's, 103
potato and mushroom pie (woodland torte), 111
tomato tart, Piret's, 109

☙ R
Rabbit
liver terrine, 142
with prune sauce, 172
terrine with tomato coulis, 143
Raisin rolls, 348
Raspberry(ies)
Melba sauce, 287
vinaigrette, 90
vinegar, 70
vinegar, chicken breasts sautéed with, 179
Ratatouille, 89
Ravigote dressing, 75
Ravioli, spinach with meat filling and cream sauce, 230
Red and green pepper salad, 88
Red onion relish, Jerrie Strom's, 155
Red onions and sweet peppers, roasted, 209
Red pepper confit, 157
Red pepper sauce, sweet, scamorze pizza with, 120
Red or white vinaigrette, Piret's, 72
Relish
onion, tart, Diana Kennedy, 155
red onion, Jerri Strom's, 155
red pepper confit, 157
tomato, 156
Rice. See Wild rice
Ricotta and almond tart, 263
Rillettes
duck, 153
pork, 152
salmon, Paula Wolfert's, 151
Robiolla and walnut filling for Brie, 30

Rolls. See also Croissants
cinnamon walnut, Piret's, 347; raisin, 348
Roquefort
and herbs, Brie with, 27
sauce for filets mignons, 237
turnips stuffed with, 208
and walnut butter, 335
Roux-based sauces, about, 321
Rum babas, 274
Rum syrup, 275

☙ S
Salad(s)
artichoke heart, 83
beet, cold, with sour cream–orange dressing, 83
cabbage, green, 95
carrot-ginger, 84
carrot, Piret's Moroccan, 88
cauliflower vinaigrette, 80
charcuterie, about, 67
chèvre with walnuts, 97
chicken, with potatoes and beets, 92
couscous, 93
cow-muzzle, 12
cucumber, 27
cucumbers, creamy, with dill, 87
duck breast and cèpes, 44
duck, roasted, 45
endive, walnuts, and goat cheese, 79
green bean, Jack Monaco's, 19
green bean, with shrimp and fresh tomato vinaigrette, 82
lentil, Marie-Christine Forester's, 77
lima beans vinaigrette, 76
Mediterranean, 94
noodle, Hugh Carpenter's pon-pon, 40
orange and onion, with raspberry vinaigrette, 90
pasta, with capers and basil dressing, 96
pasta, with smoked salmon and sun-dried tomatoes, 39
pea and snow pea, with basil dressing, 84
pepper, red and green, 88
ratatouille, 89
summer, Anne Otterson's French, 91
tomato and sorrel, 85

Salad(s)—*Continued*
    tomatoes and basil with garlic
        vinaigrette, Dee Biller's, 86
    tonnato, 95
    tortelloni, 78
    watercress and orange, 90
    white bean, 78
    winter, 81
Salad dressing(s). *See also* Vinaigrette
    basil, 84
    dill, 87
    ravigote, 75
    sour cream–orange, 83
Salmon. *See also* Smoked salmon
    with beurre blanc, 222
    gravlax with mustard sauce and
        cucumber salad, 26
    with moutarde de meaux and tomato
        beurre blanc, 224
    rillettes, Paula Wolfert's, 151
    steaks with caper beurre blanc, 226
    terrine, 145
Sauce(s). *See also* Flavored butters
    about, 320–21, 325
    béarnaise, 327
    béchamel, 324
    beurre blanc. *See* Beurre blanc
    brown, 324
    cornichon or caper for boiled beef, 163
    cream for pasta, 37
    cream, tortellini with, 193; variation,
        194
    dessert. *See* Dessert sauces
    green peppercorn, veal with, 244
    green, pompano with, 227
    herb, for fish and poultry, 323
    hollandaise, 326
    horseradish, for boiled beef, 163
    mayonnaise. *See* Mayonnaise
    meat, Italian, 202
    mustard, for calf's liver, 165
    mustard, for gravlax, 27
    mustard, for shrimp scandia, 30
    mustard, veal with, Anne Otterson's,
        243
    onion, lamb roast with, 246
    porcini cream, "combed" pasta with
        sausage and, 194

prune, rabbit with, 172
red pepper, sweet, scamorze pizza with,
    120
roasted red onions and sweet peppers,
    209
Roquefort, for filets mignons, 237
roux-based, about, 321
scallop, fettuccine with, 229
shrimp for fettuccine, 35
tarragon mustard, for pork chops, 167
tomatillo, for pizza verde, 119
tomato. *See* Tomato sauce
velouté, 322
vinaigrette. *See* Vinaigrette
watercress, chicken breasts stuffed with,
    235
wine vinegar, red, for roasted chicken,
    236
Sauerkraut-pork casserole (choucroute garnie),
    248
Sausage
    about, 122
    and apple stuffing for crown roast of
        pork, 247
    basic, 123; variations, 124
    boudin blanc, 128
    crépinettes, 124
    fennel, fragrant, 127
    lamb, 126
    lamb, pizza, 117
    and leek pie, 112
    and porcini cream sauce, "combed" pasta
        with, 194
    pork, 125
    seafood, Patty McDonald's, 129
Savarin(s), 276. *See also* Babas, about, 274
Savory cheesecake, Montrachet tart, 264
Savory choux paste, 278; gougères, 278
Scallop(s)
    coquilles Florentine, 32
    sauce, fettuccine with, 229
    soup, cream of, 50
    Vesuvio, Jack Monaco's, 34
Scamorze pizza with sweet red pepper sauce,
    120
Scampi alla fresca, 174
Scotch-espresso topping for vanilla ice cream,
    Marcella Hazan's, 294

Sea bass. *See* Bass

Seafood. *See also* name of seafood
    lasagne, 228
    sausage, Patty McDonald's, 129

Shark, thresher, for fish soup, 47

Shellfish, court bouillon for, 319

Shiitake mushrooms. *See also* Wild
  mushrooms
    rolled flank steak with mushrooms, 241
    striped bass with, 223
    three-mushroom pizza, 116

Shrimp
    -buttermilk soup (cold), Becky's
      Klodniak, 62
    coquilles Florentine, 32
    fish soup, 47
    marinated, stuffed with chèvre, 31
    sauce for fettuccine, 35
    scampi alla fresca, 174
    scandia, Maurice Moore-Betty's, 30

Smoked salmon and goat cheese pizza, 115

Smoked salmon and sun-dried tomatoes, pasta
  salad with, 39

Snail butter, 41

Snails, escargots Piret's, 41

Snapper with caviar beurre blanc, 222

Snapper, for fish soup, 47

Snow pea and pea salad with basil dressing,
  84

Sole with caviar beurre blanc, 222

Sole fillets baked in parchment, 174

Sorbets. *See also* Ice Creams
    carrot with dill, 301
    cucumber, 302
    pineapple in cucumber cups, 299; sugar
      veil for, 300
    strawberry, 298

Sorrel soup. *See* Watercress soup

Sorrel and tomato salad, 85

Soup(s). *See also* Stocks
    artichoke and chestnut, cream of, 24
    broccoli, cream of, 53
    clam chowder, New England, 52
    fish, 47
    fish, Mediterranean with garlic, 48
    gazpacho (cold), 59
    Klodniak, Becky's (cold), 62
    minestrone alla Diana, 60

    mushroom, cream of, 53
    mussel, Piret's, 51
    onion, Piret's, 57
    peach, with champagne (cold fruit), 63
    potato and Cheddar cheese, 52
    scallop, cream of, 50
    tomato consommé, 61
    watercress, 54

Sour cream–orange dressing, cold beet salad
  with, 83

Spaghetti
    Italian meat sauce for, 202
    and meatballs, Frank Munger's, 6

Spiced vinegar, 71

Spinach
    coquilles Florentine, 32
    lasagne with cheese and basil stuffing,
      196
    pasta, 188
    ravioli with meat filling and cream
      sauce, Nadia Frigeri's, 230

Spread(s). *See also* Flavored butters
    cheese, boursin-style, 177
    chicken liver, 150
    duck rillettes, 153
    pork rillettes, 152
    salmon rillettes, 151
    tapenade, 154

Squash (chayote) Don Javier, 205

Squid, calamari Belajack, 43

Steak. *See also* Beef fillets
    au poivre, George Munger, 9
    flank, braised stuffed, 239
    flank, rolled with mushrooms, 241

Stew
    boiled beef with vegetables, 162
    chicken in red wine sauce, 181
    eggplant, with lamb and pine nuts, 171
    Flemish beef, 164
    Mexican, Strom and Jenkins', 250
    veal, 169
    veal shanks Trieste-style, 170

Stocks
    about, 312–13
    brown, 313
    brown, reduction, demi-glace and glace
      de viande, 315
    chicken, 317; concentrated, 318

Stocks—*Continued*
    court bouillon for poached fish, 319
    fish, 318
    veal, 316
Strawberry
    mousse cake, 269
    sauce supreme, 305
    sorbet, 298
Striped bass. *See* Bass
Stuffed dishes. *See* Chicken breasts, Tomatoes, Turnips
Stuffing
    apple and sausage, for crown roast of pork, 247
    cranberry, for crown roast of pork, 248
Sugar twists (puff pastry), 344
Summer salad, French, Anne Otterson's, 91
Sun-dried tomatoes. *See* Tomatoes
Swordfish with moutarde de meaux and tomato beurre blanc, 224
Swordfish steaks, lemon-soy, with avocado butter, 173
Syrup, simple, 267
Syrup, rum, 275

❧ T

Tagliarini with prosciutto and green peas, 191
Tagliatelle
    pasta with cream sauce, 37
Tapenade, 154
Tarragon mustard sauce for pork chops, 167
Tarragon vinaigrette for vegetables, 74
Tart onion relish, 155
Tart(s). *See also* Quiche
    about, 257
    apple with Calvados, 260
    country, with apples, 261; other fruit variations, 261
    kiwi, 258; other fruit variations, 259
    lemon curd, 262
    Montrachet (savory cheesecake), 264
    onion, Piret's, 108
    ricotta and almond, 263
    tomato, Piret's, 109
Terrine(s). *See also* Galantine, Pâtés
    about, 130–31
    de campagne, 139
    duck, with green peppercorns, 141

    duck, with raisins, 140
    rabbit liver, 142
    rabbit, with tomato coulis, 143
    salmon, 145
"Those tomatoes", 206
Three-mushroom pizza, 116
Toast rounds, garlic, 28
Tomatillo sauce for pizza verde, 119
Tomato(es)
    baked stuffed, 207
    and basil with garlic vinaigrette, Dee Biller's, 86
    beurre blanc, 333
    beurre blanc, salmon with, 224
    (cherry) "those", 206
    consommé (hot or cold), 61
    coulis for rabbit terrine, 144
    mayonnaise, 329
    pasta, 189
    purée, cold, 201
    relish, 156
    salsa for Mexican stew, 251
    sauce with bacon, 201
    sauce, basic, 199; variations, 200
    sauce, fresh, 200
    sauce for lasagne, 197; herb, mushroom, sausage variations, 198
    and sorrel salad, 85
    sun-dried, pasta salad with smoked salmon and, 39
    tart, Piret's, 109
    vinaigrette, fresh, 82
Tommies (cookies), 284
Tonnato (tuna) salad, 95
Tortellini with cream sauce, 192
Tortelloni salad, 78
Tourte au chou (cabbage pie), 110
Trifle. *See* Zuccotto Frigeri
Trout, cold, poached with caper vinaigrette, 8
Tuiles (cookies), 283
Tuna (tonnato) salad, 95
Turkey, cranberry stuffing for, 248
Turnips stuffed with Roquefort, 208

❧ V
Vanilla
    ice cream, modern Kansas farm, 293; authentic, 293

ice cream topping, Scotch-espresso, Marcella Hazan's, 294

mint ice cream, Lorenzo and Olga's, 294

sauce, mixed-fruit cake with, 272

Veal

with green peppercorn sauce, 244

with mustard sauce, Anne Otterson's, 243

and pork, galantine of, 146

scallops with lemon juice, Nadia Frigeri's, 243

shanks Trieste-style, 170

stew, 169

stock, 316

Vegetable(s). *See also* name of vegetable, Salads

boiled beef with, 162

chicken Glasgow, 183

couscous salad, 93

ratatouille, 89

soup, minestrone alla Diana, 60

tarragon vinaigrette for, 74

winter salad, 81

Velouté sauce, 322

Vinaigrette

basic, and variations, 73

basil, 75

basil, pasta salad with capers, 96

with capers, 8

cauliflower, 80; other vegetables, 80

dill, sweet, 82

dressing for chèvre salad with walnuts, 97

garlic, tomatoes and basil with, 86

lemon, with fresh herbs, 74

lima beans, 76

mint, creamy, 82

raspberry, orange and onion salad with, 90

red or white, Piret's, 72

tarragon for vegetables, 74

Vinegar(s)

about, 67–68

herb, 70

raspberry, 70

spiced, 71

varieties of, 68

⁊ W

Walnut

and blue cheese quiche, 107

and Robiolla filling for Brie, 30

and Roquefort butter, 335

wild mushroom spread on garlic toast rounds, 28

Watercress

and orange salad, 90

sauce, chicken breasts stuffed with, 235

soup, 54

White bean salad, 78

White chocolate chip cookies, Jenny Saar's, 284

White or red vinaigrette, Piret's, 72

Wild mushroom(s). *See also* name of wild mushroom

three-mushroom pizza, 116

and walnut spread on garlic toast rounds, 28

woodland torte, 111

Wild rice steamed with mushrooms, 215

Wine vinegar, red, sauce for roasted chicken, 236

Winter salad, 81

Woodland torte (wild mushroom pie), 111

⁊ Z

Zabaglione, 304

Zest of citrus fruit, about, 92

Zesty vinaigrette, 73

Zucchini, gratin of, 205

Zucchini, ratatouille, 89

Zuccotto Frigeri, 273

10127085
ISBN 0-395-39501-1